SOVIET LAW AFTER STALIN

Part II. Social Engineering Through Law

LAW IN EASTERN EUROPE

A series of publications
issued by the
Documentation Office for East European Law
University of Leyden

General Editor
F. J. M. FELDBRUGGE

No. 20

SIJTHOFF & NOORDHOFF
Alphen aan den Rijn – The Netherlands
1978

SOVIET LAW AFTER STALIN

Part II

Social Engineering Through Law

Edited by

DONALD D. BARRY, GEORGE GINSBURGS, and
PETER B. MAGGS

SIJTHOFF & NOORDHOFF
Alphen aan den Rijn – The Netherlands
1978

ISBN 90 286 0318 2

Printed in the Netherlands

TABLE OF CONTENTS

TABLE OF ABBREVIATIONS

BSSR	Belorussian Soviet Socialist Republic
BVS RSFSR	*Biulleten' Verkhovnogo Suda RSFSR* [Bulletin of the RSFSR Supreme Court]
BVS SSSR	*Biulleten' Verkhovnogo Suda SSSR* [Bulletin of the USSR Supreme Court]
CC	Criminal Code
CCP	Code of Criminal Procedure
CDSP	*Current Digest of the Soviet Press*
CJA	Commission on Juvenile Affairs
CMF	Code of Marriage and the Family
CPSU	Communist Party of the Soviet Union
FPCL	Fundamental Principles of Criminal Law of the USSR and Union Republics
FPCivL	Fundamental Principles of Civil Legislation of the USSR and Union Republics
FPCP	Fundamental Principles of Criminal Procedure of the USSR and Union Republics
FPLMF	Fundamental Principles of Law on Marriage and the Family
LG	*Literaturnaia Gazeta* [Literary Gazette]
Pravovedenie	*Izvestiia Vysshikh Uchebnykh Zavedenii: Pravovedenie* [News of the Higher Educational Institutions: Legal Science]
Rad. Pr.	*Radians'ke Pravo* [Soviet Law]
SGiP	*Sovetskoe Gosudarstvo i Pravo* [Soviet State and Law]
SNK	*Sovet Narodnykh Komissarov* [Council of People's Commissars]
Sobr. Post RSFSR (or *SSSR*)	*Sobranie postanovlenii pravitel'stva RSFSR* (or *SSSR*) [Collected Decrees of the Government of the RSFSR (or USSR)]
Sobr. Uzak.	*Sobranie uzakonenii i rasporiazhenii rabochego i krest'ianskogo pravitel'stva RSFSR* [Collected Laws and Regulations of the Workers' and Peasants' Government of the RSFSR]

Sobr. Zak. RSFSR	*Sobranie zakonov i rasporiazhenii raboche-krest'ianskogo pravitel'stva RSFSR* [Collected Laws and Regulations of the Workers' and Peasants' Government of the RSFSR]
Sobr. Zak. SSSR	*Sobranie zakonov i rasporiazhenii raboche-krest'ianskogo pravitel'stva SSSR* [Collected Laws and Regulations of the Workers' and Peasants' Government of the USSR]
Sots. Zak.	*Sotsialisticheskaia Zakonnost'* [Socialist Legality]
Sov. Iust.	*Sovetskaia Iustitsiia* [Soviet Justice]
Sud. Pr.	*Sudebnaia Praktika* [Judicial Practice]
UZ	*Uchenye Zapiski* [Scholarly Notes (followed by the name of the sponsoring institution)]
Ved. V.S. RSFSR	*Vedomosti Verkhovnogo Soveta RSFSR* [Gazette of the RSFSR Supreme Soviet]
Ved. V.S. SSSR	*Vedomosti Verkhovnogo Soveta SSSR* [Gazette of the USSR Supreme Soviet]
VLU (*ser. obshch. nauk.*)	*Vestnik Leningradskogo Universiteta, seriia obshchestvennykh nauk* [Herald of Leningrad University, Social Science Series]
VMU (*pravo*)	*Vestnik Moskovskogo Universiteta: Pravo* [Herald of Moscow University: Law]
VTsIK	(*Vserossiiskii*) *Tsentral'nyi Ispolnitel'nyi Komitet* [(All-Russian) Central Executive Committee]

INTRODUCTION

This is the second part of a three-volume publication containing the results of extensive research on legal developments in the Soviet Union since the death of Stalin. The research is being conducted by a group of specialists from the United States and several European countries under a grant from the Ford Foundation. The first volume was published in 1977, and the third volume will be published in 1979.

The theme for this volume, "Social Engineering Through Law," evolved from discussions among the participants at the conference where the papers for the first volume in this series were originally presented. The subject of that conference was "The Citizen and the State in Contemporary Soviet Law." The broad objective had been to examine the course of recent developments in the individual's relations with the state in selected areas of the law. Having done this, it seemed appropriate to look at post-Stalin legal activity from another perspective—that of the objectives Soviet legal policy-makers have had in mind, the method they have used for the implementation of those objectives, and the successes and difficulties of that implementation in practice. Thus, the concept of social engineering through law.

The papers prepared under this general theme were presented at a meeting in New York City on October 28 and 29, 1977 at the Association of the Bar of the City of New York. The body of this book contains the original papers as revised in the light of the comments made at this conference.

Many of the most important developments in Soviet law in the past quarter-century could be classified under the heading of legal reform, and this would apply in particular to the impressive codification activity that has taken place in many branches of law. Even more fundamental to Soviet law than the new codes is the new USSR Constitution. With regard to its adoption, the participants at the conference were the beneficiaries of a fortunate break in timing. The papers were largely prepared between the time of the publication of the draft of the new Constitution early in June, 1977 and its final adoption on October 7, 1977. Therefore, all of the authors had the opportunity to consider it in their papers. Two of the chapters in this book are specifically devoted to the new Constitution or parts thereof, while references to the Constitution are found in most of the other chapters. But the contributors to this volume have not concentrated on constitutional and statutory material alone. They have also examined other available data, including particularly the activity of the courts and the views of the legal scholars and other commentators on the law. These inputs are viewed as being of considerable importance in recent legal developments.

The concept of social engineering warrants brief further comment. The term has been used widely in the literature of the social sciences and the humanities. Karl Popper, who has perhaps developed the concept most fully, sees social engineering as a pursuance of "the steps open to us if we want to achieve certain results." He contrasts it with historicism (including Marxist historicism), which sees social developments as being determined by certain "forces" or "laws." Popper advocates for a democracy what he calls "piecemeal social engineering," as distinct from "holistic or utopian social engineering," which involves redesigning the society as a whole.[1]

Roscoe Pound has applied the language of social engineering to law. He has described jurisprudence as "a science of social engineering, having to do with . . . the ordering of human relations through the action of politically organized society." In such a society, community interests "are weighed against individual self-assertion, that is, against the interest in the individual life."[2] Elsewhere he describes himself as "content to see in legal history . . . a continually more efficacious social engineering."[3]

Views such as these concerning social engineering are hardly uncontroversial. They have been subject to attack from both the right and the left.[4] This is a controversy in which the authors of this volume have no wish to become involved. We cite these writings only to give the reader a perspective on social engineering as the attempt on the part of the community's leaders to shape social behavior. Whether recent Soviet efforts at social engineering through law are essentially divorced from Marxism–Leninism or represent a practical implementation of it (as Soviet spokesmen would hold) is a matter on which people will differ. There is no particular requirement that social engineering be directed at dynamic change. One of the participants at the conference suggested that an end of Soviet social engineering might well be the maintenance of the *status quo*. What united our efforts in this volume was the attempt on the part of each author to examine legal developments in his area of concern from the perspective of the aims of the policy-makers responsible for these developments.

The authors would like to thank the Ford Foundation for the financial support which made this volume possible and the Association of the Bar of the City of New York for serving as host to the conference. The participants in the conference were:

Jack A. Barnabel, North Brunswick, New Yersey
Donald D. Barry, Lehigh University
Harold J. Berman, Harvard Law School
Valery Chalidze, Khronika Press, New York City
Walter D. Connor, U.S. Department of State
Wesley A. Fisher, Columbia University

Lazar Fridman, Elmwood Park, New Yersey
Eugene D. Fryer, Charlottesville, Virginia
George Ginsburgs, Rutgers University School of Law, Camden
John N. Hazard, Columbia University School of Law
Arthur J. Heath, New York City
William Jeffrey, Jr., University of Cincinnati College of Law
Peter H. Juviler, Barnard College, Columbia University
Hiroshi Kimura, Visiting Scholar, George Washington University
Leon Lipson, Yale Law School
Yurii Luryi, The University of Manitoba Faculty of Law
Peter B. Maggs, University of Illinois College of Law
John Morie, Columbia University
Michael A. Newcity, New York City
Christopher Osakwe, Tulane University School of Law
Stephen J. Osofsky, University of Tennessee
Manfred Pieck, Creighton University School of Law
Leonid Polsky, Kew Gardens, New York
Stanislaw Pomorski, Rutgers University School of Law, Camden
Bernard Ramundo, Chevy Chase, Maryland
Logan Robinson, Visiting Fellow, Documentation Office for East European Law, University of Leyden
Cynthia Semmler, New York City
Robert Sharlet, Union College
Gordon B. Smith, Texas Christian University
Peter Solomon, University of Toronto
Zigurds L. Zile, University of Wisconsin-Madison Law School

The Editors

NOTES

1. The quotations are from Karl R. Popper, *The Poverty of Historicism* (London, 1957), pp. 43 and 66-67. See also Popper's *The Open Society and Its Enemies* (London, 1945), *passim*.

2. The quotations are from Roscoe Pound, *Interpretations of Legal History* (New York, 1923), pp. 152 and 164.

3. Roscoe Pound, *An Introduction to the Philosophy of Law* (New Haven, 1959), p. 47.

4. For an example of an attack from the right on Popper's view of social engineering see Popper, *The Poverty of Historicism*, *op.cit.*, p. 64.

A CONSTITUTION FOR "DEVELOPED SOCIALISM"

John N. Hazard*

Why open an analysis of problems of social engineering in Soviet law with examination of a Soviet constitution, albeit new? Is it not but a "largely cosmetic" document as some Westerners are saying? [1] Is it not designed solely to attract the disadvantaged of the world to the Soviet system; a document without lasting import; a document that is unenforcible against the régime and so easily amendable as to lack even a semblance of permanency? Although hailed by its promoters as a program for a new era in Soviet development,[2] of what predictive value can it be if the system is directed by pragmatists, reputed by one keen observer to be presiding over a Communist Party where ideology is dead? [3] Under such circumstances would it not be more revealing of future trends to examine behavior of mature Western societies which have moved already into what is being called the "post-industrial era?"[4] If this direction were taken, one could ignore constitutional professions of goals and ask whether "developed socialism," as proclaimed in the USSR, will lead inevitably in the same direction of "post-industrial" society. If such a trend were discerned, one could assume that Brezhnev and his colleagues would have no alternative but to float along with it, acquiescing in the impact of the inescapable social, economic, and political forces now seen to be influencing the course of events in the West.

No thoughtful person can overlook such considerations, for there is evidence to support them. Still, I am prepared to argue that in spite of the impact of elemental forces which influence Soviet society as they influence all societies, there is room for manoeuver, and the constitution presents the master plan, detailing the solutions Soviet leaders are prepared to offer to the problems they perceive to be facing them. Constitutions of the past, whether of 1918, 1923, or 1936[5] have been found by those who look back at history to have given a clue to what Soviet leaders hoped to do, and although events sometimes forced concessions, the grand lines are generally recognized as having been followed. It is my argument that the document of 1977 is no less revealing of goals among men and women who seem to me at least to be

* Research was aided by Roger Morie, at the time a student in the School of Law under a grant from the School.

more than pragmatists, being still ideologically oriented, still clinging, perhaps doggedly, to a belief system outlined for them by Marx and Engels in 1848, developed in its leadership principles by Lenin just prior to the Russian revolution, and now become an element of what have been called the distal antecedents of those who lead.

If this position be valid, there is reason to turn to the new constitution as an indication of perceived problems and projected solutions, for the constitution purports to be a program, even a "table of contents" of Soviet law as a whole, a framework in popular terms designed to inspire peoples of the Soviet Union and even the world, as well as a basic law creating a structure of government. It reads like a guide to action, and may be designed as a strait-jacket to prevent departure from current programs after the present generation of leaders passes from the scene.[6] It may be the key, newly forged by the leaders, in the expectation that Soviet society can be turned from the route of the "post-industrial era" to open a door to something more hopeful. Daniel Bell sees Soviet leadership as equally vulnerable to social forces beyond their control as Western leaders, but the Soviet communists refuse to accept his verdict.[7] To them man, armed with what Marxism has taught him, is still able to design his own future.

1. Why a Constitution?

Westerners are wont to ask "why draft a constitution to incorporate a program?" Are not the legislators, administrators, and judges of a one-party state such as the USSR sufficiently subject to the Program of the Communist Party to require nothing more to guide them? History has not indicated that all societies require a constitution to aid the governing process. The English have lived with satisfaction for centuries without a formal constitution. They have been content to rest their governmental structure and belief system upon scattered Royal rescripts, charters, Parliamentary statutes, and even conventions. New Zealanders have thought it sufficient to their needs to follow the Mother Country's example. The Israelis have preferred to do without a constitution rather than to face the disruptive struggle expected if the issue of the role of religion in the state were opened in formal manner. Many societies in the Third World have endured for years political life conducted under suspended constitutions when the military has driven the constitution makers from power. Why has the Soviet leadership consistently put its mind to constitution drafting since its assumption of power? Lenin placed his colleague Sverdlov in charge of the drafting process in 1918 after the Third Congress of Soviets assumed power from the Constituent Assembly. By July, 1918, the first constitution was ready, making permanent the structures erected on the first day of the new régime in 1917, and formalized by the Third Congress in January, 1918.

When the question of "Why a constitution?" was put in conversation to a noted Eastern European judge of the International Court of Justice some years ago, his response was a laugh. To put the question in the late 20th century was, evidently, absurd. Perhaps his mind flashed back to the history of the Russian people, to their efforts in the early 19th century to regularize the autocratic rule of the Tsar, to the Decembrists, the reformers of Alexander II's court, to the *Zemstvo* chairmen of the turn of this century, and finally to the riots of 1905 and the Basic Law of 1906.[8] Perhaps he thought of the craving of the Russian people, not only of the intellectuals, for a constituent assembly to choose a system of government after the abdication of Nicholas II. It was a craving of such intensity that not only the Provisional Government of 1917, but even the Bolsheviks sensed strongly that they had to support the elections,[9] and on achieving power they proceeded to permit the deputies to assemble in Petrograd even after the Second Congress of Soviets had set up the Soviet system on the day after the fall of the Winter Palace. They had to label the new structures "provisional" to give a sense to the public that a choice was still open.[10] Perhaps the International Court judge also remembered Sverdlov's committee to which reference has been made, and the seemingly naive expectation of some of its members that a structure like that of Switzerland or some other Western democracy could still be adopted even though Stalin was already telling his fellow committee members that the decisions of the Third Congress of Soviets were irreversible.[11] Indubitably, Russian experience played a part in public demand for a constitution.

But, one can imagine reasons why the judge of the International Court would think of other variables. He had lived long in the West, even in England. He knew Western thinking about restraints on arbitrary power, and that in all but England, these restraints had to be in a constitution. Lenin also had lived long in the West. Perhaps that is why he thought also of friends he could win for Bolshevism if he were to follow the pattern of the constitution makers. Knowing Lenin's experience, and being keenly aware of his own, the judge seems to have thought it absurd that Marxist-oriented states would not have constitutions.

The propaganda value of constitutions has also been perceived and well stated by a prominent American political scientist. He has written, "The most efficient modern device for achieving this [participation and coordination of a large number of people to function well] has been some form of 'constitutionalism.' The only alternatives are the dictatorial application of police terror and aggressive militarism."[12]

This American specialist goes on to say that terror and militarism may be functional if they provide material progress, but in cultures with experience in constitutionalism, governing through such means "has proved [to be] almost impossible because of the inordinate investment that must be made in maintaining large terrorist and military organizations." He suggests that today the behavioral sciences and behavioral drugs may facilitate manipulation of masses, but this has yet to be demonstrated.

If these reflections are valid, Lenin in 1918 was influenced by Russian tradition, by his appreciation of the propagandistic appeal both at home and abroad of a document to be read by millions, and also by the practicality of cutting costs of government by catering to the aspirations of peoples conditioned by their struggle against autocracy. He set his draftsmen to work to strengthen his hand. He knew that his Red Army was still immature, and his Chief of the Cheka was still having difficulty creating a disciplined apparatus of terror. Finally, the soviets in villages and towns were still feeling their oats. They were by no means prepared to accept a centralized disciplined system of government. Even the Communist Party was having difficulty in leading, for until mid-1918, it had to assuage the Left Socialist Revolutionaries and some of the Mensheviks who had not gone over wholly to the opposition. The system was still far from the powerful régime of today.

When federation was brought about in 1922 as a compromise measure to pacify minorities not yet ready to accept the dictum of the 1848 Communist Manifesto that "workers know no fatherland," a constitutional structure became still more important. No leadership has attempted federation without a constitution. Some framework of commanding status is necessary to bring together peoples who are still somewhat suspicious of each other's willingness to renounce efforts to dominate. Such a structure was necessary in 1789 for the United States; it was found to be necessary for Australians and Argentinians and Mexicans, all of whom were in considerable measure within the same culture. How much more was it necessary among the peoples of the former Russian Empire whose fear of the Great Russians was so great that Lenin had been forced to permit secession in 1918 to avoid the risk of losing power even over Great Russians among whom he was building his stronghold? The first federal constitution was a limited document, being composed of nothing more than the treaty of union, signed at the very end of December, 1922, and of a copy of the Soviet structure, first established in 1917 but now to be raised to the federal level to be the government of the USSR. It contained no preamble other than the treaty, no bill of rights, no electoral law defining who was to wield power. In the narrowest sense, it was "state law" and nothing more. This was, evidently, so obvious that no one challenged the term "state law;" no one suggested that a new "constitutional law" had come into existence, as some were to do 52 years later.

In the light of the 1918 and 1923 steps toward constitutional structures, which were followed immediately by redrafting of the constitutions of the four republics that had entered the federation in 1922, roots were established from which retreat would have been difficult, if not unthinkable. The terror and militarism which served Stalin in the late 1930's were not yet possible, for they would have required unacceptably high costs in government and loss of prestige in the eyes of Soviet citizens and of the peoples of the world.

2. Why New Documents Rather than Amendments?

If the argument is accepted that in light of the many variables influencing Lenin's thinking of 1918 he could not have done other than order his committee to draft a first constitution, and when he had one, to stay with constitutions forever, there is a second question to be asked? Why have there been so many constitutions? Why is it not enough to have only one, like the United States? Americans have found it possible to meet the changing needs of the times with amendments, and with the updating by interpretation which has been the work of the United States Supreme Court.

Both Stalin and Brezhnev have given their answers to why they have presented an entirely new document rather than content themselves with amendments of what they had inherited. Both spokesmen find their inspiration, so they say, in Marxist thought on law. It is a well-known position: law is superstructure reflecting an economic base. When the economic base changes with the inexorable process of change in the types of means of production and their ownership, law must just as inevitably reflect the change. After the process has been understood with mastery of the Marxist method of analysis, those who have mastered are in a position not solely to follow economic change but to influence in some measure the future course of it. In familiar American terms they are in a position to conduct social engineering. Thus, law in a Marxist oriented and properly led society can be manipulated, so Marxists hold, to avoid the impact of forces previously thought to be inexorable, and society can be prevented from falling prey to the forces of the "post-industrial era."

Stalin explained that in application of this principle, 1936 was the appropriate year for a new constitution.[13] The last vestiges of private employment for profit had been wiped out. All Soviet citizens were now members of the same class, except perhaps for the priests, at least if class is defined in the Marxian mode as determined by "relationship to the means of production." Socialism had been achieved, if it is to be defined with an eye solely to the abolition of "exploitation" of man by man. Already in 1930 Stalin had rejected the popular idea of conventional socialists that its definition had another component, that of equality of distribution, and he had legitimized a system of material incentives that he thought necessary to stimulate production in a society which had not yet eliminated capitalism from the minds of men.

The year 1936 was seen, therefore, as an appropriate date for a new beginning, for removal of the restraints placed of the franchise in the constitution of Soviet Russia in 1918, as the non-worker and non-peasant elements were now an infinitesimal part of the population. It was also an appropriate time to restructure the top echelon of the state system, as the unwieldy Congress of Soviets, which had been carried over into the Soviet era as a symbol of mass participation in policy making, was no longer necessary or desirable. A representative system patterned on parliamentary structures would be not only less unwieldy but in all likelihood more attractive to the workers of the West who were familiar with such structures.

An American, familiar with the process of amendment, might expect it to be possible to expand the franchise, as had been done by the anti-slavery and women's vote amendments, to the United States Constitution and even to alter the top echelon of the representative system as was done when United States Senators were made subject to popular election, without drafting an entirely new Basic Law. It has even been possible in the United States to expand the constitution with a Bill of Rights by amendment, and to enlarge its application greatly, as with the XIV Amendment. These are not inconsequential changes, but they have required no massive redrafting. Why has the Soviet leadership thought amendments inadequate?

The answer is not a simple one: indeed, the leadership in 1935 had only amendments in mind, for the Communist Party instructed a drafting committee to prepare amendments to the 1923 document.[14] Only some months later was the directive changed to require the drafting of a wholly new document. The reason was given that the changes, necessary because of the achievement of "socialism," required more than amendment; they required a structure that could serve as a symbol of a new stage in social development. This position is understandable, for even non-Marxists have thought it desirable from time to time to sense a new beginning. How else can one explain the five republics of France? Europeans seem not to sense the desirability of state stability; indeed, they indicate from time to time that their urge to revolt has not been satiated. They demand a new symbol to mark a new stage. Soviet leaders may have been in the same emotional tradition, intensified in its effect upon them by what they have learned from Marx as to law as reflective of the economic base.

Whatever the reason, the decision was made to draft anew. Some analysts would suggest that the motivation for change lay not alone in Marxism, but in the desire of Stalin to perpetuate his name. In a sense, in spite of his great power, he was living in Lenin's shadow. This was a help in holding the loyalty of masses whose reverence for Lenin knew no bounds, but after more than a decade and a half of rule alone, it was time to begin casting a shadow of one's own. It was time to create "Stalinism" to bracket with "Leninism." Knowing what we all do of the pervasiveness of application of "Lord Acton's rule," the explanation may likely have been craving for recognition of power, and no more, but it seems likely that the rooting of the desire for a new document is to be found at a deeper level of consciousness.

With the precedent of change to reflect social development established by Stalin in 1936, it is not surprising that steps were taken by his successors to draft a new constitution after his death. George Ginsburgs has already chronicled those early efforts initiated by Nikita Khrushchev. He has demonstrated that they emerged rather slowly, and not until Stalin had been denounced in February, 1956, at the XX Communist Party Congress.[15] He has demonstrated that, just as in 1935, the first thoughts were given to amendment and not to total revision. Progress toward a new document was slow, in Ginsburgs' view, because of the new leader's desire to emphasize stability of law following upon Stalin's practice of rewriting some provision or other of the constitution at almost every session of the Supreme Soviet. To be sure, much of the rewriting was relatively inconsequential, caused as it was by the fact that the 1936 document had listed all of the Ministries and the territorial subdivisions of the country in its articles. This required amendment every time there was administrative change. But the changes were not all so inconsequential.

Ginsburgs notes that, in practice, the lawmaking agencies created in 1936 had not performed the functions originally assigned them. The Supreme Soviets in both federal and republic systems had enacted very few laws in spite of their monopoly on lawmaking. Their attention seemed to have been limited to the law on the economic plan, and the law on the annual budget. The great bulk of norms had emerged as edicts of the Presidia of the federal and republic Supreme Soviets, denominated "provisional" to be sure and submitted to the respective Supreme Soviet later for confirmation, but put into effect immediately as if they were "law." During wartime years the Supreme Soviet was moribund, and legislation was left to the Presidium. Even after the war, the Supreme Soviet rarely met twice a year as required by the 1936 Constitution. This lethargy at the top extended to the Supreme Soviets of the republics, and even to those in the provinces, cities, and villages.

Ginsburgs chronicles additional inadequacies of practice: no procedure for passing laws was stipulated in the constitution; no specification indicated who or what had the right of legislative initiative; at lower levels, the assemblies of the soviets were inadequately protected against usurpation of authority by their executive committees, so much so that deputies ceased attending meetings in spite of the discipline under which they were supposed to live. Even the permanent committees of the assemblies, supposed to debate policy before meetings of the assemblies, attracted little interest because their sessions were directed by the executive committee or even, as Ginsburgs says, by the chief civil servant of the administrative department they were appointed to supervise. All of these inadequacies suggested reform of the constitution, but the Communist Party leaders at the outset appear to have thought that no new document was needed, only amendment.

Not until the XXI Communist Party Congress in 1959 was there evidence of a change in attitude toward drafting. Krushchev told the Congress that the events of the preceding years required reflection in the constitution, these being: expansion of the socialist system to much of the world, and development of the Soviet economy so that building a communist society had become a practical task. Voroshilov a week later elaborated on change, referring to evolution of the collective farm structure, to the alteration in the federal organs of administration, to the expansion of the republics' competency, to the increasing activity of trade unions and social organizations.

The first step toward a completely new document was taken in 1962 when Khrushchev appointed a drafting committee of 97 members under his chairmanship to prepare a text, telling the Supreme Soviet that there must be a completely new Basic Law. He spoke after many comments had already been published in the Soviet law reviews, indicating what needed to be done. Ginsburgs has chronicled these articles and summarized the proposals. Perhaps the most imposing was a paper by P. S. Romashkin, Director of the Institute of State and Law of the USSR Academy of Sciences.[16] With the 1977 document before us, it can be noted that many of its innovations were suggested by Romashkin and his fellow authors in the long years between the first suggestion of amendment and 1977.

Some of the proposals to which heed has been given are: removal of the lists of Ministries and provinces, making recurring amendment unnecessary as administrative changes are introduced to improve economic efficiency; introduction of a programmatic preamble to set forth in popular language both the course that has been followed since 1917 and the course of things to come; clarification of the role of the Presidium in its relations with the Supreme Soviet; enhancement of the prestige of soviets with emphasis upon their role as organizers of mass participation in administration; definition of the functions of committees of soviets in preparing drafts for legislation; designation of the agencies granted the right of legislative initiative; recognition of the trade unions and other social organizations as having a role to play in developing policy in the areas of their competence; and, most dramatically, elevation of the Communist Party from the secluded place it was given in the 1936 document among the organizations in which citizens might associate to a prominent place in chapter I of the 1977 draft as one of the pillars of the political system. It is now no longer merely an association of the most active and politically conscious citizens as was its position under old Article 126. It is currently declared by Article 6 to be "the leading and guiding force of Soviet society and the nucleus of its political system, of all state and public organizations."

The doctrinal revolutionary rephrasing introduced by Khrushchev into the 1961 Program of the Communist Party,[17] is reflected in the 1977 document, as all authors have said it must be ever since it was propounded to replace the phrase "dictatorship of the proletariat," hallowed since the 1848 Manifesto. The 1977 Constitution opens with the declaration that the USSR is a "socialist state of the whole people, expressing the will and interests of the working class, the peasantry and the intelligentsia, of all the nations and nationalities in the country." It is now a more broadly based system than that expressed in the 1936 document which declared the USSR to be "a socialist state of workers and peasants." The change has not been made without some opposition, one of the critics being a worker who communicated his views to the press during the summer of 1977, alleging that under the new wording the parasites and speculators of modern times could be included within the group that governs. His criticism was levelled at the change in nomenclature of the soviets, made to correspond with the restated doctrine of the USSR as a state of the whole people. Under the new phraseology, the soviets of working people's deputies have been renamed soviets of people's deputies, and to the protester the word "people" includes the dishonest as well the honest.[18]

Less arresting structural changes have been made in the document in keeping with the suggestions made by commentators between the date of beginning the new draft and its promulgation. Thus, the bill of rights has been moved forward in the document from its place near the end of the Constitution of 1936. It is now placed immediately following the 1977 statement of principles underlying the social, political, and economic structure. This puts it before the definition of the state structure, as Romashkin thought desirable to indicate the Soviet system's increased concern for human rights.

Another structural rearrangement proposed in the 1960's and reflected in the 1977 document is moving of the chapter of electoral law from its humble position in the 1936 document just prior to the provisions on arms, flag, and capital, and the amendment procedure, to a position prior to the chapter on organs of state power constituted by the elected deputies.

It is structural changes such as the last two which have attracted Western comment as "cosmetic," and "cosmetic" they are, but in a field like constitutionalism where, as the American political scientist cited earlier has said, "constitutionalism is a self-fulfilling myth that can be approximated if it is believed in and is, to that extent, 'scientifically' valid," cosmetic change may have political importance. If this be so, it becomes evident why a new document needed to be drafted, for it would have been an absurdity to introduce an amendment saying simply, "Chapter X on Fundamental Rights shall be renumbered as Part II, Chapter 7," and another saying that "Chapter XI on the electoral system shall be renumbered Part IV, Chapter 12."

3. What Are the Clues to Impending Social Change?

Not all of the 1977 Constitution is devoted to structure of state institutions. Some provisions seem designed to foretell the course of social change. These may look to Westerners as matters of detail, but to a doctrinally oriented leadership they could have social significance. Such are the clauses on collective farms, which provide clues as to what is in store for them, whether as self-directed cooperative-type structures or as state enterprises comparable to factories in their administration. Stalin declared in what was to prove to be his final major theoretical paper, published only a few months before his death, that collective farm property should be transformed into property of all the people.[19] This suggested that the collective farm structure would be transformed into state enterprise structure.

Stalin's theme was taken up after his death by commentators and also by Khrushchev, in spite of denunciation of Stalin's tactics of government. Ginsburgs tells of suggestions that the new constitution formulate the policy of synthesis of the existing two types of property by recognizing the existence of a transitional form, the inter-collective farm ownership of enterprises and mixed cooperative-state undertakings.[20] He then provides statistics demonstrating the trend of the times. Since he wrote in the early 1960's, there has been an effort to stem the transition, as collective farmers became alarmed with the amalgamation of farms, and their re-creation as great agricultural factories in enterprise form. After Khrushchev's ouster, Brezhnev found it necessary to calm farmers' fears lest production falter.

Perhaps the conflict over agricultural policy explains the 1977 Constitution's cautious omission of any pointed reference to transition. The language of Article 12 is limited to "The State shall facilitate the development of collective farm cooperative ownership and its approximation to state ownership." This facilitation has been evidenced, as all who follow Soviet agriculture know, by the introduction of guaranteed wages for collective farmers, social insurance coverage for them, and continuing amalgamation to such an extent that the mass meetings of members envisaged by the old Model Charter of 1935 were no longer possible and a new model charter had to be promulgated setting forth the new rules. Stephen Osofsky has concluded in his book on the subject that the collective farms may well be transformed into state farms,[21] and the 1977 document seems to leave the road open to such a change if "approximation" means similarity of such a nature that differences are imperceptible.

Public participation in administration is a second topic whose future is plotted. In Khrushchev's time, it became his favorite project. He pushed it to such a point that he told the XX Communist Party Congress that it was the critical step toward public self-administration, and the "withering away of the state." Ginsburgs cites authors speaking of constitutional reform suggesting that public participation meant introduction of the popular referendum, national discussion of drafts of important legislation, and heightened activity within the public organizations.[22] The 1977 document indicates that the various proposals for reform did not fall on deaf ears. There are now to be referenda and national discussion of legislation. Article 9 says:

"The principal orientation in the development of Soviet society's political system shall be the further unfolding of socialist democracy: increasing broader participation of citizens in the administration of the affairs of society, continuous improvement of the state apparatus, enhancement of the activity of public organizations, intensification of control by the people, strengthening of the legal foundation of state and social life, extension of publicity, and taking constant account of public opinion."

Clearly, the 1977 draftsmen wanted to make much of the public's role in administration as a major element of socialist democracy. They did not say, as Lenin had his 1918 document say, and as Khrushchev told the Communist Party in 1956, that this increasing participation is related to the beginning of a process of self-administration, alternatively called "withering away of the state," as socialism advances to communism, but Brezhnev added this when making his final comments on the draft and discussion.[23] Thus, although this hoary doctrine, enunciated by Marx and Engels as the inevitable result of the elimination of classes from society, is now deemphasized, it is not dead. It has only been omitted from constitutional verbiage.

4. Has "Constitutional Law" Replaced "State Law"?

Perhaps the most refreshing idea to emerge after Brezhnev assumed Khrushchev's position as chairman of the constitutional drafting committee came from two editors of a book prepared under the supervision of the late Professor V. F. Kotok.[24] The editors' position and that of Kotok as well was proclaimed in the very title of the book. Instead of being entitled *"Gosudarstvennoe Pravo"* (State Law), as all such texts had been entitled since Imperial times, it bore the title *"Konstitutsionnoe Pravo"* (Constitutional Law).

To the outsider the change in title would seem inconsequential, but the vicious attack to which the change has been subjected indicates that there is more to it than meets the Western eye. Professor Christopher Osakwe has made the issue clear for Westerners in an extensive review of the book.[25] One has the impression from the way the authors treat the topic that the dying Kotok wanted to strike one last blow for his idea, since the authors ascribe their interest in developing the theme of constitutional law to Professor Kotok and the late very well known Professor I. P. Trainin.[26]

Kotok's disciples argue that their title even goes beyond Kotok's earlier position, but presumably he agreed with their extension of his views, for his sector of constitutional problems of the USSR's Academy of Sciences, with his name included as director, is listed as critical reviewer of the manuscript. Such a task is not taken lightly in the USSR, as all specialists in Sovietology know. The authors declare that they have introduced the new name to their book because they want it to reflect what they call the full scope of the discipline. For them, and presumably for Professor Kotok, the issue is more than one of terminology; it reflects a new point of view.

In developing their theme, the authors say that they find the traditional title "state law" unacceptable for two reasons: (1) the general public identified the traditional term with all branches of domestic law, while specialists relate it only to one branch of domestic law. This makes for confusion as to what it meant since public and specialists are not thinking of the same thing when they use it. As to reason number (2), the term "state law" as understood by specialists is too narrow, failing to indicate the breadth of concern suggested by the term "constitutional law." The subject is a broad one and deserves a broad term, for the constitution is concerned with far more than the state apparatus, the structure of government. It defines the whole structure of authority in society, as evidenced by its inclusion of provisions on the role of the non-state guiding association, the Communist Party. Also, it purports to regulate a variety of social relationships, many of which cut across each others' formal boundary lines which are structured on the vertical lines of criminal law, labor law, procedural law, etc. Social relationships cannot be grouped in vertically structured compartments; they must be grouped across vertically structured branch lines in a horizontally structured discipline. Constitutional law provides just such a horizontally integrating function, and the totality of its horizontal relationships sketch out society's profile, defining the character of all relationships. Thus, it reflects the political and economic structure of society and the status of the individual. Since this broad body of relationships is clearly reflected in legal form in the constitution itself, it is appropriate to speak of "constitutional law" and not the narrower vertically structured "state law."[27]

Professor Kotok had made his argument in an article published in 1971,[28] saying that branches of law need not be defined solely according to the subject they regulate, but that it is possible also to structure branches according to the method of regulation. Thus, constitutional law acts as a depository of basic principles for the legal system of a society. Kotok seems to feel that the traditionalists obscure the nature of the constitution as the supreme law when they insist that there is no single field of constitutional law, but only a reflection of the constitution within the traditional vertically structured branches of criminal law, labor law, procedural law, civil law, etc.

Kotok's 1971 piece was paired with that of his opponent, Professor A. I. Lepeshkin, also of the Moscow Institute of State and Law.[29] The latter denied that the term "constitutional law" was appropriate, because he thought that branches of legal science could be formed only through examination of a specific sphere of public or social relationships. Since State law deals with various forms of direct national power, with the sovereignty of the Soviet state, and with the legal status of the citizen, he saw no reason to extend the discipline into other fields by creating a new name and, presumably, a new branch of law overlapping other branches.

These 1971 articles lay the basis for the new book and the attack upon it by the Lepeshkin school, an attack so vehement that it ends with the statement that the book cannot be recommended to students.[30] The outsider cannot but wonder whether there is something deeper in issue than a name, whether there is perhaps an inter-institutional power struggle between department chiefs in which one thinks the other is trying to take over a part of his work, if not become the supreme academic leader, relying for his authority on the preeminent place occupied by the constitution above the traditionally structured branches of law.

Some clue as to the possible ramifications of the argument beyond an internecine feud is provided by the new book's authors' examination of what they believe to be the sources of their constitutional law. They refer to the resolutions of the Communist Party adopted at the XX Congress on strengthening socialist legality and developing democracy, indicating that these resolutions played a very great part in expanding socialist popular participation in the exercise of authority in the country.[31] Such resolutions enhance the factual role and legal significance of constitutional norms themselves, as when the practice was begun after 1957 to submit to public discussion drafts of laws, although the 1936 Constitution was silent on the subject. The authors seem to be saying that constitutional law must include activities of the Communist Party.

Westerners may conclude that the authors are trying to insinuate–into an environment that is hostile to the idea in bald form–that constitutional law has to do with more than state institutions; its concern is democratic social relationships so broad as to constitute a new social compact. Since constitutional law is the heart of the Soviet legal system, it must stand at the center and be definitive of all other relationships. Having taken this stance, the authors are determined to defend the heartland against all incursions. This leads them to the previously unheard of proposal that the new constitution introduces a new institution of constitutional control other than that performed today by the Procurator General of the USSR. They do not propose a constitutional court, such as Tito created in Yugoslavia, but they want at least a constitutional council.[32] This would have the duty to ascertain that all lawmaking bodies, even the highest, conform to the constitution. They argue that such a radical departure from past practice is necessary, and that it is justified by transgression in the past. To make their proposal palatable, they say that the Communist Party has been struggling with "subjectivism" and "voluntarism," two terms for Stalin's and Khrushchev's methods of governing respectively, and they cite the Party's resolutions that prove it. They seem to suggest that an instrument of constitutional control might have prevented the legislation of earlier years which violated the constitution, and to accommodate which the constitution was amended years later. While such expectation may seem unrealistic to those who follow Soviet political developments from abroad, the authors have thought it fit to express it, and their argument may be a straw in the wind of change.

If the authors have opened a new door to constitutional stability to be enforced through constitutional control, their opponents are going to try to restrain them. The review of the book already mentioned attacks the authors in the same vein as Lepeshkin attacked Kotok, namely that they are upsetting the traditional system of vertical structuring of Soviet law by proposing to structure their new discipline horizontally. Further, they are concerning themselves with more than legislation. They cannot be permitted to reach into social relationships having an impact on the creation of norms, *i.e.* into the Communist Party. Further, they are criticized for failure to comprehend the programmatic nature of the constitution, *i.e.* that it is not intended for enforcement, but is a statement of aspiration. If this anti-Kotok view were taken, presumably there could be no enforcement of rights on the theory that they spring from "general principles."

A clue to thinking of top Party leadership on the Kotok argument emerged in the final stage of discussion of the new constitution when the draft was prepared for promulgation. To the surprise of Westerners, a paragraph was added to Article 6 concerning the role of the Communist Party to read, "All Party organizations operate within the framework of the USSR Constitution." This suggests that any policy change decided upon by the Party must, in the future, be routed through the amendment procedure of the constitution before being put into practice. Such a practice cannot prevent sudden change, but it will require the Party to publish its proposal in advance, thus submitting it to public scrutiny, if not telling debate, and the methods of Stalin of unheralded change will become unconstitutional. Without means of controlling the Communist Party through institutional structures, the limitation is not complete, but it suggests a trend toward stability, toward elimination of great leaps that constitute total surprise. The Communist Party seems, thus, to be establishing for the first time a policy of keeping the public informed of what it intends to do as the supreme social engineer.

5. What Shall the Constitution Include?

Having decided, apparently, that a constitution is preferable to the English type of constitunional law, and that the constitution should be a symbol of stability, although not wholly impervious to amendment or even replacement at historically important milestones, the leadership has faced the question of what to place within it. This question proved to be the major topic of discussion during the summer months when the draft was placed before the public for discussion prior to promulgation in October, for many proposals were made to increase its coverage beyond what the draftsmen had proposed.[33]

Stalin had faced the same question in 1936 when his draft was similarly put up for discussion. Critics called for a programmatic preamble such as Lenin had placed in the Russian Republic's Constitution of 1918, and for a wide variety of detail on court procedure, and even for elevation to the level of the constitution of the existing civil code's provisions on inheritance. Stalin was reluctant to increase the coverage in this way. He rejected the idea of a preamble, saying it was unnecessary in a document having as its primary purpose the definition of state structure. He wanted to omit detail, saying that a constitution was not a code of laws, but he was willing to insert a provision guaranteeing inheritance, presumably to stimulate a will to work. Beyond this, he was not prepared to go.[34]

The same desire to expand the constitution to cover a wide field re-emerged when Khrushchev called in 1962 for a new document. Romashkin's noted article indicated that pressures were strong for a preamble, setting the grand line for the future, and for inclusion of more detail on human rights than Stalin had provided.[35] Much later, when the People's Republic of China promulgated its Basic Law of 1975 with but 32 articles, it was denounced for its shortness as well as for ideological reasons.[36] The noted Soviet specialist of Chinese law, L. W. Godoshnikov, attacked the brevity, especially the abbreviation of the Bill of Rights into four articles.[37] The consensus of Soviet leaders seemed to be that a preamble and more detail was desirable, but the document that emerged in October 1977 from the discussion suggests that the draftsmen decided upon a compromise. They were prepared to introduce a preamble and some detail in their 174 articles, but they rejected incorporation of the wide variety of provisions proposed during the summer months.

The major issue of length seems to have been focussed upon demands that provisions of the various federal Fundamental Principles of law incorporated in the constitution itself. These Fundamentals had been enacted after Stalin's death as obligatory guides to the various republics in redrafting their codes of law following amendment of the 1936 document to substitute this method of indirect guidance for Stalin's 1936 provision calling for direct drafting of federal codes of law.

The issue for the 1977 draftsmen was this: what was the existing relationship between federal Fundamentals and the constitution, and how much of them should be capsulated in the new document? All those who wrote on the subject agreed that the federal Fundamentals are more than ordinary laws. An author, published before the 1977 draft, called them laws of "constitutional import," although not themselves of the universal character of the constitution. He thought that this meant that they created "rights," and he cited the provisions on medical care created by the Fundamentals of Public Health Legislation as an example.[38] Another author wanted to add to the list of norms of constitutional import the Statutes on Status of Working People's Deputies, and on USSR citizenship.[39]

An outsider may wonder what it means to declare a law of "constitutional import." Does it mean that it creates rights which cannot be withdrawn at all, or if withdrawn, the withdrawal requires extremely careful consideration? If this be their status, why need they be capsulated in the constitution, since it seems to add nothing? Some of them have been so capsulated, notably those relating to judicial structure and criminal procedure. One may wonder whether the three-judge bench is any more impregnable as a principle because it is included within the constitution than if it had remained in the Fundamentals alone. The same may be asked about the right to inherit decedents' estates, or the right to marriage. It is indeed a matter for comment that the right to divorce, which is incorporated in the Fundamentals on Marriage and the Family, is not included in Article 53 of the new constitution as marriage is. Is it any less firmly fixed in policy than marriage?

Although it is difficult to be certain what the proponents of incorporating Fundamentals into the constitution, or placing them in a category of laws of constitutional import are trying to say, the implication is present that there is perceived to be a difference in the longevity of constitutional principles and of ordinary laws or codes. The implication is present that proponents of constitutional status for a principle hope that this status will protect the principle against arbitrary change at the whim of the leader of the moment, even though there is no evident difference in the duty of the one institution of constitutional projection that exists, the Procurator General of the USSR, to protect all law, whether it be the constitution itself, the Fundamental Principles, or a simple law against any agency other than the Supreme Soviet acting as the representative of the popular will. This being the case, it begins to look as if the public thinks that the constitution is a limitation on the power of the social engineers even though its strength is in its halo, not its teeth.

6. Why a New Constitution in 1977?

A review of the many Federal Fundamentals enacted since 1958, and of other laws said to be of "constitutional import," discloses that these laws now touch almost every phase of state and citizen activity. This being the case, why was it thought necessary to introduce the constitution in the specific year 1977 to capsulate them? Would not any year earlier or later have been as suitable? Ostensibly, the occasion was the 60th anniversary of the founding of the Soviet state, and that might be reason enough, as it is well known that the Soviet leadership likes to celebrate milestones of history. There is always an amnesty at each turning point, as there was on this occasion, and there are always massive demonstrations and ceremonies in the Great Hall of the Soviets, as there were this time as well. But there have been similarly important occasions over the years, while the drafting has been continuing, which might have been chosen for promulgation. Perhaps the most auspicious prior occasion when a constitution would have seemed in order was the XXV Congress of the Communist Party in 1976. Indeed, many Soviet authors suggested that such a moment would be chosen for the unveiling of the draft, if not promulgation of the constitution itself. Two legal authors told the world that the constitution would emerge in the "nearest future,"[40] and Soviet officials and specialists suggested in private conversations that at least fundamentals for a draft would be presented at the Congress. American students in Soviet law schools said that their teachers referred to a draft that was in circulation among the specialists, and lawyers of the Ministry of Foreign Affairs indicated that the constitutional bill of rights was being updated to bring it into conformity with the United Nations Covenants of Human Rights. All was in readiness, but the date passed unnoticed except for Brezhnev's brief reference to the drafting process in his report as progressing in unhurried fashion.[41]

The assumption gained credence that there was no hurry because there were so many updated Fundamental Principles that the law was clear; because there was no intention to change the structure of governmental agencies; because general policy had been set forth in the 1961 Program of the Communist Party, and even because there was a division of opinion within the Political Buro of the Party as to whether a change was desirable in the relationship between the federal structure and the republics in view of the announced policy of bringing the various national minorities together into a homogeneous "Soviet people."

In light of the quiet that descended after the XXV Congress had passed, the appointment of new members of the drafting committee to replace those that had died or withdrawn came as a surprise in April, 1977.[42] The very fact that a draft was brought before the Party's Central Committee within a month[43] indicates that the reports of an existing draft had been correct, and that only final decision on various options was necessary to bring it into being officially. There is even indication that the final editing was done hastily, if one is to accept the explanation that the declaration that Union Republics are "sovereign" was omitted by mistake from what was then Article 75. This explanation is supported by reference to what was then Article 80, where the USSR is said to guarantee the Republics' sovereignty, and by restitution of the key word in the document finally promulgated. Perhaps one omission occurred because an earlier draft had reflected a decision to change the status of Union Republics, and when the decision was finally made to leave them as they were, the earlier draft was not revised.

It is tempting to suppose that the year 1977 was chosen suddenly for a new constitution not solely because it marked a milestone in the achievement of "developed socialism," but for another reason as well. This other reason, bizarre as it may seem, comes to mind when comparison is made with events in Yugoslavia and China, and when these events are related to a phenomenon common to all three leadership systems, namely the phenomenon of old age. Much was made in 1977 by Western political scientists of the advancing average age of Politburo members,[44] and of the precarious health of some of them. Age is evidently becoming a factor in Soviet decision making. The same is also true in Yugoslavia as Tito moves through his 80's, and it was true during Mao's declining years. Both Mao and Tito promulgated new constitutions, and these documents show they had succession in mind. It seems that they sought to bind their successors to policies which they revered by putting them into a constitution. Can the same motivation lie behind the 1977 Constitution which Brezhnev's aging Politburo prepared?

An answer to this question depends, one would suppose, upon assessment of the present leaders' confidence in the younger generation's determination to maintain their contemporary system when it achieves power. One might well have assumed some years ago that there would be no departure from current patterns after over 60 years of inculcation of the system, but revelations made in Brezhnev's report on the discussion of the draft, as well as Soviet action in 1968 to stop Czechoslovak experimentation, raises doubts as to a unity of view on future directions among the juniors within the leadership group.

Brezhnev's revelations to the Supreme Soviet—called to promulgate the constitution—were unexpected. He revealed that in the discussion there were those who proposed abolishing the federation and proceeding to the establishment of a unitary state, presumably structured to facilitate economic planning without regard to ethnic sensibilities. Secondly, voices proposed abolishing the state apparatus and putting the entire burden of administration upon the Communist Party itself, and thirdly some proposed return to the system of egalitarian pay and abandonment of the graduated material incentives which had been introduced in 1930 to encourage production. All three of these proposals appear to be reflections of an attitude which Lenin might have castigated as "left-wing childishness," since they suggest that there are persons who want to get on swiftly to the communist stage of economic and political development, as did some of the leftists in 1917.

In sharp contrast to the leftists, there seems also to have emerged a wing within the Party which favors a development something akin to that proposed by Dubček in Czechoslovakia, namely a humanization of the system by introducing limited pluralism both economically and politically. This group may favor, as did Dubček, indicative planning, worker-management, expanded private enterprise within the service trades and even in small industry, enterprise autonomy within the state sector, and perhaps even a revived socialist party. All of these steps were taken by the Czechoslovak Communist Party in 1968, not in the name of retreat from Marxist socialism, but in the name of strengthening it. In Poland and Hungary some of these steps in modified form have been taken, and they are so prominent in Yugoslavia as to excite doubts that the Soviet leadership as at present constituted would leave the Yugoslav political scene untouched if weakness develops after Tito's death. Perhaps the Soviet leadership is thinking even of what the Western European communists have been saying, notably in Italy and Spain. It may be that the constitution is to set a pattern toward which all communists are expected to move.

If these fears from the left and from the liberalizing center are really extant, it may be that the present leadership hopes through its new constitution to build a fortress in defense of the features of the Soviet system that have become "sacred": the Communist Party monopoly as vanguard leader, the totally owned state economy, the state apparatus parallelling the Party, the federal structure, the concept of centralized economic planning, the structure of centralized industrial management, the collective farm-state farm system, and support for material incentives to production. These are the features on which the leadership has been relying to effectuate its program of social engineering; these are the building blocks of a wall that will prevent, hopefully, society's drift into the "post-industrial era." If this be the aim, repetition in 1977 at the threshold of the leadership's old age may be desired to fix in the minds of the Soviet people with the freshness of newness a program from which no younger leadership generation dare stray, lest it stimulate popular opposition too strong to contain.

7. Thoughts of the Soviet Emigrés

Strange as it may seem to Westerners that Soviet leadership is concluding that a new constitution can serve as a bastion against the program of an oncoming generation with other ideas for the future, some credence to the theory is to be gained from papers written by former Soviet citizens who have reached the West. Valery Chalidze, whose paper appears in this volume, has told Americans elsewhere that protesters in Moscow appeal to the leadership to conform to the constitution because they think it revered sufficiently in the Kremlin to restrain abuse of law.[45] Alexander Volpin suggests in a 55-page analysis what he wishes as improvement in the 1936 Constitution, implying that the constitution really matters.[46] He might have thrown up his hands in despair and declared that there is no hope of adequate reform within the system.

Volpin's paper provides Westerners some insight into what may also be in the minds of colleagues who have remained behind to share in the drafting process, the more so since several of his points were touched upon in the constitutional draft made public well after his departure. Most evident is his discussion of the federal Fundaments. He wants, like those who have remained at home to write upon the subject, to see the Fundamentals in skeletal form within the constitution. He suggests that stability is his aim, for he says it is easier to revise Fundamentals than to amend the constitution. In spite of his expectation that the constitution can assure some rights, he expects no change in Party determination to maintain its role. He says, "To demand of the Soviet constitution the complete repeal of the supreme influence of that party and its ideology before its ideal (the construction of communism) is realized is to demand from this supreme power that it cease to be itself."[47]

Volpin gives a second hint as to why a constitution is useful. He proposes specifically that the Fundamental Principles of Criminal Procedure be embodied in some fashion in the constitution.[48] But, here the reason is not potential resistance of the Supreme Soviet to any proposal to weaken the protective guarantees. He sees potential resistance elsewhere, for he argues that the public generally reads the constitution as it does not read the Fundamentals, and that if the public learns its rights, it will resist retrogression.

Volpin's point of view seems to have been held by the draftsmen who incorporated some procedural guarantees in the constitution, but other procedural guarantees of the codes have not been elevated to constitutional level. Of those that have been brought upward, perhaps the most important is the 1953 edict abolishing the Special Boards of the Ministry of the Interior which had sentenced to work camps millions during Stalin's purges. Article 160 now reads, "No person shall be considered guilty of a crime and subjected to criminal punishment except by verdict of a court and in conformity with criminal law." This provision of 1953 was designed to prevent the administrative trials of dissenters authorized by Stalin's decrees which required no conformity to the criminal code and the code of criminal procedure.

8. A New Bill of Rights

Soviet ratification in 1973 of the United Nations Covenants on Human Rights,[49] and signature of the Helsinki Declaration in 1975 with its "Basket III" containing reference to rights, seem also to have influenced the draftsmen of the new constitution, for there is considerable revision of the Bill of Rights as it stood in the 1936 Constitution. Soviet legal specialists within the Ministry of Foreign Affairs began preparation of a redrafted Bill of Rights soon after adherence to the International Covenants to bring the constitution into conformity with the new obligations, and the new constitution indicates the extent to which they have been able to create conformity. It is evident that early Soviet attitudes toward rights are still so deep that complete conformity has seemed impossible. Thus, the most characteristic feature of the 1936 Bill–the limitation on rights of freedom of expression to strengthening of the socialist system–remains.[50] The draftsmen of 1977 have even expanded upon this principle by adding a very specific Article 39 declaring, "Exercise by citizens of rights and freedoms must not injure the interests of society and of the state and the rights of other citizens."

New articles obviously inspired by the United Nations Covenants concern state protection of the family, the right to housing, the right to health protection, the right to the use of the achievements of culture, and to participate in scientific, technical, and artistic creative work, the right to take part in the administration of the state and public affairs.[51] One restrictive provision of the United Nations Covenant II now also appears in the 1977 Constitution, namely the prohibition of war propaganda.[52]

An Estonian lawyer, now teaching in Austria, has provided a careful comparison of the United Nations Covenants' provisions with Soviet law and concluded that he could not expect the new constitution (not yet published at the time) to reflect several of the Covenants' provisions.[53] These were the right to strike,[54] freedom of religious education,[55] and freedom of movement.[56] He doubted that some other rights which might be copied into the new constitution could be implemented; these being freedom of scientific research, freedom of information, and the freedom to manifest one's own religion and beliefs.

The draftsmen have born out his predictions. None of the three rights questioned have been incorporated in the 1977 document, and those formulated in 1936, and under which form the restrictive practices referred to flourished.

9. Public Participation in Determining Goals

Although functioning under the vanguard principle that only the Communist Party is qualified to make policy decisions, Soviet leaders indicated their desire in publishing their draft as they had done even in Stalin's time, to obtain an indication from the general public of what it would wish to see in the program established by the constitution. A general discussion was called when the draft was published, and it continued throughout the summer of 1977. Many of the suggestions made during that discussion have already been indicated, and the full discussion has already been reported by Robert Sharlet in a survey prepared for *Problems of Communism*,[57] but relation of that discussion to the problem of social engineering may help to indicate the extent to which Soviet leadership thinks it desirable in its program-making to listen to the voice of the public. Although it is evident that radical proposals such as abolition of the federation, transfer of the state's functions to the Communist Party, and restoration of an egalitarian wage system, will evoke no affirmative response, some guide lines suggested by citizens found their way into the final draft.

Because editors of the Soviet press select for publication only those proposals which they wish to expose, it is quite impossible to discover all types of suggestions that were raised in the period of discussion. Still, those that were disclosed indicate that the public has some strong ideas, and that the leadership is prepared to give them an ear. Most important seem to have been the proposals that indicated the emergence of group concerns, such as those of youth, of women, of environmentalists, of proponents of law and order, of disgruntled workmen who wanted to make their loafing colleagues subject to trial, and peasants fearful of losing their private garden plots. Perhaps most important among these groups were the ethnics who feared for the preservation of their political identities, and well they might, if it be true, as Brezhnev reported, that some suggestions were to abolish the federation and return the state structure to the unitary one maintained by the Tsar, and favored even today by economic planners who find it economically irrational to plan regional economies along ethnic rather than economically sound boundaries.

Youths asked for a reduction in the age at which they might be elected to office to equate it with the age of 18 at which they have been permitted to vote under the 1936 Constitution. Clearly, youth wants to participate in the work of the soviets, where decisions of importance in the implementation of high policy if not in its creation are currently being made. Brezhnev reported that the Commission had agreed to accept this request for all soviets except the Supreme Soviet of the USSR, where the age would be set at 21.[58] This is a reduction from the 23 required by the 1936 Constitution, but still not what youth wanted.

Women expressed the desire to be able to work part time, so as to give attention to their families. They opposed the rule that full time was required of all workers. Brezhnev agreed that gradual adjustments might be made in the length of the working day for women with small children, and the constitution was made to read accordingly.[59]

Many proposals came from the environmentalists. Over recent years, Soviet factory managers under pressure to reduce costs have evidently taken liberties with the environment. This has enraged the scientists, and now, seemingly the general public. The drafting commission agreed to reflect this major concern in preparing its plans for economic growth to improve the human environment and added water resources to the specifically enumerated types of natural wealth.[60]

The proponents of law and order came out strongly in the summer of discussion to denounce the evils of the bureaucracy, bribery, theft of state property, loafing on the job, absenteeism, and doctoring of records. Brezhnev promised that an effort to stop this practice would be instituted, and the system of People's Control strengthened, but some revisions were incorporated.[61]

The draftsmen had already placed in their June draft a provision favoring the small private enterprisers. Whereas the 1936 Constitution had authorized handicraftsmen and individual peasants by Article 9 to engage in private undertakings *(khoziaistva)*, many had proceeded to establish service trades which had proved of great assistance to the public in hairdressing, repairing, and the like. By Article 17 of the new constitution this expanded service activity was given constitutional status, by changing the 1936 word *khoziaistva* to occupations (*deiatel'nost'*). Of course, none could employ labor, for that was prohibited not only by the article on private occupations but also by the general provision on the topic,[62] just as it had been in 1936. No published letters during the discussion challenged this small concession to private enterprisers.

The impact of public participation in discussion may be measured in part by Brezhnev's enumeration of the changes made in the draft as originally submitted. The 400,000 proposals to individual articles resulted in the addition of one new article (Article 8 on Labor collectives) and 110 amendments to existing articles. Many were primarily doctrinal, but none the less important to a doctrinally oriented leadership and public. Thus, the June draft's failure in Article 1 to classify the workers, peasants, and intelligentsia as constituting a group to be known as "working people" as they were in 1936 evoked criticism, presumably on the ground that without such a grouping it might be supposed that three classes existed in Soviet society. The proposal was accepted and the amendment made.

In contrast to the letters in the general Soviet press, focussed on economics and jobs, there was a letter from a Ukrainian intellectual to the Soviet government renouncing his Soviet citizenship after reading the draft. Published in *Le Monde* in Paris,[63] the author declared that he had been moved to act because of the pronouncements of unanimous enthusiasm made by the Soviet media, reporting on meetings which he said were monitored by the Security Police. His attack was severe, beginning with the words, "From beginning to end your constitution is a lie." Then he proceeded to detail, denouncing the declarations that the state expresses the will and interests of the people, and that power belongs to the people; that the primary aim of government is to raise the standard of living; that nationalities have the right of free development and the republics the right to secede; that elections are expressions of popular will; and even that the state seal includes sheaves of wheat when it is known that wheat has to be imported from the United States.

This letter of dissent took issue with the qualification placed in the new Bill of Rights on their exercise. He decried the reservation by the state under Article 156 of the right to close trials whenever officials decide without reference to the public that the state's interests are endangered. Finally, he said that he no longer wanted to be included among people who are said to approve the draft since, in his view, it had been dictated by the political police to whom everything is subordinated and without which the labor camps established by the régime would not last a single day. Reports subsequently told of his arrest.

10. The Interchange with Other Like-minded Draftsmen

Brezhnev called attention in his presentation speech to the fact that Soviet draftsmen had profited from studying the new constitutions of the fraternal socialist countries.[64] The evidence is strong that this is so, for many of the new provisions are to be found also in the new constitutions. In a sense this is a novelty, for at the time of the 1936 Constitution there was no other fraternal socialist country to inspect except Mongolia, and the impression from reading the record suggested that Mongolia learned from the USSR and not vice versa. The coming to power of communist parties after World War II expanded the number of fraternal states, and it became evident that while there was to be variation from the Soviet model, it was minimal. In all of them the communist party was either unique or dominant, the state apparatus was structured like the soviets, the economies were nationalized to whatever degree was possible without creating unmanageable resistance, planning was introduced into the economy under the leadership of a state committee, and it was made mandatory not only for state enterprise managers but also for agricultural cooperatives. Even the agencies of the law, the courts and procurators, were structured along the lines of the Soviet Union's counterparts.

By degrees, the conformity to the Soviet model faded away, but not without severe struggle in Poland and Hungary, during which Khrushchev and his colleagues found it necessary to admit that there were various roads to socialism, but when they thought that socialism was not the goal, limits were imposed. The intervention of Soviet troops in Hungary against Nagy and in Czechoslovakia against Dubček demonstrated that some variations were impermissible from the Soviet point of view. Only Yugoslavia adopted a widely varied system, but Tito proved strong enough to resist the pressures brought against him. Mao Tse Tung also went his own way and finally renounced his relationship with the Soviet Communist Party to begin a series of mutual recriminations, each side reading the other out of the socialist camp.

In 1957 an effort was made to reestablish a common core by issuing a declaration entitled "Basic laws applicable in all countries embarking on a socialist course." In presenting it to the West, Dan Jacobs called it "The New Communist Manifesto."[65] The common core was to be: guidance of the working mass by the working class, led by the Marxist-Leninist Party, abolition of capitalist ownership, gradual socialist construction of agriculture, national economic planning, restructuring ideology in a socialist direction, equality of ethnically differentiated peoples, and proletarian internationalism. Subsequently drafted constitutions reflected this declaration, but variations multiplied on points not within the core.

The Bulgarian Constitution was analyzed by a Soviet law review article in 1971.[66] The article noted the introduction of the principle of popular referendum which was not yet in the Soviet basic law. The Bulgarian concept of referendum even provided for such references to the people on decision of a local soviet. The Bulgarians also linked obligations with rights, and they spoke of a constitution for "developed socialism." The 1977 USSR Constitution included all of these novelties except referenda at the local level.

Two years later, E. I. Machulskii was attracted to the constitutions of the 1960's and 1970's for some of the same reasons. He noted the links in all between rights and duties, but something like Soviet pride of intervention then overcame him, for he explained that although the Soviet Constitution of 1936 made no such specific linkage, the principle underlay the 1936 Bill of Rights.[67] His paper is unusually interesting because he argues that socialist rights do not have to be granted specifically in a constitution to exist, since they arise from the basic freedom created by socialism in all socialist societies, namely the freedom from personal exploitation. From this freedom, which capitalism cannot offer, springs the socialist Bill of Rights.

This argument sounds rather like a new "socialist natural law," an argument like that of the Founding Fathers of Philadelphia who argued, when they were berated for omitting a Bill of Rights, that it existed by virtue of natural law and required no enunciation in words. If Machulskii has been understood correctly, he says that the similarity between statement of rights and duties in socialist constitutions comes not from copying among the draftsmen, but from the socialist system. Law is but superstructure; the base influences it, and when the base is the same, the Bills of Rights will be the same.

Examination of constitutions quickened in 1975 after promulgation of new Basic Laws in the German Democratic Republic, and in Hungary, Bulgaria, Czechoslovakia, and Yugoslavia. The editors of the Moscow University Law Faculty even presented the analysis of a German graduate student of his country's new document.[68] He thought memorable in the 1974 document that the Republic was working toward a "developed socialist state", as were the Bulgarians, and that the class nature of the state had been emphasized in rephrasing the prior document, which had said that the government was a government of the German people, to make it a government of workers and peasants. The reason for the change is hinted in the elimination from the prior document of the clause calling for the rationalization of relations between East and West Germany, a rationalization no longer thought likely. He also noted that the term of the legislature had been increased from the 4 years in the then-existing Soviet model to 5 years, a step which was taken in the Soviet draft of 1977.

Another author also reviewed the socialist constitutions, noting that Bulgaria had drafted a wholly new document, while Hungary had been content with a new edition of its former constitution, and Czechoslovakia had made changes with a "constitutional law."[69] At the time, this author wrote that the Soviet leaders had not yet decided what form to adopt in modernizing their document, and the author may have wanted to indicate several alternatives. She noted further that all of the new constitutions showed a tendency toward placing sovereignty in the people, exercised through the soviets, as the 1936 USSR document had done in its Article 3; that all spoke of social organizations as owning one of the forms of socialist property but independent of state and cooperative property; that the Bulgarian document spoke of the participation of workers in the administration of society; and that norms for the conduct of foreign affairs had been set by the constitutions. As has been indicated earlier, the 1977 draft introduced these innovations too.

The author went on to present the novelties in the Bills of Rights in the constitutions she had before her, all of which were later to be placed in the USSR draft of 1977: the freedom to choose a profession, the right to safe and healthy working conditions, the right to housing, the right to a ten-year education, the right to protection from unlawful interference in personal life, and the right to defense of honor and a good name. The Bulgarians also added a duty to protect the environment.

The Cuban Constitution came under review in 1976.[70] Note was taken of its unusual preamble, of its preservation of some forms of private productive property, even in the cooperatives where members continued to own their own land. The contrast with the Soviet document was explained as logical in view of the Cuban's early stage in the development of socialism. Among the rights selected for comment was the right given citizens to present complaints to the government, and a right not only to security of correspondence but to teletype, telephone, and telegraph communication as well. These rights, with the omission of teletype, were placed in the 1977 draft as well. Perhaps it was thought that since the users of teletype in the USSR could only be state enterprises, its inclusion would have looked absurd to the population.

The Cubans also introduced the restriction against exercise of a right to the detriment of the constitution and laws, the goals and existence of the socialist government, the steadfastness of the Cuban people in building socialism and communism. When the restriction on use of rights was inserted in the 1977 draft, it was of the same tenor, although not in exactly the same words.

The authors explained the change in terms of deputies from the model term of 4 years to 5 years by saying that such a term is now considered optimal in socialist countries because it corresponds to the five-year plans. This is an arresting suggestion that a model is being circulated among the socialist countries of what is "optimal." The Cubans even set forth the organization of the State Council, equivalent to the USSR's Presidium of the Supreme Soviet, as including a First Deputy President. Much has been made of this change in the 1977 USSR Constitution as creating an opening for Brezhnev to assume the position of head of state while passing to a deputy the routine duties of President of the Presidium. It may be that the thought of Soviet change first came to Brezhnev's mind in discussing with Cubans the advantage it could give to permit a Party Secretary General to hold a position that would facilitate his work as effective head of state instead of standing behind the scenes as had been traditional within the Communist Party of the Soviet Union.

When the Hungarian constitutional changes of 1972 were examined in the Soviet press by a Hungarian author in 1976, he reached some general conclusions in comparing his country's constitution with that of the Bulgarians.[71] These conclusions may have influenced thought among the Soviet draftsmen, for they seem to have followed them. He argued that qualitative changes in the societal and governmental structure required development of new constitutional provisions; that institutions of a basic character ought to be established by the constitution and not by ordinary laws; that ordinary legislation for lesser matters was acceptable, once the basic constitutional change had been made; that national plebiscites were being introduced generally; and that a constitutional court like that of Yugoslavia was unnecessary, at least in a unitary state.

Review of the literature on interchange of ideas suggests that the Soviet drafting committee, in its long years of work since 1962, was in close touch with draftsmen in other fraternal socialist countries. Perhaps this communication took the form of interchange of experts. This could have meant that Soviet specialists suggested ideas to Bulgarians, Hungarians, and Cubans, and the emergence of seeming novelties in the constitutions of these states before the 1977 draft in the USSR could have been an effort to float a trial balloon. On the other hand, the lawyers of the countries mentioned, with their very long traditions of jurisprudential thinking, may have been more imaginative than were the Soviet draftsmen, and it could be that their imaginative ideas attracted Russians who had not previously thought of such variations in form.

In light of this conclusion of interchange of ideas, whether from the Soviets outward or *vice versa*, it is disquieting to find a specialist of the reputation of Dr. George Brunner of the University of Cologne writing that he finds no evidence of "cross fertilization" of ideas on constitutional drafting, and that Soviet influence is still strong.[72] It is not hard to accept the idea that Soviet influence is still strong, at least on the common core required by the 1957 declaration, but when one sees the technical details and even some of the peripheral subjects introduced by constitutions outside the USSR, such as the ones indicated above, it is hard to believe that they were all dictated by Soviet draftsmen who had no confidence in the loyalty of their colleagues in other lands to what has come to be known as the Marxist-Leninist formulae. It stretches no imagination to suppose that, in laying out their constitutional blueprint for the years to come, the Soviet leadership has scrutinized the work of its partners in socialism. Some of their innovations have been rejected but some have been adopted. Soviet draftsmen evidently no longer want to work alone.

11. Conclusion

Soviet leaders have chosen the constitutional form to set forth their grand design, their master plan. While they might have contented themselves with isolated statutes defining their Soviet structure of government and with the program of the Communist Party to communicate to their people and the world their program of social engineering, they have not done so. Seemingly, they have found it historically necessary and politically desirable to put both governmental structure and program in their Basic Law.

One may well ask why the year 1977 was chosen to promulgate a draft that had been in committee for 15 years. Although the 60th Anniversary of the Revolution of 1917 was an appropriate occasion to erect a new milestone, it was by no means the only appropriate occasion of recent years. Had the Communist Party wished to distinguish its XXV Congress from all the others, it might have brought forth a document in 1976. Many, both within the USSR and abroad, had expected it to do so. Had Brezhnev wanted solely to glorify his own name with a document to his leadership, he might have chosen any of the preceding years after he had consolidated his power as Secretary General of the Party. He need not have waited a whole decade.

In view of the opportunities that were allowed to slip by, it is tempting to suppose that 1977 was chosen for another reason. It may have been the moment when an aging leadership, faced with challenges from some Communists as to its concept of structures and program, sensed the necessity of attempting to bind its successors to its way of political life. Brezhnev told his listeners in 1977 that voices on the left within the Party wanted to move on swiftly to "communism" with restoration of egalitarian wages, abolition of the federal structure in the interest of more rational economic planning, and even to a form of withering away of the state through transfer of its administrative functions to the Party itself. There had been also some years earlier the challenge from the Communists of Czechoslovakia with their concept of a form of liberalized communism, and this challenge was being echoed in 1977 by Communists in Italy and Spain. It may have been that Soviet leaders feared lest this attitude creep into the Soviet Party as well.

The analyst must also consider the impact of thought in the USSR on constitutions as propaganda documents of value in the ideological struggle for the minds of men. Ideology is not dead in the USSR, although concessions have been made to stimulate production, and although society has moved away from austere attitudes of the early years. If such thought is prevalent, as it appears to be, the 1977 Constitution may have been inspired in part to compete with Western ideologists, most especially in the sphere of human rights to which so much of it is devoted. Soviet spokesmen are heralding Soviet emphasis upon economic rights which they believe are craved by much of the world. The International Covenants on Human Rights were ratified in

1973, although some of the political obligations assumed in them have not been placed in the new constitution. Evidently, human rights have become a high priority item in the Soviet arsenal of propaganda instruments, and 1977 was a good year to reemphasize the topic, especially in view of the Belgrade review of the Helsinki Final Act of 1975, planned for the autumn of 1977.

Finally, note must be taken of a new type of partnership between Soviet constitutional draftsmen and those of the Communist Party States of Eastern Europe and Cuba. While in Stalin's time, his lawyers dictated to the draftsmen of other communist led states, by 1977 the relationship was less one-sided. Brezhnev reported that his draftsmen had found useful ideas among the innovations of Eastern European and Cuban constitutions of the past decade. It may be that Soviet specialists had planted some of these innovations in the minds of their Western colleagues as trial balloons prior to drafting their own document as a composite of them all, a model for future generations incorporating the most desirable elements of many communist-inspired constitutions. Yet, it may be that the imaginative Europeans and Cubans had indeed thought of innovations to improve upon structures and programs, while maintaining the principles enunciated by all communist parties in power in 1957 as a common core to which all must adhere. If this latter be so, the Soviet document appears as the confluence of several streams of thought, hopefully sufficiently supported by many communists to become a bar to any further splits such as those introduced by the Chinese. It is a final building-block in the edifice erected by Soviet leaders in the hope of preserving—after they have passed from the scene—the structures and program created by them.

NOTES

1. Christopher S. Wren, "New Soviet Charter May Allow Brezhnev to Take over Presidency," *New York Times*, June 4, 1977, p. Al, col. 1.

2. L. I. Brezhnev, "Report on the Draft Constitution," May 24, 1977, *Pravda*, June 5, 1977, p. 1., Eng. transl. in *CDSP* 29 (1977), No. 23, 6-10, and also in *Reprints from the Soviet Press*, 15 (1977), No. 1, 1.

3. See Daniel Bell, *The End of Ideology: On the Exhaustion of Political Ideas in the Fifties*, Rev. ed. (New York, 1962), p. 16, and pp. 350-352.

4. Daniel Bell has made such an effort in his *The Coming of Post-Industrial Society: A Venture in Social Forecasting*, With a new introduction by the author (New York, 1976).

5. Previous Soviet constitutions are available in English in J. F. Triska, *Constitutions of the Communist Party-States* (Stanford, 1968), pp. 2-76.

6. David Binder reports that US Government analysts have said that the Soviet constitution could be viewed "as Brezhnev's means of 'institutionalizing' his policies–including détente–and thus imposing them on his successor." See "US Analysts Say Shifts in Soviet Seek Flexibility, Better Planning," *New York Times*, June 23, 1977, p. Al, col. 1.

7. Bell, *op. cit.*, pp. xix-xx.

8. See Michael Florinsky, *Russian History and Interpretation*, 2 vols. (New York, 1955, 1958).

9. See Oliver H. Radkey, *The Elections to the Russian Constituent Assembly of 1917* (Cambridge, Mass., 1950).

10. Decree, published October 28, 1917 (o.s.), *Sobr. Uzak. RSFSR*, 1917, No. 1, item 1.

11. See G. S. Gurvich, *Istoriia Sovetskoi Konstitutsii* (History of the Soviet Constitution), (Moscow, 1928).

12. See Harvey Wheeler, "Constitutionalism," in Greenstein and Polsby, *Government Institutions and Processes*, 5 (Reading, Mass., 1975), pp. 1-91.

13. J. V. Stalin, "Report on the Draft Constitution of the USSR, November 25, 1936," Part V; Eng. transl. in J. Stalin, *Leninism* (New York, 1942), p. 379.

14. Law of February 6, 1935, *Sobr. Zak. SSSR*, 1935, No. 8, item 69. By this law, a drafting committee was proposed to the USSR Central Executive Committee with the task of revising the 1923 Constitution to incorporate two principles: (1) replace the indirect system of elections of soviets by direct elections to all levels, and (2) bring the constitution into conformity with the existing class structure of society.

15. See G. Ginsburgs, "A Khrushchev Constitution for the Soviet Union: Projects and Prospects," *Osteuropa-Recht*, 8 (1962), 191-214.

16. P. S. Romashkin, "Novy etap v razvitii Sovetskogo gosudarstva" (A New Stage in the Development of the Soviet State), *SGiP*, 1960, No. 10, 36.

17. The 1961 Program of the Communist Party of the Soviet Union, Part Two, sec. III; Eng. transl. in J. F. Triska (ed.), *Soviet Communism: Programs and Rules* (San Fransisco, 1962), pp. 97-98.

18. This criticism from a locksmith was learned in conversation with a Soviet law professor at a conference in Africa, July 5, 1977. It was not found in a reading of the

principal newspapers, and may not have been published there. For a survey of some of the discussion, see William M. Mandel, "The New Soviet Constitution," *National Lawyers' Guild Practitioner*, 34 (Fall, 1977), 97-109. See also Robert Sharlet, "The New Soviet Constitution," *Problems of Communism*, 26 (Sept.-Oct., 1977), 1-24.

19. J. Stalin, *Economic Problems of Socialism in the USSR* (Moscow, 1952), pp. 96-104.

20. Ginsburgs, *op. cit.*, p. 205.

21. Stephen Osofsky, *Soviet Agricultural Policy: Toward the Abolition of Collective Farms* (New York, 1974).

22. Ginsburgs, *op. cit.*, p. 205.

23. L. V. Brezhnev, "Results of the Nationwide Discussion of the Draft Constitution," October 4, 1977, Part II (at the end), *Pravda*, October 5, 1977; Eng. transl. in *Reprints from the Soviet Press*, 25 (Oct. 31-Nov. 15, 1977), No. 8-9, 24.

24. S. I. Rusinova and V. A. Rianzhina, *Sovetskoe Konstitutsionnoe Pravo* (Soviet Constitutional Law), (Leningrad, 1975).

25. Book Review, *Tulane Law Review*, 51 (1977), 411-422.

26. Rusinova and Rianzhina, *op. cit.*, p. 4.

27. *Ibid.*, p. 7.

28. V. F. Kotok, "Soderzhanie sovetskogo Konstitutsionnogo prava" (The Subject Matter of Soviet Constitutional Law), *SGiP*, 1971, No. 2, 108.

29. A. I. Lepeshkin, "Sootnoshenie gosudarstvennogo prava i norm sovetskoi konstitutsii" (The Relationship between State Law and a Norm of the Soviet Constitution), *Ibid*, 102.

30. M. A. Mikhaileva, "Obsuzhdenie knigi 'Sovetskoe konstitutsionnoe pravo'" (Discussion of the Book *Soviet Constitutional Law*), *VMU* (*pravo*), 1976, No. 4, 86-90.

31. Rusinova and Rianzhina, *op. cit.*, p. 8.

32. *Ibid.*, p. 61.

33. For an extensive review of the discussion, see Mandel, *op. cit.*

34. See Stalin, *op. cit.*

35. See Romashkin, *op. cit.*

36. I. Aleksandrov, "Lozungi i praktika. O novoi konstitutsii KNR" (Slogans and Practice. On the New Constitution of the Chinese People's Republic), *Pravda*, February 5, 1974, pp. 4-5; Eng. transl. in *CDSP*, 27 (1975), No. 5, 1-5.

37. L. M. Godoshnikov, "Antinarodnaia konstitutsionnaia deklaratsiia Maoistov" (An Antipeople's Constitutional Declaration of Maoists), *SGiP*, 1972, No. 2, 95.

38. D. L. Zlatopolskii, "Nekotorye osobennosti pravovoi prirody Osnov zakonodatel'stva Soiuza SSR i soiuznykh respublik" (Some Special Features of the Legal Nature of the Fundamental Principles of Legislation of the USSR and of the Union Republics), *SGiP*, 1977, No. 2, 36.

39. Shebanov, "Sistema otraslei zakonodatel'stva i osnovaniia postroeniia" (The System of Branches of Legislation and the Foundations of a Structure), *Pravovedenie*, 1976, No. 4, 15-26.

40. M. G. Kirichenko, "Uchastie uchenykh iuristov v razvitii sovetskogo konstitutsionnogo zakonodatel'stva" (The Participation of Scholar-Jurists in the Development of Soviet Constitutional Legislation), *SGiP*, 1975, No. 9, 17 at 24.

41. "Brezhnev's Keynote Address to the 25th CPSU Congress," February 24, 1976, *CDSP*, 28 (1976), No. 8, 3-32.

42. Edict of April 29, 1977, *Ved. V.S. SSSR*, 1977, No. 18, item 274.

43. Introduced by Brezhnev, May 24, 1977, *op. cit.*, note 2.

44. Full voting members of the Central Committee of the Communist Party averaged 60 years of age in 1976, and the average age of 8 out of the 15 members of the

Politburo was 72. See Stanley Rothman and George W. Breslauer, *Soviets Politics and Society* (St. Paul, New York, 1978), pp. 178, 188.

45. See V. Chalidze, *To Defend These Rights: Human Rights and the Soviet Union* (New York, 1975), p. 53.

46. See his "On the Constitution of the USSR (Report to the Moscow Human Rights Committee)" in Leon Lipson, Valery Chalidze (eds.), *Papers on Soviet Law* (New York, 1977), p. 52.

47. *Ibid.*, p. 81.

48. *Ibid.*, p. 77.

49. The USSR ratified both the International Covenant on Economic, Social, and Cultural Rights, and the International Covenant on Civil and Political Rights on October 16, 1973. See *UN Monthly Chronicle*, 1973, No. 10, 86.

50. Art. 50.

51. These Arts. are 53, 44, 42, 46, 47, 48, respectively.

52. Art. 28.

53. See Henn-Juri Uibopuu, "The Human Rights Covenants of the United Nations and the Constitutional Law of the USSR," in Lipson and Chalidze, *op. cit.*, p. 14.

54. Covenant I, Art. 8.

55. *Ibid.* Art. 13, and Covenant II, Art. 18.

56. Covenant II, Art. 12.

57. Mandel, *op. cit.*

58. Art. 96.

59. Art. 35.

60. Art. 18.

61. There was added to Art. 60, "The evasion of socially useful labor is incompatible with the principles of socialist society."

62. Art. 14.

63. July 7, 1977, p. 2.

64. Brezhnev, *op. cit.*, Part II.

65. Dan N. Jacobs, *The New Communist Manifesto and Related Documents*, 3rd ed. (New York, 1961), pp. 169-182.

66. D. L. Zlatopol'skii, "Nekotorye osobennosti pravovoi prirody Osnov zakonodatel'stva Soiuza SSR i soiuznoi respubliki" (Some Special Characteristics of the Legal Nature of the Fundamental Principles of Legislation of the USSR and of the Union Republic), *SGiP*, 1977, No. 2, 36.

67. E. I. Machulskii, "Razvitie konstitutsionnogo statusa grazhdan v zarubezhnykh sotsialisticheskikh stranakh Evropy" (The Development of the Constitutional Status of Citizens in Foreign Socialist Countries of Europe), *SGiP*, 1974, No. 11, 92.

68. "Doklad ob izmeneniiakh Konstitutsii GDR" (Report on Changes in the Constitution of the German Democratic Republic), *VMU (pravo)*, 1975, No. 6, 86.

69. N. A. Mikhailova, "Konstitutsionnoe zakonodatel'stvo zarubezhnykh sotsialisticheskikh stran perioda postroeniia razvitogo sotsializma" (The Constitutional Legislation of Foreign Socialist Countries during the Period of Construction of Developed Socialism), *Pravovedenie*, 1975, No. 3, 45.

70. E. A. Ambartsumov, E. M. Borisov, V. M. Kremnev, i P. T. Kondrashov, "Sotsialisticheskaia konstitutsiia respublika Kuba" (The Socialist Constitution of the Republic of Cuba), *SGiP*, 1976, No. 10, 85.

71. Imre Takach, "Soobshchenie–Rol' konstitutsionnogo regulirovaniia v pravotvorchestve Vengerskoi Narodnoi Respubliki" (A Communication–The Role of Constitutional Regulation of the Legislative Process of the Hungarian People's Republic), *Pravovedenie*, 1976, No. 2, 104.

72. George Brunner, "Socialist Constitutions–Recent Constitutional Developments in East European States" in Donald D. Barry, F. J. M. Feldbrugge, and Dominik Lasok, (eds.), *Codification in the Communist World* (Leyden, 1975), p. 53. For an exhaustive comparison of these constitutions, see Chris Osakwe, "The Common Law of the Constitutions of the Communist Party States," *Review of Socialist Law*, 3 (1977), No. 2. 155.

THE NEW CONSTITUTION OF THE USSR. FROM DRAFT TO LAW: AN ANALYSIS OF THE CHANGES ADOPTED

Yurii Luryi*

1. How the Draft Was Discussed

Does history know of a case, when in the discussion of the draft of a new constitution of any country, four-fifths of the adult population took part in the debate, particularly where this discussion did not take place in the form of a national referendum? On October 4, 1977, the future President of the USSR, L. I. Brezhnev, informed the Supreme Soviet that more than 140 million people took part in the discussion of the draft of the new constitution.[1] To anybody who has knowledge of how these kinds of campaigns are conducted in the USSR this figure gives some cause for reflection. Since many people participated in constitutional debates on more than one occasion, it is unclear how this participation was counted.

For example, Mr. X is at the same time a member of the Communist Party of the USSR, member of the Trade Union, director of a factory, member of the City Council, and finally, a member of a city or regional committee of the Party. (This would be a fairly common profile of a director of a factory.) Mr. Y, a somewhat more modest person, is first of all a member of the Komsomol, a member of a Trade Union, and a worker (or an engineer) in another factory. It should be self-evident that Mr. X should have participated in the constitutional debate on five occasions, and Mr. Y on at least three occasions. Mr. X should have participated in the debate on the draft at meetings of all the employees of the factory, of which he is a director, at the meeting of the City Council of which he is a member, at the meeting of the city (or regional) organs of the Party, and also at the Party and Trade Union meetings in his factory. It is also possible that he took part at a meeting of

* The author expresses his gratitude to Professor Marek Debicki of the University of Manitoba, Department of Political Science, for his assistance in translating this paper into English, and to Ms. Lee Walker, Ph.D. student in the Department of Political Science of the University of Toronto, who helped in comparing the texts of the draft and the final version of the new Constitution of the USSR.

the Komsomol organization in his factory. Mr. Y on the other hand, discussed the draft at a Party (or Komsomol) meeting, at a Trade Union meeting, and at the meeting of the so-called "working collective" of his factory. The numbers of those who participated more than once in the constitutional debate should be counted in millions. It is self-evident that the majority of the working people in the Soviet Union are members of Trade Unions, and/or of the Party and Komsomol. The working force in 1977 was approximately 104.3 million persons.[2] According to the official statistics for the year 1975, in the USSR at that time, there were 101 million Trade Union members, 15.5 million Party members, and 35 million Komsomol members.[3] One can say with certainty that most of these people participated in the constitutional debate at least two or three times. One can also assume that in many instances, people discussed the draft of the constitution not only at Trade Union, Party, and Komsomol meetings, but also at meetings of all employees in divisions, branches, and finally at meetings of all employees of every enterprise. There is no doubt that those who participated in the debate at one meeting were not excluded from considering the same draft at another meeting, and each of those meetings was concluded with a report sent to the proper organs for consideration. Therefore, people were repeatedly counted as participating in the constitutional debate. Consequently, the figure cited by L. I. Brezhnev, showing the extent of participation in the constitutional debate is completely unreliable and significantly lower in actual fact. Thus, borrowing the term from the field of industrial relations one can say that there were 140 million units of "persons per discussion," with the number of actual people being approximately one-third of this figure.

In addition to the enormous number of various meetings at which the draft of the new constitution has been discussed, it was also widely described and debated on the pages of the Russian newspapers and magazines. In the period from June to September 1977, articles about changes in the draft were to be found in all editions of newspapers and magazines–central, republic, or regional.

The newspaper *Izvestiia* revealed that during the month of July, 1977, it received 2,785 letters which contained 3,830 proposals for amendments to the constitution.[4]

Does the analysis of the letters and articles published by the newspapers give a possibility for drawing any conclusions as to the attitudes of the population of the USSR with respect to the draft of the constitution *in toto* or in specific areas? In answering this question, one has to take into consideration at least three points:

1) A great majority of the Soviet newspapers are organs of the committees of the Communist Party–central or regional. Thus, all materials published in these newspapers are subject to very stringent Party censorship.

2) Only a certain selection of the letters received by the newspapers were

actually published. Most of the published letters were specially instigated by journalists. In many instances, journalists were actually writing the letters for those who signed them. In other instances, they were helping the letter writers in preparing their letters by suggesting the main ideas. "Organization" of letters and articles in newspapers has always been part of Soviet journalism. "Organization of materials" is a professional term, which is used officially in press, radio, and television work in the USSR. Instructions pertaining to the salaries of journalists include a tariff for the "organization of material."[5] During the time of the discussion of the constitution, the extent of participation was an important indicator of the quality of ideological work. Obviously, "organization of material" by the journalists at that time was more extensive and energetic than usual.

3) Self-censorship is also important, and it is a phenomenon widely-spread not only among professional writers. The majority of the people of the Soviet Union have learned not to commit ideological or political "mistakes," in either their written or oral expressions of opinions, as this could cause them varying degrees of unpleasantness.

These are some of the reasons why a great number of letters coming from citizens and published in the newspapers cannot be taken as a true indicator of the feelings and attitudes of society towards the draft constitution. At the same time, there are areas where the analysis of the material coming from Soviet newspapers can be of importance in looking at the results.

On October 4, 1977, L. I. Brezhnev informed the Supreme Soviet that, as a result of some 400,000 proposed amendments, the Constitutional Commission decided to introduce changes in 110 articles, and to include one additional Article in the draft.[6] On October 7, he supplemented this with eleven changes which were introduced by the deputies of the Supreme Soviet directly at the session. Unfortunately, Brezhnev did not state how many amendments to the draft constitution were introduced at the session by the deputies themselves. The number of such proposals is difficult to assess, since according to Brezhnev they were introduced both orally and in written submissions to the Constitutional Committee. Brezhnev stated, however, that the editing committee of the Constitutional Committee included the *majority* of the amendments and changes introduced by the deputies. He stated that this majority consisted of *eleven changes* and amendments proposed by the deputies. Therefore, it is obvious that the remaining proposals which were not accepted consisted of not more than ten proposals. Thus, more than 1,500 deputies of the Soviet Parliament produced not more than twenty-one amendments to the draft constitution.

Comparison between the draft constitution and the finished product gives one more possibility of assessment. The draft consisted initially of 173 articles. No fewer than 233 amendments were introduced, of which 110 additions found their way into the final text, plus 80 changes and 44 deletions from the initial text (in this number, minor editorial changes are not included).

The draft consisted of nine parts and twenty-one chapters. Only Chapter 8 dealing with "emblem, flag, national anthem, and capital of the USSR" did not undergo any revisions. Comparison of the enacted Constitution of the USSR with the draft is very interesting, not only for lawyers. The accepted changes are of various natures, from minor to quite significant ones. Some of these changes seem to have a symbolic meaning. Analysis of these changes is the subject of this work, which only compares the October Constitution with its June draft.

2. The Political System

Are There Classes in the Developed Socialist Society?

The difference between the draft and the enacted constitution starts with the very first article. The draft stated that the USSR "expresses the will and interests of the working *class*, peasants and intelligentsia." In the final text, the word "class" disappeared and the passage reads "workers, peasants, and intelligentsia." Thus, the question as to the existence of "class" in the USSR remains to be answered. If there are "classes" then, how many? The answers to these questions can be found in other chapters of the constitution and in the speeches of Brezhnev. The "working class" is mentioned in the preamble, where it is referred to as "the leading force" of Soviet society. At the same time, Article 19 of the constitution states that "The State promotes ... the effacement of class differences." It is obvious from such a statement that differentiation requires the presence of at least two classes. We find reference to these two classes in the speech by the chairman of the Constitutional Commission, L. I. Brezhnev. "It is these two forms of socialist ownership of the means of production [state and collective farm] that define the nature of our national economy, and the division of Soviet society into two friendly classes–workers and peasants."[7]

It appears that the terms "peasantry" or "collective farmer *class*" do not have a well-defined meaning, which, by the way, shows the theoretical uncertainty of the concept of class in Soviet literature. On the one hand, among the peasantry there are still the so-called "individual peasants," that is, people who are not members of the kolkhozes, who individually run farms, and due to that fact, do not belong to a "friendly class." On the other hand, included among members of the kolkhozes are directors, accountants, agriculturists, engineers, and other persons who are described not as members of a class but are referred to as "white collar workers."

These were the reasons why, due to semantic difficulties, the word "class" was not applied to "peasantry," either in the draft constitution or in the final text. Since the word "class" was not applied to the peasants, for statistical balance it was not applied to the workers.

From the Dictatorship of the Proletariat to the Dictatorship of the Party

The change of text in Article 6 of the draft, speaking of the place of the Communist Party in the state, is interesting, first of all because it appears as an answer to the reaction of the West. The attention of the West was focused on this Article and was sufficiently strongly expressed to make Brezhnev feel obliged to answer some of the criticisms. "Most bourgeois commentators also greatly disliked the draft provisions that spoke of the role of the CPSU in the life of Soviet society. They created a great noise about what they called 'the proclamation of the dictatorship of the Communist Party'."[8] Nevertheless, in the final text of the constitution, there was an addition aimed at silencing this criticism. "All party organizations shall function within the framework of the Constitution of the USSR." It appears to the writer that neither the interest of the West in this particular provision, nor the indignation of L. I. Brezhnev were sufficiently grounded.

As far as the Western reaction is concerned, it is obvious that the new constitution was not designed in order to change the political system as it exists, buth rather "to entrench the basic features of the development of socialist society, and its political organization."[9] The leading role of the Communist Party in all aspects of the life of the nation is the fact of the political organization of the USSR throughout its history. This fact is obvious and well-known, due to the thousands of oral and written testimonies which appeared in the West. In the 1936 USSR Constitution (Article 126), the Communist Party was also assigned the role of "leading nucleus of all organizations of working people, as well as social and state organizations." Thus, in this area, the new constitution should not be surprising or unexpected to a Western observer.

Throughout the life of the 1936 Constitution, the Soviet Union was the state in which there was "*dictatorship* of the proletariat." That notion did not impede the statement in the constitution "that all power in the state belongs to the working people of the cities and the country" (Article 3). As stated in the preamble to the new constitution, the goals of the dictatorship of the proletariat are already fulfilled. Nevertheless, the constitution "increased the leading role of the Communist Party." In the 1977 Constitution, all power in the nation also belongs to "the people" (Article 2). L. I. Brezhnev underlined that in the new constitution, "many of the principal norms of the previous constitutions are preserved."[10] The unlimited power, which is in the possession of the leadership of the Communist Party of the USSR, is no less than in the period of the so-called "dictatorship of the proletariat." The history of the Soviet state gives every reason to believe that although the variants of the dictatorship changed (collective–"proletariat;" one-man dictatorship–Stalin; collective–Politburo of the Central Committee of the Communist Party of the USSR), dictatorship itself always was there. What embarrasses Brezhnev in the word "dictatorship"?

In his own words, "to try to counterpoise the Party and the people, to talk about the 'dictatorship of the Party' is analogous to counterpoise, let us say, the heart with the rest of the human body."[11] Marx and Lenin always were opposed to this kind of argument as the inappropriate "application of biological terminology to the description of social phenomena." They referred to this kind of argument as "empty phrases."[12] Moreover, this biological analogy is ambiguous in our time, when the heart not only can oppose the organism, but can even be replaced in order to prolong the life of that organism.

Furthermore, Lenin's theory of the "dictatorship of the proletariat" never opposed the proletariat to the remaining part of society. As early as 1919, the Program of the Communist Party explained the "leading" role of the proletariat by the fact that it is "the most concentrated, conscious, united, hardened and enlightened part of the working masses."[13] In other words, the vanguard.

In 1977, Brezhnev characterized the Communist Party of the USSR in the same manner: "the vanguard of the Soviet people, the best, most conscientious people in the whole nation."[14]

A phrase which embarrassed Brezhnev did not embarrass Lenin at the time of the dictatorship of the proletariat: "when they accuse us of dictatorship of one party, ... we say 'yes, dictatorship of one party! We are standing on this position, and we cannot abandon it' ..."[15] Lenin said these words at the time when the 1918 RSFSR Constitution was in force.

Thus, the new constitution, in the words of Brezhnev, "stands on the ground of past experience," a ground from which it is not allowed to depart. Thus, recognition by Brezhnev of the undeniable fact of the existence in the USSR of the dictatorship of the Party would mean only his agreement with Lenin. He, however, preferred to agree with Stalin, who denied the existence of the dictatorship of the Party with the same indignation.[16]

The second change in Article 6, on first glance seems to be insignificant. From the phrase referring to the fact that the Communist Party of the USSR appears to be "the leading and guiding force of Soviet society and the nucleus of its political system, as well as all governmental and social organizations," in the final text the word "all" was removed. In that way, the Party is no longer nucleus for *all* social organizations. To what social organizations might this refer? Obviously, the Communist Party of the USSR is not a nucleus of religious organizations. For those who are familiar with the activities of the agency dealing with religion, which is attached to the Council of Ministers of the USSR, it is self-evident that the Communist Party of the USSR provides a "leading and guiding" role, even in the religious organizations. Among the social organizations in which the Communist Party is not a nucleus or leading force are organizations which have appeared without the "blessing" of the Soviet government in the last ten years—for example, monitoring groups which appeared after the Helsinki Agreement, Chapters of Amnesty International, the Committee for the Defense of Human Rights, etc. Although members of these groups undergo illegal repressions of various kinds (this well-known fact does not require any special proof), nevertheless, none of these organizations were declared illegal or were disbanded by any official act. Perhaps the deletion of the word "all" is a silent admission of the fact of the existence of such social organizations. We should look at this change in connection with the other changes, particularly those introduced into Article 7 of the draft, describing organizations which "participate in the administration of state and public affairs, and in the resolution of political, economic, social, and cultural questions." Article 7 refers also to "other *mass* social organizations." The above-mentioned groups and the Committee for the Defense of Human Rights are not mass organizations, despite hidden sympathy of masses. Thus, in the final text of this article, from the statement that "only *mass* social organizations participate in the administration of the state and public affairs, and in the resolution of political, economic, social and cultural questions," the word "mass" disappeared. The text was changed to read "other social organizations." In this way, the adopted text is distinctive from the draft since it covers the Helsinki groups and the Committee for the Defense of Human Rights.

The adopted text of the constitution creates other new forms of associations:

a) The final text of the constitution introduced a new Article 8 dealing with "working collectives" and their functions. This Article replaced Article 16 of the draft. Although working collectives were known sufficiently long ago,[17] their legal characteristics were unknown until the new constitution. The analysis of this Article has to be postponed until (as has already been announced by Brezhnev) a new statute on the rights of working collectives will be enacted.[18] This act, however, will not be applicable to civil rights groups and the Committee for the Defense of Human Rights.

b) In Article 48 of the constitution, as well as "social organizations" there appears another category—"residential collectives." They are not described in the constitution however, and it is likely that these are associations which do not possess legal personality as defined by Article 11 of the Fundamentals of Civil Legislation of the USSR. The right of citizens to participate in the activities of residential collectives is not subject to limitations by virtue of Article 48. Therefore, even that article does not preclude the establishment of civil rights organizations and the Committee for the Defense of Human Rights.

It is possible to argue against this optimistic interpretation of the changes of Articles 6 and 7 of the draft, relying on Article 51 of the constitution, in which the right of citizens to unite in a social organization, which promotes their political activities and initiative, as well as the satisfaction of their diverse interests, is granted only "in accordance with the aims of building Communism." Firstly, so far, nobody has demonstrated that the activities of civil rights organizations are contrary to the above-stated principles. Secondly, it is also necessary to state that, in that article, "organs of social initiative" or residential collectives are not mentioned at all. This omission is by no means an accidental one. It appears that the changes in Articles 6 and 7 of the draft were introduced under the influence of Article 22 of the International Covenant on Civil and Political Rights, declaring the right of each and every citizen to enter into association with others.

3. The Economic System

Changes were incorporated into all ten articles of the second chapter of the draft dealing with the economic system. We will discuss here only the most important changes related to kolkhozes and also those pertaining to private economic activities.

Kolkhozes, Collective Farmers, and the Land

a) Article 11 of the draft was devoted to the property of kolkhozes and other cooperative organizations. Besides the means of production, the kolkhoz can be owner of other property according to the draft. The only limitation is that such property has to "serve the realization of their statutory functions." In the final text, the rights of the kolkhoz to own property is limited even further. The word "serving" was changed to "necessary." This change is not merely an editorial change. Property might serve, but not actually be necessary for, the realization of a function. If one takes into account that the necessary character of property is determined not by the collective farms themselves but by Party and government organs of the region, it is evident that with the change of one word, the right of kolkhozes to own and acquire property has been changed and severely limited.

b) The newspaper *Izvestiia* published on July 16, 1977, a letter of a corresponding member of the Estonian Academy of Sciences, N. Bronstein. He proposed a change in Article 11 of the draft. The interesting history of his proposal is contained in the fact that it was neither accepted nor rejected. The right of the collective farms to own land is contained in Articles 11 and 12 of the draft, and is similar or identical to the norms of the Constitution of 1936: "land held by collective farms is secured to them for free use in perpetuity." Professor N. Bronstein suggested the following addition to this phrase: "economic obligations of the kolkhozes towards the state are determined in relation to the quantity and quality of the land they hold." It is necessary to state that the amendment which he proposed accurately reflected the legal reality. Each and every kolkhoz has to fulfill the goals set by the plan enacted by the government with respect to agricultural production. The government establishes for the kolkhozes not only the amount of production, but also "the purchasing prices, and the rate of taxation," etc. The proposed amendment "reinforces the principles of economic responsibility of the agricultural enterprises." Why was this amendment not introduced into the constitution? It appears that this occurred due to political considerations. The proposed amendment is not compatible with the phrase "free use in perpetuity." Let us assume that A claims that land, which B has in free perpetuity, belongs to A, and that B on account of this is obliged to cultivate the land only in a manner permitted by A, and to sell the produce to A at a price established by A (several times lower than the market price). Is it possible to seriously consider that B received the land in perpetuity and for free usage? For these reasons, the amendment proposed by Professor Bronstein was not acceptable. Nevertheless, the idea of increasing the accent on economic responsibility of the kolkhozes proved to be tempting, and it found its manifestation in the text of the constitution: "Collective farms, as well as other landusers, are bound to utilize land effectively, to treat it with care, and to increase its productiveness."

c) The following changes in the draft also relate to land. The significance of these changes lies in the fact that they appear to be a departure from the Program of the Communist Party of the USSR. These changes pertain to the so-called "individual plots of land," on which the individuals living in the country may raise crops, animals, and poultry for their own use, as well as for the open market. The size of these individual plots is severely limited and, in 1975, amounted to 1.5% of all arable land. On this part of the land, private agriculture is undertaken by 16% of all people living in the country.[19] The great majority of people involved in such a form of agriculture are pensioners, invalids, and women with small children, rather than "normal" farmers. Nevertheless, these plots account for some one-third of all agricultural production in the USSR. Thus in 1965, they were responsible for 32% of all agricultural output (meat, eggs, vegetables, and fruits). In the period between 1971 and 1975, 16% of the rural population were responsible for the production of a greater quantity of potatoes and eggs than were all collective and state farms together. However, it is not our task to discuss the effectiveness of the Soviet system of agricultural production. For our theme, other issues are important; productivity of these personal plots started to decrease from 32% of all agricultural production in 1965, to 28.3% in 1975, and to 28% in 1977.[20]

The soft words of the Program of the Communist Party of the USSR that "the individual private plots will gradually eliminate themselves when the members of the kolkhozes will recognize that involvement in such agricultural production is unprofitable, and will voluntarily cease to involve themselves in such activity," were followed by the harsh practical policies of "persuasion." Such policies resulted in the already reported decrease in the output of this kind of agricultural production. These matters became known as people were alerted to the problem when the draft of the constitution was already finished. On May 11, 1977, *Literaturnaia Gazeta* published an article by V. Travinskii: "Letters from a Personal Plot." It is interesting to note that the newspaper earlier refused to publish this article, which was written in 1970 or 1971, and later recalled this article after the death of the journalist. The same newspaper published on August 24, 1977, an interview with a member of the All-Union Agricultural Academy, V. A. Tikhonov, and finally on September 10, 1977, *Pravda* published an article by the head of the Division of Agricultural Problems of the Institute of Economics of the Socialist State of the Academy of Sciences of the USSR, G. Shmelev: "Re: personal agricultural plots." All of these authors pointed out the importance of individual agriculture and its previous underestimation.

Finally, this debate found its way into the draft of the constitution which departed from the Program and practice of the Communist Party of the USSR: "Citizens are bound to rationally utilize the plots of land made available to them. The state and the collective farm render aid to citizens in running the subsidiary household." This amendment manifests the change in the politics of the Soviet leadership in the treatment of private agriculture. Brezhnev said during the session of the Supreme Soviet of the USSR that, although there were tendencies towards liquidation of private agriculture, or severe limitations thereof, it was, on the contrary, necessary to give them every assistance. Furthermore, he stated that the appropriate state agencies should firmly exercise the right of control given to them by the constitution, strictly seeing to it that the plots of land made available to citizens were used rationally, for the benefit of society, that "the income from auxiliary farming and individual labor activity conforms to the principles of socialism." The future will show the direction of policies resulting from these words.

Private Property and Private Initiative

In the new Constitution of the USSR, there is a chapter devoted to the rights of Soviet citizens. It would be reasonable to find in this chapter a mention of property rights of citizens. The right of an individual to own property is one of the primary rights contained in the Universal Declaration of Human Rights–Article 17. The authors of the new constitution of the USSR obviously were of a different opinion.

One is re-affirmed in this opinion by an analysis of the differences in the draft and the final text. Article 12 of the draft dealt with personal property of Soviet citizens and was included in the chapter "Economic System." It is constructed in the following manner: in the first place the forms of ownership are described; furthermore it is stated that "the right to personal property and the inheritance thereof, is protected by the law," and finally, it is stated that possession or ownership of personal property may not be used in a manner in which it will allow obtaining of unearned income or in a manner harmful to society. In the final version of this article (which became Article 13), the following changes were introduced: a) a new concept was introduced: "the basis of the personal property of Soviet citizens;" b) it was established that earned income constitutes the "basis" of personal property. Thus, the remaining property which might be in the possession of a citizen is not the basic property; c) the legal protection is granted not to the *right* to personal property, but to the property itself; d) personal property, and also the right of inheritance, from now on will be protected not by "law" but by "the state;" e) citizens are prohibited from using personal property not only in a manner "harmful to society," but also "to the detriment of its [society's] interest," and at the same time the circle of those interests is not defined. These changes produce even greater uncertainty in the area of private property and further reduce the rights of a citizen to dispose of property. These changes constitute a further expansion of the right of the state to interfere in the property of the citizens, thus further increasing the possibility of a violation of civil rights. The already uncertain term "non-labor income" was further confused by the equally uncertain term "detriment to the interests of society." For example, in Soviet civil law there are norms of compulsory redemption of authors' rights, as well as rights of inheritors to intellectual property. These apply to copyright and patent rights as well. There also exist norms permitting the government to expropriate the property of citizens with respect to houses at prices far below the market value of the property.[21]

If these norms were in conflict with Article 12 of the draft, and because of that could have been considered unconstitutional, the final version of the constitution gives them proper constitutional authority.

References to the "interests of society" are found a second time in the chapter "Economic System" in Article 17, which deals with the individual activity, *i.e.* the right to work not in a socialist enterprise or socialist agency, but to have an individual business or to work privately part time, frequently in addition to full time work in a government enterprise. We shall compare this article with Article 6 of the International Covenant on Economic, Social, and Cultural Rights, which has been in force for the USSR since 1976. Article 17 of the Constitution of the USSR states "Individual labor activity in the sphere of trades and crafts, agriculture, serving the everyday needs of the population, as well as other forms of activity based exclusively on the individual labor of citizens and the members of their families, are permitted in the USSR in accordance with the law." Article 6 of the International Covenant of Economic, Social, and Cultural Rights states "the States parties to the present convention recognize the right to work, which includes the right of everyone to gain his living by work which he freely chooses or accepts, and will take appropriate steps to safeguard this right." Thus, we can see that instead of the right to a free choice of working activity as in the Covenant, private labor activity is permitted only if it is not specifically prohibited by the law. Such a permit is obtainable from the Financial Branch of the Executive of the City Council. The numbers of people who undertake the risk of open private economic activities is decreasing every year. According to official data, less than 0.1% of the total labor force were involved in private economic activity in 1970, and this percentage decreased further in the following years. Among those who are described as involved in handicraft, are included several surprising professions. Not only those involved in agriculture and trades, but also teachers of music, doctors, dentists, and artists who are not members of the union of artists.[22] "Withering away" of the legally—officially—registered individuals working privately is a direct result of the total system of obstacles created by the government. This complicated system is re-inforced by extremely high taxes, deliberate refusals of registration, and the creation of a climate of condemnation of private "businessmen." We shall give two examples of court cases dealing with the issues pertaining to private economic activities.[23]

1) A young artist travelled into the northern Russian villages and discovered old and partly destroyed Russian icons. He restored these icons and then sold them. As a rule, he received the icons free of charge. The believers gave the icons to the artist to protect them from unvoidable destruction. They believed in him due to the fact that he was a religious man, a restorer of art. He was charged with an offense under article 162 of the RSFSR Criminal Code, which is a charge of involvement in a prohibited business. This charge, however, was not based on legal grounds, since article 162 of the Criminal Code enumerates prohibited economic activities of business. Among such prohibited activities, restoration of freely obtained objects of art and the subsequent sale of the said objects is not included. The defense counsel of the artist turned to the Ministry of Finance with an official question whether the list contained the activity of restoring or sale of icons obtained without charge. The preparation of such a list attached to article 162 is the responsibility of the Ministry of Finance. The Deputy Minister of Finance already verbally answered the attorney that he would provide him with a reply the following day, since he was obliged to consult on the matter with the organs of *KGB*. In a letter received from the Deputy Minister the following day, the following explanation was provided: Restoration and subsequent sale of icons is a criminal activity, regardless of the manner in which they were obtained. The most important question from the point of view of the defense was, however, whether such a prohibition existed prior to the time when the charge was laid? This question was not answered. Not surprisingly, the court did not find sufficient grounds to acquit the artist.

2) Some citizens in a small town near Leningrad organized a private company of builders. The residents of a near-by place were in need of an aqueduct. The work required laying down some eight hundred meters of pipe, in order

to connect the village water system to the existing mains. The village council for many years had not been able to obtain acceptance of the project by government agencies. The private construction firm proposed to the village council a plan for the system and private work. They also stated that they would finish the work in three months, at a price twenty times lower than that quoted by a government enterprise. The contract was fulfilled and the money paid. Following this, all members of the private construction firm were charged with a criminal offense. The charge was one of embezzlement of government money. The charges stated that they had obtained for their work five times as much as provided by the government schedule. In other words, if the government enterprise conducted the work, they would charge the village council twenty times as much, but pay to the workers one-fifth of the money which private workers received for the same job.

One could cite endless numbers of such examples. The following changes to Article 17 of the draft reflect the government's attitude towards private work. "The state regulates individual labor activity, ensuring its utilization in the interests of society." What the actual interests of society are is evident from a letter to *Pravda* by Dr. Zanozdra. "Life and practice show that small and urgent repairs of shoes, tailoring, repair of domestic appliance, farm machinery in many instances are conducted faster and cheaper by private men at home, who are running their own individual businesses."[24] Without the help of the government, society found a very quick way to secure its interests. The number of unregistered tradesmen greatly exceeds the number of 1/10 of 1%–which is the number officially given by the statistical agency of the government. These people conduct their activity in their free time, after their work in some socialist enterprise. Their numbers increase with much greater rapidity than the decline of the officially registered tradesmen.

4. Foreign Policy

The chapter of the constitution devoted to the foreign policy of the USSR consists of three articles. Between the draft and the final text of the constitution, there were two changes: 1) The goals of foreign policy were expanded by adding the phrase "bringing about universal and complete disarmament." This goal appears in the present day to be a utopian one, a pious and unattainable wish. 2) In describing the principles on the basis of which the relationship between the USSR and other nations are conducted, there is a change of order in the final text: "principles of sovereign equality" was moved into the *first* place. This change of order is not caused by a simple improvement of style–it is necessary to remember that, at present, the Soviet Union very frequently uses such terms as "violation of sovereignty" and "interference with internal affairs." These words are frequently used by the representatives of the Soviet Union to describe official statements and other activities of

President Carter in respect to the violation of Human Rights in the USSR, as well as activities of various Western organizations and individuals with respect to human rights in the USSR with the goal of defending the Russian dissidents in particular.

Sovereignty and Non-interference in Internal Affairs

Analysis of the text of the Constitution of the USSR leads one to the conclusion that the activities of President Carter and other leaders of Western States, as well as activities of Western organizations, are fully in conformity with the new Soviet Constitution.

According to Article 29 of the Constitution of the USSR the relations between the Soviet Union and other nations are based on "the observance of principles" not only of "sovereign equality" and "non-interference in internal affairs," but also of "respect for human rights and fundamental freedoms" as well as "the conscientious fulfillment of obligations arising from generally recognized principles and norms of international law and treaties concluded by the USSR." Among such international agreements we find, in particular, the International Covenants on Civil, Political, Economic, and on Social and Cultural Rights. From 1976, the year of ratification of the Covenant by the thirty-fifth State, the Covenants became part of the international obligations of the Soviet Union. There is no legal system in the civilized world in which the obligation of one state or party in a bilateral or multilateral agreement, is not followed by the right of the other party or parties to comment on the nature of the obligations arising from the agreement, as well as to demand the observance of the terms of the agreement. This right is based, in particular, on the principle of the sovereign equality of the parties. This principle is placed as number one among the terms on which the foreign policy of the Soviet Union is conducted, according to the new constitution.

In order to appreciate this argument in full, one has to see the treatment in the constitutional law of the USSR of the right of interference in the internal affairs of other states. It is necessary in the first place to consider the goals of Soviet foreign policy. These are stated in Article 28 of the Constitution of the USSR and among them are the following: 1) "ensuring favorable international conditions for the building of Communism in the USSR," 2) "strengthening the position of world socialism." We will not discuss which of these two principles direct the activities of the USSR, for example, in Angola, or in the conflict between Cambodia and Vietnam, or between Ethiopia and Somalia. The extend to which the "strengthening of world socialism" is consistent with the right to equal sovereignty and the principle of non-interference in the internal affairs of those states, which are capitalist and not socialist, remains an open question. Finally, by what means and on the basis of what principles should the "strengthening of socialism" in such socialist states as West Germany, England, and Sweden occur?

Perhaps the term "world socialism" is interpreted by the author too broadly and should be restricted, for example in its application to the American continent, to socialist Cuba only. Such an objection would be quite untenable. The author's interpretation is supported by Article 169 of the Constitution of 1977, in which the national emblem of the USSR is described. The emblem contains a picture of a hammer and sickle against the background of the globe, and is followed with the inscription, "in the languages of the union republics" which reads as follows: "Proletarians of All Countries, Unite!". The official Soviet translation of the constitution uses the words "Workers of the World, Unite!", whereas the Russian text of the constitution uses the word: "*Proletarians* of All Countries, Unite." Nevertheless, in not one of these republics to which the slogan is addressed, are there any proletarians. According to Articles 17 and 19 of the 1977 Constitution, there are the following classes and social groups in the USSR: "Workers, peasants, intelligentsia, and other working people." Where are those proletarians who are called to unite by the fundamental internal law of the Soviet Union? We can trace them in *The Great Soviet Encyclopedia* which speaks for the government: "Proletariat–one of the two principal classes of *bourgeois* society; Proletarians–in a capitalist society–class of hired workers." [25] Thus, the call by the Soviet government to "proletarian unity" is directed primarily towards the population of other countries–countries of the free world. The attempt to explain the preservation of this slogan by adherence to traditions would not be a successful one. The Soviet leadership was flexible enough to change the national anthem twice. Proceeding from the principle of reciprocity of sovereign authority, one must conclude that official statements of the leaders of Western countries, with regard to violations of human rights in the USSR, or protests coming from Western societies about the said violations, are not only in total conformity with the constitutional norms of the USSR, but also are far away from the real opportunities, if one compares the extent of the problem on the one hand, and the Soviet constitutional approach to the principle of "non-interference in the internal affairs" on the other hand.

5. Equal Rights of Citizens

Chapter 6 "Citizenship of the USSR–Equal Rights of Citizens" opens the second part of the constitution entitled "The State and The Individual." The greatest changes occurred in Article 35, devoted to the notion of equal rights of men and women. Besides the safeguards provided by the draft for equal rights of men and women, there are the following additions: "creating conditions allowing women to combine work with motherhood," and also "gradual reduction of working time for women with young children." At the same time, a reference to "governmental help for single mothers" disappeared from the final text. This change does not mean that the assistance for single mothers will cease to be provided. The changes are of an editorial nature. On the one hand, there were criticisms aimed at the phrase "single mother;" "in a socialist society based on collectivism, there is no place for solitude or loneliness as social and legal categories."[26] On the other hand, this assistance is secured by Article 35 which mentions "material assistance for maternity and child bearing." The notion of "the gradual reduction of working time for women" was added by two deputies, V. Nikolaeva-Tereshkova (the first female astronaut and a member of the Constitutional Committee) and V. P. Pukhova (director of a factory).[27] This reduction, according to L. I. Brezhnev, will occur "to the extent to which it will be permitted by the creation of the necessary economic conditions."[28] Although "creating conditions allowing women to combine work with motherhood," according to the text of the constitution, "secures equality between men and women," this however cannot be considered as describing the present reality. It is a statement of principle to be reached at some future date. The economic equality of women is far from being in line with declared political equality, and thus, in reality, we cannot speak of political equality.

In order to prove this contention, it is enough to use as an example the 1961 Program of the Communist Party of the USSR, which describes the concrete conditions which have to be created and to compare this statement with the present reality.[29] A good indicator is the presence or absence of women in leading organs of the Party and in government.[30] For example, there are no women among the members of the Politburo of the Central Committee of the CPSU nor among the Ministers of the USSR. Nevertheless, it is necessary to state that this change in the constitution is a favorable one, compared to the text of the Program of the Communist Party of the USSR. The program carries with it symptoms of male chauvinism in reference to the role of the female in the family: "it is necessary to secure improved conditions for the fulfillment of the *woman's domestic chores in the family*"[31] (italics added).

6. Fundamental Rights, Freedoms, and Obligations of Citizens of the USSR

Chapter 7 is devoted to the description of rights, freedoms, and obligations of citizens, and is one of the most important in the draft of the constitution. For convenience, we will divide it into five parts.

Fundamental Rights–Articles 39 to 46

The most vivid discussion occurred with respect to Article 41 of the draft, dealing with the right to rest and leisure. According to the text of the draft, this right was to be secured by a "forty-one hour working week." This was such an obvious departure from the Program of the Communist Party of the

USSR, that it could not escape careful attention. According to the program, the thirty-five hour working week was to be achieved by 1971, and in the second decade (1971-1981) the Soviet Union was to move towards "a period of even further reduction in the working week." [32] A flood of letters reached the newspapers and the offices of the Constitutional Committee. Some recommended that the constitution should avoid mention of the working week altogether. Others wanted a statement of the principle of the reduction of the working week, at least in reference to the future, so that the citizens of the USSR "with time will achieve more free time, increasing with the greater demand for leisure as a result of expanding spiritual needs." Both sides of the argument referred to "concerns of the Party and the government." [33] With respect to the working week and leisure of the members of the kolkhozes, the consensus was that this issue required further stabilization, not only through administrative regulations, but also by statute.

The unprogrammed response to these norms did not find sympathetic hearings among the drafters of the new constitution. None of these requests were granted, although there were numerous changes in the draft. The reference to a forty-one hour working week was changed into "not exceeding forty-one hours." The problem of the work time of kolkhozes was to be "regulated by the kolkhozes themselves." Whether kolkhozes will be bound by their statutes remains uncertain. Nevertheless, the demand for stability in the determination of working time and leisure time of the *kolkhozniki* was, in the final text, even farther from being met than in the draft. In discussing the changes between the draft and the final text, Brezhnev did not refer to the above issues at all, as if nothing had taken place.

Political Freedoms–Articles 50 to 52

Article 50 of the draft enumerated political freedoms which were to be granted to Soviet citizens. These included: freedom of expression, press, assembly, mass meetings, street processions, and demonstrations. The draft also stated the *purposes* for which these freedoms were granted. Exercise of these freedoms can take place only "in order to strengthen the socialist system," and in accordance with "the interests of the working people." These limitations in the exercise of political freedoms gave rise to objections. As the objections to this part of the draft were so numerous, they had to be mentioned. One of the signs of the response was obviously "inspired." The author of an article in *Literaturnaia Gazeta*, "Our Rights, Our Duties," [34] a member of the Institute of State and Law of the USSR Academy of Sciences, V. Patiulin, undertook the defense of Article 50 of the draft. From all the influx of letters he cited only one by name, and in passing, referred to two other letters in which analogous problems or questions were raised. The very fact of the appearance of this article, as well as the contents, confirms that (using the words of Brezhnev from the already cited speech of October 5, 1977) "...

behind each change in the articles there are thousands of concurring opinions." Arguments of those who spoke against the draft are interesting even in the abbreviated way in which Patiulin refers to them. The author of the cited letter was W. Fillipin. He recommended deleting from Article 50, and other articles of the draft, all mention of limitations of rights and freedoms of individuals by a preface referring to the interests of society and state. He states "these limitations can be abused in practice by aims far apart from creating a socialist society in the USSR." Further, "any irresponsible official can suppress criticism by labeling it inconsistent with the interests of the state." Dr. Patiulin states that, in the USSR, the interests of the citizens and the state are the same, and that L. I. Brezhnev assured the people that abuses of the law–which took place earlier–will not happen any more, and finally, that the Universal Declaration of Human Rights and the International Covenant on Civil and Political Rights also prescribed some limitations to the rights of citizens. He did not point out that there are great differences between limitations imposed by the International Covenant and those imposed by the draft of the Constitution of the USSR. In the Covenant, there is a reference to limitations which are in *accordance with the law*, and only if they are necessary for the safety of society or of the state. Both in the draft and in the final text of the constitution (Article 39), these limitations are with respect to matters detrimental to the interest of the state or society. Neither safety or law are mentioned as grounds for limiting political freedoms. Thus, the basic argument is that political freedoms, guaranteed to Soviet citizens, do not result from basic human rights, but only "insofar as they contribute to the goals of strengthening of the building of socialism." Man should be entitled to use his freedoms also in those instances when the exercise of these freedoms and rights does not serve the goals of strengthening governmental or political systems. It should be sufficient that the government or the society is not adversely affected by this fact. Nevertheless, the change of Article 50 of the draft, even more strongly underlined the fact that political freedoms of the citizens are granted only in accordance with "the goals of strengthening *and developing* the socialist system" (italics added). This addition is even more surprising, since it does not correspond to the preamble of the constitution, where it is stated that, in the USSR, a developed socialist society has already been built, whereas this article refers to socialism as still being in a developmental stage. Nevertheless, according to the Constitution of the USSR, Soviet citizens can use and enjoy political freedoms only in those cases when they use them in order to develop the socialist system.

Freedom of Conscience

In distinction from the draft of the constitution, where freedom of conscience is recognized as the right of citizens of the USSR, in the final text it is "guaranteed to the citizens." The concept of freedom of conscience also underwent a certain degree of change. According to the draft, this right "was a right to profess any religion, to perform religious rites, or not to belong to any religion, and to conduct atheist propaganda." The final text underwent a change, and the "right to profess any religion" was opposed by the "right *not* to profess any religion." This contrast is not objectional in essence; however, it is formally awkward. The right to profess a religion, which is not an obligation itself, implies the right not to belong to any religion. This is the only example in the constitution when a specific right is contrasted by the right to the opposite. For example, the right to belong to a social organization (Article 51) is not contrasted by the right NOT to belong to a social organization.

We will return to this topic when discussing the articles pertaining to the electoral system.

A serious violation of the freedom of conscience is contained in the second juxtaposition between the right to "perform religious rites" with the right to "conduct atheist propaganda." It is important to note that the right to conduct atheist propaganda is guaranteed to the *citizens*. Does this mean that such a right does not belong to various governmental agencies, especially established for atheist propoganda–such as the atheist branches of the Departments of Culture of the Soviets, departments of "Scientific Atheism" in universities and institutes etc.? Does this legislative change mean the end of atheist education in the schools? Official anti-religious propaganda in the USSR is conducted in an aggressive form, and in many instances it violates the freedom of conscience of the believers. In 1971, when I was a lawyer in Leningrad, I was asked for a legal opinion on the following question: Within a certain monastery, there was established a government travel agency. A guide from this agency was conducting tours around the monastery during the ceremonies. He made loud comments about the service; "You can see how the people are stupified," "Religion is an opiate of the masses! ", and other similar comments. The local authorities refused to hear a complaint from the monastery on the grounds of the principle of the freedom of anti-religious propaganda.

In reality, the broad right to anti-religious propaganda is contrasted by a prohibition of the teaching of religion. On the one hand, the wide distribution of anti-religious publications–books, journals, pamphlets, etc.–and on the other hand the extremely limited right to publication and the scarcity of such books as the Bible, Koran, Talmud, and other religious publications, point up the reality of the situation. Distribution of religious materials can only be done by special internal religious channels. Under such conditions, it is very difficult to obtain religious materials. In 1972, an employee of the Leningrad television station copied forty copies of the Koran on the station copying machine. In the USSR, the use of copying machines in a public institution is strictly limited to official business, and the employees are obliged to give a detailed account of what is being copied. This case was brought to the attention of the Party Committee in Leningrad, and also the *KGB*. The employee who copied the Koran on request from a group of Leningrad Moslems (who at the time were in possession of only one badly worn copy of the Koran) was fired. Of course, there would be no need to copy the Koran in Leningrad's television station if the Moslems were able to obtain the Koran officially.

The Soviet right to freedom of conscience is contained in Article 52 of the constitution. This right is far apart from the one contained in Article 8 of the International Covenant on Civil and Political Rights. It is a manifestation of the goals of the atheistic Program of the Communist Party of the USSR. According to the Party, religious faith is a prejudice and a remnant of capitalism in the conscience of the people. Education of the people in the spirit of the materialist world-view is considered to be one of the main targets of Communist ideology.

The Right to File a Complaint–Article 58

The draft contained the right of citizens to complain about activities of officials. This right refers to any activity of an official since the article refers to "actions which violate the law or exceed the authority of officials." Complaints about such activities can be brought not only to "their superiors," but directly to the court. The version of this article in the draft brought a great response from Soviet jurists. Professor M. Strogovich recommended an addition to the article of strict prohibition against forwarding the complaint to the person against whose activities the complaint is brought. [35] (I have many times seen complaints of citizens on the table of those against whom they were brought with a note: "prepare an answer.") A professor of the University of Tbilisi, D. Loriia, suggested an amendment in the form of administrative courts. [36] Members of the Research Institute of Soviet Legislation, I. Kuznetsov and V. Maksimovskii, wanted to expand the notion of complaints pertaining to the activity or lack of activity of officials to decisions made by governmental and social organizations. [37] Professor S. Bratus' cautioned against the mistaken conclusion that any complaint could be brought in the future, and proposed adding the following words to Article 58 of the draft: "the list of those cases where the actions of institutions and officials may be the subject of a complaint in court shall be determined by law." [38]

The third part of this article received less attention. This part referred to a specific possibility of compensation for damage caused by illegal actions of state institutions and social organizations and also officials during performance of their duties in accordance "with the limitations established by law." The Constitutional Commission did not share the view contained in the opinions of many lawyers. The right to file a complaint against "the actions" (but not against the decisions) is contained in the adopted text. This right was not expanded to include the right to a court action. In part three of Article 58, reference to the *limitations* of the right to obtain damages was eliminated. This, however, does not mean the real elimination of the limitations themselves. It is obvious that reference to the law of damages contained in articles 445 and 446 of the RSFSR Civil Code was considered by the editors of the final version of the constitution as an unnecessary one.

Obligations of Citizens of the USSR–Article 59 to 69

Article 60 of the draft creates the obligation of the citizen to involve himself in socially useful and conscientious labor. "Strict observance of labor and productive discipline" is supplemented by the statement that "avoiding socially useful work is incompatible with the principles of a socialist society." Although this addition does not directly state a responsibility for avoiding work, nevertheless, this addition avoids the possibility of conflict between the constitution and the new version of article 209 of the RSFSR Criminal Code and corresponding articles of the criminal codes in other republics.[39]

In the final text, several further obligations are stated: "to treat the wealth of the people with care"–Article 61; "to show concern for parents and to render them aid"–Article 66; concern for "the preservation of historical monuments and other cultural treasures"–Article 68.

As a whole, the duties and obligations of the citizens of the USSR, contained in Article 61, are as follows: 1) To safeguard and strengthen *socialist property*; 2) To combat theft and waste of *state and social property*; 3) To treat the wealth of the people with care. This is, however, a sort of tautological verbosity. Words like "safeguard," "combatting theft," "waste of state and social property," and "to treat the wealth of the people with care"–are similar concepts. In the absence of these phrases, could one come to the conclusion that the citizens of the USSR are *not* obliged "to treat socialist property with care," "safeguard and protect state and social property," "combat theft or waste of national wealth"?

According to Article 59 of the constitution, the exercise of citizens' rights and freedoms is inseparable from the fulfillment of their obligations. Brezhnev, in his final speech at the session of the Supreme Soviet concluding the constitutional debate, stated that rights and obligations of citizens in the USSR are "inseparable." Thus, in order to enjoy one's rights, citizens of the USSR are obliged in particular to work conscientiously, not to avoid socially useful work, safeguard and protect socialist property, and treat it with care, protect the interests of the government, enhance its power and prestige, serve in the army, be uncompromising towards anti-social behavior, protect nature and preserve its riches, and show concern for the protection of historical monuments. This is not a complete catalogue of the obligations of citizens which have to be fulfilled in order for them to exercise their rights. Living up to such tasks is not an easy matter.

7. The Union Republics–Chapter 9

In the definition of a union republic in the final text of the constitution, the word "sovereign" was added. Thus, a union republic is a "Sovereign Soviet Socialist State." This addition seems to be for the purpose of maintaining membership in the United Nations for some of the union republics. We will turn our attention mostly to the concept of sovereignty as defined in the dictionary of the Russian language: "full independence of the government in internal and external politics." This definition should be considered in the light of the differences between the jurisdiction of the Soviet Union–Articles 73 to 75 of the USSR Constitution, and the Union Republics–Articles 76 to 81. It is obvious from even a cursory analysis that the union republics do not have even partial independence in terms of internal politics, and none in terms of external politics. The union republics implement the decisions and the orders of the highest organs of state power and administration of the Soviet Union. On constitutional grounds, there is even less reason to consider the republics as independent states than states in the United States or provinces in Canada.

8. The Electoral System

In the eight articles of the draft dealing with the electoral system, nine changes were introduced. Among the most important of these are the following listed below.

The Right to Vote and the Right to Be Elected–Article 96

In the draft, the right to be elected to all soviets, including the Supreme Soviet of the USSR, was granted to all citizens over eighteen years of age. Brezhnev called this "real evidence of the concern of our society with the young people and our faith in youth." In finalizing the draft, society must have changed its attitude towards youth; the age qualification for being elected to the Supreme Soviet was increased to twenty-one years of age.

The right to vote has not been changed, regardless of the opinion of some of the jurists. "Elections of deputies shall be universal. All citizens of the USSR, upon reaching the age of eighteen, shall have the right to vote and to be elected, with the exception of persons who have, in the manner established by law, been declared to be demented." (The use of the word "demented" in the translation is not accidental. It is due to the fact that the Russian term, *umalishennyi*, used in the constitution is not the one ordinarily used as an equivalent to such terms as "mentally incompetent" or any other equivalent used in the legal description of people legally declared to be mentally ill.) There is no statute which would describe this "manner established by law," unless it is a secret statute. In the present civil law, there is no term "demented." Speaking against the usage of this term in the draft of the constitution, the Procurator for Leningrad, A. Verevkin, said: "We think that it is necessary to change in Article 95 of the draft the term 'demented' to 'legally incompetent,' since it is necessary to more precisely determine the reasons for limiting electoral rights, both from the legal and medical point of view, as well as out of tactfulness with respect to relations with the sick and their relatives."[40] Article 96 remains unchanged only because it hides from a cursory glance the widely-spread practice of deprivation of the right to vote for "politically disloyal" citizens. Further proof of this contention is contained in the following.

From May 1, 1962, when the Fundamentals of Civil Legislation of the USSR were enacted, every person upon achieving the age of eighteen is presumed to be legally capable, meaning in possession of the capability "to acquire civil rights and to undertake civil obligations." In article 8 of the Fundamentals of Soviet Civil Legislation, it is established that nobody can be declared mentally incompetent in any other way than in the manner and instances prescribed by law. Conditions for declaring a person mentally incompetent are stated in article 15 of the RSFSR Civil Code, and in Chapter 29 of the RSFSR Code of Civil Procedure. There is no other statute which prescribes deprivation of civil (including political) rights of mentally ill persons. According to Soviet civil law, the mental incompetence in a civil sense occurs when a person is, "as a result of mental illness or feeblemindedness, unable to understand the meaning of his actions and is not capable of conducting his own actions." Thus, in order to declare a person as mentally incompetent, the fact that he is "demented" (it is interesting to note that the Dictionary of Russian Language describes the word "demented" as a pejorative term describing a person), "mentally ill" or "feebleminded," "retarded" or "lunatic"–these are various meanings and words taken from the Russian Dictionary of Synonyms[41]–is absolutely insufficient. The necessary step in the process is the description of the *degree* of mental illness or retardation. Illness has to be to a degree prohibiting understanding of actions or the limiting capability of directing one's own actions. This is recognized not only by Soviet psychiatrists but is also a matter of law. "The presence of mental illness is not sufficient evidence to declare somebody mentally incompetent; in such instances, the degree or gravity of the mental insufficiency is of grave importance."[42] On the other hand, a mentally incompetent citizen can later be declared to be in possession of full mental legal capacity, not only in case of a full recovery, but also in many instances of "significant improvement of his mental health," although he still remains mentally ill. Such is the spirit of article 15, para. 3, of the RSFSR Civil Code. Illness is a medical criterion of incapacity. There is a necessity also for a psychological criterion–the inability to understand one's actions, and to conduct them accordingly. With respect to the procedure by which a person is declared mentally incompetent, and by the same deprived of citizen's rights, the law provides that this can only be done by a judicial declaration. Cases of this nature are decided by courts with the obligatory presence of the Procurator and the representatives of the government agencies of custody and guardianship. Prior to the court action, there is the requirement of conducting (by judicial order) a psychiatric examination.

The reference in the constitution to denial of electoral rights of those who are "in the manner established by law declared to be demented" goes far beyond what we have already mentioned. This is frequently extended to fully fledged citizens, even those who are mentally healthy. Traces of this can be found in the recently published "Commentary to Some Norms Dealing with Elections to Local Soviets."[43] This commentary was not written by legal scholars, but by officials of the Department in Charge of Work in the Soviets of the RSFSR Supreme Soviet. It has to be considered as a binding source of statutory interpretation. Article 15 of the Statute states "the electoral lists are not to include people who are declared to be demented in the manner established by law." Authors of the commentary enumerate and explain "the documents on the basis of which" citizens are to be omitted from the electoral lists or to be excluded from them. The authors do not refer to any statutory instrument on which this interpretation is based. The following documents are cited in the commentary: a) judicial decisions based on psychiatric examination; and b) lists provided to the executive committees of the Soviets by the provincial and municipal health authorities containing the names of persons who are in psychiatric hospitals or mental colonies.[44] Thus, in order to be denied the right to vote, it is sufficient to be placed—even for a short time—in a psychiatric hospital or a mental colony. What are the probabilities of a person being committed to a psychiatric hospital or a mental colony without medical indications prior to an election? The answer to this question cannot be constructed from an analysis of the published law, but can be found in the coordinated activities of the *KGB* and the organs administering mental health. Thousands of people who, even in their remote past, exhibited behavior considered to be "anti-social" were forced to register in out-patient psychiatric clinics. "An anti-social activity" can be considered any expression of opinion differing from the official order, disagreement with the existing order, or a determined legal fight over rights. Disagreement with local administrative organs, and many other activities, make such people in the eyes of *KGB*, "disloyal." (Political dissidents constitute only part of this population.) Such people are forcibly registered in out-patient psychiatric clinics, not only by the orders of the *KGB* but also by orders of any other governmental agencies. Specifically, this occurs in instances where there is not enough evidence for criminal prosecution, or where, for political reasons, the authorities consider a criminal trial to be undesirable. All such people, on the orders of *KGB* are placed in mental institutions a few days prior to an election, and due to this fact, are excluded from the electoral lists.[45] Deliberate deprivation of electoral rights of this large group of Soviet citizens thus denies them the right to participate "in the governance of political and social affairs in the manner established by law" and is concealed by the constitutional phrase "persons recognized in the legally prescribed manner as being demented."

Secrecy of Voting–Article 99

The draft stated that voting is to be in secret; "checking on the expression of the will of the voter is excluded." In the final text, the last word was replaced by the word "not allowed." This is a significant change; the manner in which votes are delivered is so organized that control is not excluded at all. Ordinarely, the delivery of the vote is organized in the following manner. On the ballot, the voter always sees the name of one–and only one–candidate. Article 99 of the Election Statute states that "the voter is to leave the name of the candidate for whom he is voting, and has to *cross off* the other names of the candidates whom he is rejecting" (italics added). The voter, however, cannot fulfill this norm since there are no "other names" on the ballot. Thus, if the voter, instead of following the "red carpet" from the place where he obtains the ballot form directly to the ballot box, chooses to go into the voting booth, then the goal of his departure is obvious! He can only cross off the one and only name of the ballot–the candidate of the block of the Communists and non-Party members. Obviously, most of the voters follow the "red carpet." Thus, those who depart from the "path of righteousness" are even easier to notice. The judicial practice of the USSR knows of cases of conviction of voters for putting obscene words or pictures on the ballot. It is no surprise how the guilty were found. These are all examples of instances when "control of the expression of the will of the electors" was not excluded.

Freedom of Electoral Campaigns–Article 100

In the words of the draft, "citizens and social organizations are guaranteed free and full discussion of political and other characteristics of the candidates, as well as the right to campaign in meetings and through the press, television and radio." In the final version, there is an addition stating that "expenses connected with conducting elections for Soviets of People's Deputies are borne by the state." Thus, till such a time when social organizations (in which the leading force is the Communist Party) nominate candidates, the constitution does not guarantee the right to campaign and discuss potential candidates. This analysis is based primarily on the interpretation of Article 100. The right to campaign is not elaborated further. Does the term contain the right to campaign *against* the nominated candidate? The laconic character of this norm is strange when compared with the verbosity of Article 52, which was previously discussed (Right to profess or not to profess a religion). This can be explained by the political reality in which the right to campaign is understood to be only the right to campaign *for* the nominated candidate. This is directly stated in article 90 of the RSFSR Statute on Elections. "Each organization which nominates a candidate, as well as each citizen of the RSFSR is secured the right to campaign for this candidate."[46] Only for this kind of campaign does the government provide access to the newspapers, television, and radio.

Electors' Mandate to the Deputies–Article 102

This article did not appear in the draft. In the final version of the constitution, electors give their deputies a mandate and the Soviets take account of these mandates in the formulation of the plans, and inform citizens of their fulfillment. The system of the mandate existed also in theory prior to the enactment of the new constitution, yet in practice it did not look so idyllic. The elector gave a mandate to the deputy, then the Soviet considered it, took it into account, and informed the citizen about it. A short description of the previous system is provided in *The Great Soviet Encyclopedia.*[47] "The right to provide a mandate to the deputies belongs to the meetings of the voters which are empowered to nominate candidates." What about a single ordinary Soviet citizen? "Only the proposals of citizens which pertain to the work of the Soviets or individual deputies, and which were approved by the meetings of the voters,"[48] can expect official answers. Only time will show whether this system will continue.

The discussed changes even more obviously show the discrepancy between the Soviet electoral system and the principle of the free expression of the will of the electorate contained in Article 25(b) of the International Covenant of Civil Rights. If "to elect" (*vybirat'*) means a choice between at least two candidates, then the electoral system (*izbiratel'naia sistema*) in the USSR bears the wrong name.

9. Justice, Arbitration, and Procuratorial Supervision

This section obviously was scrutinized by the lawyers–both theoreticians and those in practice. If one is to exclude various statistical and technical corrections, the main targets of the discussion were norms relating to the independence of courts, and the concept of the presumption of innocence (Articles 154 and 159). One can also mention the contribution of Professor I. M. Tkachevskii in the discussion of the role which the constitution assigns to Comrades' Courts, which hear one-third of all cases.[49] Unfortunately, neither he nor his professional colleagues discussed the role of special courts in the constitution, and neither did he discuss the number of cases which are considered by these courts.[50]

Independence of Judges

Proposals for changes in Article 154 of the draft were in two categories: attempts at greater precision in the notion of the independence of the judiciary through the concept that judges are independent and are only to obey the law, not "in general" but "in the exercise of their judicial activities,"[51] meaning "in the consideration of cases."[52] To guarantee real independence of judges, a statement has been introduced that "nobody has the right to interfere with the exercise of judicial discretion and exert any pressure on the judges or people's assessors in their conduct and in the performance of their duties in the court."[53] In order to understand the meaning of this phrase, it is necessary to remember that the text of Article 154 of the draft was a direct quote from Article 112 of the 1936 Stalin Constitution, the effectiveness of which is well-known.

None of these amendments were accepted. Article 154 of the draft entered the constitution without any change, and became Article 155.

Presumption of Innocence

Soviet jurists connect the presumption of innnocence with the content of Article 159 of the draft: "No one may be convicted of the commission of a crime as well as be subjected to criminal punishment other than by judgment of the court and in accordance with *criminal law*" (italics added). Dr. A. Boikov considered that the following significant principles of criminal procedure derived from Article 159 of the draft: a) the determination of guilt and penalties is the exclusive prerogative of the courts; b) until a judgment is delivered, there is a presumption of innocence. Nevertheless, according to Dr. Boikov, Article 159 should be changed editorially in order to make it more clear. It requires a statement which would make it self-evident that the accused is considered to be innnocent until proven guilty by a judge.[54] Dr. W. Savitskii asserts that, in fact, the principle of presumption of innocence already exists in Soviet criminal law, although it is not stated in the statutes. "Therefore, this principle is built on the analysis of various legal norms."[55] An outstanding Soviet lawyer, S. Kallistratova, argues that Article 159 of the draft reflects the principle of the presumption of innocence although "not clearly enough."[56] She also recommended a change in Article 159 of the draft to bring it into conformity with Article 40 of the International Covenant on Civil and Political Rights. Similar opinions can be found in many legal journals. These opinions, however, were not shared by the Constitutional Committee. In the constitution, this article appears without any substantive changes. Below, we give the full text of the article in juxtaposition with Article 14, para. 2, of the International Covenant on Civil and Political Rights in order to prove that the principle of the presumption of innocence is absent from the Soviet Constitution. The right to be considered innocent is much broader than the guarantee to "not be subject to criminal punishment other than by a judgment of the court." The principle of not being subject to a criminal penalty without a court judgment can also be found in substantive criminal law: "criminal punishment can only be imposed by a decision of the court," states article 3 of the Fundamentals of Criminal Legislation of the USSR. The right to be considered innocent until proven guilty means, in the first place, that only courts can establish a person's guilt in committing a criminal offense, regardless of whether the subsequent punishment will be applied. According to article 43 of the Fundamentals of Criminal Legislation in the USSR, the court in specific cases can determine that a person has committed an offense, but at the same time, can release such person from criminal responsibility or from punishment.

The right to be considered innocent, being the core of the principle of the presumption of innocence, not only protects the rights of a person to a lawful, impartial, and unprejudiced court, but also protects his *moral* right to be considered innocent. It also protects his property rights in those cases where compensation for damages is dependent on proving that it resulted from the commission of a crime. The text of Article 160 of the Constitution of the USSR repeats, with minor changes, part of article 7 of the Fundamentals of Criminal Procedure of the USSR and represents a poorly hidden negation of the principle of the presumption of innocence. V. Paniugin, a judge of the USSR Supreme Court, interprets this particular statute in the following way: "the law connects the right of the court to establish guilt with the exclusive power to impose the sentence. The investigating organs (procurator) have the right, in a procedurally proper form, to establish the fact of the commission of a crime by a certain person." [57] Application of this concept has the following consequences for Soviet labor law, which utilizes a principle of full or limited liability of workers for damage caused to their employer. One of the conditions for determining full material liability is the presence of any action or lack of action on the part of the worker which is prohibited by criminal law. [58] In such cases, the investigator for the procurator or the police, in order to increase the amount of damages or payments, reports that a particular worker has committed a crime. Subsequently, charges are dropped. However, the statement is introduced as evidence in a civil action relating to the amount of damages, and the civil court does not have the power to determine whether a criminal offense was committed. [59] In this manner, a person is considered to be guilty of a crime without a judicial decision. Another example of disregard for the principle of the presumption of innocence are the judgments passed on individuals by high Party organs and the press, long before judicial decisions. A recent example of such nature is the commission of "grave offenses" by the activist of the Human Rights movement in the USSR–Anatolii Shcharanskii, announced by *TASS* and several Soviet newspapers. [60]

Finally, when Soviet jurists explain the principle of innocent until proven guilty, they do not refer to Article 160 of the constitution or to the analogous text of article 7 of the Fundamentals of Soviet Criminal Procedure. They repeat the words of the Covenant that "the presumption of innocence [in law] is a principle according to which the accused is considered innocent until his guilt is established by a decision of the court."[61]

In 1976 when the International Covenant on Civil and Political Rights became legally binding to the Soviet Union, the USSR undertook an obligation according to Article 2 of the Covenant: to bring into conformity with the Covenant, its laws, including its constitution "to safeguard the rights recognized in the Covenant." If the draft fell far short of this obligation, the final constitutional text has even further increased this gap.

NOTES

1. *Pravda*, Oct. 5, 1977. An English translation of the new USSR Constitution by F. J. M. Feldbrugge and William B. Simons can be found in *Review of Socialist Law*, 4 (1978), No. 1, 57-84.

2. Information from the Chief of the Administration of Budget Statistics of the Central Statistical Administration of the USSR, D. Dumnov, in *Pravda*, Aug. 25, 1977.

3. *Ezhegodnik bol'shoi sovetskoi entsiklopedii 1976 g.* (Annual of the Great Soviet Encyclopedia 1976), (Moscow, 1977), pp. 14, 20, 22.

4. *Izvestiia*, Jul. 8, 1977.

5. The author worked for several years as legal advisor to the Leningrad television station and is well acquainted with such staff activity.

6. *Pravda*, Oct. 5, 1977.

7. *Pravda*, Oct. 5, 1977. Here, and in the following quotations, the emphasis is added by the author.

8. *Ibid.*

9. From the report of L. I. Brezhnev on May 24, 1977, as reported in *Pravda*, Jun. 5, 1977.

10. *Ibid.*

11. *Pravda*, Oct. 5, 1977.

12. See, for instance, V. I. Lenin, *Materializm i empiriokrititsizm* (Materialism and Empiriocriticism), (Moscow, 1951), p. 310.

13. *Programmy i ustavy KPSS* (Programs and Statutes of the CPSU), (Moscow, 1969), p. 40.

14. *Pravda*, Oct. 5, 1977.

15. V. I. Lenin, *Polnoe sobranie sochinenii* (Complete Collected Works), Vol. 39, 5th ed., p. 134.

16. I. V. Stalin, *Voprosy Leninizma* (Problems of Leninism), p. 133.

17. See, for instance, A. Zakaliuk, *Rol' trudovogo kollektiva v preduprezhdenii pravonarushenii* (The role of the Labor Collective in Preventing Violations of the Law), (Kiev, 1973).

18. Closing remarks of L. I. Brezhnev reported in *Pravda*, Oct. 8, 1977.

19. *LG*, Aug. 14, 1977. Interview with member of the All-Union Academy of Agricultural Sciences, V. A. Tikhonov.

20. G. Shmelev, "O lichnom podsobnom khoziaistve" (On Private Subsidiary Farming), *Pravda*, Sept. 10, 1977.

21. See decrees of the USSR Council of Ministers, No. 1131 of December 15, 1961, and No. 651 of August 16, 1966, and also see articles 501 and 522 of the RSFSR Civil Code.

22. *Pravda*, Aug. 22 and 25, 1977.

23. Within the personal experience of the author.

24. *Pravda*, Aug. 25, 1977.

25. *Bol'shaia sovetskaia entsiklopediia* (The Great Soviet Encyclopedia), Vol. 21, 3rd ed. (Moscow, 1975), p. 72.

26. Letter from V. Levchenko in *Pravda*, Sept. 3, 1977.

27. *Pravda*, Oct. 8, 1977.

28. *Ibid.*

29. *Programmy i ustavy KPSS, op. cit.*, pp. 172-175.

30. *Bol'shaia sovetskaia entsiklopediia, op. cit.*, pp. 18-20.

31. *Programmy i ustavy KPSS, op. cit.*, p. 172.

32. *Ibid.*, pp. 169, 170.

33. Editorial review of readers' letters in *Izvestiia*, Jul. 28, 1977.

34. V. Patiulin, "Nashi prava, nashi obiazannosti" (Our Rights, Our Duties), *LG*, Nov. 14, 1977.

35. M. Strogovich, "Prava grazhdan" (The Rights of Citizens), *LG*, Jul. 20, 1977.

36. V. Loriia, "Nuzhny administrativnye sudy" (Are the Administrative Courts Necessary), *Sots. Zak.*, 1977, No. 9, 54, 55.

37. V. Maksimovskii, "Real'nost' prav" (The Reality of Rights), *Izvestiia*, Jul. 28, 1977.

38. S. Bratus', "Pravo na sudebnuiu zashchitu" (The Right to Judicial Defense), *LG*, Aug. 3, 1977.

39. Article 209 of the RSFSR Criminal Code, as amended in 1975 (*Ved. V.S. RSFSR*, 1975, No. 33, item 698), now reads as follows:

"Systematically engaging in vagrancy or begging and also leading a parasitic way of life over a protracted period of time shall be punished by deprivation of freedom for a term of up to one year or by correctional labor for the same term.

The same actions, committed by a person previously convicted under the first paragraph of this article, shall be punished by deprivation of freedom for a term of up to two years."

40. *Sots. Zak.*, 1977, No. 9, 50.

41. *Slovar' sinonimov russkogo iazyka* (A Dictionary of Synonyms of the Russian Language), Vol. II (Leningrad, 1971), p. 521.

42. *Sudebnaia psikhiatriia* (Judicial Psychiatry), (Moscow, 1965), p. 51.

43. *Kommentarii k nekotorym stat'iam polozheniia o vyborakh v mestnye Sovety deputatov trudiashchikhsia* (Commentary to Certain Articles of the Statute on Elections to Local Soviets of Working People's Deputies), (Moscow, 1977), p. 8.

44. *Ibid.*, p. 8.

45. This information is based on the experience of the author who served for many years as legal advisor to the Chief Psychiatrist of the City of Leningrad and to several mental hospitals in the city. Those who are interested in additional sources may find them in issues of *Khronika tekushchikh sobytii* (A Chronicle of Current Events) or *Khronika zashchity prav v SSSR* (A Chronicle of Human Rights in the USSR), both published by Khronika Press, New York.

46. *Kommentarii, op. cit.*, p. 48.

47. *The Great Soviet Encyclopedia, op. cit.*, Vol. 17, p. 200.

48. *Ibid.*

49. *SGiP*, 1977, No. 9, p. 6.

50. Regarding special courts, see Yurii Luryi, "The Right to Counsel in Ordinary Criminal Cases in the USSR," in Donald D. Barry, George Ginsburgs, and Peter B. Maggs (eds.), *Soviet Law After Stalin, Part I: The Citizen and the State in Contemporary Soviet Law* (Leyden, 1977), pp. 106, 107.

51. V. Vlasov, "Nezavisimost' sudei" (The Independence of Judges), *Pravda*, Aug. 19, 1977.

52. G. Anashkin, "Pravovaia osnova Sovetskogo zakonodatel'stva" (The Legal Basis of Soviet Legislation), *Sots. Zak.*, 1977, No. 8, 52.

53. See, for example, V. Savitskii, "Demokratizm nashego pravosudiia" (The Democracy of Our Judicial Process), *Izvestiia*, Jun. 17, 1977.

54. A. Boikov, "Razvitie demokraticheskikh printsipov sotsialisticheskogo pravosudiia" (The Development of the Democratic Principles of the Socialist Judicial Process), *Sots. Zak.*, 1977, No. 8, 11, 12.

55. V. Savitskii, *op. cit.*

56. S. Kallistratova, "Nekotorye zamechanie o proekte novoi Konstitutsii SSSR" (Some Remarks About the Draft of the New Soviet Constitution), *Khronika zashchity prav v SSSR*, 1977, No. 27, 70.

57. E. S. Belinskii, V. E. Paniugin, *Material'naia otvetstvennost' rabochikh i sluzhashchikh* (Financial Liability of Workers and Employees), (Moscow, 1977), p. 46.

58. Art. 10(3) of the Statute on Financial Liability of Workers and Employees for Damage Caused to an Enterprise, Institution, or Organization, *Ved. V.S. SSSR*, 1976, No. 29, item 427. For a comparison of this statute with earlier legislation regulating this subject, see *Review of Socialist Law*, 3(1977), No. 3, 481-489.

59. See the Decree of the Plenary Session of the USSR Supreme Court, May 28, 1954, sec. 7, and of June 5, 1974, secs. 6 and 7.

60. See the thorough coverage of the Shcharanskii case in the *CDSP* during 1977 and 1978, especially *CDSP*, 29(1977), No. 9, 1-2.

61. See, for example, *Entsiklopedicheskii slovar' pravovykh znanii* (Encyclopedia of Legal Knowledge), (Moscow, 1965), p. 355, and M. S. Strogovich, *Kurs sovetskogo ugolovnogo protsessa*, tom I, *Osnovnye polozheniia nauki sovetskogo ugolovnogo protsessa* (Treatise on Soviet Criminal Procedure, Vol. I, Basic Precepts of the Science of Soviet Criminal Procedure), (Moscow, 1968), p. 147.

HUMAN RIGHTS IN THE NEW SOVIET CONSTITUTION*

Valery Chalidze

1. General Observations

Differences of formulations and a calculated tendency to use undefined terms are generally characteristic of Soviet legal drafting, particularly when the norms of law involve an ideologically significant theme. However, I probably cannot point out a Soviet law in which these unpraiseworthy techniques were used as assertively as in the new Soviet Constitution, more particularly—in the text of the constitution up to the start of the third chapter. The impression is even created that beginning with the third chapter, the draft of the constitution was prepared by jurists acquainted with legislative drafting, while the preamble and the first two chapters were prepared by party bureaucrats better adapted to writing a party programmatic document or anniversary speeches. In places, the impression is created that the absence of exclamation points in the text of the constitution is the result of a typographical error.[1] The activists of the Soviet movement in the defense of rights who took part in the discussion of the draft constitution already noted as a sorry feature the declarative and propagandistic character of the draft constitution. Those changes which were introduced during the approval of the draft did not change the nature of the text under consideration in this regard.

It must be said that—on the level of legislative drafting—the quality of the new constitution is much worse than the old, the more so if one considers that during the forty years which have passed since 1936, Soviet legislative drafting on the whole developed and, on an average, the current laws are in a technical sense superior to the laws of the 1930's. This experience gained among Soviet jurists in drafting laws was not, regrettably, used by the Consti-

* The article presented here does not claim to be any sort of full legal commentary on the USSR Constitution. These are merely a few, at times very general, observations. During work on this article, I benefited from studying many *samizdat* texts dedicated to criticism of the draft constitution (see issues 25 and 27 of *Khronika zashchity prav v SSSR* (A Chronicle of Human Rights in the USSR)). Discussions with A. Vol'pin and other colleagues were most useful.

tutional Commission in confirming the ideologically most important chapters of the constitution.

Inasmuch as in this article, I basically consider the question of human rights in the new constitution, in criticizing the language of the constitution I shall limit myself only to examples significant for my theme.

The meaning of the term "drawing together," as applied to "all nations and nationalities of the USSR" in Article 36, dedicated to the repetition of the principle of equality of rights of different races and nationalities, is entirely unclear. The vagueness of the term causes particular worry in connection with the fact that in the last decade, judging by the protests emanating from the national republics, the centralized attempt at Russification of national cultures has been intensified. Usually for interpretation, it is important in what sense the legislator uses the unclear term in another place in the text. In the given instance this method of interpretation does not help, since in Article 12 the term "drawing together" is used in just as unclear a sense in connection with the discussion of the drawing together of collective-farm and cooperative property with state property.

The sense in which the verb "to respect" is used is incomprehensible. It is encountered in Article 29, in which the expression "human rights" is mentioned for the only time in this constitution. It is stated that the relations of the USSR with other states are built, specifically, on the basis of respect for human rights and fundamental freedoms. The proposition that "respect for human rights" in the given instance signifies observance of guarantees concerning human rights would be tempting; however, a comparison of Articles 37 and 59 compels one to conclude otherwise. In Article 59 it is stated that a citizen of the USSR is obliged to observe the Constitution of the USSR and Soviet laws. However, in Article 37 it is stated that foreign and stateless persons present on the territory of the USSR are obliged to "respect the Constitution of the USSR" and "to observe Soviet laws." There is reason to assume that in the given case the requirement "to respect" is weaker than the requirement "to observe," for it is doubtful that the legislator addressed himself to foreigners with a stronger imperative governing their relation to the Constitution of the USSR than to Soviet citizens. In such a case, respect for human rights in Article 29 signifies something weaker than the obligation to observe the guarantees of human rights (it is intrinsically interesting why, speaking for the only time in this text in clear form about human rights in general, the legislator speaks about this just in connection with the relations of the USSR with other states).

The relationship between the terms "duty" and "obligation" is entirely unclear. In a purely colloquial sense, duty rather signifies a moral imperative, and obligation a legal one. An attempt to interpret the terms "duty" and "obligation" in the constitution from this point of view will lead to difficulties. For instance, a citizen of the USSR is "obliged" to observe the Constitution of the USSR. At the same time, it is "a duty of a citizen of the USSR to struggle with thefts and dissipation of state and social property." It would seem that the word "obliged" is a more powerful imperative, but it is difficult to assume that "duty" signifies a weaker imperative since it is stated (Article 31): "The duty of the Armed Forces of the USSR before the people is to reliably defend the socialist Fatherland . . . . " We encounter a still more powerful imperative, namely, the combination of duty and obligation in Article 68: "Care for the preservation of historical monuments and other cultural values is the duty and obligation of citizens of the USSR."

I will note here yet another ideologically useful technique of legislative drafting which, on first glance, may give an impression of inaccuracy. (In studying, however, one should operate on the premise that carelessness in the text is minimal; in general, my acquaintance with Soviet laws convinces me that those places—which seem to project our appearance of inaccuracy in legislative drafting—in fact contain certain conveniences for interpretation in accordance with the political goals of the moment.) I have in mind now the fact that in certain places rather important things are spoken of not in the form of a norm but as if off-hand, for instance in a participial expression. For instance, in Article 6, in the first paragraph there is reference to the Communist Party of the Soviet Union; in the second paragraph an abbreviated name is mentioned, obviously of the same party, "Communist Party," and this name is preceeded by the participial expression "armed with Marxism-Leninism." Is not entirely clear what purposes the legislator pursued mentioning so casually the ideological basis of the activity of the Communist Party—might this not be an attempt to protect the Communist Party from "revisionism" tendencies?

It is also not entirely clear what was the hidden purpose of calling the status of a citizen of the USSR "a title" and casually calling this title high: "A citizen of the USSR is obliged to observe the Constitution of the USSR and Soviet laws, to respect the standards of Socialist conduct, to bear honorably the lofty title of citizen of the USSR." It is difficult for me to say in the given case what advantage for vague interpretation the authorities will derive from such a formulation. As far as citizens of the USSR are concerned who do not wish to bear their high title of citizens of the USSR with honor or to consider this status a title or a high title—this article of course gives them reasons for discussion.

Amusing examples from the area of legislative drafting could be multiplied in discussing the constitution, but I will not linger on this. I will note, taking advantage of the occasion, that as in the former, in this constitution the religious term "sacred duty" has remained with respect to the defense of socialist society, but it is pleasant to note that, in distinction from the old constitution, the term "enemy of the people" is not now used.

2. Communist Leadership

Although this question is more related to the theme of political structure, nevertheless since it is also important for discussion of the theme of human rights in the new constitution, I will mention it keeping in mind that it has already engendered criticism by many people, in particular the activists of the Soviet movement in defense of human rights. This criticism, though, involved Article 6 of the draft constitution which was supplemented in the final version with a third very important paragraph. Now this article reads as follows:

> "The leading and guiding force of Soviet society and the nucleus of its political system, of all state and public organizations, is the Communist Party of the Soviet Union. The CPSU exists for the people and serves the people.
>
> The Communist Party, armed with Marxism-Leninism, determines the general perspectives of the development of society, in the course of the domestic and foreign policy of the USSR, directs the great constructive work of the Soviet people, and imparts a planned systematic and theoretically substantiated character to their struggle for the victory of Communism.
>
> All party organizations shall function within the framework of the Constitution of the USSR."[2]

In *samizdat*, the critics even stated that there is open contradiction between this article (in the draft, *i.e.* without the third paragraph) and Article 1:

> "The Union of Soviet Socialist Republics is a socialist state of the whole people expressing the will and interests of the workers, peasants, and intelligentsia, and of the working people of all the nations and nationalities of the country."

I do not see such a contradiction, particularly now that Article 6 has been supplemented by the third paragraph. From the historical point of view, it may be said that the introduction of Article 6 in the constitution is an attempt (but only an attempt) to legally confirm the usurpation of power by the Bolsheviks, which took place in 1918. During the course of almost 60 years from the time of the dispersal of the Constituent Assembly, it could be observed that the Communist Party is in fact the leading and directing force of the Soviet state, and indeed is the nucleus of its political system, though I would have preferred not to use indefinite terms as "directive force" and "nucleus of the system." In the course of all these decades, the actual position of the Communist Party in the system of authority was always much more powerful than was noted in the laws. The same is also true now. It is intrinsically interesting why almost 60 years were needed even for such an unclear attempt to legalize this usurpation. Of course, the answer suggests itself that for consideration of international prestige it is impossible even now to inscribe in the constitution something everyone knows, namely, that the whole plenitude of authority in the Soviet Union belongs to the Communist Party of the Soviet Union; among western admirers such a norm in the constitution would completely destroy the illusion of a state of the whole people. However, I am not entirely convinced that this is the sole reason and that this should end the analysis of the question of why almost 60 years were required for such a cautious attempt to legalize the usurpation of power by the Bolsheviks, but I will not develop this theme here.

Article 6, however, besides the diffuse formulations on the primacy of the Communist Party in the Soviet political system, contains in its final form a very important norm: "all party organizations shall function within the framework of the Constitution of the USSR." On the one hand, this norm is important because it follows that even the Communist Party shall act within the framework of the Constitution of the USSR and, so far, possible attempts by the Communist Party to place itself formally above the law are not recognized as legal in the constitution. On the other hand, this norm is extraordinarily important in that it clearly recognizes the possibility of the existence of other party organizations separate from the Communist Party of the USSR. One may answer me in this regard that the legislator had in mind Communist Party organizations, since he placed this norm expressly in the article dedicated to the CPSU; this, however, is no argument–reference is to *all* party organizations. The fact that, earlier in this article, the discussion concerned specifically the Communist Party does not limit the generality of the third paragraph of the sixth article–the more so that, in the constitution, there are examples of articles dealing, even in a single and not in separate paragraphs, with the most varied matters; for instance, in Article 24 in the second paragraph "The state encourages cooperatives and other public organizations to provide all types of services for the population. It encourages the development of mass physical culture and sports."

I noted this as an interesting overt mention of *other* party organizations; the actual freedom to found other parties is contained in Article 51 on the rights of citizens to unite in public organizations.

3. Reservations to Guarantees of Rights

I already have said that the term "human rights" is used only once and then in connection with foreign policy principles. However, a whole chapter is dedicated "to the basic rights, freedoms, and obligations of citizens of the USSR." This is a verbose list of certain basic rights, social and economic rights, and duties of citizens. Soviet jurists have often noted with satisfaction that in the Soviet Constitution (in the old constitution, but this also applies to the new one) there are not only guarantees of rights, but also indications of what assures these rights. It is this that makes the enumeration of a few rights so verbose. However, the guarantees of rights in the constitution are usually accompanied not only by an indication of what assures the given rights but also by certain *reservations* and *explanations*. Among *explanations* I include expressions of the type "in accordance with the interest of the people and for the purposes of strengthening and developing the socialist structure, citizens of the USSR. . . " (are guaranteed, in the given instance, the freedoms of speech, press, assembly. . . etc.) Such explanations preceding the guarantees of rights have already been discussed by the activists of the movement in the defense of human rights. It is clear from the grammar that the sense of such an expression is only in the explanation, that the very fact of guarantee of these rights corresponds to the interests of the people and to the purposes of strengthening and developing the socialist order. The usual attempts by Soviet jurists to consider such constitutional explanations as reservation and to point out that the given freedom is guaranteed only in the event it is used in accordance with the interests of the people and for the purposes of strengthening and developing the socialist order are grammatically groundless.

However, beside such explanatory expressions, direct reservations are also encountered in the constitution. In particular, Article 59 contains a general reservation: "Realization of rights and freedoms is inseparable from the performance by a citizen of his obligations." This reservation has disturbed critics, but speaking in general it means absolutely nothing new for practice and has perhaps an indoctrinational significance, but not a legal one. I, of course, cannot deny that some illiterate bureaucrat will, in practice, use this reservation so as to arbitrarily limit the rights of someone on the basis that he did not fulfill some obligation. However, the laws containing rules on the limitation of rights in punishment for being remiss in fulfilling obligations are sufficiently well known, and the given article cannot be interpreted as license for the arbitrary deprivation of any rights for the non-fulfillment of any obligation whatsoever. I think this is nothing more than a not wholly successful attempt to philosophically justify the existence, in a legal system, of laws granting punishments for slighting obligations.

Another reservation which also disturbed the critics of the draft is contained in Article 39: "The use by citizens of rights and duties must not cause harm to the interests of society and the state, nor to the rights of other citizens." It may seem that this reservation provides a constitutional basis for the article of the criminal law on anti-Soviet agitation, under which many are accused for participation in the free exchange of information. However, in this criminal code article, it is by no means presumed that the punishable agitation or propaganda must cause *injury* to the interests of the state: it is sufficient if the actor has as his *purpose* the causing of injury (*i.e.*, the undermining or weakening of Soviet power). In courts, the accusation usually avoids proper proof of the fact that the actor had such a purpose, but, with respect to the fact that *actual injury was done* to the interests of the state, no serious discussion arises at all, for even the law does not require this. In our time, when in many countries there has for decades been endorsed the use of the freedom of speech not limited by worry about the interests of the state, the accusation that by free speech one will cause actual harm to the interests of the state may be countered by reference to the fact that, even if there were a purpose of causing such a harm, the actor made the attempt with inappropriate means. I would say, on the contrary, that the reservation of Article 39 of the constitution places in doubt the legality of the effect of the article of anti-Soviet agitation, *i.e.*, pursuant to the general principle that the limitations of rights in the laws should not be harsher than indicated in the constitution if there is such rich indication in the constitution. And if the constitution speaks of the impermissibility of *causing injury* to anything by means of the use of rights, then the law must not punish merely because the actor had the purpose of causing such injury. This reservation may be broadly used propagandistically, but I also see in it nothing insurmountable for the plenitude of the use of rights. Of course, this reservation may be used by the agencies of state authorities with greater success than the previous one in attempts to limit the rights of citizens. (In this regard, the Soviet authorities do not like to enter into discussions with citizens about just what the interests of society and the state are, preferring to consider themselves authorized experts on what these interests are.) However, in practice it will hardly introduce anything new.[3]

The reservation on obligation in Article 62 also entailed the disapproving criticism of participants of the movement in the defense of human rights: "A citizen of the USSR is obliged to safeguard the interests of the Soviet state, to aid the strengthening of its power and prestige." Here with still greater definiteness, I can say that this rule concerning an obligation, speaking generally, by itself in no way limits any rights. The proclamation of the obligation in the constitution merely serves an educational significance, if the law does not prescribe punishment for neglecting this obligation. Up to now, in any event, Soviet criminal laws do not provide punishment for infractions such as the failure to aid the strengthening of the prestige of the Soviet state. I think that the introduction of such amendments to the criminal legislation cannot be expected in the near future. It is a different matter that, in suitable cases, accusers will cite this article of the constitution in accusatory speeches in political trials, but this does not mean that the presence of such an article in the constitution will cause any significant changes in legal practice. Something in this article reminds me of the repealed article of the old Criminal Code on the discrediting of authority. In fact, worry about the authority of the state is, perhaps, a matter for the state itself and this article must apply, properly speaking, to state employees who by their acts may cause harm to the authority of the state. By himself, a citizen of the USSR who is not a state employee does not after all represent the state legally, and any of his actions can cause injury only to his own authority but not to the authority of the state. What the rulers in the given case may have in mind as causing injury to the authority of the state is the publication of information, for instance, on the violation of human rights in the Soviet Union. I consider that, from the point of view of mankind in general, such publication is rather an expression of the concern on the part of the citizen for the authority of the state, for making public information on the activity of those officials who cause harm to the authority of the state. However natural such a train of thought maybe, it is hardly likely that Soviet state bureaucrats will agree with it.

In general, apparently, one should not think that the declaration of obligations in the constitution must necessarily entail the confirmation of this obligation in the criminal legislation. In the old 1936 Constitution in Article 130, in the list of obligations there is the following not entirely clear formulation: "Every citizen of the USSR is obliged . . . to act respectfully toward social duty." In the forty years during which this constitution was in effect, the Criminal Code was not supplemented by an article punishing for the nonfulfillment of this obligation. But, it would seem, this formulation was used for indoctrinational purposes.

I can note from the text of the constitution, and also from other documents, that the Soviet legislator is somehow especially afraid of the abuse of rights, although in principle this problem exists also in other states, but there they attempt to solve it by the compilation of a sufficiently complete and exact list of prohibitions limiting the use of rights in those cases where the use of rights leads to an impermissible collision with the interests of society or of other persons. For various reasons, the Soviet legislator is apparently unable to provide a sufficiently precise list of such limitations, and reservations such as Article 39, para. 2, are introduced into legislation not out of indoctrinational considerations but also out of considerations of convenience in limitating rights in those instances when, for reasons of prestige, the legislator wishes to avoid the overt limitation of a right in the given area. However, the introduction of such reservations will not introduce anything new into Soviet practice. Of course, procurators will cite them with pathos in accusatory speeches. But, they previously cited propaganda documents with the same success.

4. Equality

Article 34 reads:

> "Citizens of the USSR are equal before the law, without distinction of origin, social or property status, race or nationality, sex, education, language, attitude to religion, type and nature of profession, place of residence, and of other circumstances.
>
> The equal rights of citizens of the USSR are guaranteed in all spheres of economic, political, social, and cultural life."

The guarantee of nondiscrimination, independent of "other circumstances," looks rather inaccurate. This may seem to be rather heavy-handed legal humor,[4] but behind such a strange guarantee there obviously are fully understandable considerations of the authors of the constitution. The fact is, in accordance with agreements ratified by the Soviet Union, the absence of discrimination must be guaranteed not only in accordance with indicia listed in the constitution but also, for example, in accordance with the index of political beliefs. It is easy to understand that the Soviet legislator had his reasons not to mention openly in the constitution the equality of rights independently of political beliefs. However, as is well known, the constitution is not only an internal normative document but also the facade of the state. It is easy to imagine a situation where a Soviet citizen, who is protesting against discrimination on grounds of political belief, is shown this article and told "see, political beliefs are not mentioned here." And, conversely, it is easy to imagine a situation where, at an international conference, the Soviet Union is subjected to criticism for the absence of a guarantee of equality independently of political beliefs—in this case, the Soviet representative can cite the expression "other circumstances" and assure his gullible partners that political beliefs indeed are included in these other circumstances. The equality of citizens, independently of race and nationality, is mentioned twice in the constitution but this is not the only double guarantee. Article 36 is especially dedicated to racial and national equality, and what is very important in this article is the indication of the possibility of using the native language and the languages of the other peoples of the USSR. To what degree this guarantee will be reflected in opportunities for the development of national cultures is difficult to say, considering the intensification of the process of Russification in the republics. It is clear, moreover, that this article is applicable directly for the protection of the rights of prisoners to conduct correspondence and conversations at meetings in their native language—a natural blessing the enjoyment of which is often impeded by the administration of camps.

5. Basic Rights

Freedom of Speech, of the Press, of Assembly, of Meetings, and of Street Processions and Demonstrations

Article 50 of the new Soviet Constitution states:

> "In accordance with the interests of the people and in order to strengthen and develop the socialist system, citizens of the USSR are guaranteed freedom of speech, of the press, and of assembly, of meetings, and of street processions and demonstrations.
>
> The exercise of these political freedoms shall be assured by putting public buildings, streets and squares at the disposal of the working people and their organizations, by broad dissemination of information, and by the opportunity to use the press, television, and radio."

In comparison with Article 125 of the old constitution:

> "In conformity with the interests of the working people and for the purpose of strengthening the socialist system, citizens of the USSR shall be guaranteed by law:
>
> a) freedom of speech;
> b) freedom of the press;
> c) freedom of assembly and meetings;
> d) freedom of street processions and demonstrations.
>
> These civil rights shall be offered by placing, at the disposal of the working people and their organizations, printing presses, stocks of paper, public buildings, streets, communications facilities, and other material requisites necessary for the exercise of these rights."

I would say that the new constitution is more cautious in listing how these rights are assured. For example, it no longer speaks of providing the working people and their organizations with printing presses and stocks of paper, and speaks simply of ensuring the possibility of use of the press. However, I do not know if this has any great practical significance. What is more important: in distinction from the old constitution, now the listed rights are called *political.* This is done without emphasis, off-handly, but it is extremely essential, since in international documents on human rights, such rights are preferably considered *civil* rights (in the Convention on the Elimination of All Forms of Racial Discrimination, ratified by the Soviet Union, among civil rights there are mentioned in particular the right to freedom of beliefs and their free expression, and the right to the freedom of peaceable assemblies and associations). This is more important than may appear at first glance since if a right is recognized as civil in Soviet legislation, then a citizen may claim its judicial defense in a civil judicial proceeding, in as much as there is no special mandate for the administrative defense of such a right. In legal literature, there has long been apparant a tendency toward considering freedom of speech and the other rights analyzed here as political. Now this tendency has triumphed in the text of the constitution. Paradoxical though it may be, the presence of guarantee of a right in the constitution does not at all assure the judicial protection of these rights.

However, consideration of this theme is distracting me from the theme begun on the material guarantees of rights; certain other rights guaranteed in the constitution are connected with freedom of speech. Article 49 guarantees the *right of citizens* "to submit proposals to state bodies and public organizations for improving their activities, and to criticize shortcomings in their work." This norm is by no means a guarantee of a right to criticism of the activity of state institutions, although it is stated in the same article that persecution for criticism is forbidden. This article if formulated most carefully and provides merely a right to submit proposals for *improvement* of the activity of state institutions, and also the right to criticize *shortcomings* in their work. Criticism directed at what the authorities do not consider shortcomings may, in practice, be recognized as other than that to which a right is guaranteed in Article 49. Exactly in the same way, a proposal not for the improvement of the activity of institutions, but, for example, for the cessation of a certain type of activity of some institution, also may turn out to be unprotected by this article. It is not hard to guess that such fine points of formulation may prove important in practice. I have a strong impression that the current edict of the Presidium of the Supreme Soviet of April 12, 1968, "On the Procedure for the Consideration of Proposals, Statements, and Complaints of Citizens" guarantees a broader scope of rights to citizens in connection with application to state agencies than Article 49 of the constitution. In any event, discussion there concerns the right of citizens to apply with any proposals, and not only with proposals for the improvement of the activity of state and public organizations.

> "Citizens of the USSR, in accordance with the objectives of building communism, are guaranteed freedom of scientific, technical, and artistic creative work. . ." This article is important in itself although, in the listing of that which is guaranteed by this freedom, the constitution limits itself to an indication of such state measures as are entirely compatible with state control over creative work."

The Right to Enjoy Cultural Achievements

This right is guaranteed by Article 46, and in listing that which is guaranteed by this right, particular indication is made of "general access to the cultural treasures of the fatherland and of the world that are preserved in state and other public collections." This is an extraordinarily important promise, practically outlawing the special restricted collections in libraries and the closed reserves in museums, with, however, the one reservation–that, in practice, discussion can arise as to what state collections consider treasures of culture and what they do not. In any case, this article facilitates discussion with the authorities for those who, being in the Soviet Union, wish to defend their right to freedom of receipt of information.

The Right of Association

In the 1977 USSR Constitution, Article 51 reads as follows:

> "In accordance with the objectives of building communism, citizens of the USSR have the right to associate in public organizations that promote political activity and initiative, and the satisfaction of their manifold interests. Public organizations are guaranteed conditions for the successful performance of the functions defined in their charters."

If one compares this article with Article 126 of the old constitution, one can see that the norm concerning the right of association has been subjected to a more substantive reworking in comparison with the changes in the article concerning freedom of speech and others (compare Article 125 of the old and Article 50 of the new constitution), and not only because mention of the Communist Party is transferred from the article on the right to association to the first chapter (Article 6). In comparison with the article on freedom of speech, this article contains somewhat more detailed explanation than the corresponding article on the right to association in the old constitution. I think that the authors of the constitution were given the task of formulating the article on the right to association more carefully in connection with the fact that, in the last seven years, public associations not controlled by the state have been formed in the Soviet Union. At one time, when the first such association was formed that was recognized by international organizations–the Committee on Human Rights, I had a discussion with the procuracy with respect to the legality of the foundation of the Committee on Human Rights and I specifically cited the constitution. Nothing in the formulation at that time prevented me from justifying the legality of the formation of the Committee on Human Rights in the Soviet Union. Since then, several additional independent public associations have been formed that are widely known in the west including the "Amnesty International" group, and the Moscow, Ukrainian, Lithuanian, Georgian, and Armenian groups of support for the implementation of the Helsinki accords in the USSR. This extraordinarily important activity of the Soviet participants in the movement for the defense of human rights apparently causes the authorities uneasiness, and it could have been expected that the article on the right to association in the new constitution would be formulated more cautiously. I cannot see so far that there would be more difficulty using the article of the current constitution on the right to association to justify the legality of the creation of independent public organizations. What is clear is that there is no list of types of public organizations that featured in the former Article 126, which, however, obviously does not limit the right to create organizations of any type.

Trade unions are mentioned in the new constitution only as something already existing, whereas in the old constitution (Article 126) they were mentioned among those organizations in which citizens had the right to join. Perhaps this is important if one supposes (and such a supposition is not without foundation), that the authorities do not want to focus particular attention of the citizens on the possibility of creating free trade unions not controlled by the state. Such a possibility exists. The right to the creation of free trade unions is guaranteed by the Convention on the Right of Association ratified by the Soviet Union, and the right to association in trade unions is expressly guaranteed in Article 2 of the Fundamentals of Labor Legislation. So far, no instances are known of the organization of a free trade union not controlled by the authorities; however, it is known that persons with the same type of occupation at times are placed in conditions in which they can not work in state institutions (for instance, unofficial artists and also scholars who have been deprived of work and are attempting unsuccessfully to obtain permission to emigrate). In such conditions, it is understandable that the authors of the constitution had no desire to emphasize the right of citizens to create free trade unions independent of state control. However, the omission of this right in the constitution does not limit it, and citizens of the USSR in accordance with Soviet law may create trade unions even when a trade union of employees of a given specialty already exists.

Religious Freedom–Article 52

> "Citizens of the USSR are guaranteed freedom of conscience, that is, the right to profess any religion or to profess none, and to conduct religious worship or atheistic propaganda. Incitement of hostility or hatred on religious grounds is prohibited.
>
> In the USSR the church is separated from the state, and the school from the church."

This article of course is far from guaranteeing religious freedom to citizens, the more so because freedom of atheistic propaganda is explicitly guaranteed but there is no freedom of religious propaganda. With respect to the almost identical formulation of this article in the draft constitution, the members of the Christian Committee for the Defense of the Rights of Believers in the USSR–O. G. Iakunin, V. Khaibulin, and V. Kapitanchuk–addressed a statement to the Constitutional Commission in which the draft was subjected to criticism from the point of view of the guarantee of religious freedom. Considering that the ruling role of the atheist Communist Party was declared in the new constitution in such explicit form, the authors of this statement noted that the guarantee of religious freedom must be properly featured in the constitution and also proposed the following other possibilities:

> "1) The ruling party shall exclude from its Charter the provision obliging each of its members 'to conduct a decisive struggle against religious survivals.' 2) It shall officially recognize the compatibility of communism and religion. 3) The thesis of the possibility in principle of religion under communism shall be introduced into the text of the new Constitution of the USSR."

The authors of this statement considered the situation so serious for believers that they declared: "If this draft is adopted, then believing citizens will in all seriousness face the torturesome question: Can they, without harm to their religious conscience, remain citizens of a state which has legislatively declared atheism as its goal?"

Inviolability of Private Life–Articles 55 and 56

> "Citizens of the USSR are guaranteed inviolability of the home. No one has the right, without lawful grounds, to enter a home against the will of the persons residing in it."
>
> "The personal life of citizens, secrecy of correspondence, telephone conversations, and telegraphic communications are protected by law."

These articles do not require commentary, but perhaps what is needed is to express regret concerning the absence of legislation exhaustively listing instances when it is possible to infringe the inviolability of private life and the absence of regulations defining the procedure for such infringements in all cases.[5] But from the very beginning, I have not set as my goal the evaluation of the conformity of the guarantees of the constitution to practice; this is a theme for another work. Nevertheless, the fact that these articles are in the constitution is important in and of itself.

6. Conclusion

I have noted here certain changes in the constitutional system of guarantees of rights. The reader will also find, in the constitution, guarantees of procedural and socio-economic rights–I will not linger on this.[6]

In conclusion, I will say that although the constitution may be criticized for many things with respect to how and how fully human rights are formulated in it, one should however remember that in the constitution the legislator usually does not claim to give an exhaustive list of guarantees of human rights. Besides the constitution, there is other legislation: Soviet laws, the Conventions on Human Rights, and international agreements ratified by the Soviet Union. The obligations of the USSR under these agreements remain in force, and in the constitution the readiness of the USSR to conscientiously fulfill such obligations is confirmed (Article 29). Thus, the Soviet Union cannot rely upon the absence in the constitution, for instance, of the right to freely leave the country, as a basis for ignoring this right, for it is found in the Convention on Human Rights. However, the current constitution, like the old one, gives many possibilities for discussion with the authorities in case of violation of human rights.

In the USSR there are people who have already been conducting this discussion actively for more than ten years, and naturally even if the formulations of the constitution are loose and vague, they will use them for the justification of their demands for the defense of human rights.

Unfortunately, the constitution in practice may be used only for such discussion. In Soviet law there is no procedure for defending one's constitutional right in court if this right is not repeated in another law for which a judicial procedure for its defense is provided.

NOTES

1. The exclamation point in the description of the seal of the USSR relates not to a norm of the constitution but to the slogan reproduced on the seal (Article 169).

2. Besides the addition to the third paragraph, there is another important change compared to the draft: the word "all" has been removed from the first paragraph in connection with the reference to public organization; in any case, there is in the constitution no longer any open pretense that the Communist Party is the nucleus, say, of the independent Helsinki groups.

3. A similar, although theoretically perhaps worse, reservation is contained in Article 5 of the Fundamentals of Civil Legislation: "Civil rights are protected by law, with the exception of cases when they are exercised in contradiction with the purpose of these rights in a socialist society in the period of the building of communism." It is important to emphasize that here the legislator indicates merely the limits of the *protection of rights*, and these limits are narrower than the limits of *use* of rights which are discussed in Article 39 of the constitution.

4. Unfortunately, the formulation in the corresponding articles of the Convention on Human Rights is equally lame.

5. The well known activist in defense of human rights, A. Vol'pin, once noted that the secrecy of correspondence is observed in the Soviet Union because the *KGB* does not reveal the contents of the letters which it reads. After reading the draft of this article, A. Vol'pin asked me to emphasize that this was said by him ironically.

6. Without getting into a detailed discussion of the guarantees of social and economic rights, I will note with pleasure Article 40 where it is stated that the right to work includes:

> "the right to choose a profession, type of occupation and work in accordance with inclination, ability, vocational training, and education, with due account of the needs of society."

(I emphasize that reference here is to the *right* to consider social needs and not that these needs can limit the right of selection of type of occupation.)

In Article 60, there is also mention of work in the area of socially useful activity *selected* by the citizen himself.

THE SOVIET UNION, 'JUS COMMERCII,' AND INTERNATIONAL LAW: THE CASE OF THE MOST-FAVORED-NATION CLAUSE*

George Ginsburgs

Certainly, one of the most interesting developments on the Soviet scene since the death of Stalin has been the political leadership's growing awareness of and responsiveness to the pressure of consumer appetites. The problem has been met in part by adjusting domestic priorities to handle these new exigencies. But, a sustained effort has also been made to tap the resources of international trade in order to help satisfy some of the citizenry's demands, where home production proved incapable of slaking the mass thirst for goods and services, or pinch-hit for the Soviet economic apparatus in sectors where the latter simply was not equipped to cater to the population's needs. This increased reliance on foreign trade has, in turn, prompted the Russians to pay greater attention to the matrix of legal rules governing the international flow of commodities and spurred them to seek, on occasion, to alter the applicable norms so as better to advance the commercial interests of the USSR.

This is a case, then, where the Soviet régime is currently engaged in an experiment in "legal engineering" on the international plane. Conditions here, it should be pointed out at the very outset, are somewhat different than in the domestic context. In domestic law, the phenomenon of "legal engineering" involves devising a legal rule to achieve a desired socio-juridical objective and testing its application with a view to achieving maximum effectiveness in

* The present essay draws heavily on the previous work of American specialists on Soviet law concerning the function of the most-favored-nation clause in Soviet foreign trade relations. The reader is referred, in particular, to two earlier pieces: H. J. Berman, "Legal Framework of Trade between Planned and Market Economies: The Soviet-American Example," *Law and Contemporary Problems*, 24 (1959), 482-528, and M. Domke, J. N. Hazard, "State Trading and the Most-Favored-Nation Clause," *American Journal of International Law*, 52 (1958), 55-68. Furthermore, I wish to acknowledge my indebtedness to Professor Berman's incisive commentary on the present article in his role of official rapporteur at the New York session which discussed the original version of this paper.

attaining the designated goal. The emphasis in these circumstances is on the elaboration of an appropriate substantive norm and the most suitable method of its implementation. An established mechanism for rule-making already exists in each country and, hence, no serious problems arise as regards either the right institutionalized procedure for promulgating the corresponding rule, once the choice is made, or further adapting its contents in the course of subsequent enforcement.

In international law, however, the concept of "legal engineering" has a much broader meaning. On the one hand, just as in domestic law, the operation features an effort to enunciate a new rule of (international) law or amend an earlier rule with the intention of accomplishing particular ends. On the other hand, given the decentralized nature of the international legal system, the process by which the backer (or backers) of the proposed formula seeks (or seek) to gain for it the status of a recognized norm of international law is at least as important for purposes of "legal engineering" as its material component. In short, in the arena of international law, the technique of "legal engineering" embraces both the procedural and substantive aspects of norm-creation and the present essay will address itself to each of these dimensions in tracing the Soviet bid to redefine the role and function of the familiar most-favored-nation clause in conjunction with an attempt to introduce into the current corpus of international law the novel notion of "jus commercii."

1. Brief Historical Excursus

The Bolshevik regime emerged from its seminal years traumatized by the economic blockade and other means of economic warfare which it experienced at the hands of the rest of the international community. As a result, the leadership's chief concern was to escape from the quarantine as quickly as possible by vindicating its right to trade, *i.e.*, to enjoy full access to available import and export opportunities, and to a fair share of the international commercial exchange.[1] The emphasis in those days was on the very basic business of getting a chance even to engage in trade relations with foreign countries, without much thought yet to what technical terms would be used if the occasion arose. The critical question was whether Soviet Russia would be allowed to enter the international trade stream at all and when and not what particular rules it intended to follow in that event.

Not surprisingly, then, care was taken from the start to deal with this key issue, and several of Soviet Russia's earliest agreements contained clauses intended to make sure that peace was duly restored on the economic front. The Treaty of Brest Litovsk, for instance, already included a provision stipulating that:

> "The Contracting Parties are agreed that, with the conclusion of peace, the war terminates also in the field of economy and finance. They engage not to participate either directly or indirectly in measures having for their aim the continuance of hostilities in economic or financial spheres, but to hinder such measures within the boundaries of the territories of their states by all means in their power."[2]

This innovative formula designed to combat "economic aggression" became a prototype for Soviet treaty practice during the period which preceded the USSR's admission into the League of Nations. Thus, in the Treaty of Friendship and Neutrality between the USSR and Turkey, of December 17, 1925, the signatories pledged themselves, *inter alia*, "not to participate in any alliance or agreement of a political character with one or more other powers directed against the other Contracting Party."[3] A supplementary protocol explained that the expression "of a political character" likewise embraced "all such financial or economic agreements between powers as are directed against the other Contracting Party."

An analogous commitment is recorded in the Agreement on Neutrality and Non-Aggression between the USSR and Germany, of April 24, 1926,[4] whereby both states declared that, "if a coalition will be formed among third countries for the purpose of submitting one of the Contracting Parties to an economic or financial boycott, the second Contracting Party will not join such a coalition." Similar language occurs in the Treaty of Neutrality and Non-Aggression between the USSR and Afghanistan, of August 31, 1926,[5] and the Treaties of Non-Aggression between the USSR and Lithuania, of September 28, 1926,[6] between the USSR and Latvia, of February 5, 1932,[7] and between the USSR and Estonia, of May 4, 1932.[8] Furthermore, the Treaty between the USSR and Latvia took the added precaution of giving the safeguard retroactive effect. After noting that the parties were bound not to adhere to "any treaties, conventions or agreements aiming at an economic or financial boycott of either of the Contracting Parties," it confirmed that the current agreement did not modify any international rights and obligations arising out of previous agreements entered into by the signatories "insofar as such treaties did not include any elements of aggression within the meaning" of the present convention. Hence, should there be in the older treaties articles sanctioning resort to economic aggression, the expectation now was that the corresponding provisions would have to be brought into conformity with the spirit and letter of the latest accord.

Finally, the Treaties of Non-Aggression between the USSR and France, of November 29, 1932,[9] and between the USSR and Italy, of September 2, 1933,[10] sound the same theme, with all concerned resolving that they would not "become a party to any international agreement of which the effect in practice would be to prevent the purchase of goods from or the sale of goods or the granting of credits to the other Party and not to take any measure which would result in the exclusion of the other Party from any participation in its foreign trade."

The data prompt several observations. *First*, the pattern here is so consistent that this activity must clearly be viewed not as a series of *ad hoc* improvisations but as the outgrowth of a settled policy line. *Second*, the initiative for these arrangements obviously emanates from the Soviet side: none of Moscow's partners had to fear collusion between the Soviet régime and a third party apt to affect their economic interests adversely (unless one had in mind Russia's sole ally–Mongolia–a remote contingency at any rate and a negligible economic factor even so); whereas, for the Kremlin, the prospect of collaboration within capitalist circles to the economic detriment of the Soviets looked very real indeed. *Third*, the fact that the subject of "economic aggression" cropped up in a succession of quintessentially political agreements already served to establish an organic link between the economic and political spheres which was and remains a fixture of the Communist canon and, of course, also reflected the initial Soviet exposure to economic warfare plainly motivated by political considerations.[11] *Fourth*, the choice of such key documents as treaties of neutrality and non-aggression to air the issue is not accidental either and effectively underscores the crucial importance attached by the Soviet régime to the economic aspect of its international relations. *Fifth*, the insertion of economic matters into inter-state agreements regulating recognized institutions of international law forcefully made the point that international economic activities, too, or at least certain types of international economic activities did not hinge merely on the discretion of the respective state but were governed by norms of international public law which prescribed various rules of official conduct in this area as well. The conceptual association was thus counted upon to extend the writ of international law, which traditionally focussed almost exclusively on political affairs, to the domain of economic foreign policy that hitherto had been left to the members of the international community to manage virtually as they saw fit.

Compared to the definite views espoused by the Soviet leadership in this department, its position on assorted technical terms of international trade was at first much less precise. The attitude towards the most-favored-nation clause, for instance, ranged from mutely passive to mildly critical. On the one hand, the principle appears as a regular feature of Soviet treaty practice. Yet, the record seems to indicate that the reason for this phenomenon was that Soviet negotiators routinely acquiesced in the demands of the other party (especially true in the case of the secessionist states) to be guaranteed privileged access to the Russian market. Contrary to subsequent claims, the Soviets themselves did not at this stage of the game show any visible enthusiasm for the whole idea or behave in a manner calculated to create the impression of anything but indifference about whether this or another procedure was followed.[12]

Doctrine, in fact, questioned the relevance of the clause under the new conditions where foreign trade was envisaged as a state monopoly. The principal advantages of the most-favored-nation clause derived from preferential rates of customs duties, and most Soviet experts saw no purpose in maintaining these levies since all phases of import and export traffic were now concentrated in governmental hands and nothing more would be achieved by such a system than to reshuffle funds from one state agency to another. Under the circumstances, the impact of the most-favored-nation clause was bound to be slight, and donating that status represented little else than a gesture of goodwill which Soviet diplomats were willing to make since the material cost was low in any event. Even so, readiness to grant this trade concession literally on request did cause some unhappiness, and the extension of an unconditional most-favored-nation régime to Germany, for example, was faulted for being unprofitable for the USSR presumably because no attempt was made to extract a *quid pro quo* in a situation where the "capitalist" partner believed that he was obtaining a benefit and should have been asked to pay for it by consenting to reciprocal compensation.[13]

In short, the Soviets used the most-favored-nation clause during this period as bait: the foreigners lusted after the alleged benefits the status would secure them on the Soviet scene, and the lure could be exploited to induce them to break ranks with their fellow capitalists and enter into commercial relations with Soviet Russia. The Soviet response was purely instinctive, however, perceiving the technique as an expedient tool and resorting to its practical application as occasion arose, without benefit of an analytical framework that would vest the operation with a sense of theoretical legitimacy, tactical coherence, or strategic vision.

Incidentally, the same holds true for instances where the Soviet Union met with discriminatory trade practices abroad and took appropriate countermeasures. Thus, a Resolution of the Council of People's Commissars of October 20, 1930, recommended that the People's Commissariat for Foreign and Domestic Trade take steps with regard to countries that established a special régime for trade with the USSR which did not extend to other countries. The proposed remedies included complete cessation or maximum reduction of orders and purchases from these countries, a halt to the use of their shipping, and so forth.[14] Again, in 1935-1936 a number of states created obstacles in connection with Soviet wishes to earmark sums earned through export to buy items needed at home. The Council of People's Commissars reacted on January 16, 1936, by issuing a Resolution providing for the reduction of export to countries whose financial-currency legislation or administrative regulations did not guarantee Soviet organizations full freedom to utilize receipts from export to settle accounts on obligations incurred by these organizations or Soviet trade missions, regardless of when these debts were contracted.[15] Similarly, the Resolution of the Council of People's Commissars of September 8, 1939, authorized the People's Commissariat for Foreign Trade to: 1) limit or prohibit the export of goods and the delivery of goods already *en route* from the USSR to countries where legislative and administrative rules, as well as administrative and court practice or the enactment of financial restrictions, produced unfavorable conditions for Soviet foreign trade; 2) prohibit export abroad of goods not paid for by the purchasers.[16]

Today, Soviet spokesmen claim that these measures constituted acts of retorsion instituted in response to *unlawful* attempts at discrimination against trade with the USSR. The current pitch, interestingly enough, is not that the responsible capitalist states had in these cases adopted unfriendly or unfair policies *vis-à-vis* the Soviet Union to which the latter reacted in kind, *i.e.*, one discretionary decision matched by another and usually leading to the repeal of both. Instead, Soviet commentators now claim that discrimination *per se* in the conduct of foreign economic relations is contrary to public international law and affords the injured party the right to resort to legal reprisals, which is what the USSR is said to have done on the occasions just mentioned.[17] However, the contemporary record shows no evidence of such motivation: rather, Moscow seems throughout to have dealt with a practical problem by practical means without indulging in any fancy theorizing about the legal propriety of the whole affair. Its sole intent then appeared to focus on the choice of a suitable antidote to cure the current affliction in purely pragmatic terms, without getting embroiled in complicated legal debates. On both counts, therefore, major virtues were subsequently discovered and retrospectively attributed to the most-favored-nation and non-discrimination concepts that originally had been neither noticed nor advertised.

With only minor modifications, the preceding pattern persisted after the USSR's entry into the League of Nations, except, of course, that the Soviet régime's admission into the elite circles of the international community even before that signal event already gave it ample opportunity to promote its pet theses and let it experiment with new formats to gain general recognition for its schemes. Taking advantage of these improved channels of communication, Soviet spokesmen continued to emphasize the interconnection between politics and economics. From the pulpit of the League and in the councils of a succession of international conferences convened to deal with pressing issues of global diplomacy, Soviet representatives hammered at the theme of the indivisibility of political and economic peace, stressing that unbridled economic nationalism naturally tended to spill over into conflict by more lethal means and preaching economic pacification as an indispensable corollary of any viable political and military security system.[18]

The various meetings held in the early thirties, spurred by the worldwide economic crisis, provided the Soviet Union with a chance to vent some of its most impassioned oratory on behalf of "economic normalization" through concerted international action. The highlights of the Soviet campaign were the session of the European Commission of the League of Nations in May 1931, and the International Economic Conference in London in the Summer of 1933. In the former forum, the Soviet delegation tabled a draft of a universal pact of economic non-aggression that was discussed by a special committee which, however, made no attempt to follow up on the idea. The project called on all states "to renounce all discrimination in their mutual relations and to consider as incompatible with the principles of the present protocol the adoption or application in the respective countries of a special regime directed against the interests of one or several countries signatories of the protocol or not applied to all other countries."

On the latter occasion, the representatives of the Soviet Union redoubled their efforts. Repeatedly reminding the assembled dignitaries of the USSR's past exertions to win approval for a treaty of economic non-aggression, senior Soviet diplomats pointed out that the need for instituting such safeguards had since become only more acute because measures of economic aggression, instead of declining, had gradually proliferated and constantly took a new form. They, therefore, appealed for an economic truce involving not just a commitment not to resort to novel weapons of economic war but also a pledge to lay down existing arms. To consolidate the peace, the Soviet Union's spokesmen recommended the endorsement of a resolution (June 15, 1933) obliging all participating states mutually to abolish, without regard to the reasons for their enactment, all legislative and administrative measures previously imposed and currently in force smacking of economic aggression and discrimination.

In a companion move (June 20, 1933), the Soviet delegates sought to revive their plan for the conclusion of a protocol of economic non-aggression. The up-dated version prescribed, *inter alia*, the renunciation by states of "all forms of discrimination" and forbade the "imposition and application of a special régime directed against any state and worsening the conditions governing that country's trade compared to the conditions observed with respect to the trade of all other countries." The document next listed the types of economic discrimination that henceforward would be barred: "discriminatory customs duties established for one country, general prohibitions or special conditions for import or export aimed at a particular country, special railroad rates, special imposts levied on commercial vessels, special conditions for the admission of economic organizations, all kinds of boycott of one country's trade by medium of governmental or administrative measures." Finally, the text stipulated that all measures of discrimination in force in the signatory countries had to be repealed from the moment the present protocol entered into force for the corresponding state. [19]

A noteworthy aspect of Soviet attendance at the deliberations of both these bodies was the emergence in that connection of the most-favored-nation principle as a significant feature of Soviet diplomacy. Appropriately enough, not much was made of the development at the time, except that Soviet commentators now began referring to the clausula as a "fundamental principle of mutual economic relations" in the history of Soviet contacts with the West.[20] As previously mentioned, the claim is factually incorrect, but the shift did reflect the enhanced role of the concept at this stage of the game which prompted indulgence in the common Soviet practice of elevating the status of a currently popular tactic by forging the myth of its unassailable position as a permanent fixture of Soviet repertory from the very start. At first, the efforts to tamper with the record did not go beyond the sort of bare assertion just quoted.[21] How greatly the picture has changed in the intervening years and how far the process of inflating the importance of the most-favored-nation rule has since progressed can best be appreciated by the way in which these events are being treated in recent Soviet literature. Indeed, the focus has switched quite dramatically, and in their analysis of the record Soviet commentators today dwell equally, if not more, on the value of a technical tool—such as the most-favored-nation concept—to foil the nefarious schemes of the USSR's enemies and defend the interests of the Soviet Union as on the spectacle of grand policy pronouncements that hitherto had attracted the bulk of lay and scholarly attention both at home and abroad.

In that vein, modern discussion of these experiences devotes considerable space, for instance, to Litvinov's warning at the May 1931 session of the European Commission that deviation from the most-favored-nation principle in the guise of extending "preferential tariffs and privileges to particular countries or groups of countries would mean the division of Europe into economic groups and camps, destined not to cooperate with but to struggle against other similar groupings, with the stimulus for the struggle being supplied not so much by economic as by political impulses." At the September meeting of the Commission, the USSR's chief delegate voiced his objections in even sharper tones, declaring that "preferences amount to legalized discrimination, aggravating contradictions between countries," and thus constitute a "clearly expressed form of economic war."[22] The current accent on these dicta is not accidental and obviously reflects the prevailing Soviet perception of the most-favored-nation clause as a prime weapon in the fight to disrupt "hostile economic groupings," a view projected backward to the origins of the Soviet order for purposes of legitimation.

How sincere were the Soviet motives in advancing these propositions throughout the thirties is hard to tell. One can sense in the Kremlin's behavior during those years a strain of fear that the capitalist world would be apt to seek escape from the current economic crisis by venting its frustrations on the USSR. There is no doubt that the Soviet leadership was still haunted by the memories of the régime's initial encounter with a hostile international environment, when it had its first taste of economic sanctions. Marxist habits of thought operated further to intensify these apprehensions by attributing to the capitalists a natural propensity to resort to economic aggression against a class enemy to get themselves out of a tight corner.

In addition, however, it seems safe to conclude that the Soviets now also engaged in a calculated game. The theme of universal peace had enormous mass appeal then, and the Soviets were determined to cash in on its popularity. With the world's economy in disarray, extending their propaganda efforts into the economic realm by calling for economic pacification offered the Soviets a unique chance to broaden their campaign, tap a major new source of international anxiety, and pose as the sole champion capable of saving humanity from the scourge of economic warfare. In short, existing conditions were such that they both caused the Russians genuine worry for the solidity of their own position—prompting feverish activity in favor of collective security as a prophylactic measure—and contributed to a feeling of euphoria on the part of the Russians at the sign of the chaos reigning in the bourgeois camp—encouraging bold affirmative action to exploit these difficulties to Moscow's advantage. The depth of Soviet attachment to the policies it presently advocated must be gauged in the light of these conflicting commitments, a mix of candor and expediency.

In closing, it must be pointed out that, in terms of tangible accomplishments in this area, the pre-war record can boast of very few successes. The League's performance on the economic front produced meager results. Functionally and temperamentally, the organization was in fact ill-equipped to tackle urgent economic problems and, instead of proposing solutions for the world's economic woes, its random collection of specialized boards and commissions concentrated on gathering raw data and pursuing statistical research. The assignments of the individual agencies lacked the scope to permit the elaboration of comprehensive policy recommendations of the kind so desperately needed at this stage of the game to pull the international community out of the economic nosedive, and no institutional effort was made to pool this information for immediate practical application. Thus, the Soviets themselves concede that their attempts to transform the League of Nations into an effective tool of economic as well as political cooperation to meet the exigencies of the member states proved largely in vain. [23]

At another level, though, a different picture emerges. Mankind was slowly awakening to the extent of the mutual influence between economics and politics. The Soviets, due to their own early experience and Marxist orientation, were far ahead of the pack in this respect and were instrumental in cultivating greater awareness of this relationship. While it did not gain general recognition for its theories on the subject of the economic underpinnings of the political structure or manage to get its views translated into valid rules of international law, the Soviet régime plainly made its fellow governments a lot more conscious of the de-stabilizing effect of economic extremism on the world political system. In the process, the notion that economic affairs might properly fall within the jurisdiction of an organization such as the League of Nations and undergo formal international regulation instead of being considered the private province of each state's willpower no longer sounded as exotic as it once did. On the psychological plane, the impression is that the Soviets pursued a course which relied on hypnotic repetition of certain propositions to lead to the ultimate acceptance of the unusual as normal, operating on a principle no more sophisticated than if an assertion rang familiar enough it would then routinely be stamped as indeed true. On balance, the net score on the substantive side may have been disappointing, but the Soviets had reason to derive some satisfaction from the progress registered in fostering new attitudes here.

Finally, although the Soviets failed to get their program "enacted" into law, its highlights are worth recalling to fill in the background of the Soviet Union's current agenda. According to the scenario drawn up by a leading Soviet exponent of international law:

> "The first stage to be reached is the urgent necessity of winning, by medium of a solemn agreement, universal recognition for the principle of the illegality of economic war. Economic war awaits its Pact of Paris that must banish it from international relations and "outlaw" it.
>
> The second task that is called for is the precise treaty definition of proscribed weapons of economic warfare, the most complete attempt at which was made in the draft protocol submitted by the delegation of the USSR at the London Conference. It is sufficient to remember the prohibitions and restrictions "permitted" by the Convention of November 8, 1927, "for the abolition of prohibitions and restrictions on import and export" to realize that any suppression of economic war would be futile as long as the concept of the latter has not been strictly concretized by a convention defining the various proscribed forms of international economic aggression.
>
> ***
>
> It would be truly superfluous to invoke fresh arguments to prove that economic security and political security are intimately linked and indissoluble in mankind's present conditions.
>
> If the men in charge of the destiny of people are today, with few exceptions, virtually unanimous in recognizing that political security can only be guaranteed by a collective and organized system embracing all nations prepared for active collaboration in defense of the cause of

peace, one may be allowed to think that the same system must be applied for safeguarding economic security.

Doubtless, it would be too rash to maintain that once a convention of economic non-aggression signed, heavenly harmony would replace today's fierce economic struggle. But it is evident that any practical step made in this direction will significantly contribute to the appeasement of international conflicts and consequently to the removal of the terrible specter of war.

A special task rests here on all men working toward the rapprochement of peoples and the development of the most generous of sciences—that of international law; the enormous difficulties of general disarmament stem from the problem of material disarmament—the destruction or limitation of weapons of war: armies, navies, canons; the sole weapons of economic struggle are legislative and administrative acts. Economic disarmament is primarily juridical disarmament, and the duty of legal counselors in all countries is to contribute to its success."[24]

2. The Post-War Situation

Although interest in international economic matters has remained a constant feature of the Soviet diplomatic repertoire, much of the specific style and tenor of Soviet concern with the subject in the pre-war period no longer fitted conditions on the world scene after 1945 and so has been dropped from current usage. For example, the heavy accent on the theme of economic non-aggression in the earlier phase tended to create an impression of excessive Soviet fear and vulnerability that did not square with the image the USSR was presently trying to project of a recognized superpower, in the economic as well as in the military sphere. The clauses in the USSR's old bilateral treaties relating to economic "peace-keeping" had proved their value when the USSR functioned in virtual isolation and had good reason to beware of the effect of possible collusion between its capitalist opponents on its economic position. Now, however, the Soviet Union had acquired its own coterie of "socialist" friends, and treaty provisions—explicitly barring special economic relations with any country at the expense of another member of the global community—could get in the way of plans to develop closer ties within the "socialist" fraternity.

In any event, these considerations had little practical relevance in the immediate post-war years. With the onset of the "Cold War," commercial exchange between the USSR and the capitalist countries nearly came to a standstill, and the task of elaborating basic principles of trade policy was shelved since the prevailing circumstances hardly warranted such an effort. Soviet spokesmen were mostly content to denounce the economic measures adopted in the West in the course of the confrontation in the cliché-ridden language of those days that uniformly pictured all steps taken to halt Soviet encroachment as an imperialist conspiracy spearheaded by Washington's dream of establishing its global hegemony.[25]

A noticeable shift in attitudes occurred in the early fifties. The International Economic Conference held in Moscow on April 3-12, 1952, for instance, marked renewed attention on the part of the USSR to problems of international trade. The speeches of the Soviet representatives at that meeting dealt essentially with *ad hoc* problems of stimulating commercial traffic between the USSR and the rest of the world and did not address themselves to policy questions, but there were repeated calls for the dismantlement of discriminatory barriers as an indispensable first step toward the revival of trade contacts between all countries. Artificial, politically motivated impediments to the free flow of goods and services across state borders were blamed for much of the world's economic disruption, the slow pace of postwar reconstruction, and the imbalances and hardships in national living standards occasioned by the maintenance of restrictive trade practices. Hence, the prompt elimination of these egregious obstacles was deemed imperative to restore the natural movement of commodities that would greatly benefit the whole of mankind.[26]

The death of Stalin lent further impetus to this trend. Already in 1954, the Soviet Union began agitating in the Economic Commission for Europe and the Economic and Social Council for reforms designed to improve the existing system of international trade. Soviet proposals pressed for an end to economic, administrative, and commercial-political restraints on European trade, urged the convocation of international conferences of governmental experts to recommend means of broadening international trade, and advocated the creation of an International Trade Organization intended to ensure the effective regulation of economic cooperation and the systematic expansion of commercial ties between states. The following years witnessed a dramatic surge in Soviet diplomatic activity in this domain: in the Economic Commission for Europe, the Economic and Social Council, and the United Nations General Assembly, Soviet representatives sponsored a succession of projects aimed at restructuring the prevailing pattern of international trade relations through the adoption of novel normative principles and the establishment of new supervisory machinery. At every opportunity, Soviet delegates tabled draft treaties, resolutions and declarations in which they pushed their concept of a revamped world economic order based on a different set of rules from what had hitherto been accepted as valid precedent in this area. The most-favored-nation clause featured prominently on the Soviet agenda.[27]

Khrushchev's campaign in the mid-fifties to promote the ideals of peaceful coexistence added momentum to the enterprise. Quite obviously, the switch to the latest precepts created an incomparably more propitious atmosphere for the bid to convince the world of the advantages of doing business with the

Russians than had the previous climate of confrontation. The current "soft-sell" theme, which stressed pacific competition between the rival political systems, readily adapted itself to the notion of economic accommodation by the medium of mercantile exchanges conducted on reciprocally profitable terms. By the same token, the Soviets derive many of their strongest arguments in favor of a revised international economic code from what they claim to be the postulates of peaceful coexistence.

The most authoritative Soviet definition of what constitutes peaceful coexistence appears in the present Party Program. According to this formula, peaceful coexistence entails: renunciation of war as a means of settling disputed issues between states, their solution by means of negotiations; equality, mutual understanding, and trust between states, respect for each other's interests; non-interference in domestic affairs, recognition of the right of each people independently to decide all questions concerning its country; strict observance of the sovereignty and territorial integrity of all countries; development of economic and cultural cooperation on the basis of full equality and mutual benefit.[28]

Note the explicit reference to "development of economic and cultural cooperation on the basis of full equality and mutual benefit," for Soviet legal commentators rely on this proposition to forge a direct link between trade, which they identify as the principal form of economic cooperation,[29] and the requirements of peaceful coexistence. The usual reasoning here is that international trade and economic connections contribute to the normalization of relations and the growth of rapport between countries, and create a specific material stake in the continuation of such relations and the preservation of peace.[30] Although Soviet spokesmen concede that economic elements alone cannot prevent the outbreak of war, they do assign to this factor a significant role in abating international tensions and deciding controversial problems through amicable methods.

The pitch, then, is that since states now must abide by the norms of peaceful coexistence, they are obliged to trade with one another because such exchanges foster the objectives of peaceful coexistence, which, in turn, means that every state has to follow a policy on international trade positively calculated to raise the quantitative and qualitative level of its share in order to comply with its duty to fulfill the desiderata of peaceful coexistence.[31] Conversely, the extent of a country's pursuit of the right kind of trade is looked upon as a true index to the depth of its commitment to the values of peaceful coexistence, so that its failure to perform satisfactorily on that count is treated as *prima facie* evidence of contravention of the spirit and letter of peaceful coexistence, and its actions aimed at imposing constraints on its foreign trade operations are judged to be in open violation of the peremptory norms associated with the concept of peaceful coexistence. In short, going by this scenario, a state is presumed to owe it to other states to maintain an optimal economic liaison with them and, therefore, to take affirmative steps to achieve that end. Given that the grant of most-favored-nation status in trade matters customarily tends to encourage commercial initiative [32] and the refusal of that privilege has the common effect of inhibiting business contacts, the logical conclusion is that a state is legally bound to let its trading partners enjoy a most-favored-nation régime in commercial affairs if it wants to live by the canon of peaceful coexistence.

Language use is geared to relay the same message. Indeed, calling international trade a prime species of economic cooperation has some very definite practical implications. Mercantile mores have traditionally been inspired by self-serving considerations, exploiting natural advantages to drive a hard bargain and to maximize one's profits within a context still acceptable to both parties. Cooperation, on the other hand, presupposes not a chase after the greatest possible unilateral benefit, but a readiness to compromise in order to guarantee a fair return to all sides. Thus, the attitude, the calculus and the *modus operandi* are quite different, depending on whether the people involved decide to function as competitive businessmen or as members of a "team" and, of course, the rules of the game change accordingly. At a recent conference, for instance, a Soviet lawyer quite seriously lectured me on the impropriety of capitalist entrepreneurs levying 6% or more interest on commercial loans to socialist countries because, he claimed, a rate that high did not jibe with the notion of cooperation. He made no allowance whatever for the fact that commercial activity has historically followed the path of charging what traffic would bear, since he was plainly bent on applying not the old values, but criteria reflecting a divergent, and often antipodal, table of priorities. Again, a congenial *modus vivendi* along these lines is presumably best achieved through routine access to the most-favored-nation status, whereas denial of that treatment or an attempt to extort a special *quid pro quo* for licensing such an arrangement allegedly smack of the exploitative past practices of the discredited bourgeois era.

As the foregoing suggests, while international trade is desirable, not just any kind of trade fits the bill. Commercial dealings between states must also meet certain objective standards, in particular, the two named in the Party Program's description of peaceful coexistence—full equality and mutual benefit. The former requirement, we are told, signifies that in their economic interactions all countries, independently of their social system, economic power, general level of development, character of their economic order, etc., must abstain from resorting to any sort of political and economic coercion, unilateral demands, enslavement of one country by another. [33] Quite obviously, a trade policy which draws invidious distinctions between countries by awarding or withholding most-favored-nation rank at will does not square with the sense of equality, and when entry into the preferential class is determined on political grounds, the whole procedure further runs afoul of the prohibition against "coercion."

An additional point that Soviet sources insist on in this connection is that this equality of economic opportunity be real and not just formal,[34] which is one of the reasons why they rather focus on the parity of socio-economic systems than individual state units.[35] The trouble with the second approach, as far as the Soviets are concerned, is that it leaves open the possibility of treating as like entities which are put in the same category. Thus, the notion of equality could in theory be satisfied if a capitalist state, say, treated all fellow-capitalist states in identical fashion on the scale of the legal régime of international commerce and then dealt evenhandedly with all its socialist trading partners, but on terms that differed from those applied to the first contingent.[36] As long as a uniform standard prevailed within each generic group, it could be argued that the principle of equality remained inviolate, except that such an outcome would hardly be satisfactory to those who thereby found themselves relegated to an inferior position by dint of some *a priori* classification scheme. Having had a personal taste of this experience, the Russians, as already mentioned, stress instead the equality of competing socio-economic systems in a conscious bid to plug this vexing loophole. The next step, not too surprisingly, is to claim that once a state opts to bestow the most-favored-nation grade on one business associate it must, for the sake of equality, assume an analogous commitment *vis-à-vis* the rest.[37]

The other component–mutual benefit–is said to mean that every country is free to purchase what it wishes and sell what it can, taking into account its national interests and currency and financial capabilities.[38] Typically, the dictum is couched in the affirmative in the sense that a state's right to purchase what it wants on foreign markets appears, in light of this phrasing, to preempt the corollary right that one might expect to inhere in each state to sell what it pleases and to whom it pleases. The slant, of course, is by no means accidental, for it fits perfectly the USSR's continuing needs as a shopper on the international scene. Be that as it may, the analysis logically leads to the conclusion that mutual benefit is best served when all artificial measures that obstruct a country's access to external channels of supply are removed. This also applies to denial of most-favored-nation régime, since the net effect of such refusal is to impose an extra burden on the flow of commercial traffic between the respective parties and, thus, significantly hobble the freedom of the state so treated to engage in trade on optimal terms which, by definition, are most likely to ensure "mutual benefit."

On substantive grounds, the gist of the Soviet attempt to distill positive rules fixing the legal basis of inter-state trade from the phenomenon of peaceful coexistence may strike the independent observer as singularly unimpressive. With regard to the procedural side of the operation, the performance is of higher quality and accordingly deserves a few additional words, especially since the pattern followed here seems to be part of a general Soviet technique for promoting the creation of new principles of international law to replace the antiquated norms reflecting a bourgeois ethos. The trick is to start with an abstract and innocuous proposition that, perhaps for this very reason, is universally acceptable (*e.g.*, sovereignty, equality, and so forth) and then to spin out a succession of progressively more elaborate equations—each of them incrementally grafting concrete content onto the preceding formula—to cap the sequence after a series of unobtrusive steps, none of which often raises serious objection on its own, with a specific prescription aimed at achieving a particular end by enunciating a fresh rule.

Never mind that the chosen line of reasoning is not the only one possible and that an alternative chain of analysis could be developed with just as much, or even more, claim to logic and coherence; nor that the consensus which surrounds the original amorphous premise is apt to break down either from the outset or at some intermediate stage, once the mechanism of building a detailed case is put in motion and all concerned confront the job of selecting from a wide assortment of appropriate incrustations for the central theme. The point is to take unfair advantage of the situation by being the first to launch a version and let the opposition challenge your interpretation if inclined to do so. Primacy is frequently mistaken for legitimacy and, in any event, having easily seized unoccupied terrain, one forces the competition to work hard to recover lost ground, in the face of uncertain results. What gave and indeed still gives the Soviets a marked edge on this occasion is the fact that the concept of peaceful coexistence on which hinges this entire script is their brainchild and the accident of parenthood allegedly forges a special bond in determining the character of the offspring—*i.e.*, authorship is tantamount to recognition of a valid stake in defining the final product.

To compound the problem, the Soviet Union's rivals were largely content tacitly to acquiesce in the idea of peaceful coexistence and showed no enthusiasm for exploring its potential ramifications, thereby leaving the Russians at liberty to fill the vessel with contents of their own picking, except that the West could always demur at Moscow's reading of the record. However, periodically registering a dissent from somebody else's opinion is quite different from instituting positive action to propound a distinct thesis and is a far less effective method of waging the contest over whose views should prevail in shaping the operative frame of reference. Virtually by default, then, the Russians have had a field-day here, although the outcome bears the imprint of their sectarian vision which is not shared by those very circles which are the target of the campaign. By going this route, the Soviets may have acquired a powerful propaganda weapon and undoubtedly have tapped the sympathies of the Third World in mounting their assault on capitalist "privileges," but it is to the storehouses of the bourgeoisie that the Kremlin is seeking entry and an adversary approach based on pressure tactics has less chance in accomplishing that goal than what otherwise might be gained through suasion. In short, the very magnitude of the Soviet success in capturing control of the task of drafting an official exegesis of the canon of peaceful coexistence has led to the project's failure as a practical experiment in proselytization and only managed to split the audience into rival camps, without a common agenda. In the wake of this Pyrrhic victory, the companion economic norms that Moscow has so strenuously championed now look destined to remain either bargaining counters or distant desiderata or private by-laws governing business dealings among the USSR and its close friends and associates.

Most of the elements identified with peaceful coexistence concurrently rate as general principles of international law or norms of international customary law. They are also cited in that additional capacity to buttress the Soviet argument,[39] and since the two versions show considerable overlap, instead of repeating the story in full only the latter's distinguishing features will be noted.

Thus, the Soviets set great stock by the rule of non-discrimination[40] which they describe as an outgrowth of the principle of the sovereign equality of states.[41] Both allegedly represent imperative norms of international law;[42] conduct incompatible with either *ipso jure* constitutes a flagrant violation of contemporary international law.[43] Although the concept of non-discrimination has its roots in the notion of the sovereign equality of states and, hence, is ancillary to it, the Soviets assign it a separate role from that played by the parent proposition. As mentioned earlier, a major flaw in the formula of sovereign equality–in the Soviet estimate–is that it has allowed some countries to draw socio-economic differentiations while claiming to afford equal treatment according to species, as it were.

The injunction against discrimination cures this defect in that it prohibits any activity which ensues in the elevation of certain states above the rest, especially in matters of trade, and consequently makes illegal policies which sanction preferential status for particular recipients while denying others the same benefits on whatever pretext, the socio-economic alibi included.[44] Applied literally, this doctrine would spell the end of the most-favored-nation clause whose primary rationale has always been that a state may, purely at its own discretion, see fit to grant to select trading partners extra economic opportunities unmatched in its relations with less privileged company.[45] In fact, this is precisely the direction in which the Russians have recently been moving and perhaps nothing illustrates the shift better than the changing tone and tenor of Soviet writing about the right connection between the whole issue of non-discrimination and the most-favored-nation article.

In 1960, for instance, a Soviet legal expert discussed the topic at considerable length and, in essence, endorsed the traditional view that the most-favored-nation clause and the principle of non-discrimination could exist simultaneously without conflicting. The most-favored-nation item, he concluded, qualified as an *ad hoc* reward by medium of treaty marking a special degree of intimacy between the states involved. In a sense, the arrangement did derogate from an absolute standard of non-discrimination, but it was a permissible concession stemming from an overt act of sovereign will expressed in appropriate provisions of an agreement. The notion of non-discrimination was, therefore, limited to routine circumstances not subject to conventional regulation and here it did operate as a customary norm imposing on a state the duty to behave evenhandedly towards all its trading partners who were not entitled to any formal dispensation. This dichotomy is, of course, quite familiar, and the scheme propounded by the Soviet author would pass muster in most legal quarters.[46]

How far things have since progressed may be judged by the same writer's efforts in a 1968 work to adapt to the latest line. Simply recognizing the parallel existence of the two categories mentioned above and justifying the gradation by reference to treaty norms versus customary practice is no longer an acceptable procedure. Expected to bridge the contradiction, our hero fudges by trundling out the threadbare Marxist *deus ex machina* of "the unity of opposites" to explain how the dialectic manages to fit all the disparate pieces into a harmonious entirety. Or, to quote verbatim,

> "the progressive nature of the most-favored-nation regime *inter alia* lies precisely in that, by equating the rights of states enjoying that régime through the progressive expansion of their [*i.e.*, the constituents'] radius (thanks to the conclusion of further new treaties) it eventually transforms the privileged regime into a common one, into a regime for all, *i.e.*, into a non-discriminatory regime; on the basis of the common regime which arose in this manner there begins to form a more privileged regime, and so forth. Thanks to this, increasingly more intense forms of international economic cooperation develop. Accordingly, this principle has nothing in common with economic groupings of states, but is directed against such groupings."[47]

The proposed escape-hatch, then, is to look at those states which have received most-favored-nation status from another state as merely a spearhead for the residue: the image is that of scouts sent ahead to establish an advance position on an upper plateau where the main body of troops is scheduled soon to join them, at which point the process repeats itself. The gap is thus temporary and presumably is tolerable—indeed perhaps is even constructive—given that the mechanism is ultimately slated to function in such a way as to lift everybody by stages to ever higher rungs of economic rapprochement—by definition, a desirable goal. Presto, the dilemma is resolved by simple proclamation that what appears unequal is but a prelude to yet greater equality and what seems divided is just a herald of still closer unity. Remember, though, that the scenario rests throughout on the crucial assumption that the synthesis will proximately produce the universalization of the most-favored-nation terms and this anticipated result contains the real clue to the whole *roman à clef*.

In the final analysis, of course, the Soviet argument is persuasive only if one accepts the initial premise, namely, that these general principles of international law which Soviet spokesmen invoke in order to draw the ensemble of subsidiary conclusions crucial to their case do, in fact, apply to the realm of international economic affairs. Yet, that is precisely the issue that the Russian scribes never address themselves to *in substantia*, preferring instead to act as if the truth of the proposition were incontestable and so universally recognized as to require neither discussion nor demonstration. Others may find this version utterly unconvincing, and for good reason. Whatever merits the Soviet salespitch may have *de lege ferenda*, it certainly does not reflect the precedent set in the field of international commercial practice, and if that corpus of rules is now being discarded in favor of a different repertoire, evidence of the existence of a consensus approving the switch must still be adduced. That critical item is exactly what the Soviets fail to provide when they prate about a current code of public international law on trade and economic cooperation and, thereby, seem deliberately bent on confusing wish with reality. The rhetorical approach does make sense when empirical proof is lacking, and the record would suggest that the Soviet choice of *modus operandi* effectively attests to awareness of the importance of this missing element in the equation and accounts for Moscow's decision to go the alternate route.

This feature probably explains why the Soviets have tried so hard to find, in the inventory of positive law, some additional pegs on which to hang their thesis. Not surprisingly, the United Nations Charter has been pressed into service.[48] The technique is to string together whatever language randomly appears in the text that bears on the present subject. To begin with, Soviet sources like to point out that the Charter pays much more attention to economic problems than did its predecessor–the Covenant of the League of Nations–and attribute this phenomenon to the influence of the USSR at the time the statute was being drafted.[49] Thus, they claim, there was from the first a conscious desire to get the United Nations deeply involved in social and economic matters and to vest the organization with ample authority in these fields.

In witness of this intention, Soviet commentators recite the passages in the preamble which express the members' determination "to promote social progress and better standards of life in larger freedom" and "to employ international machinery for the promotion of the economic and social advancement of all peoples." They next skip to Article 55 which notes that:

> "With a view to the creation of conditions of stability and well-being which are necessary for peaceful and friendly relations among nations

> based on respect for the principles of equal rights and self-determination of the peoples, the United Nations shall promote:
> a) higher standards of living, full employment, and conditions of economic and social progress and development;
> b) solutions of international economic, social, health, and related problems. . ."

The capstone of the edifice is Article 56 whereby all members pledge themselves to take joint and separate action in cooperation with the Organization for the achievement of the purposes set forth in Article 55. Surveying the picture, Soviet lawyers have no trouble arriving at the conclusion that "contemporary international law prescribes to states the development of friendly relations, principally in the economic domain; specifically, it prescribes, in accordance with Article 56 of the UN Charter, the implementation by states of mutual economic cooperation (and, hence, international trade) 'for the achievement of the purposes set forth in Article 55.' " [50]

The resulting scenario recapitulates the already familiar ingredients. Relying on the aforecited formulations in the preamble and the companion injunction "to live together in peace with one another as good neighbors," Soviet legal experts extrapolate from these hortatory pronouncements binding norms, fixing the duty of member states to further commercial exchange and economic cooperation on equitable terms, and shun any measures which might hinder such traffic or worsen the conditions under which it must operate. In that context, non-discrimination is a *sine qua non* and its logical culmination, as we have seen, is equal access to most-favored-nation treatment. If nations are now bound, by virtue of the modern canon of international law as enshrined, *inter alia*, in the United Nations Charter, to do everything in their power to encourage trade and economic intercourse on a global scale, then quite obviously pursuing policies that do not affirmatively advance these goals runs counter to the agenda and amounts to a dereliction of legal responsibilities. [51] Nor do the Russians neglect to emphasize the usual theme in this connection that not only are the individual states bound to observe these principles but that the Organization is officially entrusted with supervising their behavior and initiating positive steps to regulate international economic activity to the end of fulfilling the commitments enunciated in its constitution. [52]

Once again, however, the proposed interpretation encounters a host of difficulties. *First*, just to mention a few of the more obvious objections, these ethereal concepts in the United Nations Charter may not have been meant to do more than inspire beautiful thoughts. *Second*, even if they were designed as programmatic guidelines, the situation would call for a concerted effort to impart these vaporous dicta proper substantive content. *Third*, a unilateral attempt to indulge in a nakedly partisan reading of the vague language of these grand declarations was certainly not calculated to gain them the kind of universal following that alone would make sense within the framework of the worldwide organization. And, *fourth*, assuming general agreement on the need to give practical effect to these fuzzy exhortations, the fact remains that this job could be accomplished in a variety of different, often diametrically divergent, ways. For, a large assortment of perfectly reasonable contingency plans could easily be squared with the Charter's rhetorical flourishes and each of them, regardless how unlike the rest, successfully defended as what the authors of the document must have had in mind when they crafted the parent articles.

Quite understandably, the emergence of UNCTAD and the thrust of its performance has boosted Moscow's hopes to win fresh recognition for its views. Although at first the Soviets sounded disappointed that their scheme for a formal International Trade Organization[53] was aborted in favor of UNCTAD, they soon reconciled themselves to the substitute arrangement and put all their energies into making good use of the new forum to promote their plans. In many respects, the tactic has proved its mettle, and the record shows that the Kremlin can indeed derive considerable comfort from the way its position on these issues has frequently been endorsed by a large proportion of UNCTAD's membership.

The resolutions that have emanated from UNCTAD's sessions espouse, for instance, the general principles long championed by the Russians as desirable features of an overhauled international economic order. This has been accomplished primarily through intense lobbying with the massive bloc of Third World countries and steady solidarity of the socialist camp with the latter's initiatives, but, whatever the actual methods, the outcome has tended to vindicate many Soviet claims about how the existing international trade structure ought to be revised.[54] Noteworthy among these was the decision reached at UNCTAD's Geneva meeting (1964)[55] opposing discrimination stemming from dissimilarities in socio-economic systems and prescribing that accommodations in trade terms observe that requirement. The move had the effect, at least in theory, of resolving a chronic Soviet complaint that the postulate of sovereign equality had been arbitrarily interpreted in the West to fit *a priori* categories and so penalized certain countries assigned to a "lower" division compared to those enjoying higher ranking. Presumably, "class" discrimination *per se* was forthwith prohibited instead of mere discrimination between equals, however defined.

A second significant innovation involved the formula adopted on the same occasion declaring that international trade must be mutually advantageous and must be conducted on the basis of the most-favored-nation régime; in the cadre of this trade, it was further urged, no measures were to be instituted that could cause injury to the trade of other countries. Thus, a device—that in the past had amounted to a purely voluntary concession awarded by one country to a chosen trading partner to mark the special intimacy of their relationship—was now turned into a general proposition of international economic activity and, by that token, was also vested with an added juridical dimension. According to Soviet legal scholars, the old treaty norm thereby acquired the supplementary quality of a recommendatory norm, meaning that a policy that previously had just been legally sanctioned was henceforward elevated into a principle backed for inclusion in international agreements.[56] The magnitude of the alleged metamorphosis can hardly be exaggerated and should the Soviet contention be accepted as valid, the bottom line would be the virtual transformation of a discretionary *modus operandi* into a mandatory procedure. If refusal of most-favored-nation status was already pictured as suspect before then on grounds of violating the injunction against discrimination, nothing could under the present standard warrant such denial in the future.

The third item of the lot concerns the preferences which UNCTAD's documents sought to establish on behalf of developing states, calling on the developed countries to offer them all privileges they granted each other without expectation of a *quid pro quo* and without extending these extra rights to the remaining developed countries, and without any obligation on the part of the developing countries to let their more advanced cousins share in the preferential arrangements they entered into between themselves. To the Soviets, these rules spell a major departure from precedent in that they mandated, "besides the traditional exemptions previously permitted by international law from the most-favored-nation principle by indicia of subjects of international law (for neighboring countries, for border trade, etc.),"[57] an additional important exception for the benefit of developing countries which was not only condoned but, in fact, recommended.

So far, one cannot quarrel with this view. What does raise eyebrows is the concurrent Soviet bid to portray these cases as entailing the sole authorized exclusions in this context, going on from there to argue that the attempt of some Western countries to utilize the medium of "closed economic groupings" to forge preferential ties within their own circles, while refusing equal opportunities to external trading associates under the pretext that the most-favored-nation clause did not cover this contingency, ran counter to the above norms and figured as a gross violation of the applicable law.[58]

UNCTAD's positive proposals furnished a welcome shot in the arm to Moscow's persistent campaign against all Western plans for institutionalized regional cooperation, since until now the Soviets had had to rely on the much weaker ammunition provided by the general principles of international law to wage that battle. Earlier, for instance, a number of Soviet legal commentators had discussed the "customs union" reservation to the most-favored-nation concept without really committing themselves on the subject. Subsequently, the issue became more controversial and their response turned more equivocal. A stock tactic was to deny the right of Western states to withhold from third partners the special privileges conferred on members of such a "community" (even when the former could invoke the most-favored-nation rule) on grounds that these entities—*e.g.*, the Common Market—represented a "political" and not a customs unit.[59]

Why a blueprint for general integration should be allowed a more limited impact than a joint experiment in creating a unified customs zone is not clear, save that formally speaking the broader project did not explicitly bill itself as a "customs union" and the historical record refers only to the latter. The argument may make very little sense, but at least it keeps alive the notion that an old-fashioned "customs union" might, *in extremis*, be recognized as reason for suspending the operation of the most-favored-nation clause *vis-à-vis* the outside clientele as regards "internal" concessions.[60] However, some Soviet lawyers have, as of late, taken a harder line and have flatly asserted that even a bona fide "customs union" cannot serve as an alibi. They could cite no material evidence to support their claim and instead engaged in highly abstract philosophical discourse to make their point.[61] Then UNCTAD came along and, since its pronouncements seemed to lend a degree of credibility to this chapter of the Soviet scenario, local spokesmen were encouraged to redouble their efforts to prove that the dynamics of Western models of regional organization conflicted with the normal functioning of the most-favored-nation principle, leading to the logical conclusion that the principle must prevail.[62]

In short, just as in the thirties, the most-favored-nation formula was thrown into the breach in a bid to checkmate the growing tendency toward economic rapprochement within the bourgeois world, wielded as a crowbar to pry open the doors of the various capitalist clubs and preserve the Soviet Union's stake in trading with the individual members on the most advantageous terms possible which would be effectively destroyed once the respective partners managed to present a solid front.

In the final analysis, of course, the success of the whole enterprise hinges on Moscow's ability to persuade its listeners of the juridical soundness of its script. The job, as it turns out, is not an easy one, for it requires the Soviets to show why the recommendations emanating from UNCTAD's sessions should be viewed as possessing legally binding force. While each Soviet author offers his variations on the central theme, the gist of their collective pitch is that the legal value of the official communiques issued by UNCTAD conferences resides in the fact that the bulk of their provisions is inherently declarative of the imperative norms featured in the code of peaceful coexistence and articulated in the United Nations Charter, as well as rooted in the general principles of international law. Hence, according to Soviet specialists, UNCTAD's documentary output has simply clarified and concretized what to all intents and purposes was already an established part of the corpus of international law.[63]

This ingenuous explanation overlooks several difficulties. For example, the thesis rests on the key assumption that the propositions contained in the texts approved by UNCTAD are inherently repetitive of existing rules and that is precisely what accounts for their veracity and validity. Yet, the record indicates that a significant proportion of the states attending these meetings felt that the opposite was true, namely, that the majority had usurped its powers to define and/or refine in order to legislate *de novo*, and in the end voted against proposals which, in the opinion of this faction, did not restate the old law so much as extensively revise it or fill large portions of it with a substantive content for which no precedent could be discovered.[64] Absent a consensus on the crucial issue that the current version is an accurate and authentic interpretation of past practices, one is quite free not to accept the Soviet contention in favor of that finding.

Furthermore, the question intrudes about the need to stage this elaborate exercise if the record was so limpid and the sole result was a virtual reiteration of something that was common knowledge. Curiously enough, the thought has also occurred to a few Soviet writers and their answer sheds light, perhaps unconsciously, on the trouble they have maintaining their present position. Thus, the thrust of their response is that such a reaffirmation of the rules was incumbent because the behavior of certain states in recent years tended to cast serious doubt on whether these principles were still operative, given that they openly pursued policies at odds with the prescribed standards.[65] The obvious retort is that, under the circumstances, the alleged canon either rates as a figment of somebody's expedient imagination or indeed lapsed by dint of systematic non-compliance and, in the second eventuality, the situation demanded not mere replication, but full-scale resurrection.

Next, no matter what weighty moral-political role Soviet authors may attribute to the views expressed through UNCTAD's corporate channels,[66] none of them ventures to suggest that the organization was competent to promulgate new rules governing items entrusted to its jurisdiction by means of balloting procedure. The product of the institution's deliberations could claim to derive legitimacy from prior recognized sources, but not from an *ad hoc* act of will of a plurality of the assembled states, except possibly on an occasion where unanimity happened to reign.

A final crucial problem awaits solution. Even assuming that UNCTAD's recommendations faithfully echoed valid principles of international law, did the latter cover the same ground? The query is prompted, of course, by the realization that the principles now being applied to commercial affairs might heretofore have operated only in other domains. In this particular instance, as mentioned earlier, the norms referred to shaped the political behavior of states, while governments continued to conduct business abroad free of these constraints. Significantly, Soviet spokesmen themselves admit as much when they note that UNCTAD's work bears evidence to the *extension* of these principles into the area of international economic law.[67] However, a development of that scope plainly qualifies as a substantial innovation in light of the established precedent and, again, the step calls for near unanimity in order to aspire to normative potency.[68] Without quasi-universal backing, the experiment must fail and an objective verdict in this case cannot hold otherwise.

3. Concluding Remarks

The striking feature of the picture is the persistence of the theme in Soviet doctrine and practice. The pattern's consistency testifies to the enduring importance of this element in the Soviet decision-making process, reflecting continued Soviet vulnerability in this sector and Moscow's determination to solve the problem through manipulation of the rules observed in the current system of foreign trade. The tactics used by the Kremlin to achieve that end have evolved over the years in step with shifts in the diplomatic environment and changes in the USSR's own capabilities, but the goal has remained the same throughout. Since the thirties, the most-favored-nation clause has become an increasingly trusted weapon in the Soviet arsenal designed, on the one hand, to block the coalescence of "closed" capitalist economic groupings that would automatically lead to a serious deterioration in the USSR's bargaining position and, on the other hand, to improve the USSR's commercial prospects by evening the balance through the device of guaranteeing the Russians access to the most generous business terms available. While there is no doubt that Soviet economic power has grown manifold since the pre-war period and that the Soviet Union today is no longer the beggar it once was in the international marketplace, the Kremlin's constant concern with the potential threat of bourgeois economic collusion directed against the interests of the USSR corroborates our impression of the Soviet Union as the underdog in the match, committed, *inter alia*, to revising the pertinent rules in order to tip the scales in its favor.

The emergence of the Third World, which shares the USSR's economic handicap *vis-à-vis* the industrialized Western community, has provided the Soviet Union with valuable allies in pursuing its plans for overhauling the structure of international trade and operating it in accordance with a new set of regulations. In posing as the devoted champion of the underdeveloped countries in their crusade for a bigger slice of the earth's economic pie, the Soviet Union has benefited from some marked differences in the political "life-styles" of the capitalist and socialist régimes. For example, the so-called "bourgeois" countries rely heavily on legislation to run their affairs, which means that, on the whole, their performance can readily be checked by consulting the statutory record. Discrepancies between how a capitalist government manages its import and export activities and whatever international yardstick is supposed to fix the appropriate standards are, thus, plainly visible and invite instant criticism. By contrast, the socialist states can afford to project the most benign official image since real authority lies with the administrative controls which function anonymously in the background where the entire process is safely hidden from prying eyes.

Take the following incident. After supporting the Third World's demands at UNCTAD's 1964 session for preferential treatment of exports from these countries, the Soviet Union rushed to comply with this "recommendatory norm"[69] by repealing on January 1, 1965, all customs duties on goods originating from developing states, including manufactured items. In light of the USSR's monopoly of foreign trade and the centralized nature of its foreign trade apparatus, the above reform *per se* signifies nothing, until and unless the corresponding bureaucratic agencies are instructed to step up purchases from the countries concerned. Absent a profit motive and given the constraints imposed by the national plan of economic development, a reduction in the price of certain foreign commodities alone cannot supply an effective incentive that would, by itself, result in a reorientation in the flow of trade. However, outwardly, Moscow's gesture overfulfilled expectations, and so the Russians can and do draw everybody's attention to the grand facade and bask in the admiration of those naive enough to confuse fiction with fact. In a private enterprise milieu, such a measure would be bound to have definite practical repercussions and awareness of the consequences has prompted Western governments to move slowly on this front, furnishing the Soviets with ample opportunity to lambast them for deliberately failing to meet their international "obligations."

The same can be said of regional integration schemes in East and West. The mechanism of rapprochement in the West is essentially dependent on legal techniques, and the law serves both to further convergence and consolidate the piecemeal gains registered in the drive toward unification. The gradual dismantling of internal customs barriers and the shift toward the free traffic of goods within the incipient community is an indispensable tool for promoting assimilation. The implementation of the project through legal methods is a highly visible undertaking, an easy target for sniping on grounds of instituting discrimination between states based on the criterion of membership in the association. Again, the socialist Commonwealth can avoid these pitfalls. Publicly, it can eschew introducing preferential arrangements relating to customs levies[70] and still induce greater economic rapport within the fraternity by pulling any one of a myriad administrative levers at its command and by this camouflaged route conveniently bypassing the overt legislative circuitry.

In going about this job, the Soviets, as noted, have proceeded in thoroughly unorthodox fashion, advancing views on how norms are created in international law that verge on the revolutionary and then seeking through equally novel means to translate these theories into practice. The results can, at best, be described as uncertain, although Soviet sources profess considerable satisfaction at the progress made in establishing a code of international public economic law, even if, as is occasionally conceded, so far only in embryonic form.[71] A curious aspect of the scenario is what made the Russians adopt an adversary approach in this episode. For it is clear that, with the aid of the Third World, the Soviets have here managed to fashion an impressive battering-ram. To many outside observers, however, a more conciliatory attitude would seem to hold greater promise of success, since they doubt that resort to confrontation is likely to win the Russians entrée into the bourgeoisie's good graces. This leaves us with the intriguing problem as to the reasons that might have motivated the Soviets to act as they have and the following hypotheses, singly or in combination, might help account for their mode of behavior:

1) Although the Soviets are concerned with improving their access to capitalist markets, they can weather the West's displeasure with these strong-arm tactics better than the developing countries can and are prepared to foot the bill, if need be, in exchange for the Third World's gratitude for loyally backing the latter's inflated demands, counting on a sense of mounting crisis to increase the underprivileged nations' desperation and commensurately enhance the USSR's ability to influence their conduct.

2) The more extreme the demands that the Soviet Union encourages the Third World to press against the West, the sharper the dividing line between the two antagonists and the more dramatic the Soviet Union's solidarity with the poorer nations and opposition to the "moneybags."

3) Losing hope of getting the West to treat the Soviets benignly through friendly suasion, the Soviets could be figuring that, in cooperation with the radical fringes of the international community, they would have a better chance of extorting concessions from the West and, indeed, that by swinging to the far pole they would guarantee that the middle-ground to which both sides would eventually have to gravitate to resolve the dispute would end up being more favorable to them.

Meantime, the stalemate continues, with the West taking cover behind old legal ramparts and the Soviets, jointly with their motley collection of allies, experimenting with new legal assault weapons in a bid to breach the walls and penetrate the inner citadel.[72] Whatever the outcome of the struggle, the legal arena is bound to witness some fierce skirmishing, and the relevant law's visage may and, in fact, is quite apt to emerge profoundly affected by the encounter.

NOTES

1. B. E. Shtein, *Torgovaia politika i torgovye dogovory Sovetskoi Rossii 1917-1922gg.* (Trade Policy and Trade Treaties of Soviet Russia 1917-1924), (Moscow-Petrograd, 1923), p. 193.

2. Article 9, Appendix 2, of the Peace Treaty between the RSFSR and the Central Powers of March 3, 1918. Text in *Dokumenty vneshnei politiki SSSR* (Documents of the Foreign Policy of the USSR), Vol. 1, pp. 125-146; Eng. transl. in L. Shapiro (ed.), *Soviet Treaty Series* (Washington, D. C., 1950), Vol. 1, pp. 5-11.

3. *Sobr. Zak. SSSR*, 1926, II, No. 26, item 170; *Dogovory o neitralitete, nenapadenii i o soglasitel'noi protsedure, zakliuchennye mezhdu Soiuzom SSR i inostrannymi gosudarstvami* (Treaties of Neutrality, Non-Aggression and on Conciliation Procedure Concluded between the USSR and Foreign States), (Moscow, 1934), pp. 100-101.

4. *Sbornik deistvuiushchikh dogovorov, soglashenii i konventsii, zakliuchennykh SSSR s inostrannymi gosudarstvami* (Collection of Treaties, Agreements, and Conventions Concluded by the USSR with Foreign States and in Force), Vol. 4, pp. 16-18 (hereafter abbr. as *SDD*); *League of Nations Treaty Series*, Vol. 53, pp. 387-396 (hereafter abbr. as *LNTS*).

5. *Sobr. Zak. SSSR*, 1928, II, No. 3, item 16; L. Shapiro (ed.), *op. cit.*, pp. 322-323.

6. *Izvestiia*, September 30, 1926; *Dogovory. . .*, pp. 48-50.

7. *SDD*, Vol. 7, pp. 6-8; L. Shapiro (ed.), *op. cit.* (Washington, D. C., 1955), Vol. 2, pp. 47-48.

8. *Sobr. Zak. SSSR*, 1932, II, No. 23, item 251; *LNTS*, Vol. 131, pp. 297-307.

9. *Izvestiia*, November 30, 1932; *Dogovory. . .*, pp. 132-134.

10. *Sobr. Zak. SSSR*, 1933, II, No. 30, item 261; *SDD*, Vol. 8, pp. 8-10.

11. Such clauses occasionally also cropped up in commercial pacts. See, for instance, Article 6 of the Temporary commercial agreement between the USSR and the United Kingdom of April 16, 1930. *SDD*, Vol. 6, pp. 37-43; L. Shapiro (ed.), *op. cit.*, Vol. 2, pp. 20-21.

12. Cf., I. M. Kulishcher, *Mezhdunarodnye torgovye dogovory* (International Trade Treaties), (Peterburg, 1922), Part II, pp. 40-119. Likewise, E. Korovin, "Uslovie naibolshego blagopriiatstvovaniia v dogovorakh RSFSR" (The Most-Favored-Nation Clause in the Treaties of the RSFSR), *Sovetskoe pravo*, 1922, No. 3, 30-41.

13. B. E. Shtein, *op. cit.*, pp. 124-125; 179; 182.

14. *Sobr. Zak. SSSR*, 1930, item 557.

15. *Sobr. Zak. SSSR*, 1936, No. 3, item 28.

16. *Sobr. Post. SSSR*, 1939, item 403.

17. *E.g.*, E. Usenko, "Printsip nediskriminatsii i printsip naibolshego blagopriiatstvovaniia v mezhdunarodnykh ekonomicheskikh otnosheniiakh," (The Principle of Non-Discrimination and the Principle of Most-Favored-Nation in International Economic Relations), *Vneshniaia torgovlia*, 1960, No. 7, 19 (hereafter abbr. as *VT*).

18. See E. Korovine, "Les Pactes de Non-Agression Economique et la Préservation de la Paix," *New Commonwealth Quarterly*, 1935, No. 3, 203-204.

19. *Vneshniaia politika SSSR*, Vol. 3, pp. 636-637.

20. E. Korovine, *op. cit.*, 206.

21. Cf., A. S. Korolenko, *Torgovye dogovory i soglasheniia SSSR s inostrannymi gosudarstvami* (Trade Treaties and Agreements of the USSR with Foreign States), (Moscow, 1953), p. 126.

22. Cited in I. Genin, "Krizis printsipa naibolshego blagopriiatstvovaniia v torgovoi politike kapitalisticheskikh gosudarstv," (Crisis of the Most-Favored-Nation Principle in the Trade Policy of the Capitalist States), *VT*, 1933, No. 19, 14-15.

23. E. S. Pchelintsev, "Mezhdunarodno-pravovye voprosy ekonomicheskogo i sotsial'nogo sotrudnichestva gosudarstv (Po materialam Ligi Natsii)," (International Law Questions of Economic and Social Cooperation of States (On the Data of the League of Nations)), in *Voprosy mezhdunarodnogo prava* (Questions of International Law), (Moscow, 1963), *UZ* Instituta mezhdunarodnykh otnoshenii, seriia iuridicheskaia, vyp. 16, pp. 177-217.

24. E. Korovine, *op. cit.*, 213-214.

25. See, for instance, V. I. Lisovskii, "Amerikanskii 'zakon 1948 goda ob ekonomicheskom sotrudnichestve' i mezhdunarodnoe pravo," (The American "1948 Law on Economic Cooperation" and International Law), *SGiP*, 1948, No. 8, 28-35; K. Ia. Chizhov, "Ekonomicheskaia ekspansiia SShA–ugroza suverenitetu gosudarstv," (The Economic Expansion of the USA–Threat to the Sovereignty of States), *ibid.*, 1951, No. 6, 47-61; *idem*, "Dva mirovykh rynka i sovremennoe mezhdunarodnoe pravo," (Two World Markets and Contemporary International Law), *ibid.*, 1953, No. 1, 36-51.

Interestingly enough, Soviet commentators now have to contend here with colleagues who strive to push back the record of Soviet initiatives on behalf of "progressive" norms of international economic law right back to the end of the Second World War in order to enhance the USSR's merits in this domain. See, for instance, V. Mordvinov, I. Ornatskii, "Organizatsiia Ob"edinennykh Natsii i problemy mezhdunarodnoi torgovli," (The United Nations Organization and Problems of International Trade), *VT*, 1960, No. 11, 3-4. On the other hand, V. Fomin, "Mezhdunarodnaia torgovlia–vazhnaia forma mirnogo sosushchestvovaniia gosudarstv," (International Trade–Important Form of Peaceful Coexistence of States), *VMU (pravo)*, 1965, No. 2, 36, correctly notes that ". . . in the past a definite negative influence was exerted on the business ties of our country by the cult of Stalin's personality. As is known, the influence of the cult of the personality expressed itself, in particular, in that the development of comprehensive mutually advantageous business ties between the USSR and capitalist countries was sometimes held back without any reason."

26. *Mezhdunarodnoe Ekonomicheskoe Soveshchanie v Moskve, 3-12 aprelia 1952g.* (International Economic Conference in Moscow, April 3-12, 1952), (Moscow, 1952). Likewise, V. I. Lisovskii, "Vneshneekonomicheskie sviazi Sovetskogo Soiuza sluzhat delu mira (K sozyvu Mezhdunarodnogo ekonomicheskogo soveshchaniia)," (The International Economic Ties of the Soviet Union Serve the Cause of Peace (On the Occasion of the Convocation of the International Economic Conference)), *SGiP*, 1952, No. 3, 23-29.

27. *E.g.*, Iu. N. Kapelinskii, *Torgovlia SSSR s kapitalisticheskimi stranami posle vtoroi mirovoi voiny* (Trade of the USSR with Capitalist Countries after the Second World War), (Moscow, 1970), pp. 20-27; N. G. Sysoev, A. A. Sentiuleva, *Obshcheevropeiskoe ekonomicheskoe sotrudnichestvo, Vozmozhnosti i deistvitelnost'* (All-European Economic Cooperation, Potentialities and Actuality), (Moscow, 1961), pp. 33-45.

28. *Kommunist*, 1961, No. 16, 52-53.

29. Cf., the statement by N. S. Khrushchev: "What is economic cooperation? It is trade. . . We are for trade, and that is peaceful cooperation." *Pravda*, March 24, 1960. The same theme was broached by Mikoian at the 20th Party Congress: "We are of the firm opinion that solid peaceful coexistence is unthinkable without trade, which is a good basis for it after the emergence of two world markets as well." *Rech na XX s"ezde*

KPSS (Speech at the 20th Congress of the CPSU), (Moscow, 1956), p. 17.

Also, V. Mordvinov, I. Ornatskii, *op. cit.*, 10; A. P. Korotaev, "Ekonomicheskie soglasheniia SSSR so slaborazvitymi stranami," (Economic Agreements of the USSR with Underdeveloped Countries), *VT*, 1959, No. 5, 43; V. M. Pochkaeva, *Pravovye voprosy ekonomicheskogo sotrudnichestva gosudarstv v sisteme OON, Ekonomicheskaia Komissiia OON dlia Evropy* (Legal Questions of Economic Cooperation of States in the UN System, The UN Economic Commission for Europe), (Moscow, 1962), pp. 4-5.

30. V. V. Fomin, *op. cit.*, 31, 35; *idem, OON i mezhdunarodnaia torgovlia (Pravovye voprosy)*, (The UN and International Trade (Legal Questions)), (Moscow, 1971), p. 15; B. M. Pinegin, *Nasushchnye problemy mezhdunarodnoi torgovli, K itogam Konferentsii OON po torgovle i razvitiiu* (Vital Problems of Internationl Trade (On the Results of the UN Conference on Trade and Development)), (Moscow, 1966), pp. 3, 63; I. S. Glagolev, *Mezhdunarodnaia bezopasnost' i ekonomicheskoe razvitie, Bor'ba SSSR za mir i sokrashchenie voennykh raskhodov* (International Cooperation and Economic Development, The Struggle of the USSR for Peace and the Reduction of Military Expenditures), (Moscow, 1974), p. 161.

31. V. Mordvinov, I. Ornatskii, *op. cit.*, 9-10; V. I. Lisovskii, *Mezhdunarodnoe pravo* (International Law), (Moscow, 1970), p. 263; G. M. Veliaminov, *Pravovoe regulirovanie mezhdunarodnoi torgovli, Opyt IuNKTAD* (Legal Regulation of International Trade, The Experience of UNCTAD), (Moscow, 1972), pp. 8, 162.

32. O. Bogdanov, "Printsip naibol'shego blagopriiatstvovaniia v torgovykh dogovorakh Anglii," (The Most-Favored-Nation Principle in the Trade Treaties of England), *VT*, 1960, No. 4, 34; O. Kozhevnikov, E. Medvedev, "Naibol'shee blagopriiatstvovanie–osnova uspeshnogo razvitiia vzaimovygodnoi torgovli," (Most-Favored-Nation Treatment–Basis of Successful Development of Mutually Beneficial Trade), *VT*, 1969, No. 3, 23.

33. V. N. Polezhaev, *Vneshniaia torgovlia–vazhnyi faktor mirnogo sosushchestvovaniia* (International Trade–Important Factor of Peaceful Coexistence), (Moscow, 1962), p. 5. Also, V. V. Fomin, *op. cit.*, note 25 above, 34.

34. *E.g.*, G. M. Veliaminov, *op. cit.*, pp. 177-178.

35. Cf., V. V. Fomin, *op. cit.*, note 25 above, 34, where the author notes that "the principle of equality of both systems penetrates the principle of equality of states." Likewise, R. L. Bobrov, "Printsip ravnopraviia dvukh sistem v sovremennom mezhdunarodnom prave," (The Principle of Equal Rights of the Two Systems in Contemporary International Law), *SGiP*, 1960, No. 11, 43-44.

36. G. M. Veliaminov, *op. cit.*, pp. 190-191. Likewise, B. M. Pinegin, *op. cit.*, pp. 73-83.

37. G. M. Veliaminov, *op. cit.*, p. 222. See, too, A. S. Korolenko, *op. cit.*, p. 126; V. N. Polezhaev, *op. cit.*, p. 10; B. M. Pinegin, *op. cit.*, p. 93.

38. V. N. Polezhaev, *op. cit.*, p. 6. Also, V. V. Fomin, *op. cit.*, note 30 above, pp. 139-141.

39. V. V. Fomin, *op. cit.*, note 30 above, p. 12.

40. V. Mordvinov, I. Ornatskii, *op. cit.*, 8.

41. For example, M. Pochkaeva, "Diskriminatsiia v torgovle i mezhdunarodnoe pravo," (Discrimination in Trade and International Law), *VT*, 1968, No. 9, 20; *Kurs mezhdunarodnogo prava* (Course Book on International Law), (Moscow, 1968), Vol. 6, p. 230.

42. See, V. I. Menzhinskii, I. V. Shapovalov, "Razrabotka v OON pravovykh printsipov mezhdunarodnogo torgovogo sotrudnichestva," (Elaboration in the UN of the Legal Principles of International Trade Cooperation), *Pravovedenie*, 1969, No. 3, 104.

43. *Ibid.* In similar vein, G. Veliaminov, "Diskriminatsiia–tormoz mezhdunarodnoi torgovli," (Discrimination–Brake on International Trade), *VT*, 1971, No. 11, 48, 50.

44. Cf., G. M. Veliaminov, *op. cit.*, note 31 above, p. 190; *idem*, *op. cit.*, note 43 above, 51.

45. V. V. Fomin, *op. cit.*, note 30 above, p. 47; G. M. Veliaminov, *op. cit.*, note 31 above, p. 223. Compare, E. T. Usenko, "Most-Favored-Nation Treatment in Soviet-American Trade Relations," *Denver Journal of International Law and Policy*, 1975, No. 5, 243: "The significance of this [the most-favored-nation] treatment in international trade is so great that, without its establishment and observance, normal relations cannot exist between the countries concerned."

46. E. T. Usenko, *op. cit.*, note 17 above, 21-22.

47. *Kurs mezhdunarodnogo prava*, p. 259. Equally obscure is the sense of the statement on p. 260: "The most-favored-nation treatment is a principle of a high order presupposing, as a direct pre-condition for its existence, observance of the principle of non-discrimination. Most-favored-nation treatment is a supplement to non-discrimination or, in other words, a sort of 'superstructure' on it. That is why violation of the principle of non-discrimination is, at the same time, also a denial of the principle of most-favored-nation treatment. But from this, it follows that both principles represent a barrier in the path of discrimination." One can only wonder if the tortured style is an unwitting true mirror here of the violence done to substance.

A minority view in Soviet legal literature has sought to avoid these complications by flatly equating the most-favored-nation (mfn) treatment with non-discrimination. See, for example, D. M. Genkin, "Printsip naibol'shego blagopriiatstvovaniia v torgovykh dogovorakh gosudarstv," (The Most-Favored-Nation Principle in the Trade Treaties of States), *SGiP*, 1958, No. 9, 22, 26. This approach has been criticized by the majority apparently out of considerations that, by reducing non-discrimination to mfn, the Soviet Union would be deprived of a second line of defense. Should it fail to obtain mfn, there would be no argument left for the right to equal treatment under the common régime applicable to trading partners without special treaty arrangements.

48. *E.g.*, V. V. Fomin, *op. cit.*, note 30 above, p. 11; G. M. Veliaminov, *op. cit.*, note 31 above, pp. 19-21.

49. V. V. Fomin, *op. cit.*, note 30 above, pp. 27-28; *idem*, "OON i nekotorye pravovye voprosy mezhdunarodnoi torgovli," (The UN and Some Legal Questions of International Trade). *Sovetskii ezhegodnik mezhdunarodnogo prava 1964-1965* (Soviet Yearbook of International Law 1964-1965), (Moscow, 1966), p. 320 (hereafter abbr. as *SEMP*); S. B. Krylov, *Istoriia sozdaniia OON* (History of the Creation of the UN), (Moscow, 1960), p. 65.

50. V. V. Fomin, *op. cit.*, note 25 above, 36. Also, *idem, op. cit.*, note 49 above, pp. 320-321, and V. I. Menzhinskii, I. V. Shapovalov, *op. cit.*, 107.

51. M. Pochkaeva, *op. cit.*, note 41 above, 20; V. V. Fomin, *op. cit.*, note 30 above, pp. 31-32; G. M. Veliaminov, *op. cit.*, note 31 above, pp. 208-213.

52. V. V. Fomin, *op. cit.*, note 25 above, 36; *idem, op. cit.*, note 49 above, pp. 321-322.

53. V. Mordvinov, I. Ornatskii, *op. cit.*, 9; V. V. Fomin, *op. cit.*, note 49 above, p. 323; B. M. Pinegin, *op. cit.*, pp. 125-151; A. Ia. Nekrasov, *SSSR i razvivaiushchiesia strany v OON* (The USSR and the Developing Countries in the UN), (Moscow, 1970), p. 8; *OON i aktual'nye mezhdunarodnye problemy (k 20-letiiu OON)*, (The UN and Current International Problems (On the Occasion of the UN's 20th Anniversary)), (Moscow, 1965), pp. 213-229; Iu. Ogarev, "Sozdanie mezhdunarodnoi torgovoi organizatsii–nastoiatel'noe trebovanie zhizni" (Creation of the International Trade Organization–Insistent Requirement of Life), *Mirovaia ekonomika i mezhdunarodnye otno-*

sheniia, 1964, No. 2, 82-94; V. V. Fomin, "K voprosu o sozdanii Mezhdunarodnoi torgovoi organizatsii," (On the Question of Creation of an International Trade Organization), *SGiP*, 1965, No. 5, 125-130; *Sovetskii Soiuz i Organizatsiia Ob"edinennykh Natsii (1961-1965gg.)*, (The United Nations and the United Nations Organization 1961-1965), (Moscow, 1968), pp. 302-316.

54. V. I. Menzhinskii, I. V. Shapovalov, *op. cit.*, 102.

55. See, for instance, L. Lobanov, "Konferentsiia OON po torgovle i razvitiiu," (The UN Conference on Trade and Development), *SEMP 1964-1965*, pp. 405-409; V. Spandarian, "K itogam Konferentsii OON po torgovle i razvitiiu," (On the Results of the UN Conference on Trade and Development), *VT*, 1964, No. 8, 3-6.

56. Cf., G. M. Veliaminov, *op. cit.*, note 31 above, p. 224, where the author claims that UNCTAD's action (in 1964) became "a landmark point on the road to the universalization of the principle of most-favored-nation treatment and its progressive investiture with a *jus cogens* quality." Also, *idem*, "Printsip naibol'shego blagopriiatstvovaniia," (The Most-Favored-Nation Principle), *VT*, 1970, No. 10, 50.

57. G. M. Veliaminov, *op. cit.*, note 56 above, 51.

58. M. Pochkaeva, *op. cit.*, note 41 above, 23-24; G. M. Veliaminov, *op. cit.*, note 56 above, 51-52.

59. V. Mordvinov, I. Ornatskii, *op. cit.*, 3; B. M. Pinegin, *op. cit.*, pp. 102-104.

60. *E.g.*, S. Mai, "O rezhime naibol'shego blagopriiatstvovaniia," (On the Most-Favored-Nation Regime), *VT*, 1955, No. 1, 18.

61. *Kurs mezhdunarodnogo prava*, pp. 267-269. See, too, G. M. Veliaminov, "The Legal Basis of All-European Economic Co-operation," in *All-European Economic Co-operation* (Moscow, n.d.), p. 77.

62. V. V. Fomin, *op. cit.*, note 30 above, p. 156; B. M. Pinegin, *op. cit.*, pp. 93-94; V. Gorskii, "Torgovaia politika EES–orudie diskriminatsii sotsialisticheskikh stran," (The Trade Policy of the EEC–Weapon of Discrimination against the Socialist Countries), *VT*, 1969, No. 12, 23-27.

63. V. I. Menzhinskii, I. V. Shapovalov, *op. cit.*, 107, where the authors argue that the principles adopted at the Geneva conference represent, in the main, either universally recognized principles of international law or propositions stemming from these principles and developing them. In both cases, they claim, "the juridically obligatory nature of these principles for states is unquestionable, inasmuch as the effect of universally recognized norms of international law extends to the entire aggregate of international relations, including the commercial ones as well." Hence, they conclude, "the fact that individual developed capitalist countries voted at the conference against some of these principles or abstained in no manner frees them from the duty to observe these principles because they belong to general international law–*jus cogens.*"

In similar vein, V. V. Fomin, *op. cit.*, note 49 above, p. 328, although the author adds that the Geneva conference also advanced new principles, including a new interpretation of the principles of mutual advantage and most-favored-nation treatment, exceptions to the mfn principle and a completely new interpretation of the principle of freedom of trade (Third General Principle). These new principles, according to him, "acquire an important moral-political significance." In his subsequent writings, V. V. Fomin tilts further in favor of the juridical force of the majority of the principles endorsed by the Geneva and New Delhi conferences of UNCTAD. See, for instance, his *IuNKTAD: mezhdunarodnaia organizatsiia po torgovle i razvitiiu* (UNCTAD: International Organization for Trade and Development), (Moscow, 1970), p. 76, and *op. cit.*, note 30 above, pp. 115-117. G. Veliaminov, *op. cit.*, note 43 above, 50, attributes to UNCTAD's decisions aimed against discrimination "important moral-political character" and "great juridical significance." In his book, *op. cit.*, note 31 above, pp. 115-117, Veliaminov takes a somewhat more equivocal position, but ultimately concludes that, although the countries that did not vote in favor of particular principles at the Geneva conference and did not formally recognize them, nevertheless they "recognized the effectiveness of these principles" at the New Delhi meeting, and generally speaks of the normative character of the decisions and recommendations emanating from the 1964 and 1968 sessions and "their definite recommendatorily obligatory significance." V. M. Gevorgian, in E. P. Pletnev (ed.), *Diplomatiia i ekonomicheskoe razvitie* (Diplomacy and International Development), (Moscow, 1965), pp. 212, 228, flatly affirms the normative nature of these documents and their binding character, at least for the states that attended the meetings.

64. On occasion, one also senses in the writings of Soviet specialists a readiness to concede the novelty of many of these ideas in order better to contrast the "bad old days" with the "improvements" now effected under Soviet prodding and, of course, to enhance the USSR's merits in that connection. See, for instance, B. M. Pinegin, *op. cit.*, p. 127. Similarly, V. I. Menzhinskii, I. V. Shapovalov, *op. cit.*, 105, note the "further development and concretization" of the right of each state freely to dispose of its natural resources through the addition of the right freely to trade and the new principle of international law concerning mutual benefit. V. V. Fomin, *op. cit.*, note 30 above, p. 110, speaks of the conference "deciphering" the principles of the UN Charter and, in some instances, supplementing them with reference to the international trade relations of states.

65. *Kurs mezhdunarodnogo prava*, p. 234. V. M. Gevorgian, *op. cit.*, p. 215, goes so far as to claim that the attempt of the Western powers to cite their past treaty practice regarding foreign trade "as some kind of source of law . . . is nothing else than a bid to raise inequality to the level of an international legal principle" which "contradicts the UN Charter and international law as a whole." More cautiously, G. Veliaminov, *op. cit.*, note 43 above, 51, observes the importance of UNCTAD's rearticulation of certain older rules to prevent, for example, "the possibility of incorrect interpretation of the principle of non-discrimination."

66. Thus, see B. M. Pinegin, *op. cit.*, p. 138; V. V. Fomin, *op. cit.*, note 49 above, p. 328, and "Razvitie mirovoi torgovli i printsipy mezhdunarodnogo prava," (The Development of International Trade and the Principles of International Law), *SEMP 1968* (Moscow, 1969), p. 287.

67. V. M. Gevorgian, *op. cit.*, p. 214; V. I. Menzhinskii, I. V. Shapovalov, *op. cit.*, 104; V. V. Fomin, *op. cit.*, note 30 above, p. 124.

68. Cf., the interpretation proposed by V. I. Menzhinskii, I. V. Shapovalov, *op. cit.*, 107, as cited in note 63 above, to get around this difficulty.

69. The concept of "recommendatory norm" formulated by Veliaminov represents a curious innovation. The notion itself seems to rest on a contradiction in terms in that a norm is either binding, in which case it is not recommendatory, or it is recommendatory, in which case it is neither a norm nor binding. The author's own thesis is somewhat confused, but appears to boil down to the following. The "recommendatory norms" elaborated by UNCTAD, *i.e.*, those whose legal status is somewhat uncertain because of their novel character, *ought* to be given effect by all participating states and so it is incumbent on the states concerned to take appropriate measures to put them into practice. If and when a state proceeds accordingly, other states do not have the right to object to the impact of its action on their interests. For example, UNCTAD called on every developed state to adopt a preferential treatment for the foreign trade of underdeveloped nations, without extending similar privileges to developed countries, and when an industrialized state, say, the Soviet Union, revises its trade rules in line with this recommendation, other industrialized states ostensibly cannot protest against such steps. Why this should be so, however, it is not clear: if the scheme is not based on an existing

rule of international law and merely amounts to an option, no matter how authoritatively endorsed, there is no reason for a third country whose interests are adversely affected by the project not to take issue by citing contrary provisions of positive international law. *Viz.*, G. M. Veliaminov, *op. cit.*, note 31 above, pp. 122-123, 141-145, and 227; *idem, op. cit.*, note 43 above, 51, and "Konferentsiia OON po torgovle i razvitiiu i mezhdunarodnoe pravo," (The UN Conference on Trade and Development and International Law), *SEMP 1969* (Moscow, 1970), pp. 157-161.

70. G. Veliaminov, *op. cit.*, note 56 above, 51.

71. V. M. Gevorgian, *op. cit.*, pp. 212, 230; V. I. Menzhinskii, I. V. Shapovalov, *op. cit.*, 107, 109; V. I. Lisovskii, *op. cit.*, note 31 above, p. 259; V. V. Fomin, *op. cit.*, note 30 above, p. 105; B. M. Pinegin, *op. cit.*, pp. 126ff.; G. M. Veliaminov, *op. cit.*, note 31 above, pp. 16, 151-155; M. Pochkaeva, "Mezhgosudarstvennye ekonomicheskie otnosheniia i mezhdunarodnoe pravo," (Inter-State Economic Relations and International Law), *VT*, 1970, No. 4, 55.

72. For an eloquent plea by a leading Polish international lawyer in favor of the restructuring of the existing format of international economic activity, see M. Lachs, "Natsionalizatsiia i razvitie mezhdunarodnykh ekonomicheskikh otnoshenii," (Nationalization and the Development of International Economic Relations), in *Problemy mezhdunarodnogo prava* (Problems of International Law), (Moscow, 1961), p. 154.

IMPROVING THE LEGAL MECHANISMS FOR ECONOMIC CHANGE*

Peter B. Maggs

1. The Problem

How can Soviet law be made into an effective mechanism for engineering the rapid modernization of the economy of the USSR? The following discussion will examine the difficulties involved in making Soviet economic law a dynamic instrumentality for change, and the attempts being made to overcome these difficulties.

Legal systems in general and European legal systems in particular are fundamentally conservative by nature. The European tradition of codification is antithetical to rapid change. The effort required for proper codification means that a good code cannot be drafted overnight, and means that a code, once enacted, is typically expected to stay in force for decades if not for centuries. Such methods may have been satisfactory in prior eras, but they face serious problems in a society with rapidly changing economic structures. Knowledge of the law has traditionally been transmitted during a few years of formal legal education. Lawyers in the past have expected much of this knowledge to last a lifetime. Thus changes must be made not only in the laws, but in the system of dissemination of information about the laws and of legal education, if those laws are to be executed in practice.

Like most industrial societies, the Soviet Union has concentrated production under a few large organizations. While these organizations are government ministries rather than private corporations, in many ways they have both the incentives and the means to resist legal change characteristic of the giant corporation of the United States. What has happened to date has been that, while the scholars in Moscow have been debating such questions as the need for an economic code, nearly all of the actual operative rules have been made in the form of regulations issued by the ministries affected.[1] This self-regulation has had both positive and negative effects. The rules have

* The author wishes to acknowledge the extremely useful criticisms and suggestions of Professor Stanislaw Pomorski and the other participants in the discussion of this paper at the conference on Law and Social Engineering in the USSR.

shown real understanding of the problems involved, for those who have drafted them have been involved in the day-to-day operation of the particular industries. However, the individual ministries have consistently used the power of self-regulation delegated to them to further their own interests at the expense of other state organizations and/or the Soviet public, and they have largely ignored the legitimate needs of outsiders to know the content of the regulations.

Soviet writers on legal subjects are well aware of the maxim *nemo judex in causa sua*, and they frequently criticize the present locus of the rule making power for such matters as transportation and electricity. But is there a better solution? American experience has seemed to show that the choice may not be between self-regulation and impartial regulation, but between self-regulation and de-regulation with freedom of entry. Time and again, our experience with "independent" regulatory agencies has been that they have come under the influence of the regulated industry, and have ended up as the spokesman and protector of existing industry interests. On the other hand, regulatory bodies that umpire between strong competing interests may combine the ideal attributes of knowledgeability and impartiality. There are a number of different patterns. The one seen, probably quite correctly, as ideal by Soviet legal analysts is that of State Arbitration (*Gosarbitrazh*), which, being attached directly to the Council of Ministers of the USSR, is both legally and actually independent of any particular industrial ministry.[2] What is seen as the worst example are industries such as electricity, where an industrial ministry has a monopoly on the production of a product or service, sets the legal regulations governing its sale, and sells it under those regulations.

In addition to more conservative elements which it shares with other European legal systems, the Soviet legal system is subject to a number of additional conservative forces. These include traditions of secrecy, the tendency to treat legislation as embodying scientific truths, restrictions on freedom of discussion, and a veneration for deceased leaders and the elderly. These forces trace their origins far back in Russian history and are unlikely to be dissipated soon.

2. Economic Legislation as an Information System

Some Soviet commentators have recently suggested an entirely new approach to the whole question of economic legislation. This approach involves the treatment of the system of economic law as a system for the gathering and transmission of information, a system many of whose functions will be automated over the next few years.[3] The advocates of this approach contend that reform efforts can only be succesful if all of the elements of the information systems are taken into account. In many ways, the current reform efforts are finally being directed in a coordinated manner throughout this information system. This approach gives them some hope of succeeding where other attempts have failed. The discussion below will show how efforts at improving the codification, publication, distribution, and indexing of legislation, as well as the education and placements of specialists in economic law are being coordinated.

The Need for Legislation Reform

"Is the department of codification asleep. . . ?"[4] *–Lenin*

Soviet and foreign observers are universally in agreement with the assessment of the state of Soviet economic legislation given in a 1974 speech by General Secretary Brezhnev:[5]

> "Unfortunately, for a long time these questions have not been allotted enough attention, and as a result many unsolved problems have piled up. In every branch of the national economy, thousands of different rules and instructions are in force. Just try to figure them out! Moreover, many of these instructions have become outdated, contain unjustified limitations, and overdetailed regulation."

However, there are broad disagreements over the causes of the cures for this situation. Within the Soviet Union, various groups appear to be actively maneuvering to obtain an improved position in the new order of economic legislation which Secretary Brezhnev has been demanding.

The problems of organization of the Soviet system of legislation are by no means peculiar to the Soviet regime or to the Russian people. Similar problems existed in Czarist Russia, and similar problems exist in other countries at a like stage of economic development. Mikhail Speransky, the great Russian codifier of the ninetheenth century,[6] discussing how the legislation of Russia was becoming uncontrollable, made remarks which might well be applied to the situation in the USSR of the 1970's.[7]

> "Here it would not be excessive to note that, if the edition of a Complete Collection of our Laws at the present time already has presented not insignificant difficulties, then after the passage of a few years it would be still more complicated, and finally it might become almost unattainable."

The problem seems to be common in countries whose economic development has outstripped their legal development. Compare for instance the following description of the situation in Brazil.[8]

> "Instead of amending basic code provisions, Brazilian practice has been to adopt supplemental legislation, which, in turn is amended and re-amended. Generally one is forced to read a host of separate statutes

> and decrees regulating a given subject (and many others as well) and then undertake the jigsaw job of piecing together the provisions still in force to arrive at the governing law."

However, the present state of the system of organization and communication of economic legislation in the USSR has gone through a somewhat unusual evolution. In many developing countries, there has been steady progress from a system of uncodified, unpublished, and unindexed economic regulations to a system where such regulations are codified, published, and indexed. The Soviet Union has gone through a series of cycles, with a disruption of the system of dissemination of economic regulations in the 1917 revolution followed by the reestablishment of a workable system by the late 1920's and early 1930's, which in turn was largely destroyed by pervasive secrecy and the shift of emphasis to criminal law in the Stalinist period of the late 1930's and the 1940's. The effects of Stalinism on the system of organization and dissemination of information about economic regulation were so devastating that it will be the end of the 1970's before the degree of order prevailing in 1907 or 1937 is again reached.

Soviet scholars now see a steady improvement ahead for the system of organizing and disseminating economic legislation. The successful completion of the *Collection of Laws in Force of the USSR* is to be followed over the next 5 to 10 years by the preparation of a *Code of Laws of the USSR*; access to legislation is to be improved by the introduction of a modern computerized retrieval system. New cadres of specialists in economic laws are to be trained. It remains to be seen if the historical cyclical pattern will reassert itself, or if the technical organization of Soviet legislation will in fact continually be improved.

The Economic Law Debate

There have been repeated disputes among Soviet legal scholars over the question of whether the law governing economic regulations should be organized separately into some sort of economic code, or should be codified together with other law under traditional legal categories such as civil and administrative law. Both to the outside observer and, apparently, to top Soviet Party leaders, this debate has appeared to have had the very negative effect of distracting attention to highly theoretical problems while ignoring the immediate needs of the economy for the rapid achievement of some sort of ordering of the mass of economic legislation, its publication, and its widespread distribution. The Party-enforced deadlines for the publication of the *Collection of Laws in Force of the USSR* and the *Code of Laws of the USSR* seem to have been successful in forcing Soviet legal scholars to turn at least some of their attention to the prompt solution of practical problems of the organization of legislation.

Only a brief interpretative account of the history of the development of the Soviet economic law theory will be given here, both because so much has been written on the subject elsewhere,[9] and because of the contention, outlined above, that the whole debate is actually peripheral to what is happening in the reform of economic legislation. In an article published in 1970, Dr. Hans-Georg Heinrich divides the development of Soviet theory on economic law into the "classical" period of the 1930's; the post-Stalin debates ending with the passage of the Fundamentals of Civil Legislation in 1961; and the revival of the debate after the 1965 economic reforms.[10] The revived debate begun in 1965 still continues, now centering around the draft code of economic law published in 1970[11] and debated in various fora since then.[12]

The economic law school of the late 1920's through the late 1930's was far more radical in its ideas than have been any of its successors, and it suffered a far more radical fate. When such legal theorists as Gintsburg, Pashukanis, Stuchka, and Amfiteatrov split economic law away from civil law into an independent discipline, they did so with the express purpose of preparing for the withering away of civil law governing the legal relations between private individuals and private property ownership. As John Hazard pointed out in his introduction to a volume on Soviet legal philosophy, their attempts to carry out their theories in practice posed a direct threat to Stalin's new emphasis on material incentives.[13] The post-Stalin advocates of the creation of a system of economic law separate from the system of civil law have carefully avoided any hint of a connection between the creation of a separate field of law dealing largely with private property rights and an intention to limit those rights. Rather, the proponents of the economic law approach have insisted that their sole goal was to improve the functioning of the Soviet economy.

The first great debate over economic law was settled by Vyshinskii's purge of the economic law advocates in the late 1930's. Not surprisingly, the issue was not raised again until after Stalin's death, when a second debate opened in connection with a discussion of the form that the recodification of Soviet civil legislation was to take.[14] This debate was ended only temporarily with the decision to include economic law matters in the new civil codes of the 1960's.

Beginning soon after the ouster of Khrushchev in the mid-1960's, the issue was raised again and found a vigorous champion in Professor V. V. Laptev of the Institute of State and Law whose concepts were, in turn, strongly opposed by a number of Soviet scholars, particularly Professors S. N. Bratus' and O. S. Ioffe. Two main topics took on importance in the economic law debate which has been conducted since 1965. The *first* was the issue of whether or not an "economic code" should be enacted to serve as the central legal document in a reformed system of economic legislation; *second*, if such a document was enacted, should it precede or follow the enactment of laws consolidating other branches of economic law.

The view that the first task of economic law reform is the enactment of an economic code has been strongly supported by Professor V. V. Laptev.[15] Others have argued for enactment of Fundamental Principles of Economic Legislation.[16] They and Laptev agree that the traditional categories of civil and administrative law are outdated and that a new category of law—"economic law"—has arisen.

As proposed by Laptev, the Economic Code would consist of the following divisions:[17]

I. General Provisions
II. Participants in Economic Relations
III. Property of Economic Organizations
IV. Planning of Economic Activity
V. General Provisions on Economic Obligations
VI. Economic Sanctions
VII. Research and Technological Work Activity
VIII. Construction Activity
IX. Supply and Sales Activity
X. Freight Transfer Activity
XI. Credit and Accounting Activity
XII. Other Economic Obligations
XIII. Protection of Economic Rights

Laptev argues that a new code or fundamental principles of economic law should be at the center of the whole economic law reform effort. Some critics have noted that the draft code cannot really serve as the center of such a reform because it excludes such important branches of economic law as financial, land, labor, and collective farm law. Laptev answers these critics with the argument that no general principles could be developed if so broad an area were covered.

Arguing against the existing scheme of the dominance of civil and administrative law, Laptev suggests that the combining of legal rules governing state enterprises and citizens in a single code leads to such a high level of abstraction that the provisions are of little use.

Furthermore, he argues that the general principles of civil law are often found in the republic codes and thus lack the uniformity necessary for economic legislation. For the same reason, he opposes the suggestion that economic legislation follow the pattern of other recent codifications with Fundamental Principles enacted at the all-union level, followed by codes at the republic level.

Much of the recent debates has turned on the issue of whether or not, in fact, "economic law" exists as its own principles. Laptev argues that it does and includes such basic concepts as those of "economic organization," "economic competence," "economic obligation," and "economic sanction."

The opposing camp has presented numerous counterarguments.[18] It contends that Laptev is mistaking an area of social activity for a branch of law, and that economic law lacks the basic unifying characteristic of legal technique that is necessary for a branche of law.[19] Thus, for instance, they argue that civil law is characterized by the regulation of horizontal relations between parties such as contractual rights, while administrative law is regulated by vertical relations such as the authority to give commands. In a 1959 pamphlet, Ioffe traced back some of these views to their Western European origins.[20]

The anti-codification school argues that economic law lacks any general principles suitable for incorporation in a general part of the code.[21] Many of the reasons they advance are essentially similar to those advanced in arguing that economic law is not an independent branch of the law. Since economic law involves a large number of different techniques of regulation, and since general parts of a code should be based on regulatory approaches applicable throughout the code, there is no room for a general part in an economic code, yet it is of the essence of a code to have a general part.

As a final, fall-back argument, the opposition argues that codification is premature. First, they say, the various branches of economic law, such as construction law, banking law, etc., should be made the subject of comprehensive legislative enactments. Only then, they suggest, in light of the content of those new legislative enactments, would it be possible to make an informed decision on whether or not there should be an economic code, and only with this preliminary work done, could a useful code be produced.[22] They argue that the emphasis of recent Party and government decrees on broad areas of legislative reform and the omission of any command to issue an economic code favor their position.[23] In a joint article, Professor V. P. Gribanov, chairman of the civil law department of the Moscow University Law Faculty, and Professor O. S. Ioffe, chairman of the civil law department of the Leningrad University Law Faculty, argue that the whole thrust of the new decree is that reform is needed throughout the socialist sector, not just in those areas covered by the draft economic code.[24] They point out also that the area of finance, which is specifically mentioned as one of the high priority areas, does not even fall within the area covered by the draft code. They also point out that the Labor Code, mentioned in the decree as one of the recent achievements, does not fall within the economic code. The authors of this article also put considerable emphasis on the new role of the Ministry of Justice, perhaps wishing to emphasize the correspondingly reduced influence of the Institute of State and Law of the USSR Academy of Sciences, which has been the center of the "economic law" school.

The Current State of Economic Legislation

Secretary Brezhnev's criticism of the state of Soviet economic law is well deserved; however, in fairness he should have mentioned the major progress that has taken place in the area of economic legislation in the last dozen years. While no basic code of economic legislation has been enacted and the *Code of Laws of the USSR* is not yet completed, major progress has been made in codification. There has been some success in attacking both of the problems mentioned in the Brezhnev speech, the disorganization of legal rules and their multiplicity.

The first steps involved the passage of a large number of major legislative acts dealing with specific organizations, institutions, and areas of economic law. These acts include, to name but a few of the more important ones: the Statute on the Production Combine,[25] the Statute on State Arbitration,[26] the Statute on the Procedure for Presentation and Consideration of Claims,[27] the Statute on Discoveries, Inventions, and Innovation Proposals,[28] the Statute on the Permanent Production Conference,[29] the General Statute on All-Union and Republican Industrial Combines,[30] the Decree on Certain Measures for the Further Improvement of the Management of Industry,[31] the Fundamental Principle of Legislation on Labor,[32] the Fundamental Principle of Land Legislation,[33] and the Statute on the Socialist State Production Enterprise.[34]

Several important trends of Soviet legislative reform in the 1970's may be traced to a Party and Government decree of December 23, 1970.[35] This decree gave a more important role to the Ministry of Justice in legislative reform, provided for the publication of a *Collection of Legislation in Force of the USSR*, and called for the ending of the Stalinist secrecy which had surrounded much of the area of current economic regulation. Some of the improvement in access to legislation was immediate, with the beginning of publication of the *Bulletin of Normative Acts of Ministries and Departments of the USSR*, and with the opening of the *Collection of Decrees of the Government of the USSR* to general subscription; some took years, as in the case of the longer-term project of the *Collection of Legislation in Force of the USSR*.

On June 25, 1975, the Central Committee of the CPSU and the Council of Ministers of the USSR, responding to Brezhnev's criticism, issued a joint decree demanding a speed-up of the process of putting economic law in order.[36] It certainly appeared that, as in 1959, the Party leadership had lost patience with some of the scholastic argument that was going on in legal circles and was seeking to get some clear steps taken to clean up the economic legislation mess. The first priority task was set as the "elimination of the multiplicity of legal acts on one and the same question, containing contradictions, discrepancies, unjustified restrictions, and petty regulation cramping the initiative of enterprises and organizations." The decree also picked particular areas for priority: planning, construction, finances and credit, material and technical supply.

The Ministry of Justice was given a new and very important role as the coordinating body for this project. The Ministry, in cooperation with other interested agencies, was to coordinate the work, setting up legislative drafting plans for the coming 2 or 3 years, and drawing up guidelines for the drafting process. The Ministry, along with the All-Union Institute of Soviet Legislation, was also to speed up work on the *Collection of Legislation in Force of the USSR* so that the whole collection would be published by the end of 1976.

The process of law reform now taking place follows closely the pattern of nineteenth century codification. This is first the compilation of a complete collection of laws, followed by the publication of a *Code of Laws* (*Svod Zakonov*). However, those responsible for this process generally agree that it would be impossible for the *Code of Laws* to contain more than the highlights of economic legislation. Therefore, this stage will have only limited effect on organizing and clarifying economic legislation.[37]

Another reform was meant to correct a problem long complained about by Soviet legal scholars, that of *sub silentio* repeal of regulations. Once again, a requirement was emphasized that, "as a rule," drafts of legislation submitted to the Council of Ministers should contain a list of legislation to be repealed. Particular attention was given to those agencies such as *Gosplan*, *Gosstroi*, and the financial agencies which have the power to issue legal acts binding on other governmental agencies. These organizations were required to put their own houses in order during 1976. The republics were instructed to carry on a similar reform.

The 1970 and 1975 decrees mark a major shift in the *de facto* locus of legislative power. The Ministry of Justice, which was only reestablished in 1970, is given the primary responsibility for coordinating the drafting of economic legislation. No mention is made of the law schools, whose professors played a major role in the drafting of previous economic legislation. The Ministry appears not only to have received a guiding role in the effort to reform economic legislation, but also to have ensured itself a much more important place in the development of new economic legislation.[38]

Recodification of Regulations at the Ministry Level

Perhaps the greatest flaw of the advocates of the "economic law" school is that they tend to underestimate the great *de facto* power of the various ministries.[39] The following incident illustrates this power. The Nevinnomysskii Chemical Combine brought an action in *arbitrazh* for 34,757 rubles in damages caused by a power outage against the Nevinnomysskii State District Electric Power Station. It sought not only the penalty provided by the Rules on the Use of Electrical Energy of eight times the normal electric charge for the time of a power outage, but also sought to recover the actual damages resulting from the power outage under the general rules on damages of Article 36 of the Fundamentals of Civil Legislation. *Arbitrazh* held that the provisions of the Rules did not exclude the additional recovery of actual damages and ruled for the plaintiff. A few days later the Ministry of Energy and Electrification of the USSR added a new Paragraph 81-a to the Rules, providing that recovery should be limited to the penalty stated in the rules.[40] This is but one example of the insistence by powerful ministries upon making the rules governing their affairs, and in many cases in making the rules governing their relationships with other ministries. The unrealistic aspect of the idea of an economic code is that it would set up rules, such as the general right to recover actual damages in case of breach of contract, which would deprive these ministries of their favored position. Of course, it would be possible to adopt an Economic Code which had a number of escape clauses allowing ministries to pass regulations derogating from the Code, however such a code would be of much less value as means of unification and reform of the law.

Thus, what real reform is taking place and is likely to take place is at the Ministry level. There will be a *Code of Laws of the USSR*, and there may be an Economic Code; however, codification at this level is likely to be far less significant in solving the problems of economic law than the quieter work now going forward in numerous individual ministries and organizations to recodify, index, and publish departmental regulations. The problem is complicated by three factors. *First*, most ministries have the power to issue regulations within the sphere of their competence that are binding upon organizations subordinate to other ministries. *Second*, many regulations are issued jointly by several ministries, or organizations, and require the cooperation of these organizations for their reform and codification. *Third*, many regulations issued by no longer existing organizations, such as the Council of Labor and Defense, the Economic Conference (which was attached to the Russian Republic Council of People's Commissars from 1920 to 1936), and the Supreme Council of the National Economy are still in force. A complete solution of the problem of administrative codification in the last two cases may eventually require the creation of some sort of centralized codification agency.

The State Bank is a prime example of those agencies which have the power to regulate both their own internal affairs and their relations with others. The main function of the Bank is supervision of the legality of economic transactions. The Bank is ensured the chance to play this supervisory role in almost all transactions because of legislation requiring that payments be made through the Bank, and because working capital of enterprises and economic associations is kept so low that they must rely upon bank loans for their regular operations. Its all-pervading supervisory function has made the State Bank the source of an immense mass of economic legislation. Not long ago, there were over 80 official bank "instructions" in force and over 1000 "Circular Letters." Major recodification efforts have been underway at the Bank to simplify this situation. The Bank has adopted a plan for the reissue and unification of its instructions during the five-year period 1976-1980. During this period, the 80 instructions are to be reduced to 13 instructions by combining instructions concerning related fields of industry, and by including, where possible, all relevant rules in instructions dealing with a given industry rather than with a given type of financial transaction.[41] A significant step toward publication was made with the issuance of a *Systematic Index of Instructional Materials of the Administration of the State Bank*.

Important reform and codification steps have been taking place at *Gosarbitrazh*. A collection of instruction directives of *Gosarbitrazh* has been published, including all directives in force through 1976.[42] This publication was preceded by major recodification work which allowed the combining of 35 old instructions in 18 new instructions, and included the updating of all the instructions to reflect changes in legal policy. Another important area of activity has been the issuance of a large number of new Special Conditions of Supply. (These are rules which provide detailed terms governing the particular features of supply relationships in different industries.) Since 1969, at least 40 Special Conditions of Supply have been issued or reissued. Special conditions of supply for consumer goods are issued by *Gosarbitrazh* acting alone, while those for producer goods are issued by *Gossnab* acting together with *Gosarbitrazh*. Soviet commentors have pointed out that there is some question about the latter practice, which in essence allows *Gossnab* to regulate its own supply relations.[43]

A problem complicating the ongoing practice of recodification at the ministerial level is the common practice of issuance of joint decrees by various interested organizations. Thus, for instance, the regulations of September 10, 1976, On a New Form of Brigade Economic Accountability in Construction-Brigade Contracting, were approved by the State Committee on Matters of Construction, the State Planning Committee, the State Committee on Labor and Social Matters, the Ministry of Finance, and the Construction Bank, and were agreed to by the All-Union Central Council of Trade Unions.[44] It is fairly clear why the consent of these various organizations was needed for the issuance of this legislation; however, the issuance in this form of numerous decrees greatly complicates reform and recodification efforts. Any change in these regulations would come normally with the consent of all concerned. Since there are thousands of such multi-agency decrees outstanding, involving every conceivable combination of existing and defunct agencies as issuing bodies, real reform could come only in one of two ways. *First*, the convening of many overlapping inter-agency committees to consolidate and reenact legislation of this type. *Second*, the assumption by the Council of Ministers of its role as higher agency, and the recodification of this legislation at the Council of Ministers level. The first approach is impossibly complex to realize in practice. The second approach would involve a transfer of power away from the Ministry level to the Council of Ministers, a transfer sure to be resisted by the Ministries, and which the present staff structure of the Council of Ministers would probably be unable to handle.

The whole problem of the volume of Soviet legislation is related to another question, that of the level in the Soviet hierarchy where certain types of decisions should be taken. As is pointed out in an article by A. M. Iakovlev,[45] the two questions are inextricably linked, since the only way the volume of legislation can be reduced is by giving more independence to the ultimate operating organizations at the bottom of the pyramid.

Physical Access to Economic Legislation

A minimum requirement of any legal information system is that those affected by legislation have physical access to that legislation. There are a number of possible methods of providing such access, including direct distribution of legislation to affected organizations, various forms of publication, and computer networks. Each method involves particular costs and benefits. However, because of the inherent conservatism of the legal system and the difficulty of budgeting the funds and manpower needed for changeover to more efficient methods, the Soviet Union has tended to lag substantially behind most economically developed countries in providing access to legislation. During the early 1970's, serious efforts began to overcome this gap. At first, these efforts were aimed toward publication; more recently, emphasis has shifted toward the improvement of the distribution of legislation in unpublished form.

For many years, much or most of Soviet legislation and administrative regulations were not published but were merely distributed to those supposed to be affected. Given the high value traditionally placed by governments of Russia upon secrecy, and the savings in printing and distribution cost, it is not surprising that this method flourished, particularly under Stalin, when secrecy was valued even more highly than usual, and competing demands for economic resources were great. As Soviet commentators have been first to point out, such a system has serious drawbacks. First, too narrow a group may receive the legislation. Some of those directly affected may fail to get it, many of those indirectly affected will certainly not receive the information, and legal scholars and economists who should be analysing and criticising the legislation may have difficulty obtaining it. In addition, the savings from smaller printings and mailings will be largely offset by the extra expenses of maintaining files of large number of individual items at each receiving location.

For all of these reasons, once the Stalinist restrictions of secrecy were removed, the Soviet legal system moved in the early 1970's toward publication. Here, there were two needs: publication of current legislation, and publication of legislation previously distributed directly. Both were met to some extend—the first by the establishment of a number of new periodicals of legislation and by widening opportunities for subscription to existing legislative periodicals; the second, by the publication of a large number of specialized collections of legislation in various fields.

A move away from publication toward direct distribution of legislation may be noted in the late 1970's. Neither the *Collection of Legislation in Force* nor the various ministerial collections have been published in the sense of being sold in bookstores or being available to library users without special permission. Rather, they have apparently been printed or mimeographed and have been distributed in the traditional direct distribution pattern to the perceived ultimate users. One can only speculate on the motives for this partial return to the secret legislation system so prevalent in earlier Soviet and Russian history. One possibility is that the procedures for securing approval for the declassification of previously secret legislation would have been so time-consuming that it would have been impossible to meet the deadlines set by the Party for legislative reform other than by compiling collections "for official use only." A more sinister hypothesis is that a substantial proportion of the unpublished legislation contains norms whose content is kept secret because publication would be embarrassing for the Soviet leadership domestically or internationally. Finally, the rather poor record of publication as a means of distribution of legislation in the USSR makes the alternative of publication relatively less attractive.

Publication, particularly publication in book form, involves a substantial time delay between the passage of legislation and its availability to those subject to the legislation. In this respect, it may actually be inferior to the method of direct distribution to affected parties. The typical delay between the adoption of an administrative regulation and its appearance in the *Bulletin of Normative Acts* (if it is, indeed, selected for publication there) is five to six months. This does not compare favorably with average one month delay achieved by the *Bulletin of Financial and Economic Legislation* published in Moscow in the 1930's, and certainly does not compete with the one day delay of publications of the Bureau of National Affairs, a leading United States commercial legal publisher.

It may be that Soviet censorship controls have prevented the Soviet Union from regularly publishing legal information in the form which most other advanced industrial countries have found necessary to enable their lawyers to keep up with the rapidly changing government bureaucratic regulations on economic activity. This is a simple technique not requiring huge data banks or powerful computers. It involves the distribution of legal information in the form of looseleaf volumes with the publication of regular supplements thereafter. The incredible backwardness of the Soviet Union in this regard may be explained by the impossibility, under such a system, for central censorship and secrecy authorities to determine what each volume contains at any given point of time. Alternatively, it may be explained by some basic flaws in the system of incentives for innovation in the publishing industry which has prevented this development. (It might be noted that in Yugoslavia, which has competing legal publishers, such services are commonplace.) After this paper had been typeset, legislation was adopted ordering the publication of the *Code of Laws of the USSR* in looseleaf form.

Soviet authorities are beginning to consider a method, now starting to attain acceptance in other countries, for the distribution of texts of legal materials, namely the use of computer networks to provide access to the text of legislation stored in automated data retrieval systems.[46] Such a system could, if properly managed, avoid the delays typical of conventional publication or distribution. It could also serve as the basis for a search system providing access to legislation. It could serve only indirectly to aid in legislative reform and identification of repealed provisions by making easier the identification of all legislation dealing with given subject matter. Finally, by concentrating access to legislation in a single computer system, it would provide maximum control over such access.

A related, but much more radical approach is the current attempt by various Soviet scholars to make a great leap forward, ahead of the slow process of making economic legislation accessible to and understandable by humans by directing it instead at machines. For the past half dozen years, Soviet scholars in law and economics have been asked to lend their efforts to the development of "automated systems of management" at all levels of the Soviet economy. One aspect of this automation will be to restructure the vast number of documents which flow between various Soviet organizations, both planning and contractual documentation. Since computers cannot handle the necessary decisions unless the rules involved are expressed in an extremely concrete manner, a complete reexamination of large areas of economic legislation—with a view of providing the required detailed concrete instructions—has become necessary.

As more and more of the reform of economic legislation becomes concerned with the question of how to make it intelligible to machines rather than to humans, many of the historical approaches to codification may become irrelevant.[47] The whole European codification movement was an attempt, and in some countries a surprisingly successful one, to reduce law to general principles which could be understood by the educated citizen. Development of generalizations, even at the expense of some oversimplification, is essential to human understanding of a complex area. The nature of computers, however, is to demand concrete detail—computers cannot go far in understanding abstract general principles. On the other hand, computers will faithfully administer instructions of incredible complexity that would be beyond human ability to perform without error. Thus, draftsmen's attention increasingly will have to turn to detail.[48]

Finding the Relevant Economic Legislation

Finding the relevant economic legislation is not an easy matter in the Soviet Union, even once access is attained to all of the legislation in force. The development of finding aids for legislation has suffered from excessive decentralization. Typically, each Ministry and the legal office of each major enterprise has maintained a card file indexing legislative enactments. This has been necessary because centrally-made indexes have been non-existent or hopelessly incomplete. The amount of indexing materials published for sources of economic law in the USSR each year is certainly less than that produced in the United States each week, and quite possibly less than that produced in the United States on the average working day.

The inevitable result is a largely inadequate and duplicative effort in the area of indexing. Proposals now suggested to automate or semiautomate this system on a local basis, would only be throwing good money after bad. Clearly what is needed is some strict centralization of the process of indexing or of otherwise creating access to legislative materials.

Work is under way, in connection with the planned publication in a centralized way of major collections of legislation, to also publish indexes to this legislation. This will mark a major advance, and may limit the necessity for locally-maintained indexes, but only to the extent that the centrally-produced indexes are published in a timely manner.

An alternative to publication of indexes, and one with the advantage that full centralized control is maintained, is the creation of indexes in a single copy with access through a computerized retrieval system. This alternative has found much favor among Soviet legal scholars, and there has been at least one major experimental implementation of such a system. A second possibility, which has not to date been seriously considered by the USSR, is the implementation of a system of storage of full text of legislation with retrieval through an index containing all important words in the text. The reason why such a system has not been given really serious consideration is because the USSR does not yet produce domestically the type of computer hardware necessary for the economical operation of a really large data retrieval system.

Legislation in 1978 authorized purchase of foreign computer equipment for preparation of the new *Code of Laws of the USSR.* It seems quite possible that, over a ten to fifteen year timeframe, computer retrieval will supplant conventional sources of and indexing for legislation. Computers will provide no answer to the most basic problem, however, that of legislative reform to modernize and clarify legislation.

Economic Law and Legal Education

Recent years have seen a continual effort to keep the supply of lawyers to the economy even with or ahead of the growing mass of legislative material. During the period from 1970 through 1975, the number of lawyers working as legal advisors to organizations engaged in economic activity more than doubled, reaching a total number of over 50,000. At least one republic, Estonia, has reached a level of one lawyer for every two thousand enterprise employees.[49]

Important efforts are also being made in law training for executives.[50] The demand for law graduates for service as enterprise counsel substantially exceeds the supply in most places. As one Soviet commentator explains, this is the result not so much of lack of law graduates, but of the interaction of the structure of the legal education system and the rules concerning job placement. At Soviet higher educational institutions, graduates of the day division are virtually guaranteed employment according to the specialty that they have acquired, but most must repay the state for their free education by accepting a job from a list of positions which are deemed most needed by the economic planners (even if the job is in a distant location) and by remaining there for several years. Many young lawyers who take such jobs remain thereafter, either because they like the job, or because they are from rural areas and restrictions on movement to major urban areas prevent their seeking more interesting places to live.

All institutions for legal education are located in large cities. Most of them have large evening and external divisions. As a result, about 60% of the law students are in these divisions rather than in the day division. (This mix is unusual for Soviet higher education, which in general is full-time day division education.) Because standards of living are substantially higher in larger cities, and because stable residence is a Russian tradition, few of the students in evening or correspondence divisions are interested in obtaining jobs in the smaller cities and towns where legal counsel for enterprises and economic institutions are in shortest supply. Unlike students of the day division, they are not subject to compulsory assignment. (Nor could they practically be made subject to such assignment–if forced to choose between obtaining a night-school diploma and being sent to Siberia, or foregoing the diploma and perhaps losing the chance for a job promotion, most Moscow evening students would quit the University.) As a result of this, there is a substantial surplus of lawyers available in cities with law schools, and a critical shortage elsewhere.

Many of the prime movers of the economic law philosophy in the 1930's were law professors, and the development of the ideas of economic law has been closely related to the development of legal education. John Hazard has related how "economic law" came to dominate the law school curriculum in the 1930's at the expense of traditional civil law subjects. After Vyshinskii's purges, the curriculum and the law schools were reorganized. The department of civil law became the largest and most influential department in most law schools, and the subject of economic law as such was banished from the curriculum with its subject matter parceled out to an inadequate number of hours in the courses on civil and on administrative law.[51] By the mid 1960's, the study of "economic law" had again become established at law schools, text books were once again issued for economic law, and in some instances new departments of economic law were organized at law schools. All of these steps would appear to be reasonable reactions to the fact that an increasing number of law school graduates were finding jobs in the economic law sector. However, these developments must have represented a threat to traditional civil law departments. It is perhaps not surprising that one of the most serious opponents of the whole economic law movement has been Professor O. S. Ioffe, chairman of the department of civil law at Leningrad and author of numerous civil law textbooks. The new decree would appear to mean even further emphasis in legal education on the whole area of economic law, so that both further editions of textbooks in the area, including probably specialized textbooks in subfields of economic law, and further development of civil law departments may be expected.

3. Conclusion

Despite many difficulties, the USSR seems to be slowly progressing toward a systematization of economic law and of the means of dissemination of information about it. If present trends continue, by the late 1980's a reasonable standard of codification, publication, and dissemination will have been achieved. Then, attention can be concentrated fully on the substantive dilemma of economic law, that of matching the productivity of the most advanced capitalist countries with a socialist economic system. However, the increasing trend toward the distribution of legislation in the form of classified documents or through a limited-access computer system could seriously threaten the ultimate goal, that of optimizing the system of economic regulation. While the Soviet Union has allowed a substantial range of free speech to lawyers and economists wishing to engage in constructive criticism of economic legislation, such criticism can hardly be meaningful or useful unless those concerned have access to all relevant legislation and can quote from it in their published works. Otherwise, Soviet economic law could suffer the sad fate of Soviet criminology, which was reduced to meaningless generalizations by the secrecy classification of criminal statistics.

While great progress has been made toward giving economic law questions a fair share of law school curricula, the problem of maldistribution of lawyers specializing in economic law cannot be fully solved until more progress is made on one of the most basic problems in the Soviet Union—the difference in the quality of life between the city and the countryside, and between the small town and the major urban center.

NOTES

1. D. M. Rutman and Iu. S. Tsimmerman, "Normotvorcheskaia deiatel'nost' promyshlennogo ministerstva i upravlenie otrasl'iu" (The Rulemaking Activity of the Industrial Ministry and the Management of the Branch), *SGiP*, 1972, No. 4, 87.

2. A. Ia. Grun, "Uchastie gosudarstvennykh arbitrazhei v sovershenstvovanii zakonodatel'stva" (The Participation of State Arbitration Organizations in the Improvement of Legislation), *SGiP*, 1976, No. 11, 28.

3. M. I. Braginskii, "Pravovoe regulirovanie informatsionnykh otnoshenii v usloviiakh ASU" (Legal Regulation of Information Relations under the Conditions of an Automated System of Management), *SGiP*, 1976, No. 1, 38; A. F. Shebanov, A. P. Shliakhov, and S. S. Moskvin (eds.), *Pravovaia informatsiia* (Legal Information), (Moscow, 1974).

4. *Leninskii sbornik* (The Lenin Collection), Vol. 35 (Moscow, 1945), p. 352.

5. L. I. Brezhnev, *Vse dlia blaga naroda, vse vo imia chelokeva-Rech' na vstreche s izbirateliami Baumanskogo izbiratel'nogo okruga g. Moskvy 14 iiunia 1974 g.* (Moscow, 1974), p. 15.

6. See the discussion of Speransky and his work in H. J. Berman, *Justice in the USSR*, Rev. ed., enl. (New York, 1963), pp. 206-212.

7. M. Speransky, *Obozrenie istoricheskikh svedenii o Svode zakonov* (Survey of Historical Information on the Code of Laws), (St. Petersburg, 1833), p. 157.

8. K. S. Rosenn, "The *Jeito*: Brazil's Institutional Bypass of the Formal Legal System and its Developmental Implications," *American Journal of Comparative Law*, 19 (1971), No. 3, 514, at 540.

9. The most thorough discussion is in Eberhard Schneider, *Das Wirtschaftsrecht in kommunistischen Rechtsdenken*, (Köln, 1964); also see L. Ia. Gintsburg, "Nauka grazhdanskogo (khoziaistvennogo) prava v SSSR v 1929-1931 gg." (The Discipline of Civil (Economic) Law in the USSR in 1929-1931), *Pravovedenie*, 1976, No. 6, 97.

10. H. G. Heinrich, "Zur Entwicklung der sowjetischen Wirtschaftrechtstheorie," *Osteuropa-Recht*, 16 (1970), 25-46.

11. *Khoziaistvennyi kodeks SSSR (Proekt osnovnykh polozhenii)* (Economic Code of the USSR (Draft of Basic Provisions)), (Moscow, 1970).

12. In addition to the numerous articles and books cited in other notes, there was an important open discussion of the Code at the Institute of State and Law in Moscow. The discussion is summarized in T. E. Abova, "Obsuzhdenie proekta Osnovnykh polozhenii Khoziaistvennogo kodeksa SSSR," *SGiP*, 1973, No. 8, 137, and is reported in full in *Obsuzhdenie proekta Osnovnykh polozhenii Khoziaistvennogo kodeksa SSSR* (Consideration of a Draft of the Basic Provisions of the Economic Code of the USSR), (Moscow, 1973).

13. J. N. Hazard, "Introduction", in H. W. Babb (ed.), *Soviet Legal Philosophy* (1951), xvii.

14. V. S. Tadevosian, "K proektu Osnov grazhdanskogo zakonodatel'stva Soiuza SSR i soiuznykh respublik" (On Draft of the Fundamental Principles of Civil Legislation of the USSR and the Union Republics), *Sots. zak.*, 1960, No. 8, 47; V. S. Tadevosian, "Nekotorye voprosy sistemy sovetskogo prava" (Certain Questions of the System of

Soviet Law), *SGiP*, 1956, No. 8, 99; discussed in J. N. Hazard, "The Withering Away of the State: The Function of Law," *Survey*, Oct. 1961, 72.

15. V. V. Laptev, "Poniatie khoziaistvennogo zakonodatel'stva i puti ego sovershenstvovaniia" (The Concept of Economic Legislation and Ways for Its Improvement), *SGiP*, 1976, No. 7, 72; *Teoreticheskie problemy khoziaistvennogo prava* (Theoretical Problems of Economic Law), (Moscow, 1975); V. V. Laptev, "Sub"ekty khoziaistvennogo prava" (Subjects of Economic Law), *SGiP*, 1975, No. 4, 80; V. V. Laptev, "Ekonomika i khoziaistvennoe pravo" (Economics and Economic Law), *Kommunist*, 1975, No. 1, 53; V. V. Laptev, "K kodifikatsii khoziaistvennogo zakonodatel'stva" (Toward the Codification of Economic Legislation), *SGiP*, 1974, No. 10, 75; V. V. Laptev, *Predmet i sistema khoziaistvennogo prava* (The Subject and the System of Economic Law), (Moscow, 1969).

16. S. S. Alekseev and V. F. Iakovlev, "O sovershenstvovanii khoziaistvennogo zakonodatel'stva (Obshcheteoreticheskie voprosy)" (On the Improvement of Economic Legislation (Problems of General Theory)), *SGiP*, 1975, No. 6, 43.

17. Laptev, "K kodifikatsii. . . ," note 15 above.

18. Reports of several lively debates about economic law have been published: L. A. Kuz'micheva and V. I. Zhukov, "Obsuzhdenie monografii 'Teoreticheskie problemy khoziaistvennogo prava' " (Evaluation of the Monograph *Theoretical Problems of Economic Law*), *Pravovedenie*, 1977, No. 2, 146; *Obsuzhdenie proekta Osnovnykh polozhenii Khoziaistvennogo kodeksa SSSR* (Consideration of a Draft of the Basic Provisions of the Economic Code of the USSR), (Moscow, 1973).

19. S. N. Bratus' (ed.), *Sistematizatsiia khoziaistvennogo zakonodatel'stva* (The Systematization of Economic Legislation), (Moscow, 1971); See particularly O. S. Ioffe, "Poniatie i sistema khoziaistvennogo zakonodatel'stva" (The Concept and System of Economic Legislation), in S. N. Bratus' (ed.), *Sistematizatsiia khoziaistvennogo zakonodatel'stva* (The Systematization of Economic Legislation), (Moscow, 1971), p. 48.

20. O. S. Ioffe, *Pravovoe regulirovanie khoziaistvennoi deiatel'nosti v SSSR* (Legal Regulation of Economic Activity in the USSR), (Leningrad, 1959).

21. O. S. Ioffe, "Obshchaia chast' i sistematizatsiia khoziaistvennogo zakonodatel'stva" (The General Part and the Systematization of Economic Legislation), *SGiP*, 1974, No. 10, 82-87.

22. Essays in Bratus', note 19 above.

23. S. N. Bratus', "O putiakh sistematizatsii khoziaistvennogo zakonodatel'stva" (On Ways for the Systematization of Economic Legislation), *SGiP*, 1975, No. 9, 52-60.

24. V. P. Gribanov and O. S. Ioffe, "Puti razvitiia sovetskogo khoziaistvennogo zakonodatel'stva" (Ways for the Development of Soviet Economic Legislation), *Pravovedenie*, 1975, No. 6, 45.

25. Polozhenie o proizvodstvennom ob"edinenii (kombinate), approved by decree of the Council of Ministers of the USSR, March 27, 1974, *Sobr. Post. SSSR*, 1974, No. 8, item 38.

26. Polozhenie o Gosudarstvennom arbitrazhe pri Sovete Ministnov SSSR, approved by decree of the Council of Ministers of the USSR, January 17, 1974, No. 60, *Sobr. Post. SSSR*, 1974, No. 14, item 19.

27. Polozhenie o poriadke pred"iavleniia i rassmotreniia pretenzii predpriiatiiami, organizatsiiami i uchrezhdeniiami i uregulirovaniia raznoglasii po khoziaistvennym dogovoram, approved by decree of the Council of Ministers of the USSR, October 17, 1973, *Sobr. Post. SSSR*, 1973, No. 23, item 128.

28. Polozhenie ob otkrytiiakh, izobreteniiakh i ratsionalizatorskikh predlozheniiakh, approved by decree of the Council of Ministers of the USSR, August 21, 1973, *Sobr. Post. SSSR*, 1973, No. 19, item 109.

29. Polozhenie o postoianno-deistvuiushchem proizvodstvennom soveshchanii, approved by decree of the Council of Ministers of the USSR and the All-Union Central Council of Trade Unions, June 18, 1973, *Sobr. Post. SSSR*, 1973, No. 15, item 80.

30. Obshchee polozhenie o vsesoiuznom i respublikanskom promyshlennykh ob"edineniiakh, approved by decree of the Council of Ministers of the USSR, March 2, 1973, No. 140, *Sobr. Post. SSSR*, 1973, No. 7, item 32.

31. Postanovlenie TsK KPSS i Soveta Ministrov SSSR, "O nekotorykh meropriiatiiakh po dal'neishemu sovershenstvovaniiu upravleniia promyshlennost'iu" March 2, 1973, *Sobr. Post. SSSR*, 1973, No. 7, item 31.

32. Osnovy zakonodatel'stva Soiuza SSR i soiuznykh respublik o trude, *Ved. V. S. SSSR*, 1970, No. 29, item 265.

33. Osnovy zemel'nogo zakonodatel'stva, *Ved. V. S. SSSR*, 1968, No. 51, item 85.

34. Polozhenie o sotsialisticheskom gosudarstvennom proizvodstvennom predpriiatii, approved by a decree of the Council of Ministers of the USSR of Oct. 4, 1965, *Sobr. Post. SSSR*, 1965, No. 19-20, item 155. Translated in full in *CDSP*, 17 (1965), No. 42, 3-10.

35. "Ob uluchshenii pravovoi raboty v narodnom khoziaistve" (On the Improvement of Legal Work in the National Economy), Decree of the Central Committee of the CPSU and the Council of Ministers of the USSR of Dec. 23, 1970, *Sobr. Post. SSSR*, 1971, No. 1, item 1; *Biulleten' Ministerstva vysshego i srednego spetsial'nogo obrazovaniia SSSR*, 1971, No. 5, 8.

36. Decree of the Central Committee of the CPSU and the Council of Ministers of the USSR, June 25, 1975, "O merakh po dal'neishemu sovershenstvovaniiu khoziaistvennogo zakonodatel'stva" (On Measures for the Further Improvement of Economic Legislation), *Sobr. Post. SSSR*, 1975, No. 16, item 98.

37. A. E. Kozlov, "Uchenyi sovet o sovershenstvovanii khoziaistvennogo zakonodatel'stva" (The Research Council on the Improvement of Economic Legislation), *SGiP*, 1976, No. 6, 138.

38. L. M. Rutman, "Normativnye akty ministerstv i vedomstv v sisteme khoziaistvennogo zakonodatel'stva" (Normative Acts of Ministries and Departments in the System of Economic Legislation), *SGiP*, 1975, No. 11, 50-57.

39. S. Pomorski, "The Soviet Economic Associations: Some Problems of Legal Status and Organization After the 1973 Reform," *Review of Socialist Law*, 2(1976), No. 3, 129.

40. V. V. Laptev (ed.), *Teoreticheskie problemy khoziaistvennogo prava* (Theoretical Problems of Economic Law), (Moscow, 1975), p. 281.

41. M. L. Kogan, "Sovershenstvovanie zakonodatel'stva o kreditovanii narodnogo khoziaistva" (Improvement of the Legislation on Providing Credit for the National Economy), *SGiP*, 1976, No. 9, 72.

42. *Sistematicheskii sbornik instruktivnykh ukazanii Gosarbitrazha pri Sovete Ministrov SSSR* (Systematic Collection of Instructive Directives of State Arbitration Attached to the Council of Ministers of the USSR), (Moscow, 1976).

43. M. M. Braginskii, "O sovershenstvovanii zakonodatel'stva po material'no-tekhnicheskomu snabzheniiu" (On the Improvement of the Legislation on Material and Technical Supply), *SGiP*, 1977, No. 3, 70.

44. *Biulleten' normativnykh aktov*, 1977, No. 2, 3.

45. A. M. Iakovlev, "Pravo i adaptivnaia funktsiia sistemy regulirovaniia promyshlennogo proizvodstva" (Law and the Adaptive Function of the System of Regulation of Industrial Production), *SGiP*, 1975, No. 3, 19.

46. E. V. Boldyrev and V. N. Ivanov, "Problemy sovershenstvovaniia sistemy pravovoi informatsii" (Problems of Improving the System of Legal Information), in *Problemy*

sovershenstvovaniia sovetskogo zakonodatel'stva: Trudy 4 (Moscow, 1977), p. 149.

47. I. L. Bachilo and S. V. Katrich, "Osnovnye napravleniia razrabotki organizatsionno-pravovogo obespecheniia ASU" (Basic Directions of Development of the Organizational and Legal Arrangements for an Automated System of Management), *SGiP*, 1975, No. 8, 48.

48. O. S. Ioffe, "ASU i zakliuchenie dogovora postavki" (The Automated System of Management and Conclusion of the Supply Contract), *Pravovedenie*, 1974, No. 2, 33.

49. M. P. Vyshinskii, "Sovershenstvovanie khoziaistvennogo zakonodatel'stva i voprosy podgotovki iuridicheskikh kadrov" (The Improvement of Economic Legislation and Questions of the Preparation of Legal Cadres), *SGiP*, 1977, No. 6, 59.

50. E. A. Agaeva, "Podgotovka kadrov rukovoditelei i pravovoe obespechenie deiatel'nosti predpriiatiia" (Preparation of Cadres of Managers and Legal Support for the Activity of the Enterprise), *Pravovedenie*, 1977, No. 2, 18.

51. Hazard, note 13 above, at xxxi.

AUTOMOBILIZATION AND SOVIET LAW: REFLECTIONS ON CERTAIN ASPECTS OF SOVIET AUTOMOBILE LAW

Christopher Osakwe

1. Introduction: An Overview of the Problem

To the Soviet policy makers, the term "automobilization" is bound to conjure an image both of relief on the one hand, and of problems on the other. As any observant Western visitor to the USSR knows, intra-city public transportation in the Soviet Union is annoyingly inefficient, grossly overburdened, and unnecessarily overbureaucratized. Any assistance that "private" transportation could provide in this regard would be more than welcome both by the state planners and by the enduring Soviet consumers.

As if to aggravate the problem of inadequate public transportation in the USSR, in 1967 the entire country switched over to a five-day work week, thus freeing two days for rest and leisure for the average Soviet worker.[1] If universal experience is to serve as any indication of what this free time is going to be used for, one would say that the Soviet workers, in addition to engaging in that great Soviet national pastime–"abuse of vodka", would also plan more family picnics, weekend trips to the countryside, family outings, and group travels, including intra-city and even inter-republic driving. To meet these leisure demands, the Soviet government will have to provide not only more camping sites and inter-city amusement parks, but also a stepped up inter-city ground transportation to move people to and from these weekend vacation spots.

As part of its programmed response to these emerging consumer demands of the increasingly more sophisticated Soviet citizens, the Soviet government recently reaffirmed its commitment to a long-term plan aimed at producing more automobiles than are presently available in the heavily regulated Soviet automobile market. In taking this step, the Soviet government hopes to kill two birds with one stone–it hopes to remedy the present inadequacy in its intra-city and inter-city public transportation system by siphoning a minimal portion of the passengers into the private automobiles; secondly, it hopes, willy-nilly, to satisfy the demands of many Soviet citizens who have long yearned for some of the advantages that come with individual ownership of personal means of transportation, *i.e.*, individual comfort and the avoidance of the scheduling headaches that generally accompany reliance on public transportation.

Soviet official policy toward automobilization is reflected in the following two reports. In his report[2] to the USSR Supreme Soviet on October 27, 1976, N. K. Baibakov, the Deputy Chairman of the USSR Council of Ministers and Chairman of *Gosplan* of the USSR, stated that: during the current five-year plan (1976-1980), the USSR plans to put into operation 61,500 kilometers of paved highways, not counting other state and local highways which will also be expanded or improved; that the five-year plan contemplates a considerable increase in the number of private automobiles; that the five-year plan contemplates the increase in the production and sale of other major consumer goods like television sets, radio sets, tape recorders, refrigerators, vacuum cleaners, clocks, motorcycles, and many other miscellaneous synthetic products of household use.

The second report is an extensive interview[3] granted to an *Izvestiia* correspondent on March 10, 1977, by the RSFSR Minister of Construction and Exploitation of Automobile Highways, A. A. Nikolaev, in which he disclosed a comprehensive plan to construct new highways throughout the republic and to renovate existing ones. In his words, the RSFSR 9th five-year plan calls for the construction and renovation of 50,000 kilometers of paved highways throughout the republic.

In what looked like a general survey of Soviet automobile policy in historical perspective, *Izvestiia* published a fully-illustrated article[4] in which it pointed out the following interesting facts: on November 7, 1924, the Soviet government proudly paraded through the Red Square in Moscow the first ten automobiles ever to be produced by Soviet automobile manufacturing plants. Then these automobiles were called *AMO-F15*, but today they are marketed under the name of *ZiL*; in 1925 the production of heavy duty trucks commenced at the Iaroslavskii Automobile Plant; on January 1, 1932, the Gorkii Automobile Plant commenced production of automobiles; in August 1970, the Volga Automobile Plant began production of *Zhiguli*, and on December 28, 1976, the 3 millionth *Zhiguli* rolled off the conveyor belt at the Volga Plant; in 1976 Soviet automobile plants produced 2,025,000 automobiles; in 1977 the USSR hopes to produce 2,071,300 automobiles, *i.e.*, at the rate of 5,647 automobiles per day; by 1980 the Soviet plan calls for the production of 2,296,600 automobiles per year, *i.e.*, at the rate of 6,275 automobiles per day. It becomes quite clear that the Soviet Union is determined to enter the automobile age by the 1980, assuming all goes well with the current five-year plan.

Even though Soviet automobilization policy is overtly designed to meet the transportation needs of the ordinary Soviet citizens, one gets the impression, from reading the Soviet press, that some citizens are not very happy with the inevitable side effects of automobilization on the Soviet way of life. In letters to the newspapers *Pravda* and *Izvestiia*, Soviet citizens have complained about the fact that the proliferation of automobiles will lead to the creation of a new class of social parasites generally referred to by the complaining citizens as *chastniki*.[5] Other complaints have raised the question of environmental pollution[6] associated with automobilization. A third group of complaints point to the fact that the construction of automobile garages will of necessity impede the construction of sports facilities and children's playgrounds.[7] To this litany of automobile woes, one may add traffic congestion which is already becoming noticeable in the streets of Moscow, Leningrad, Kiev, and Odessa.

Somehow, First Secretary Leonid Brezhnev seemed to have anticipated some of these citizen complaints. In his report to the 25th Congress of the Communist Party of the Soviet Union, First Secretary Brezhnev warned against some of the inevitable impact of massive automobilization on the ideological stability of his fellow Soviet citizens.[8] He specifically noted:

> "We have achieved a great deal in our quest to improve the material welfare of the Soviet people. We shall continue, in the future, to address ourselves to this task. It is necessary, however, that the growth of material wealth should be accompanied constantly by a lift in the moral and cultural levels of the people. Otherwise, we shall end up with attitudinal recidivism and petty bourgeois psychology in the general public. We must not lose sight of this possibility."[9]

In this regard, one must point out the ambivalence of Soviet policy toward automobilization. On the one hand, communist ideology regards the ownership of a personal automobile as a manifestation of a reprehensible, un-socialistic individualism. But on the other hand, Soviet policy makers seem to reason that the Soviet government decision to meet the individualistic demands of the Soviet consumers may be rationalized as being only a benign ideological concession to Soviet consumerism. In other words, they feel that socialism and automobilization are not antagonistically contradictory.

To buttress this fact *Izvestiia*, in a 1976 article,[10] noted that at the time there were over 16,000,000 private automobiles, motorcycles, and mopeds in the USSR, and that by the end of the current five-year plan (1976-1980), this figure would be increased by 5-6 millions. Within this scheme of growth, a special effort if being made by the Soviet government to develop automobiles that are suited not only for city driving conditions, but also for rural driving. One such example of the latter, *i.e.*, automobiles designed for rural use, is *VAZ-2121* which "combines high ruggedness with the comfort of the *Zhiguli*".[11] Among the most popular lightweight automobiles presently being produced by Soviet automobile plants are the *Volga*, *Moskvich*, *Zhiguli* (which goes by the name of "Lada" in foreign markets), and *VAZ-2121*.

From the above discussion, it seems clear to this writer that the Soviet Union is on the threshold of a modest automobilization of the entire Soviet society. The overall impact of this policy on the Soviet Union will be three dimensional: *first*, it will have to be reconciled with Soviet communist ideology; *second*, it will bring about substantial changes in the way of life of the ordinary Soviet citizens; *third*, it will act as a catalyst for Soviet law reforms in those areas of the law which are directly concerned with the use and ownership of automobiles.

As already noted above, the impact of the policy of automobilization on communist ideology is evidenced by the fact that the Soviet policy makers are now willing to regard individual owners of automobiles not as non-socialist, petty bourgeois, individualists, but as hard-working, law-abiding, well-intentioned, Soviet socialist consumers. In addition to such official reconciliation of the policy of automobilization with communist ideology, the Soviet government will have to take its case to the people. It will have to recondition the people into accepting the fact that individuals who own automobiles are not necessarily *chastniki*.

The anticipated impact of the automobilization of the Soviet way of life could be more difficult to measure. It could conceivably transform the society from a country of bus and train riders into a nation on wheels. The newly acquired freedom of movement is bound to spill over into other aspects of Soviet life yet to be determined. Furthermore, since it takes some money to maintain an automobile in operational form, if the Soviet government allows too many of its citizens to own automobiles, it may be faced in the not-too-distant future with a workers' demand for wage increase.

To a great extent, Soviet law and its enforcement in the 1980's will be greatly influenced by the present Soviet automobile policy. The thesis of this study is that the present Soviet law, which was basically shaped in the 1960's, is not equipped to respond to the needs of a nation on wheels, which the USSR plans to become upon the completion of the automobilization policy in the 1980's. The impact of this policy on Soviet law will be two-fold: *on the one hand*, automobilization will generate more caseload for the courts and the administrative agencies, as well as for the other dispute-settlement mechanisms within the Soviet state; *on the other hand*, the proliferation of automobiles will create new problems which will, in turn, call for practical solutions either in the form of the adoption of new statutes, or modification or abrogation of the existing laws or regulations.

Among the areas of Soviet law that will be directly and immediately affected by this policy of automobilization are the following: *criminal law*–there will be an increase in automobile thefts and break-ins, drunken driving, joy riding, etc. New criminal statutes are bound to be enacted to handle the inevitable problem to be created by moonlighting taxi drivers (*podpol'nyi* or *samozvannyi taksist*); the *law of torts*–there will be more automobile accidents, and this will prompt the Soviet law maker to reexamine the present law of torts and automobile insurance; law governing sales and leases of automobiles; law governing the ownership, exchange donation, and inheritance of automobiles; *administrative law*—there is bound to be more "*samovol'noe stroitel'stvo avtostoianki*," *i.e.*, the erection of garages by private individuals without the permission of the appropriate city authorities, more violations of domestic passport rules, more persons operating automobiles without a license or with an expired, revoked, or suspended driver's license, more temptations to operate vehicles that are technically not-road-worthy, more pressure on the state automobile inspection (*GAI*) to step up its policing of the automobile inspection rules, a proliferation of unlicensed private automobile repairmen, an increase in the "fixing" of traffic tickets, more automobile-related acts of petty hooliganism, etc.

Other side effects of the Soviet automobilization policy will include: the need to expand highway construction throughout the USSR, to construct more gasoline filling stations, more motels for the inter-state travellers, more eating places along the highways, more two-way telephone call booths, etc. In other words, the impact of automobilization on Soviet reality will be enormous.

This study, however, will focus only on the catalytic effects of the Soviet automobilization policy on Soviet law, to the exclusion of all the other anticipated impacts on the Soviet way of life or ideology. [12]

For reasons of space and thematic coherence, the following analysis will focus on *three* aspects of Soviet automobile law: [13] the constitutional foundations of the right to own personal automobiles in the USSR; Soviet criminal law as it relates to the use and operation of the automobile; and those aspects of Soviet law of torts dealing with automobile-related injuries. All other aspects of Soviet law, that will somehow be affected by automobilization, will be grouped under one heading and analyzed only fleetingly. A concluding section of the study will serve both as a brief synthesis of the foregoing discussions, as well as a projection of the changes in automobile-related laws that will be or ought to be made by Soviet lawmakers in the next decade.

2. The Constitutional Foundations of the Right To Own a Personal Automobile in the USSR

The USSR Constitution of 1977 [14] expressly recognizes three forms of property ownership: socialist property, personal property, and a limited form of private property. Under Article 9 [15] of the Constitution, socialist property—which is the leading form of ownership in the USSR—consists of property belonging to the state, as well as property belonging to collective farms and cooperative organizations. Article 10 [16] then goes on to list specific items that constitute state property. These include: land, minerals, waters, forests, the basic means of production in industry, construction, and agriculture, assets of banks, state-run trade organizations, public utilities and other transport and communication, state-run undertakings, most urban housing and other property necessary for state purposes. The clear implication of the listing of these items in Article 10 is that the right of ownership of these items is exclusively reserved to the state. Thus, land, for example, can neither be owned by a social organization nor by an individual citizen. Article 12 [17] lists articles that may be owned by collective farms and cooperative organizations. Under Article 20 of the Fundamental Principles of Civil Legislation of the USSR and the Union Republics (FPCivL), property owned by other socialist organizations, the Young Communist League (*Komsomol*) etc., is also considered to be socialist property. [18]

Article 18 of the USSR Constitution expressly recognizes as a separate form of economic activity, "individual labor in handicrafts, farming, and property ownership and other forms of activity based exclusively on the personal work of individual citizens and the members of their family." The recognition of this form of private enterprise, and the private property rights accompanying it, has been a half-hearted concession by the Soviet government to the acquisitive instincts of the Soviet peasantry. A crucial limitation on this form of private property has been that it must derive from the individual labor of the members of the collective farm household to the total exclusion of the labor of outside persons.

Article 13 of the USSR Constitution of 1977 recognizes personal property as the third form of property ownership in the USSR. The two types of personal property recognized under Soviet law today are individual property and the property of a collective farm household, both of which are designed to serve the same purpose, *i.e.*, to satisfy the consumer needs of the respective owners. Items that may be owned as personal property include, but are not limited to, articles of everyday use, personal consumption and convenience, the implements and other objects of a small agricultural operation, a house, and earned savings. Article 13 also recognized the right of citizens to inherit personal property.

The right of personal property under the USSR Constitution is further clarified in the FPCivL. Under Article 9 of the FPCivL, citizens may own, bequeath, inherit, and donate personal property, or exercise any other rights connected with personal ownership of such property. Under the same provisions of the FPCivL, property right includes the right to own, use, or dispose of the property, in accordance with procedures established by law.

From the foregoing discussion, it follows that there have been three major limitations on personal property rights in the Soviet Union, *i.e.*, material, quantitative, and procedural. The material limitations flowed from the provision of Article 6 of the USSR Constitution, according to which individuals could not own any of the items listed therein. Thus, the constitutional right to own personal property has not included the right to own land, or mineral deposits, or factories, or any other items, the exclusive ownership of which is vested in the state.

The quantitative limitations flow directly from article 25 of the FPCivL. Under its provision, the following limitations are imposed on the quantity of the same items that an individual may own: no citizen may own more than one dwelling house;[19] the law of the individual union republics may impose a limitation on the size of living space that an individual may own;[20] the laws of the individual union republics may limit the number of heads of cattle that an individual collective farm household may own, as well as the heads of cattle that an individual citizen may own;[21] the law of the individual union republics may provide that an individual member of a collective farm household may not individually own items which, under the collective farm charter, may be owned only by the collective farm itself. Thus, for example, the RSFSR, pursuant to the authority granted it under article 25 of the FPCivL, provides in article 113, par. 2 of the RSFSR Civil Code that a member of a collective farm may not personally own an item which, under the collective farm charter, may be owned only by the collective farm itself. Also, under article 110 of the Civil Code of Estonia, a member of a collective farm household may not own any additional dwelling house.

The procedural limitations on the right of personal property flows from the provisions of articles 19 and 25 of the FPCivL, respectively. Under article 19 of the FPCivL, as already indicated above, any exercise of the right of ownership must comply with the procedure established by law, whereas, under article 25, para. 1 of the FPCivL, no item of personal property may be used to derive unearned income.[22]

Soviet commentators uniformly subscribe to the above interpretations of the relevant constitutional provisions, as well as to the provisions of the relevant federal and state statutes dealing with the right and nature of personal property in the USSR.[23] A typical Soviet commentary on the subject was given by one Soviet writer, A. A. Rubanov, in a recent article which explored the socio-legal aspects of the right of personal ownership in the USSR.[24] He noted:

> "Two factors concerning the nature of personal property in the USSR are generally recognized: Firstly, personal property is economically the by-product of social property to the extent that personal property derives from the investment of individual labor in the public means of production. Secondly, the uses of personal property have a utilitarian character and, as such, must not lead to the accumulation of unearned income. Accordingly, the personal property of a Soviet citizen is fundamentally different from private, capitalist property which, as is well known, constitutes the basis for the exploitation of man by man."[25]

In another passage, the same author went on to discuss the dialectical relationship between personal and socialist property in the USSR. He stated:

> "In the Soviet society, personal property relationship is only a link in the system of property relationships. All elements of this system are mutually dependent. Personal property is economically a derivative of socialist property. However, between personal and socialist property there exists a reverse relationship. The essence of this reverse relationship consists in the fact that as long as individual needs are directly satisfied out of personal property, the latter plays a major role in the rejuvenation of the individual worker within the socialist society. Such rejuvenation of the socialist worker creates one of the essential conditions for the growth of socialist property. Socialist property is the product of the labor of society's people."[26]

By the same reasoning, another Soviet commentator, R. O. Khalfina, stated that personal property affords the owner "the fullest freedom, as an owner, to use that portion of social product placed at his disposal for the satisfaction of his material and cultural needs in consonance with his tastes, idiosyncracies, and inclinations."[27]

A group of Soviet commentators sums up Soviet attitude towards personal property in the following passage:

> "In a socialist society, personal property is a special form of consumption of social product. By the virtue of its utilitarian character, personal property cannot serve as a source of the exploitation of man by man. As society advances towards communism, [however,] the individual demands of citizens will be satisfied to an increasing extent through the resources of social funds . . . Personal property is a derivative of socialist property not only because the latter is the source of the former, that is, individual labor within the socialist economy is the source of personal property, but also because the evolution and development of personal property is totally determined by the development of socialist property. Under socialism, the welfare of individual citizens depends upon the welfare of the entire socialist society as a whole; the growth of social production multiplies the personal property of individual workers."[28]

The essence of Soviet law of personal property ownership is captured in Article 12 of the 1977 Constitution of the USSR which provides that "property, which is situated in the personal ownership and use of individual citizens, may not be used either to derive unearned income or to the detriment of the society."

When one translates all that has been said so far to fit the specific situation of the individual automobile owner in the USSR, the following general principles of law stand out: *first*, the USSR Constitution of 1977 recognizes the right of any citizen to own an automobile. This right, however, like all other rights under the Soviet constitutional system, is not an absolute right. Under Soviet constitutional law of property ownership, the only right that is absolute is the right of the state to define the terms and conditions under which individual citizens may own property; *secondly*, the constitutional right to own an automobile is circumscribed by two major limitations–on the one hand, it may not be used to derive an unearned income which is the same thing as saying that it may not be used to generate unsocialist profits and, on the other hand, the exercise of the rights of ownership of an automobile must conform to the procedures established by law; *thirdly*, there are no *de jure* quantitative limitations on the number of automobiles that an individual citizen may own at any given time. Thus, the constitutional right to own an automobile includes the right to own more than one personal automobile. However, the prohibitive costs of buying and maintaining an automobile in the Soviet Union may tend to impose *de facto* quantitative limitations on such ownership; *fourthly*, since personal property is the by-product of socialist property and since income earned from working in the socialist economy is the immediate source of the personal automobile, a Soviet citizen who does not engage in socially-useful labor, *i.e.*, does not earn his living from working within the socialist economy, arguably does not have a constitutional right to own an automobile. In other words, the right to own an automobile is contingent upon a demonstration that the automobile so acquired is either the direct result of income earned in the socialist economy or of lawful inheritance or donation.[29] Any citizen who acquires a personal automobile with parasitic or unsocialist income does not acquire, let alone retain, any vested right in such automobile since such property is subject to forfeiture by the state.[30] The legal rationale for forfeiture of property acquired by unsocialist income is different from the rationale for forfeiture of property used to derive unearned income. In the former instance, forfeiture is predicated upon the fact that the owner of the automobile never had legal title to the automobile to start with, *i.e.*, the purchase of the automobile with speculative income is void *ab initio*; whereas in the latter instance, the forfeiture is based on the doctrine of abuse of right.[31]

Having established that a Soviet citizen's constitutional right to own an automobile is derivative and conditional, we shall now proceed to see how this right has been protected as well as circumscribed by provisions of Soviet criminal law.

3. Automobilization and Soviet Criminal Law

As already noted above, in this study a massive automobilization of the Soviet society will inevitably have two-fold effects on Soviet criminal law: on the one hand, it will lead to more incidents of violations of the provisions of the Criminal Code; on the other hand, it is bound to precipitate the enactment of more criminal statutes designed to criminalize certain hitherto noncriminal abuses of the automobile. It is equally possible that the Soviet lawmaker may experiment with a decriminalization of certain automobile-related offenses now being considered to be criminal. If this happens, there may or may not be any net increase either in the number of automobile-related crimes in the Criminal Code or in the caseload of the criminal courts.

Among the prominent provisions of the RSFSR Criminal Code which deal with automobile-related offenses are the following: article 144 (which covers theft of personal property, including the automobile); article 149 (which deals with intentional destruction of personal property); article 153 (which criminalizes private entrepreneurial activity or activity as a commercial middleman); article 154 (which deals with speculation, including speculation in automobiles); article 162 (which criminalizes the act of engaging in prohibited trade, including the person-to-person sale or exchange of automobiles); article 211-1 (drunken driving); article 211-2 (which criminalizes the intentional granting of a seal of approval to a technically defective transport vehicle); article 212-1 (joy riding); and article 213 (which deals with violations of rules governing the operation of motor vehicles.)

By contrast, violations of the following two provisions of the RSFSR Criminal Code may be facilitated by the ownership and operation of a personal automobile: article 197 (which criminalizes any unauthorized entry into a border region), and article 198 (dealing with violations of internal passport rules). Let us take a close look at each of the above provisions of the RSFSR Criminal Code and hazard a guess as to the potential effects of automobilization upon each one of them.

RSFSR Criminal Code Provisions which Directly Deal with Automobile-Related Crimes [32]

1) *Article 144: Theft of Personal Property*

Under article 144 of the RSFSR Criminal Code, the secret stealing, *i.e.*, theft, of personal property of citizens is a crime. As already pointed out above, the automobile is a permissible item of personal property under Soviet law. Therefore, theft of personal property as contemplated by this provision of the Criminal Code is an intentional crime, and therefore can never be committed through negligence.

A leading Soviet commentary on criminal law defines the theft of personal property as "the intentional, unlawful appropriation of property which belongs to another person from the possession of such owner with the intention of unlawfully converting such property to the ownership of the person who stole it." [33] It follows, therefore, that if the defendant negligently appropriated a personal automobile belonging to another person, his action does not fall under article 144. Obviously, the question as to whether the defendant acted intentionally or negligently in appropriating a personal automobile belonging to someone else is a question of fact, which has to be proven by the prosecutor. If the defendant stole an automobile without knowing to whom it belonged–the state, a social organization, or an individual–he must be charged under article 144 if, in fact, the automobile belonged to an individual. Conversely, if he stole an automobile believing that it belonged to an individual owner when, in fact, it belonged to the state or to a social organization, such action must be charged not under article 144, but under article 89 of the RSFSR Criminal Code.

At the same time, if the defendant appropriated the automobile without the intention of retaining ownership over the automobile, but rather, only with the intention of using it and returning it to the owner, the action would not be qualified as theft under article 144, but rather may come under article 212-1 of the Criminal Code. In other words, appropriation of a personal automobile belonging to another person without the intention of retaining ownership over the vehicle is not punishable under article 144 of the RSFSR Criminal Code.

Also, the contributory negligence of the owner of the automobile, *e.g.*, his failure to lock the car when parked or leaving the ignition key in an unattended automobile, etc., neither negates nor mitigates the criminal responsibility of the defendant in action under article 144. [34]

2) *Article 149: Intentional Destruction or Damaging of Personal Property of Citizens*

Under article 149 of the RSFSR Criminal Code, it is a crime to intentionally destroy or damage the personal property of citizens thereby causing significant loss to the victim. This provision covers not only breaking into, but also any other intentional damage or destruction of a personal automobile. Like article 144 before it, article 149 contemplates intentional action on the part of the defendant.

Article 149 on its face does not define what is meant by "significant loss". We can only deduce from that the fact that it is left to the court, on a case-by-case basis, to determine the substantiality of the loss depending on the circumstances of each case. One Soviet commentator, however, seems to suggest that under no circumstance may a loss of 100 rubles or less be regarded as a significant loss for the purpose of article 149. [35] Regardless of whether or not the court classifies loss suffered by the victim as "significant loss," the victim may pursue a separate cause of action in tort against the tortfeasor to recover damages. [36]

3) *Article 153: Private Entrepreneurial Activity, and Activity as a Commercial Middleman*

Article 153 of the RSFSR Criminal Code contemplates two separate but interrelated crimes–private entrepreneurial activity by utilization of state, cooperative, or other social forms, and activity as a commercial middleman carried on by private persons as a form of business for the purpose of enrichment.[37] Under a strict reading of the provisions of article 153, the following activities would qualify as a crime: the sale of private automobiles by a private entrepreneur through the outlets provided by state or other socialist enterprises, or through a dummy state enterprise or other socialist enterprise; acting as a commercial middleman in any commercial transaction involving an automobile, *e.g.*, the sale or exchange of automobiles.

As this writer has noted elsewhere, "the activity as a commercial middleman is criminalized only if it contains the following two factors: [first,] if it is engaged in as a form of business, *i.e.*, for the individual this is considered to be a regular source of income; [secondly,] if it is engaged in, even though not as a form of business, but with the intention of reaping unreasonable profit, *i.e.*, such profit that is in no way commensurate with the quality and quantity of the labor put into the service."[38]

Given the present procedural restrictions on the sale of automobiles in the Soviet Union, the activities of a commercial middleman are bound to flourish in an era of massive automobilization. By the same token, the Soviet government is most likely going to step up the fight against such anti-socialist parasitism. One possible cost-effective way in which such battle is going to be waged by the state will be to increase the maximum punishment for automobile-related article 153 crimes from its present level.

4) *Article 154: Speculation*

Article 154 of the RSFSR Criminal Code defines speculation as the buying up and reselling of goods or any other articles of value for the purpose of making a profit.[39] For there to be a criminal action under article 154, the intent to resell for profit must be present at the time of purchase of the goods or other articles of value. It makes no difference, for purpose of criminal liability, whether the speculator ultimately realized any profit from his operation or, in fact, whether he actually suffered a loss. Intent to make profit refers to his state of mind at the material time that he set out to buy the goods. Thus, if Ivanov sets out to buy an automobile with the intent to resell it and to reap a profit therefrom, he has committed the crime contemplated under article 154 at the moment that he resold the automobile to a third party.

In a society like the Soviet Union where the demand for private automobiles is much higher than the supply, automobile speculation readily becomes a common practice. As a matter of general practice, speculation in automobiles normally goes hand-in-hand with the crime of private entrepreneurial activity described in article 153 above. Also, speculation in automobiles, of necessity, involves the conduct proscribed in article 162 of the RSFSR Criminal Code.

In the view of this writer, automobile speculation will pose one of the greatest problems for the Soviet authorities in an age of automobilization. Unless the Soviet government is willing to relax its laws regarding the sale of automobiles, automobile speculation is bound to flourish not only in the renowned black markets of Soviet Georgia and Armenia, but also in the European republics of the USSR. This writer's guess, however, is that the Soviet government, for ideological reasons, will not relax the fight against speculators. Instead, punishment for large scale speculation in automobiles will most likely be increased possibly to include capital punishment.

5) *Article 162: Engaging in a Prohibited Trade*

Under article 162 of the RSFSR Criminal Code, it is a crime to engage in a trade concerning which there is a special prohibition, if such act does not entail administrative liability or if it is committed after the imposition of an administrative penalty.[40] Thus, in order to invoke the provision of article 162, it must be shown that there is a special law which prohibits such a trade and that the defendant engaged in such prohibited trade as a form of business.

Among automobile-related trades that are specifically prohibited by law are the following: illegal operation of taxi service with the use of a private automobile;[41] person-to-person (retail) sale of automobiles as a form of business;[42] acting as the commercial middleman in any commercial transaction involving the automobile, *e.g.*, sale, purchase, or exchange of an automobile;[43] the unauthorized use of a personal automobile for the commercial transportation of goods as a form of business.[44] In all of these instances, it requires more than one violation in order to bring the defendant's action under the purview of article 162 of the RSFSR Criminal Code.

As in the case of speculation under article 154, violation of article 162 of the RSFSR Criminal Code is bound to flourish in the Soviet Union in an era of large-scale automobilization. As a result of this, the Soviet authorities will be forced either to relax the ban against some of the activities described in the foregoing paragraphs or to decide not to invoke sanctions for a substantial portion of these violations. In this writer's view, the Soviet government's reaction in this instance would be to retain the present bans against unauthorized private uses of the automobile. The writer also believes that, for manpower reasons, as well as for reasons of law enforcement priorities, the procurator's attitude toward article 162 violations will be governed more and more by a policy of selective enforcement and prosecutorial discretion.

6) Article 211: Violations of Rules of Save Movement or Operation of Transport by Persons Who Drive Transport Vehicles

Under article 211 of the RSFSR Criminal Code, it is a crime for any operator of a motor vehicle, whether or not the operator of the vehicle does so for a state or social organization, or as the owner of the vehicle, to violate a rule designed to protect the safety of the movement and operation of motorized vehicles, if such violation results either in less grave or light bodily injury, or in substantial material loss to a victim. The same action resulting in the death or grave bodily injury of the victim entails a more severe punishment under the provisions of para. 2 of article 211 of the Criminal Code.

As can be seen from the above provisions, an element of the crime in article 211 is a violation of some specific rules or regulations relating to the safety of vehicular movement or operation. Among such rules are the following: Rules Regarding the Technical Exploitation of Vehicles; Rules Regarding The Protection of Automobile Highways and Highway Installations, etc. Among the violations specifically criminalized by article 211 of the Criminal Code are the following: speeding (*i.e.*, travelling in excess of the posted speed limits); illegal turns or backups; moving in the wrong direction in a one-way street; operating a vehicle which is mechanically not road-worthy; violations of rules governing the weight of loads or loading procedures, etc.

In addition to establishing a specific violation of a rule in force, the prosecution, in order to invoke article 211, must also show that the violation resulted either in physical injury or in substantial material loss to the victim.

> "The question as to what constitutes substantial material loss shall be determined by the court, on a case-by-case basis, by taking into consideration not only the actual amount of the damage caused, but also all other concrete circumstances of the incident, particularly the cost of the damaged property, the size and costs of the repair of such object, the material (financial) situation of the victim, etc."[45]

In a 1969 decree issued by the Plenum of the RSFSR Supreme Court, it was stated that in examining automobile-related crimes where the qualification of the crime depends on the substantiality of the material loss suffered by the victim, the court must not confine its findings to a vague reference to the fact that the victim suffered substantial material loss, but rather must indicate the exact amount of the material loss as well as the motivation for the defendant's action which the court relied upon in reaching its determination of substantiality of the material loss. The question as to whether or not a particular material loss is substantial or not must be made by the court on a case-by-case basis by looking at all the relevant circumstances of each case.[46]

But one Soviet commentary took the unequivocal position that "material loss to the tune of 100 rubles may not be considered to be substantial, because generally such minor losses do not involve highway accidents and as such, in the absence of any other consequences contemplated by law, criminal liability shall be excluded."[47]

Obviously, in order to establish criminal liability under article 211 of the Criminal Code, there must be established a causal connection between the violation of the pertinent road safety rule and the injury or damage suffered by the victim. Prosecution of a defendant under article 211 does not extinguish the right of the victim to institute an action in tort to recoup his damages.

For purposes of article 211 of the Criminal Code, the term "transport means" includes only such automative transportation means which by law must be registered with the *GAI* before their operation on the highways and for which an operator's license is required.[48] These include: buses, pleasure cars, trucks, trolley-buses, streetcars, motorcycles, motorscooters, tractors and other agricultural automotive machines snow cleaners, street sweepers, etc. Conversely, this term does not include bicycles and mopeds.

The crime contemplated under article 211 generally is based on negligence. The violation of an automobile safety rule which results either in the death of or the physical injury to the victim would be qualified not as negligent homicide under article 106, nor as negligent infliction of bodily injury under article 114, but rather as an article 211 crime. By contrast, if the violation of the said rules is intentional and results in physical injury to or in the death of the victim or in damage to personal property, the action would be appropriately qualified under the Criminal Code provisions dealing with intentional homicide (article 102, 103), or intentional infliction of personal injury (article 108, 109), or intentional destruction of personal property (article 149). In these latter circumstances (*i.e.*, in the case of the intentional use of the automobile to commit the crimes in the afore-mentioned provisions of the Criminal Code), in addition to the punishment prescribed in the respective Criminal Code articles, the automobile must be confiscated by the state as required under article 86 of the RSFSR Code of Criminal Procedure.

Where necessary, the court may revoke or suspend the operator's license of the person convicted under article 211 of the Criminal Code. Even where the operator of a motor vehicle did not violate any specific road safety rule or regulation, he is under an obligation to render assistance to any victim of an automobile accident in which he is involved. Failing to do so, he may face criminal prosecution under the provisions of article 127 of the RSFSR Criminal Code.

In the view of this writer, the Soviet government should give some thought to decriminalizing a first-time commission of the crime in article 211, para. 1. This particular provision could be adequately handled through administrative sanctions, coupled with the already-recognized right of the victim of such accident to sue for damages in a separate civil action. To criminalize any conduct that could, with equal effectiveness, be handled administratively is to trivialize the criminal justice system.

7) *Article 127: Leaving in Danger*[49]

Under article 127 of the RSFSR Criminal Code, it is a crime for any person to fail to render necessary assistance to another person who is in danger of death, if such aid could have been rendered by the guilty person without serious danger to himself or to other persons. Under the provisions of this article, it is also a crime for a person to fail to inform the appropriate authorities or persons of the necessity to render aid to a person in need of such aid. It is, even more so, a crime if the person who failed to render aid has himself placed the victim in the said danger.

Thus, if an operator of a motor vehicle, without any apparent violation of any specific automobile safety rules or regulations, is involved in an automobile accident in which another person is injured or killed, such operator has a legal duty to render assistance to the victim, or if he could not render such assistance himself, he has a legal obligation to report the incident to the appropriate authorities immediately so that medical assistance may be rendered to such victim. A hit-and-run driver would therefore be prosecuted under both article 127 and article 211, if his operation of the vehicle entailed any violation of automobile safety rules or regulations.

It is in the interest of Soviet public policy to retain the provisions of article 127 as they presently are. Therefore, in the view of this writer, no significant impact on article 127 is expected from the Soviet automobilization policy. There may very well be more violations of the provision of article 127.

8) *Article 211-1: Driving Transport Vehicles While Drunk*

Under article 211-1 of the RSFSR Criminal Code, it is a crime for a person to drive a motor transport vehicle or any other self-propelled machine[50] while in a state of intoxication, if such a person had been previously deprived of his operator's license in an administrative proceeding or had no valid operator's license to start with, and had been subject to administrative sanction within the past twelve-month period for such violation.

The apparent meaning of the provision of this article of the RSFSR Criminal Code is that any first-time offense involving any of the above-listed violations *per se* would not be actionable under article 211. A prior administrative sanction is a prerequisite for criminal action under article 211. Thus, if Ivanov were to be deprived of his operator's license in connection with the commission of another crime, *e.g.*, the crime in article 211, and he thereafter operates a motor vehicle in a state of intoxication, he would be subject to administrative sanction rather than to a criminal sanction under article 211-1. This is so for the simple reason that the previous deprivation of his operator's license was the result not of an administrative proceeding, but of a criminal proceeding.

It should be noted that in order to invoke article 211-1 it is not necessary to show that the operation of the vehicle resulted in any accident or damage to life or property. The mere operation of a vehicle in a state of intoxication, where the operator had been previously denied of his operator's license in an administrative proceeding or had been administratively sanctioned within the past twelve months for driving without a valid license, is a crime. It is equally important to note that if a person was deprived of his license to operate a bus in a previous administrative hearing, he is chargeable under article 211-1 if he thereafter operates any other motorized vehicle, other than a bus, in a state of intoxication.

For purposes of article 211-1, the state of intoxication of the operator may be induced either by use of alcoholic or any other intoxicant, *e.g.*, narcotic drug. Soviet commentators take the position that the crime under article 211-1 calls for criminal intent and not just criminal negligence.

In the light of the present Soviet government battle against alcoholism, it is not expected that the rule in article 211-1 of the Criminal Code will be relaxed in any form. In a country where alcoholism is already a chronic problem and bad driving is almost a national trait, large-scale automobilization, coupled with a lax rule against drunken driving, could decimate the entire Soviet population within a very short period of time. The Soviet government would like to avoid such a national disaster.

9) *Article 211-2: Approving the Operation of a Technically Defective Transport Vehicle*

The provision of article 211-2 is specifically aimed both at the officials of the technical maintenance divisions of transport organizations, or of state or social organizations that operate a large fleet of automobiles, and at the officials of the State Automobile Inspection (*GAI*) bureaus, *i.e.*, officers responsible for certifying the road-worthiness of an automobile through the issuance of a "brake tag." Under the relevant provisions of this article of the RSFSR Criminal Code, it is a crime for any responsible official of a state automobile inspection bureau to give approval for the operation of a motor vehicle which is known to be technically defective, if such action results in any of the causally-connected consequences specified in article 211 of the Criminal Code. It is also a crime under article 211-2 for the private owner of an automobile to permit a third party to operate his automobile which is known to him to be technically not road-worthy, if such action results in any of the consequences contemplated under article 211 of the Criminal Code.

10) *Article 212-1: Driving Away Means of Motor Transport (Joy Riding)* [51]

Under article 212-1 of the RSFSR Criminal Code, the driving away of a motor vehicle belonging to another person without the purpose of stealing it is a crime. This provision is designed to discourage joy riders who deprive an individual owner of an automobile of the use of his automobile but with the limited intent of using it and returning it to the owner, or at least abandoning it in such a way that it could be readily repossessed by the owner. The crime is deemed to be completed from the moment that the joy rider moves the automobile away from the spot where it was parked by the owner, whether by driving it away or by pushing it. If in removing the automobile from its parking spot the joy rider violates any of the rules contemplated in article 211 of the Criminal Code, he must be charged both under article 211 and article 212-1 of the Criminal Code. Only persons who have attained the age of 16 may be charged with the crime under article 212-1, which, by the way, calls for direct intent. If, however, the defendant appropriated the automobile with the intention of retaining ownership over it, he shall be charged appropriately under article 144 of the Criminal Code.

Joy riding is a problem which plagues all modern automobile societies. Soviet punishment for joy riding, at the present time, is not out of tune with what it is in other countries, notably in the United States. It is therefore not expected that the Soviet goverment, under the pressures of automobilization, will relax or lift the provisions of article 212-1 of the Criminal Code. If any charges are to be made at all in this regard, they would most probably be in the direction of increasing the punishment for joy riding.

11) *Article 213: Violation of Rules Governing Transport*

Under article 213 of the RSFSR Criminal Code, the violation of rules designed for the safety and the orderly movement of automotive vehicles, if such violation results in the loss of human life or other grave consequences, is a crime. As in the case of article 211 which we discussed above, violation of specific safety rules or regulations is a prerequisite for criminal responsibility under article 213. But unlike the crime in article 211, the subject of the crime under article 213 could be a pedestrian, a bicyclist, or an operator of any other non-motorized vehicle, whose violation of the safety rules directly caused the automobile-related accident. It could also be a passenger in the automobile that was involved in the accident.

Thus, for example, in the case of "P" the Criminal Division of the RSFSR Supreme Court held that article 213 of the RSFSR Criminal Code establishes liability of citizens for the violation of operative rules designed for the safety and the orderly movement of automotive vehicles. The subject of this crime could be a pedestrian or passenger, or any other person who violates any of the rules hereby contemplated.[52] Only persons who have attained the age of 16 may be charged under the provisions of this article. In the view of this writer, no major changes should be expected in the 1980's with regard to the provisions of article 213.

Criminal Law Enforcement of the Soviet Internal Passport System: Articles 197 and 198 of the RSFSR Criminal Code

One of the major advantages of owning a personal automobile is the ability to move about not only within the city limits, but also across republic lines, free from the restraints necessarily imposed on the traveller by the scheduling and routing of public transportation. An automobilist who lives in Leningrad could take his entire family to Riga or Vilnius on an extended weekend stay. Alternatively, he could just prefer to drive to a scenic site outside of Leningrad, even though no buses or trains are routed through such areas. In this regard, the private automobile could be seen as the one instrument that could inject a true meaning into a Soviet citizen's constitutional freedom of travel within his own country.

Like all the other freedoms recognized under the Soviet constitutional system,[53] however, the freedom of travel is not and never was intended to be absolute. It is limited by statutory provisions of Soviet organic laws, as well as by practical realities of Soviet life. Articles 197 and 198 of the RSFSR Criminal Code constitute an integral part of the institutionalized limitation on the freedom of Soviet citizens to travel, even inside the USSR. The institutionalized limitation referred to here is the Soviet internal passport system.

The Statute on the Passport System in the USSR was promulgated into law by a decree of the USSR Council of Ministers on August 28, 1974.[54] The new Soviet passport system contemplates three types of registration of persons: *propiska* (*i.e.*, residence registration–the most permanent form of registration of citizens which indicates the place of permanent residence of the registrant of his prolonged stay at a particular locality); *vypiska* (*i.e.*, departure registration which is required whenever a registrant leaves his place of permanent residence to travel elsewhere. Upon arrival at the new place of permanent or temporary residence, the citizen is required to go through a new registration); *registratsiia* (*i.e.*, registration for a temporary stay away from the place of permanent residence).

Under article 1 of the Statute,[55] "all Soviet citizens who have attained the age of 16 are obliged to obtain the passport of the citizen of the USSR". Under article 5 of the Statute, the validity of the passport is not limited to any time period, but when citizens attain the ages of 21 and 45 years, respectively, new passport photographs corresponding to this age shall be inserted into the passport in order to validate it. Article 6 requires citizens to undergo three types of registration as described in the foregoing paragraph–*propiska, vypiska*, and *registratsiia*.

Article 7 charges the following persons with the responsibility of overseeing citizen compliance with the rule in article 6: heads of housing offices; housing administrators; persons in charge of apartment houses and hotels; chairmen of housing construction or *dacha* construction cooperatives; directors or managers of hotels, sanatoriums, rest homes, pensions, tourist parks, hospitals, boarding houses for the aged and the handicapped, boarding homes for children, and other similar institutions in which persons, who are subject to residence registration, are situated; house owners and other persons in whose jurisdiction there are dwelling buildings or premises. Control over the implementation of the passport system, under article 8 of the Statute, is vested in the executive committees of the local councils of working peoples' deputies, as well as agencies of internal affairs.

Under article 23 of the Statute, "citizens who change their place of residence, as well as those who depart to another locality for temporary residence for a term exceeding one and a half months, except those departing on a business trip, on holidays, for a *dacha*, for rest or recuperation, are obliged to register their departure before leaving." But under article 22 of the Statute, even a temporary residence in a different locality of less than one and a half months is subject to registration.

Article 25 of the Statute provides that "for residence registration in population centers located in a frontier zone, a permit for entry into this zone to be obtained in accordance with the established procedure shall be submitted to an agency of internal affairs at a place of residence before exit to the frontier zone." Under article 27, if a residence registration is denied, the unsuccessful registrant is obliged to leave the population center where he was denied registration within seven days of such denial. Article 34 of the Statute contemplates two types of sanctions for violations of these rules: administrative fine of up to 10 rubles for minor (routine) violations, and criminal punishment for malicious violations.

Two provisions of the RSFSR Criminal Code serve as an implementation of the general provisions of the Statute on the Passport System of the USSR. These are articles 197 and 198 of the Criminal Code. Under article 197, violations of rules of entry into or leaving or registration in a border region or zone, if committed after the imposition of an administrative sanction for a similar violation, is a crime. By the same token, article 198 regards as a crime any malicious violation of passports rules in localities where special rules of registration have been introduced and if the violator has already twice previously been subjected to an administrative sanction therefor.

A cursory look at the Soviet internal passport system immediately creates the impression that unsupervised individual, inter-city automobile travel inside the Soviet Union, far from being encouraged, is at best only to be tolerated by the Soviet government. Full compliance with the requirements of these domestic passport rules will undoubtedly have chilling effect on the freedom of travel by Soviet citizens. If the Soviet Union decides to go ahead with full automobilization, Soviet law enforcement authorities must brace up to cope with an inevitable increase in violations of these passport rules. Alternatively, the Soviet government may elect–this is unlikely however–to dismantle these artificial barriers to free travel within the USSR. If the Soviet policy makers were to learn just one lesson from the American automobile experience, it is that free motoring and domestic passport mentality are incompatible ideals. The one must yield to the other. To pursue both goals would be eternally contradictory. From what this writer can discern, it appears that the Soviet government is determined to operate its automobilization policy within the framework of a domestic passport system. Only time will tell how successful such an experiment will be.

4. Automobilization and Soviet Law of Torts

The Nature of the Problem

Without any doubt, the impact of automobilization on Soviet law will be most felt in the areas of torts and insurance. Automobile accidents constitute the single largest source of tort liability in the Soviet Union after industrial accidents. Whereas a socialist organization's liability from industry-related injuries to workers is covered under workmen's compensation law, which requires all production enterprises to carry sufficient liability insurance,[56] the liability of a private automobilist resulting from the operation of a motor vehicle is presently not covered by any insurance policy issuable to the motorist himself. On a voluntary basis, the owner of a personal automobile may insure his property, *i.e.*, his automobile, against loss or damage. Such automobile insurance policy which is issued only by the state insurance agency, *Gosstrakh*, covers only loss of or damage to the automobile and nothing else. It does not cover the liability of the motorist to a third party, for example.[57] On a voluntary basis, however, a private citizen may insure himself against death or injury from any accident, including automobile accident.[58]

Thus, it seems to this writer that the *first* major defect of the present Soviet automobile insurance policy, or lack of it, is the failure of Soviet law to require the individual automobile operator to contribute directly to the costs of hospitalization of automobile victims and to the funds for the compensation of such victims for lost wages as a result of an automobile accident.

The *second* inadequacy of the present Soviet automobile liability law is that it operates a two-tier system for determining the liability of the motorist in the event of an automobile accident. The first tier is that in a one-car accident the owner of the automobile is held to strict liability, *i.e.*, liability without fault. This is based on the fact that the automobile is an ultra-hazardous instrumentality.

By contrast, when two or more automobiles are involved in an accident, liability of the parties is not based on strict liability, but rather on the doctrine of fault. In other words, the owner of the automobile whose fault caused the accident shall be held to pay compensation to the victims thereof. To establish liability under this system, it is necessary to go through the time-consuming and accusatory process of establishing which of the two operators was at fault. If it is established that both drivers were contributorily negligent, the court shall take into consideration the degree of fault of both parties in computing damages. This unnecessary process could be discarded by switching to the system of no-fault automobile insurance policy.

The experience of the United States has been that there is growing dissatisfaction with fault-based automobile liability law.[59] As of 1975, no-fault automobile insurance laws had been enacted in sixteen US states, most of which pay personal injury benefits but not property loss. A proposed US federal law would require each state to have a no-fault law, while limiting medical and rehabilitation expenses to $ 100,000. This policy would also cover lost wages and salaries up to $ 12,000. If the bill passes, states would have up to three years, from the time the federal law goes into effect, to enact laws that equal or surpass the federal guidelines. Failing to do so, the federal limits would apply until non-complying states passed their own versions of the no-fault laws.[60]

A leading American authority on no-fault automobile insurance policy gives this explanation of the no-fault policy:

> "Under no-fault laws, each motorist is required to insure himself (and his passengers and pedestrians injured by him) for out-of-pocket losses (medical expense and wage loss but not for pain and suffering), regardless of who is at fault in the accident or even whether there was a defect in a product. In return, each motorist (now assured of payment of his losses by his own insurance company) is required to waive—at least to a certain extent—any claim against the other driver based on the latter's fault. In other words, in return for being assured payment of his out-of-pocket loss to at least a modest extent, the motorist must waive to a corollary extent his right to be paid based on fault for all his out-of-pocket losses, plus pain and suffering."[61]

The obvious advantages of such no-fault automobile policy are numerous—it eliminates unnecessary court costs and attorney's fees, it cuts down on the time needed to process claims, it expedites payment to the needy victims, court dockets would be unburdened because there would be no need for litigation and benefits would be more equitable. In an age of massive automobilization, the no-fault automobile insurance policy makes a lot of sense.

This portion of our study proposes to predict changes that may be introduced by Soviet law makers in the sphere of automobile accident compensation law in the next decade. At the present time, there are three alternatives available to the Soviet government: *first*, it may either choose to retain the present system which not only contemplates a two-tier system for the determination of the liability of a motorist, depending on whether he was involved in a one-car or in a two-car automobile accident, but also which fails to provide for direct motorist participation in sharing the costs of automobile accident compensation payments; *second*, it may instead adopt a system of social insurance as a method of compensating all victims of automobile accidents[62] and thereby abandoning all concepts of tort and automobile liability; or, *finally*, it may switch to a no-fault automobile insurance system.

This writer believes that the Soviet Union cannot afford to operate under its present system of automobile liability and accident compensation in an era of even a modest automobilization. The present system encourages reckless driving and places a heavy burden on the social insurance system. Of course, the Soviet government can choose to modify the present system by simply requiring all motorists to obtain, at the least, liability insurance, coupled with a scheme which graduates the insurance premium payments in direct correlation to the motorist's driving record. This may be an acceptable solution to the Soviet automobile accident problem in the 1980's.[63]

By contrast, the system of social insurance will not only tend to further encourage reckless driving, but, more importantly, it will place an intolerable financial burden on the state. It is highly doubtful if the Soviet government will ever return to this hitherto rejected system of social insurance.

The third, and perhaps most cost-efficient alternative, is for the Soviet government to adopt a no-fault automobile insurance policy. A no-fault automobile insurance law will not pose any constitutional problem under the Soviet constitutional system.

What follows below is a brief analysis of those provisions of Soviet law of torts[64] dealing with private automobile-related tort liability. The analysis consists of a brief discussion of the doctrine of strict liability in contemporary Soviet law. This is followed by a fleeting discussion of only those absolute defenses which are applicable in an action for automobile-related tort. These include: lack of proximate cause, intentional act on the part of the victim, *force majeure*, unlawful act of a third party, and the running of the statute of limitation.

Strict Liability in Soviet Law: A General Analysis[65]

Under the general principles of tort liability contained in article 444 of the RSFSR Civil Code, for there to be a cause of action, it must be shown that the four elements of tort are present, *i.e.*, that the victim suffered a material harm, that the tortfeasor acted unlawfully, that the wrongful act of the tortfeasor is causally connected with the material harm suffered by the victim, and that the tortfeasor acted with fault.[66] The failure to show any of these elements will relieve the defendant of all tort liability.

As a general exception to the rule in article 444 of the RSFSR Civil Code, however, article 454 of the RSFSR Civil Code contemplates the possibility of tort liability without fault on the part of the tortfeasor.[67]

Under the general rule of article 454 of the RSFSR Civil Code, any person who causes material harm to another person by engaging in an activity involving the use of an ultrahazardous instrumentality, *i.e.*, an instrument which poses a source of increased danger to the surrounding environment, is held strictly liable even if he acted without fault. Such strict liability is rationalized by the fact that any person who knowingly engages in activities involving extraordinary danger to the surrounding environment takes the risk that such activity may cause harm to other persons, even if it can be shown that such person (the tortfeasor) acted with utmost care.

The general principle of strict liability under Soviet law was articulated by the Plenum of the USSR Supreme Court in a highlight decree which was handed down in 1963.[68] The decree stated in part:

> "In contrast to article 88 of the FPCivL [this corresponds to article 444 of the RSFSR Civil Code] according to which a tortfeasor is considered not liable for harm caused if it is established that he acted without fault, article 90 of the FPCivL [which corresponds to article 454 of the RSFSR Civil Code] provides that a juridical person or an individual, whose activity is connected with a source of increased danger for the surrounding vicinity, is strictly liable for the harm caused through the use of such source of increased danger, unless it can be shown that the harm was caused by an irreversible force of nature or through the contributory intentional act of the victim himself."[69]

Article 454 of the RSFSR Civil Code reads as follows:[70] "Organizations and citizens whose activities involve increased dangers for their neighbors (transport organizations, industrial enterprises, builders, motorists, etc.) are bound to make good any harm caused by such source of increased danger . . ." There is an on-going debate among Soviet writers as to whether article 454 of the RSFSR Civil Code as quoted above contemplates two independent bases of strict liability, *i.e.*, engaging in activities which involve increased danger to the neighbors, and the mere ownership of sources of increased danger, or whether it contemplates only one basis of strict liability, *i.e.*, engaging in activities which involve increased danger to the neighbors because of the fact that the instrument used in such activity is a source of increased danger to the neighboring vicinity.

One school of thought among Soviet writers–the majority school–takes the position that a source of increased danger *per se* is not a basis for strict liability, but rather that strict liability results from activity connected with the use of a source of increased danger. In other words, no activity in itself would constitute a basis for strict liability, just in the same way that no source of increased danger *per se* would constitute a basis for strict liability. Only activity involving the use of a source of increased danger should result in strict liability for the person engaging in such activity. A representative of this school of thought, Professor O. S. Ioffe, explains his position as follows:

"In the text of article 454 of the RSFSR Civil Code reference is made, on the one hand, to activities which pose an increased danger to the surrounding vicinity and, on the other hand, to specific objects which by their very nature are a source of increased danger. . . It cannot be a source of increased danger until it is put in motion or otherwise acted upon by man's activity. . . Thus, the factor taken into consideration by the law in imposing liability for use of instrument of increased danger is not the object itself, but rather man's activities connected with the object. But for man's activities to qualify as constituting increased danger, such activities must be related to the use of certain objects without which such activities would loose such special character. The list of such objects, albeit an incomplete list, is given in article 454 of the RSFSR Civil Code." [71]

A second school of thought in Soviet doctrinal law takes the position that article 454 of the RSFSR Civil Code contemplates two independent bases for strict liability: "activities which involve increased danger," and "sources of increased danger" even where the latter is not in use at the time that the material harm occurred. Among proponents of this theory are L. A. Maidanik and N. Iu. Sergeeva, [72] O. A. Krasavchikov, [73] and A.A. Sobchak. [74]

This writer supports the position espoused by Professor Ioffe, *i.e.*, the majority position in Soviet law. In doing so, however, the meaning of "activity" as suggested by another Soviet author, Professor Krasavchikov, is also adopted by this writer. According to Krasavchikov, "the law imposes liability on the owner of a source of increased danger in connection with the latter's use, creation, storage, and transfer, etc., of the corresponding source of increased danger as a result of which activity increased danger is created for the surrounding vicinity." [75] He goes on to state that the term "activity" as used in article 454 of the RSFSR Civil Code includes not just the ordinary use, but also the creation (*i.e.*, construction, erection, wiring, installation, etc.); storage (*i.e.*, refrigeration, burial, *e.g.*, of nuclear waste, disposal, *e.g.*, of explosive materials); transfer (*i.e.*, transportation by land, sea, or air); and all such related exploitative handling of the source of increased danger. [76]

The law itself does not define what may qualify as a source of increased danger for purposes of strict liability under article 454 [77] of the RSFSR Civil Code. The law, however, does list, albeit inexhaustively, certain activities which, by their very nature, are to be considered to involve increased danger to the surrounding vicinity. In addition to those activities that are listed in article 454 of the RSFSR Civil Code, Soviet doctrinal law generally lists the following activities as falling within the category of ultra-hazardous activities: storage of radioactive, inflammable, or poisonous materials; quarrying; sand digging; loading or unloading of goods. [78] In addition to all of these activities, a specific statute may create strict liability for persons or organizations which engage in certain other types of activities. One such statute is the USSR Air Code of 1961,[79] as amended by a Decree of the Presidium of the USSR Supreme Soviet issued on March 13, 1973.[80] A second statute which contemplates strict liability for persons who engage in certain types of ultra-hazardous activities is the 1929 USSR Merchant Shipping Code.[81] As to what constitutes a "source of increased danger," Professor Krasavchikov's 1973 study is perhaps the most authoritative statement on the subject.[82]

In all situations where the law contemplates strict liability, the owner of the source of increased danger is the one liable for harm resulting from the use of the source of increased danger. This point is further explained by Professors Genkin and Kunik in the following passage.

> "For harm caused through the use of a source of increased danger, the owner of such instrument shall be strictly liable even when the harm resulted from the technical operation of the source of increased danger by someone else other than the owner. Thus, in the case of harm, caused through the use of an automobile, the owner is liable and not the non-owner, who happens to be driving the automobile at the time of the injury. The person driving the automobile may be criminally liable if his actions contain the indicia of a crime."[83]

As used in the above passage, the term "owner" means "either the juridical person or the individual who exercises either the right of ownership or the right of operational control over the automobile."[84] If the operator of the automobile was operating it in the course of his employment for the owner, the owner of the automobile shall be vicariously liable[85] for harm caused by the operator. Having compensated the injured third party, however, the owner of the automobile may seek indemnity[86] from the employee only if the latter was negligent in the operation of the vehicle.[87]

There are situations in which the owner of the automobile would not be vicariously liable for the harm caused by the operator, *e.g.*, if the owner of the automobile contractually transferred the automobile to another party to be used for the benefit of that party. This is the situation when the owner of an automobile transfers it to a renter,[88] to an independent contractor, or to a bailee. In such cases, the transferee-operator of the automobile is considered to be the owner of the automobile for the purposes of tort liability resulting from harm caused by the operation of the automobile.[89] Also, if the operator of the automobile took control of the automobile, *i.e.*, a thief, a joy-rider, etc., the operator himself shall be held liable for any harm that is caused through the use of the automobile.[90] If, however, the owner's negligence contributed to the unlawful possession of the automobile by the third party, *e.g.*, through negligent storage or failure to lock the car, etc., both the negligent owner and the unlawful operator shall be liable *in solido* under article 180 of the RSFSR Civil Code for harm so caused through the operation of the automobile.[91] Presumably, however, the owner of the automobile may seek indemnity from the unlawful operator for any contribution paid by him (the owner) under the general principles of article 456, para. 1 of the RSFSR Civil Code.[92]

The Plenum of the Supreme Court of the USSR consolidated all of the above principles into one decree which was handed down in 1963.[93] In the pertinent provisions of the 1963 decree, the Plenum stated:

> "By the term 'owner of a source of increased danger,' one means the juridical person or individual who effectively exploits the instrument of increased danger either by virtue of the right of ownership or by right of operative control, or by virtue of other legal bases, *e.g.*, through a contract of rent, lease, independent contractor, or any other temporary contractual transfer of effective control to the transferee. A person is not considered to be the owner of a source of increased danger for the purposes of tort liability, resulting from use of such instrument of increased danger, if the person is operating the instrument by virtue of a contract of employment with the owner of the instrument, *e.g.*, a chauffeur, bus driver, locomotive driver, crane operator, etc. The owner of the instrument of increased danger is not liable for harm caused by the use of the instrument if it is shown that he lost possession of the instrument not by his fault, but as a result of the unlawful act of the operator-third party."[94]

The Plenum went on to add that if, however, the owner's negligence proximately contributed to the third party's unlawful possession of the automobile, both the owner and the unlawful possessor are liable *in solido, i.e.*, jointly and severally.[95]

From the above discussions, it follows that the rule in article 454 of the RSFSR Civil Code is an exception to the general rule governing tort liability under article 444 of the RSFSR Civil Code. The exception, however, relates only to the element of fault. For there to be a cause of action under the strict liability statute, the other three elements of tort must still be present, *i.e.*, it must be established that the victim suffered a material harm, that the harm was the result of the wrongful act on the part of the tortfeasor, and that the harm suffered was causally connected with the act of the tortfeasor.

Defenses in a Tort Action Involving the Use of the Automobile

Even where all the elements of liability are present, the tortfeasor may still avoid liability totally or have his liability mitigated if certain defenses are available to him. In the words of Professor Krasavchikov, "[b]y 'defenses' in an action for tort, one means such legal facts the existence or absence of which is considered by law either as a ground for full relief of the defendant from liability or as a ground for the reduction in the amount of compensation to be paid by the tortfeasor to the victim of the tort."[96]

For the purpose of convenience, we shall divide all the available defenses in Soviet law into two categories–absolute defenses and relative defenses. Of interest to us in this study are only the absolute defenses.

1) *Absolute Defenses*

These include all those defenses which, if successfully pleaded, will lead to a total release of the defendant from all liability regardless of whether such liability is based on fault or whether it is based on strict liability. These include the following:

a) Lack of Proximate Cause

For there to be liability for tort, it must be established that there was a causal connection between the wrongful act of the defendant and the injury or damage suffered by the victim. It follows, therefore, that if the act of the defendant is casually removed from the injury there cannot be liability. This lack of proximate cause [97] as an absolute defense in an action for tort is based upon the provisions of article 444 of the RSFSR Civil Code.

b) Intentional Act on the Part of the Victim

In all tort claims, including tort based on fault or on strict liability, if the intentional act by the victim contributed proximately to the causation of the harm, the tortfeasor shall be released from all liability. [98] The Plenum of the USSR Supreme Court adopted this position when it decreed in 1963 that "[i]n all cases the contributory intentional act on the part of the victim constitutes a basis for releasing the tortfeasor from liability." [99] In doing so, the court clearly distinguished the victim's contributory intentional act from his contributory gross negligence. Whereas, the former operates as a basis for the total release of the tortfeasor from liability, the latter shall operate only as a basis for a proportionate reduction in the damages. [100] It is true, of course, that the court in its discretion may release the tortfeasor from all liability if it is found that the victim's gross negligence contributed proximately to the causation or to the aggravation of the harm. But the difference lies in the fact that if the victim's intentional act contributed proximately to the causation of the harm, the defendant shall be released from all liability by operation of law, whereas the release from all liability is discretionary if it is established that the victim's gross negligence proximately contributed to the causation or aggravation of the harm. [101]

c) Insurmountable Act of Nature (*Force Majeure*)

A tortfeasor is released from strict liability under article 454 of the RSFSR Civil Code if it is shown that the injury was the result of an insurmountable force of nature, [102] *e.g.*, flood, earthquake, hurricane, etc. Since the law itself does not list those forces that may qualify as insurmountable forces of nature, it follows that "[t]he question as to whether a particular phenomenon qualifies as an insurmountable force of nature shall be decided in each case depending upon the concrete conditions of the locality at the time of the incidents. For example, in some cases, a phenomenon may qualify as an emergency and objectively as an insurmountable force, while in another situation the same phenomenon may be surmountable and therefore would not qualify as an insurmountable force of nature."[103] In other words, the concept of insurmountability varies with time, place, and surrounding circumstance.

A statute, however, may create liability even where an insurmountable force of nature was found to have contributed proximately to the causation or aggravation of the harm. When this happens, the insurmountable force of nature argument does not operate to release the tortfeasor from strict liability.[104] One example of such statute is the USSR Air Code.[105]

d) Unlawful Act of a Third Party

Under the Soviet strict liability statute, it is settled law that if the harm was caused through the unlawful act of a third person, the owner of the source of increased danger is not liable, unless it is shown that the negligence of such owner contributed proximately to the unlawful possession of the ultra-hazardous instrumentality by the third party. In the latter situation, both the owner of the instrument and the unlawful operator as of the time the harm was committed are subject to liability *in solido* to the injured party. Such owner may in turn bring an action for indemnity against the third party for any material loss suffered.[106]

e) Statute of Limitations

A plaintiff cannot maintain an action in tort if the statute of limitations has run. Upon making the determination that the statute of limitations has run, the court must dismiss the suit either acting on its own or at the request of the defendant. However, if the court finds that the plaintiff's failure to file suit within the prescribed time limit in attributable to an excusable reason, the court may proceed, in its discretion, to hear the case.[107]

5. Miscellaneous Provisions of Soviet Law That Are Likely to be Affected by Automobilization

In the foregoing sections of this study, we have examined the anticipated impact of automobilization on three broad areas of Soviet law–constitutional law, criminal law, and the law of torts and automobile insurance. In what follows we extend the inquiry to other technical aspects of Soviet law, *i.e.*, sales, lease, donation, exchange, and inheritance of automobiles.

Law of Sales (New Automobiles) [108]

The sale of automobiles in the USSR is governed by the same general principles of contract of sales that are embodied in articles 237-254 of the RSFSR Civil Code. Article 237 of the RSFSR Civil Code defines a contract of sales as a consensual, mutual, non-gratuitous agreement whereby the seller undertakes to transfer the ownership of the object of the contract to the buyer who, in return, undertakes the reciprocal obligation to accept the good and to pay for it the sum agreed upon by both contracting parties.

In the case of the sale of a new automobile in the Soviet Union, the seller, by law, is generally a state organization. Under article 240 of the RSFSR Civil Code the price of the good sold by a socialist organization, *i.e.*, state, cooperative, and social organizations, must conform to the price fixed by the state for such commodity, unless in those instances where the law establishes an exception. Since there are no known exceptions with regard to the sale of automobiles, it follows that the selling price for a new automobile by a state organization generally should conform to the state price list. What this means in terms of Soviet economic realities is that, without regard for actual cost of production, the Soviet government artificially manipulates the price of commodities entrusted to its exclusive right of sale. Depending on the current economic policy of the state, the price of a commodity could be higher or lower than the real market price. In the case of the automobile, it so happens that Soviet government policy at this time is to artificially inflate the price of family-size cars so as to discourage many potential buyers. [109]

Soviet law grants to state organizations the exclusive right to sell new automobiles in the USSR, to the exclusion of all private car dealers, including even those Western corporations which collaborated with the Soviet government in the manufacture of these automobiles. It will be unrealistic to expect at this time that the Soviet Union will relax such ban against private participation in the marketing of new automobiles in the Soviet Union.

Law of Sales (Used Automobiles)

The sale of used automobiles in the Soviet Union presents a different problem of its own. Because the automobile is a deficit item in the Soviet Union, the sale of used automobiles by one private person to another private person is prohibited by law. Such sale must be processed through a state commission store which acts as a middleman (a broker) between the seller and the buyer. In doing so, the commission store collects about 70% of the selling price as its commission.

Strictly speaking the state commission store, in selling the automobile to B, is not acting as the agent of A, because even though the store sells the automobile to B in the interest of A, the store does so in its own name. The status of the state commission store is that of a pure independent contractor or a broker, rather than that of an agent acting for an undisclosed principal.

The store acts in the interest of A in negotiating the sale of the automobile to B.[110] But also, the commission store assumes all risks connected with the sale of the automobile to B.

The law requires that the commission contract between A and the commission store be in writing.[111] The sale price to be demanded by the commission store in selling the automobile to B is to be determined by the agreement between A and the commission store, but under no circumstance must such agreed upon selling price (between A and the state commission store) exceed the state-fixed "bluebook" value of the automobile. If the state commission store sells the automobile for less than the price agreed upon with A, the store has to make up the difference to A.

It is an open secret that Soviet citizens who desire either to sell or buy a used car will do anything to circumvent the state commission store. The result of such "civil disobedience" by Soviet citizens is that the automobile black market flourishes throughout the Soviet Union. In an age of automobilization, the Soviet government will be forced to relax the rules governing the sale of used automobiles. The first change that must be made will be to permit private citizens to sell and buy used cars without having to go through the state commission stores. The state could institute a system of registration of all such private sales for the purpose both of keeping record of all automobiles that change ownership, and of collecting sales tax on all such private sales.

Law of Lease of Automobiles

Article 275 of the RSFSR Civil Code defines lease as the temporary transfer of operational control over a consumer object by the owner (or by the organization that exercises the right of operational ownership over such object) to a lessee for a consideration. Under present Soviet law, only state agencies may lease automobiles. It is a crime for an individual owner of an automobile to lease his automobile to a third party for a fee or in exchange for any other article of value. Also, an individual lessee of an automobile is under an obligation not to sublet the automobile so leased to him by the state rental agency. The lease agreement must be in writing, and the lessee is obligated to compensate the lessor for any damage to the automobile, other than the normal wear and tear associated with the operation of the vehicle.

It is not expected that the Soviet Union will relax the rules governing the lease of automobiles in the foreseeable future. But it is inevitable that car rentals will increase in the Soviet Union in the 1980's.

Law Governing Donation, Exchange, and Inheritance of Automobiles

No major changes are likely to take place in the areas of donation, exchange, and inheritance of automobiles. The present Soviet law of donation permits the unilateral gratuitous transfer, *i.e.*, donation, of automobiles from one citizen to another, as long as the act of donation–where the retail price of the automobile is in excess of 500 rubles–is notorized. However, if the act of donation is a camouflage for another illegal transaction, *e.g.*, person-to-person sale of automobile, person-to-person exchange of one automobile by the ostensible donor for another automobile or for something else of value to be received from the apparent donee, etc., the donation will be null and void.

Under the present law governing exchange of consumer goods, all forms of commodity exchanges between private individuals *inter se* are categorically prohibited by Soviet law. Any such exchange must be accomplished through the intermediary of the state commission store. By insisting that all commodity exchanges should go through the state trade mart, the Soviet government is assuming a very burdensome responsibility of policing citizen compliance with such laws. This burden could be readily shed by deregulating all commodity exchanges, with a few exceptions, and instead requiring that all private exchanges of consumer items be registered with the state.

Finally, subject to the respective laws of inheritance,[112] an automobile owner may bequeath his automobile to another person. In this regard, no changes are reasonably expected in the next decade of Soviet law reforms.

6. Some General Conclusions

According to apologists of the Soviet legal system, Soviet law is revolutionary by nature. Unlike bourgeois law, which is conservative by nature and is used in essence to preserve the *status quo*, Soviet law serves as an instrument of social engineering, as an instrument for paving the way for the ultimate demise of law itself, as an instrument for building the new Soviet man. Since there will be no laws under full communism, it follows that there will be no notion of crime, tort, contract, or succession under that lawless system. However, until the Soviet people reach that promised land, law has an immediate role to play in the realistic world of the contemporary Soviet Union.

An inescapable part of that Soviet realism is the projected automobilization of the Soviet society. Admittedly, the purpose of this policy is not to put two automobiles in the driveway of every Soviet home. The goal is a modest one–to enable as many Soviet citizens who wish to own personal automobiles to do so without creating a pervasive un-socialist private property psychosis. Whether the Soviet government likes it or not, Soviet society cannot totally avoid the impact of automobilization. The direct sources of such automobiles are both international as well as domestic.

Today, Soviet frontiers are more open to foreign tourists than they have ever been before in the 60 years existence of the Soviet State. Foreign travelers visit the Soviet Union by all modern means of transportation–by air, sea, rail, and, of course, by road. Some even cross into the Soviet Union on foot. But a great number of those who visit the USSR by road do so in private automobiles. Throughout their stay in the Soviet Union, these foreigners operate their private motor vehicles on Soviet roads. And as such they expose both themselves, their passengers, and pedestrians to the risk of personal injury or damage to property as a result of the operation of the motor vehicle. The contemporary Soviet Union can no longer afford to close its gates to the foreign motorists.

On the domestic scene, the direct source of motor vehicles is the announced Soviet policy of automobilization. The next decade is bound to witness a substantial growth in the material wealth of Soviet citizens. Not only will the long-deprived Soviet citizen then be able to own television sets, refrigerators, radios, washing machines and dryers, but also most of them will then be able to afford an automobile, which will replace the color television set as the ultimate status symbol in Soviet society.[113] This will inevitably lead to an un-socialist stratification of the Soviet Society into "haves" (those who have personal automobiles) and "have-nots" (those who cannot afford to own a personal automobile).

Ownership and operation of a motor vehicle in the Soviet Union raises a host of questions not only of constitutional law, law of torts, contracts, and property, but also of administrative law and criminal law. Present Soviet law crystallized essentially in the 1960's, and, therefore, in the view of this writer, its norms are ill-suited to handle the problems of the remaining two decades of this century, particularly the automobile-related problems.

As an illustration of the enormity of this problem, let us take just the tort aspect of the ownership and operation of a motor vehicle. The following problems immediately arise in one's mind: the general duty of care in the operation of a vehicle; liability for injuries to pedestrians (particularly children), bicyclists, and motorcyclists; liability to invited guests of the operator of the vehicle; owner's vicarious liability where the vehicle is operated by another person; the owner's responsibility to maintain the vehicle in operating condition. Of particular interest to the foreign motorist is the question of his liability under Soviet law for the negligent operation of his vehicle inside the Soviet Union, as well as the question of compensation for damages that he may suffer as a result of the negligent operation of a motor vehicle by a Soviet motorist. Of equal importance to him is the question of conflict of laws in an automobile accident case in which he is either the plaintiff or defendant.

The newly-adopted Constitution of the USSR has reaffirmed the constitutional foundations of the right of individual citizens to own automobiles. In doing so, however, the 1977 Constitution seems to have stressed the critical point which was left out of the 1936 USSR Constitution, *i.e.*, that the right to own a personal automobile is not and never will be regarded as an absolute right. Since the essence of ownership of a personal automobile is to satisfy the consumer needs of the owner as well as those of the members of his immediate family, the 1977 Constitution of the USSR, in Article 12, makes it very clear that any citizen who uses his personal automobile, either to derive unearned income or to further anti-social purposes, places such automobile in danger of confiscation by the state. This writer believes that the 1977 Soviet Constitution contains adequate provisions to guide the evolution of a Soviet automobile law for the next two decades.

Since the 1977 Constitution of the USSR has endorsed the idea of a constitutional right to own a personal automobile, it follows that Soviet criminal law will continue to protect the property rights of citizens with regard to the automobile. In the late 1980's this writer expects that the provisions of Societ criminal law dealing with the ownership and use of the automobile not only will, but, in fact, must undergo a few, albeit minor, changes. One should expect to see not only an intensification of the anti-speculation campaign, but also an increase in criminal punishment for convicted automobile black-marketeers. Similar changes, involving a stepping up of the enforcement of the law against violators, as well as a possible increase in the punishment upon conviction, are envisaged in relation to private entrepreneurial activity, actions as a commercial middleman, engaging in prohibited trade, and drunken driving. In all the other areas of Soviet criminal law dealing with automobile crimes, one should expect at least a preservation of the *status quo* or possibly a change, either in the direction of decriminalization of some of the crimes or the adoption of a policy of selective non-enforcement of suspected violations by the procurator.

In the area of tort liability, contemporary Soviet law is grossly inadequate to serve Soviet needs in the 1980's and 1990's. First, the Soviet Union should consider requiring all motorists to carry a liability insurance. It will be more preferable if they elect a no-fault automobile insurance policy. Second, the Soviet Union should consider adopting a guest statute that would strictly limit the liability of the owner or operator of a motor vehicle for injury or death caused to an invited gratuitous guest.

One other critical area of the law where the Soviet government can afford to relax its present anachronistic rules is in the realm of the sales of used cars. There is no compelling reason why the Soviet government should insist upon handling all used car sales through the inept state-run commission stores. The present system is not only inefficient, but, more importantly, it causes underground used-car markets to flourish throughout the USSR. If the Soviet government's purpose in insisting on the commission sales procedure is to keep record of all used car sales and to collect sales taxes on such sales, the same purpose could be achieved by simply requiring that all private sales of used cars be notarized. The same requirement could be imposed on private citizens who whish to exchange their automobiles either for other automobiles or for something of value.

In the area of the domestic passport system, one cannot reasonably expect any major changes to be brought about by automobilization. The Soviet government is apparently determined to subject the pleasures of the individual motorist to the real or imaginary national security interests which the domestic passport system is designed to protect.

Whether or not these projected law reforms take place, one thing is certain, *i.e.*, that the Soviet Union will never be the same again once the automobilization policy is fully implemented by 1980.

The automobile will present Soviet law with one of its greatest challenges in the decades ahead. Let us hope that the Soviet lawmakers will respond by developing a responsive automobile law, by which we mean a law which is substantively cost efficient, procedurally uncomplicated, and ultimately motivated by a pro-consumer policy.

NOTES

1. See "Five-Day Week Brings Weekends Without Services," *CDSP*, 19 (1968), No. 50, 3-4.

2. N. K. Baibakov, "O gosudarstvennom piatiletnem plane razvitiia narodnogo khoziaizstva SSSR na 1977 goda" (On the State Five-year Plan for the Development of USSR National Economy for the Year 1977), *Pravda*, Oct. 28, 1976, pp. 2-3.

3. "Avtomobil'nye Dorogi Rossii–Interv'iu po pros'be chitatelei" (Automobile Highways of Russia–An interview at the Request of Readers), *Izvestiia*, Mar. 11, 1977, p. 2.

4. "Oktiabr', vremia, liudi" (October, Time, and People), *Izvestiia*, Feb. 13, 1977, p. 5.

5. "Avtomobil', televizor i serdityi diadia" (Automobile, Television, and the Angry Uncle), *Izvestiia*, Sept. 25, 1976, p. 5. In a reply to the above complaint, *Izvestiia* pointed out that it is not only erroneous to refer to owners of personal automobiles as *chastniki*, but that, in fact, it is highly insulting to use the term *chastnik* in reference to a working person.

6. *Id.*

7. "Dom dlia avtomobilia" (A Home for the Car), *Izvestiia*, Sept. 15, 1976, p. 2.

8. *Izvestiia*, Sept. 25, 1976, p. 5.

9. *Id.*

10. "Chtoby ne bylo proisshestvii" (So That There Would Be No Accidents), *Izvestiia*, Nov. 25, 1976, p. 5.

11. See "VAZ: esche odna novinka" (VAZ; Just One More Novelty), *Izvestiia*, Apr. 6, 1977, p. 4. The production plan calls for the production of 15,000 *VAZ-2121* by the end of 1977.

12. Because it is written under the constraints of space, this study has also chosen to omit many other aspects of Soviet automobile law, such as the responsibility of foreigners who operate motor vehicles inside the USSR. The writer hopes to undertake, at some later time, a supplementary study devoted to these and other related questions of Soviet automobile law.

13. The term "Soviet automobile law" is used in this study to refer to a totality of those general principles of Soviet law that directly relate to the ownership, operation, and abuses of the automobile. Not being an independent branch of Soviet law, Soviet automobile law draws upon the legal norms operating in the other established branches of Soviet law such as: constitutional law, criminal law, law of contracts and torts, property law, the law of successions and donations, administrative law, and the law of insurance.

14. At the time of this writing, the USSR had just adopted a new state constitution which replaced the 1936 Stalin Constitution. The 1977 Constitution of the USSR protects the rights of personal property in Article 12. The language of Article 12 of the 1977 Constitution directly corresponds to the provision of Article 10 of the 1936 Constitution. For an English translation of the 1977 USSR Constitution by F. J. M. Feldbrugge and William B. Simons, see "Constitution (Fundamental Law) of the Union of Soviet Socialist Republics." *Review of Socialist Law*, 4 (1978), No. 1, 57-84.

15. Article 9 of the 1977 USSR Constitution corresponds to Article 5 of the 1936 Constitution.

16. Article 10 of the 1977 Constitution corresponds to Article 6 of the 1936 Constitution.

17. Article 12 of the 1977 Constitution corresponds to Article 7 of the 1936 Constitution.

18. Unlike Article 5 of the 1936 Constitution, which failed to explicitly list property belonging to social organizations as socialist property, Article 9 of the 1977 Constitution does so, thus eliminating the former need to fall back on Article 20 of the FPCivL in order to complete the list in Article 5 of the 1936 Constitution.

19. This limitation applies to members of the same family who are living together.

20. For example, in the RSFSR each individual is entitled to 9 sq. meters of living space (article 106 of the RSFSR Civil Code). In the Ukraine the housing norm is 13.65 sq. meters per person, whereas in Soviet Georgia and Azerbaidzhan the housing norm is 12 sq. meters per person. The RSFSR law (article 316 of the RSFSR Civil Code), just as the laws of the other 14 republics, grants exemption from its housing norm to certain privileged persons. For example, the following individuals are entitled to more living space under RSFSR law either because of their standing in society or because of their professional needs: heroes of the USSR: heroes of socialist labor: laureates of all levels of the medals of honor, and persons recognized by the state for their service to science, the arts, or technology; members of the Union of Artists of the USSR and the union republics; writers; artists; composers; architects; movie actors and directors; peoples' artists of the USSR; inventors; scientific workers with at least a doctor's degree: scientific workers holding the following university titles–associate professors, senior research associates, full professors, corresponding members of the USSR Academy of Sciences and academicians. In other words, just about every Soviet citizen of any social standing, but not the members of the proletarian class, peasants, and low echelon civil servants.

21. Under article 112 of the RSFSR Civil Code, there is a quantitative limitation on the right of individuals to own head of cattle.

22. Details of these procedural limitations are discussed in the section of this study dealing with sales and leases of automobiles, as well as the section on succession and donations of personal automobiles.

23. For a comprehensive Western analysis of the nature and legal regulation of property rights in the USSR, see J. N. Hazard, W. E. Butler, and P. B. Maggs, *The Soviet Legal System–Fundamental Principles and Historical Commentary*, 3rd. ed. (Dobbs Ferry, NY, 1977), pp. 361-414.

24. A. A. Rubanov, "Sotsial'nye aspekty prava lichnoi sobstvennosti v SSSR" (The Social Aspects of the Right of Personal Property in the USSR), *SGiP*, 1973, No. 9, 25-32.

25. *Id.*, 25.

26. *Id.*, 27.

27. R. O. Khalfina, *Pravo lichnoi sobstvennosti* (The Law of Personal Ownership), (Moscow, 1964), p. 33.

28. A. A. Piontkovskii, P. S. Romashkin, and V. M. Chkhikvadze (eds.), *Kurs sovetskogo ugolovnogo prava* (Treatise on Soviet Criminal Law, hereafter cited as Piontkovskii, *et al., Treatise*), Vol. 5 (Moscow, 1971), 283-286.

29. For a general review of the current Soviet law on forfeiture, see C. Osakwe, "Forfeiture," in F. J. M. Feldbrugge (ed.), *Encyclopedia of Soviet Law* (hereafter cited as: Feldbrugge (ed.), *Encyclopedia*), Vol. 1 (Leyden, 1973), pp. 288-290.

30. Article 17 of the USSR Constitution of 1977 permits individual handicraftsmen

to engage in limited private enterprise, as long as they do not exploit outside labor. Personal property acquired with the proceeds of such private enterprise is accorded equal protection with all other legitimate personal property rights under articles 115 and 134 of the RSFSR Civil Code. Also, Soviet law permits Soviet citizens to render personal services to foreign establishments operating inside the Soviet Union (foreign embassies and consulates, press corps, foreign trade delegations, business corporations, etc.). Payments received for such services are considered to be "earned" income for purposes of Soviet personal property laws.

31. For a general discussion of the concept of abuse of right in Soviet law, see C. Osakwe, "The Common Law of the Constitutions of Communist Party-States," *Review of Socialist Law*, 3 (1977), No. 2, 155-217, at 190-196.

32. With the exception of article 127, which is a logical sequel to article 211, these provisions of the RSFSR Criminal Code are discussed here in the numerical order in which they appear in the Code. No attempt was made to group them into thematic headings, *e.g.*, violations related to ownership rights, violations of safety regulations, and violations of rules governing the sale of automobiles.

33. Piontkovskii, *et al., Treatise*, note 28 above, Vol. 5, p. 296.

34. The RSFSR Criminal Code contemplates other forms of stealing of personal property in articles 145 (open stealing), 146 (assault with intent to rob), 147 (swindling), and 148 (extortion). All of these provisions, *mutatis mutandis*, apply to the theft of personal automobiles.

35. Note 45 below.

36. For a detailed discussion of the general principles of Soviet law of torts, see the section of this paper dealing with automobilization and the law of torts.

37. For a detailed discussion of the elements of the crime in article 153 of the RSFSR Criminal Code, see C. Osakwe, "Contemporary Soviet Criminal Law: An Analysis of the General Principles and Major Institutions of Post-1958 Soviet Criminal Law," *Georgia Journal of International and Comparative Law*, 6 (1976), 437-492.

38. *Id.*, 481.

39. For a detailed discussion of the elements of the crime of speculation under article 154 of the RSFSR Criminal Code, see *id.*, 482-483.

40. For a detailed discussion of the elements of the crime in article 162 of the RSFSR Criminal Code, see *id.*, 484-485.

41. In the case of "D," the USSR Supreme Court held that a person who uses his private automobile to transport passengers for a consideration only on one occasion would not be covered by article 162 of the RSFSR Criminal Code, because, in the Court's view, article 162 calls for a "systematic activity" on the part of the defendant. Case of "D," *BVS SSSR*, 1960, No. 8, cited in G. Z. Anashkin, I. I. Karpets, and B. S. Nikiforov (eds.), *Kommentarii k Ugolovnomu Kodeksu RSFSR* (Commentary to the RSFSR Criminal Code) hereafter cited as: Anashkin *et al., Kommentarii*), (Moscow, 1971), p. 347, n6.
Under the Edict of the Presidium of the RSFSR Supreme Soviet issued on June 19, 1968, entitled "Ob usilenii administrativnoi otvetstvennosti za narushenie pravil dvizheniia po ulitsam gorodov, naselennykh punktov i dorogam i pravil pol'zovaniia transportnymi sredstvami" (On Increasing the Administrative Penalty For Violation of Rules of Highway Safety on the Streets of Cities, Populated Areas and on Roads, as well as of Rules Governing the Operation of Means of Transportation), the one-time use of a personal automobile for the transportation of passengers for a consideration is an administrative offense. *Ved. V. S. RSFSR*, 1968, No. 26, item 1009.

42. See: Section 4 of "Pravila registratsii nekooperirovannykh kustarei i remeslennikov" (Rules Governing the Registration of Non-cooperative Artisans and Handicrafts-

men) which was adopted by a Decree of the USSR Council of Ministers on June 30, 1949, with amendments of April 22, 1958, *Sobr. Post. SSSR*, 1958, No. 7, item 24, amendments of June 3, 1963, *Sobr. Post. SSSR*, 1963, No. 12, item 12.

43. *Id.*

44. *Id.*

45. See Anashkin *et. al., Kommentarii*, pp. 451-452.

46. Decree of the Plenum of the RSFSR Supreme Court, "O sudebnoi praktike po delam o prestupleniakh, sviazannykh s narusheniiami pravil ikh bezopasnosti dvizhenii i ekspluatatsii transportnykh sredstv a takzhe s ugonom" (On Judicial Practice Regarding Crimes Connected with Violations of Rules of Highway Safety and of The Use of Means of Transportation, as well as with their Unauthorized Operation), Oct. 22, 1969, *BVS RSFSR*, 1970, No. 1, item 4.

47. I. I. Gorelik, M. R. Levutanus, G. B. Astanovskii, and A. Beliaev, *Prava i otvetstvennost' peshekhodov*, (The Rights and Responsibility of Pedestrians) hereafter cited as Gorelik *et. al., Rights*), (Moscow, 1976), p. 78.

48. Anashkin *et al., Kommentarii*, p. 452.

49. For a detailed discussion of the elements of the crime in article 127 of the RSFSR Criminal Code, see Osakwe, note 37 above, pp. 478-479.

50. The term "transport vehicle or any other self-propelled machine" is used in the same context that it had been used under article 211 above.

51. Article 211-2 of the RSFSR Criminal Code covers other types of crime which are not related to the operation of a personal automobile and, as such, are irrelevant to the topic of this study. For a general commentary on article 211-2, see Anashkin *et. al., Kommentarii*, pp. 455-456.

52. Case of "P", *BVS SSSR*, 1962, No. 11.

53. For a general discussion of the fundamental freedoms granted under the Soviet Constitutional system, see Osakwe, note 31 above. See also C. Osakwe, "Equal Protection of Law Under The Soviet Constitutional System," *Netherlands Studies in Comparative Law*, 2 (1975), No. 2, 159-211.

54. Decree of the USSR Council of Ministers approving the Statute on The Passport System of the USSR, Decree No. 677, of August 28, 1974. See *Sobr. Post. SSSR*, 1974, No. 19, item 109. Sections 4, 6, 8, and 19-38 of the Statute went into effect on January 1, 1976. For an English language translation of the statute by William E. Butler, see "Soviet Passport Legislation," *Review of Socialist Law*, 2 (1976), No. 1, 47-65. For a synoptic update of the predecessor passport legislations of the USSR, see R. Beermann, "Passports," in Feldbrugge (ed.), *Encyclopedia*, Vol. 2, pp. 489-491.

55. All citations to the 1974 Statute on the Passport System of the USSR are to Butler's English translation of the Statute, note 54 above.

56. For a general discussion of the various types of insurance policies in the USSR, see L. A. Motiler (ed.), *Gosudarstvennoe strakhovanie v SSSR* (State Insurance in the USSR), (Moscow, 1971).

57. For a general discussion of Soviet insurance law, see *id.*, pp. 120-123; B. Rudden, "Insurance," in Feldbrugge (ed.), *Encyclopedia*, Vol. 1, pp. 323-326, B. Rudden, *Soviet Insurance Law, Law in Eastern Europe*, Vol. 12, (Leyden, 1966).

58. For a general discussion of the coverage offered by a personal (life) insurance policy under Soviet Law, see E. A. Motiler (ed.), note 54 above, pp. 231-250.

59. For a general review of the trend toward no-fault automobile insurance in the United States, see O'Connell, "Torts," in Gillers (ed.), *Looking At Law School: A Student Guide From the Society of American Law Teachers* (1977), pp. 108-122.

60. See "Gallup Poll: Public Split On Merits of No-Fault," *The Times-Picayune* (New Orleans, La.), Sept. 15, 1977.

61. O'Connell, note 59 above, p. 116.

62. The social insurance system is not a totally new idea to the Soviets. It prevailed in the Soviet Union during the early period. See Law on Social Insurance, Decree of October 31, 1918, in *Sobr. Uzak.* (Collected Statutes) 1918, I, 906. For a general discussion of the early Soviet social insurance system, see A. E. Tay, "The Foundations of Tort Liability in a Socialist Legal System: Fault Versus Social Insurance in Soviet Law," *University of Toronto Law Journal*, 19 (1969), 1. At the present time, it appears that a social insurance system is successfully being tested in New Zealand. The New Zealand experiment is approvingly cited by Professor O'Connell in his survey of the comparative law of torts. See O'Connell, note 59 above, p. 116.

63. Back in the 1960's, Soviet writers openly debated the question of whether Soviet motorists should be required to carry a third-party liability insurance policy. Some writers strongly urged the imposition of such requirement on all motorists, while others argued for a retention of the *status quo*. For a general survey of this Soviet debate, see A. P. Nozdriadkov, ' O strakhovanii grazhdanskoi otvetstvennosti vladel'tsev individual'nogo transporta" (On the Insurance of Civil Liability of Owners of Personal Automobiles), *SGiP*, 1977, No. 8, 72.

64. For a general discussion of the general principles of Soviet law of torts, see: A. Adahl, "Torts," in Feldbrugge (ed.), *Encyclopedia*, Vol. 2, pp. 677-680. Among the classic works on the Soviet law of torts by Western students of Soviet Law are the following: B. Rudden, "Soviet Tort Law," *New York University Law Review*, 42 (1967), 583; W. Gray, "Soviet Law of Torts; The New Principles Annotated," in Lafave (ed.), *Law in the Soviet Society* (Urbana 1965), p. 180; J. N. Hazard, *Communists and their Law: A Search for the Common Core of the Legal Systems of the Marxian Socialists States* (New York, 1969), pp. 381-416; D. Barry, "Governmental Tort Liability in the Soviet Union," *Rutgers Law Review*, 20 (1966), 300; D. Barry, "The Motor Car in Soviet Criminal and Civil Law," *International and Comparative Law Quarterly*, 16 (1967), 56; J. N. Hazard, W. E. Butler, and P. B. Maggs, *The Soviet Legal System–Fundamental Principles and Historical Commentary*, 3rd. ed. (Dobbs Ferry, NY, 1977). A great bulk of the modern Soviet statutory law of torts may be found in the following statutes: Osnovy Grazhdanskogo Zakonodatel'stva Soiuza SSR i Soiuznykh Republik (The Fundamental Principles of Civil Legislation of the USSR and the Union Republics) adopted on December 8, 1961, articles 88-95, (hereafter cited as USSR FPCivL 1961), *Ved. V.S. RSFSR*, 1961, No. 50, item 525; 1964 Civil Code of the RSFSR, articles 444-471; Rules Governing the Compensation of Workers by Enterprises, Institutions, and Organizations For Personal Injuries and Other Injuries to Health, adopted jointly by the State Committee on Questions of Labor and Wages of the USSR Council of Ministers and the Presidium of the All-Union Central Committee of Trade Unions on December 22, 1961 (hereafter cited as Rules Governing Compensation For Personal Injuries 1961), *Ved. V.S. SSSR*, 1961, No. 41, item 420. The general provisions of the FPCivL have been re-enacted in the RSFSR Civil Code, as well as in the civil codes of the other fourteen Soviet union republics. Purely for the sake of convenience, all civil code references in this study are made to the RSFSR Civil Code. Where other Soviet writers or the Soviet Courts make reference to the FPCivL in passages cited in this study, a cross reference will be given to the corresponding provisions of the RSFSR Civil Code.

65. The discussion of strict liability here is not confined only to those provisions of the doctrine that are relevant to the use of the automobile.

66. For a general discussion of the bases of tort liability under article 444 of the RSFSR Civil Code, see Rudden note 64 above; Adahl, note 64 above.

67. For a more detailed discussion of the doctrine of strict liability in Soviet Law,

see O. S. Ioffe, *Obiazatel'stvennoe pravo* (The Law of Obligations), (Moscow, 1975), pp. 801-809.

68. Decree of the Plenum of the Supreme Court of the USSR "O sudebnoi praktike o vozmeshchenii vreda" (On Judicial Practice Regarding Compensation for Damages), Oct. 23, 1963, amended by a decree of Mar. 30, 1973; amendment in: *BVS SSSR*, 1973, No. 3, 13 (hereafter cited as Decree of the USSR S. Ct. Plenum); Decree of the Plenum of the Supreme Court of the RSFSR, "O nekotorykh voprosakh voznikshikh v praktike sudov pri primenenii norm grazhdanskogo Kodeksa RSFSR reguliruiushchikh vozmeshcheniia vreda" (On Certain Questions Which Arise in the Practice of Courts Regarding the Application of Norms of the RSFSR Civil Code Governing Compensation for Damages), Feb. 7, 1967, *BVS RSFSR*, 1967, No. 4, 7 (hereafter cited as Decree of RSFSR S. Ct. Plenum). All subsequent citations to these two decrees are to the extracts contained in: A. Iu. Kabalkin (ed.), *Grazhdanskoe Zakonodatel'stvo–Sbornik Normativnykh Aktov* (Civil Legislation–A Collection of Normative Acts), (Moscow, 1974), pp. 943-955 (Decree of the USSR S. Ct. Plenum) and pp. 955-958 (Decree of RSFSR S. Ct. Plenum), respectively.

69. *Id.*, 945.

70. Article 454 of the RSFSR Civil Code. For an English language translation of the 1964 RSFSR Civil Code, see A. K. R. Kiralfy, *The Civil Code and the Code of Civil Procedure of the RSFSR 1964, Law in Eastern Europe*, Vol. 11 (Leyden, 1966), pp. 11-150.

71. O. S. Ioffe, note 67 above, p. 804. Professor John Hazard also supports this position. See J. N. Hazard, note 64 above, p. 394.

72. L. A. Maidanik and N. Iu. Sergeeva, *Material'naia otvetstvennost' za povrezhdenie zdorov'ia* (Material Responsibility For Causing Injury to Health), (Moscow, 1968), p. 48, as cited in Ioffe, note 67 above, p. 804.

73. D. A. Krasavchikov, *Vozmeshchenie vreda, prichinennogo istochnikom povyshennoi opasnosti* (Compensation for Injury Casued by a Source of Increased Danger), (Moscow, 1966), p. 16, cited in Ioffe, note 67 above, p. 804.

74. A. A. Sobchak, "O poniatii istochnika povyshennoi opasnosti v grazhdanskom prave" (On the Concept of Source of Increased Danger in Civil Law), *Pravovedenie*, 1964, No. 2, 144-145, as cited in Ioffe, note 67 above, p. 804.

75. A. A. Krasavchikov (ed.), *Sovetskoe grazhdanskoe pravo* (Soviet Civil Law), Vol. 2 (Moscow, 1973), pp. 345-346.

76. *Id.*

77. The pertinent provisions of article 454 of athe RSFSR Civil Code are reproduced.

78. E. A. Fleishits and O. S. Ioffe, *Kommentarii k grazhdanskomu kodeksu RSFSR* (Commentary to the Civil Code of RSFSR), 2nd rev. ed. (Moscow, 1970), p. 676.

79. Air Code of the USSR adopted by the Presidium of the USSR Supreme Soviet on December 25, 1961. *Ved. V. S. SSSR*, 1961, No. 52, item 538. An English translation of the USSR Air Code can be found in *Law in Eastern Europe*, Vol. 14 (Leyden, 1967), pp. 86-115.

80. Edict of the Presidium of the USSR Supreme Soviet, Mar. 13, 1973. The text of the decree is given in Kabalkin (ed.), note 68 above, p. 929.

81. 1929 USSR Merchant Shipping Code, as cited in D. M. Genkin and I. A. Kunik (eds.), *Sovetskoe grazhdanskoe pravo* (Soviet Civil Law), (Moscow, 1967), p. 497. An English translation of the 1929 Code appears in *Law in Eastern Europe*, Vol. 4 (Leyden, 1960).

82. A. A. Krasavchikov, note 75 above, pp. 345-347.

83. Genkin and Kunik, note 81 above, p. 504.

84. *Id.*, 504.

85. For a general discussion of vicarious tort liability in Soviet law, see Rudden, note 64 above.

86. For a general discussion of the action for indemnity in Soviet law, see Rudden, note 64 above.

87. See Fleishits and Ioffe, note 78 above, p. 677.

88. A person who rents an automobile from a rental agency may in turn hold the rental agency liable in an action for indemnity, if it is shown that the rental agency failed to maintain the automobile in a good mechanical condition and failed to warn the renter of the fact that the automobile was not in a good condition when it was rented. See Fleishits and Ioffe, *id.*, pp. 677-678.

89. See Ioffe, note 67 above, p. 804.

90. See Ioffe, *id.* See also Fleishits and Ioffe, note 78 above, pp. 677-678.

91. See Fleishits and Ioffe, *id.*, p. 678.

92. See Ioffe, note 67 above, p. 804.

93. 1963 decree of the USSR Supreme Court Plenum, note 68 above.

94. *Id.*, at 945.

95. *Id.*

96. Krasavchikov, note 75 above, p. 334.

97. For a general discussion of the doctrine of proximate cause in Soviet law, see Rudden, note 64 above.

98. See generally Ioffe, note 67 above, pp. 807-808.

99. Decree of the USSR Supreme Court Plenum, note 68 above, 950.

100. For a general discussion of the bases for the award of diminished damages see Rudden, note 64 above.

101. Ioffe, note 67 above, p. 828.

102. See Ioffe, *id.*, p. 807-808.

103. Fleishits and Ioffe, note 78 above, p. 678.

104. Ioffe, note 67 above, p. 808.

105. USSR Air Code, note 79 above.

106. For a general discussion of strict liability in Soviet law, see section on strict liability in the section on the law of torts.

107. For a general discussion of the statute of limitations in Soviet civil law, see Rudden, note 64 above.

108. For a general discussion of the law of sales in Soviet law, see Z. Szirmai, "Sales," in Feldbrugge (ed.), *Encyclopedia*, Vol. 2, pp. 596-597; Z. Zile, "Retail Trade," in Feldbrugge (ed.), *Encyclopedia*, Vol. 2, pp. 590-592.

109. Based on national average take-home pay in January 1976, a Soviet worker requires 37.5 months of work time in order to earn enough money to buy a compact car in Moscow. By contrast, his American counterpart requires 6.9 months of work time in order to earn enough money to buy a compact car in Washington, DC. Also, a Soviet worker requires 190 minutes of work time in order to earn enough money to buy 10 gallons of regular gasoline; cf. US worker's 91 minutes of work time. Figures are cited in: "Russia's 60 years of Communism: Success or Failure?," *US News and World Report*, Oct. 24, 1977, 42-66, at 53. The same source states that real income in the Soviet Union now averages $ 208 a month per person. *Id.*, 43.

110. For a general discussion of the law of commission contracts in Soviet law, see D. Winter, "Commission Agents," in Feldbrugge (ed.), *Encyclopedia*, Vol. 1, pp. 136-140.

111. See article 404 of the RSFSR Civil Code.

112. The bulk of RSFSR inheritance law is codified in articles 527-561 of the RSFSR Civil Code.

113. It is estimated that as of 1977, 6 out of 10 families in the Soviet Union owned refrigerators; 7 out of 10 owned washing machines. By 1975 the estimate was that there were television sets in 8 out of 10 homes; whereas a mere 4% of families in the USSR owned an automobile. These figures are contained in: "Russia's 60 Years of Communism: Success or Failure?," *US News and World Report*, Oct. 24, 1977, 42-66, at 44.

CONSUMER PRODUCT QUALITY IN SOVIET LAW: THE TRIED AND THE CHANGING

Zigurds L. Zile*

1. Introduction

Almost a decade and a half ago, I wrote an essay on various aspects of law and the distribution of consumer goods in the Soviet Union.[1] This earlier work described and analyzed the organizational structure of Soviet trade in consumer goods, transmission of consumer demand to producers, devices for shaping consumer demand, protection of buyers' interests, in particular with respect to the quality of service and merchandise, and the extent and function of illicit private trade. The present article is, in a way, a continuation of the earlier work, but in only one of its aspects–consumer product quality.

My assessment of the situation in the early 1960's contained the following generalization:

> "The poor quality of products is a disgrace to the Soviet economy. Added to a lack of ways and means for eliminating defects, it at times borders on disaster. Obtaining spare parts for producer goods presents a major problem for managers and their staffs. The need is even more neglected in the area of consumption. The cost in terms of time and energy wasted by a factory to hunt down a certain gear or by a teacher to find a tiny screw for the frame of his eyeglasses is incalculable. Furthermore, defects in machines and gadgets that are supposed to work constitute an interminable source of frustration. One can easily imagine the annoyance felt by a Soviet viewer whose set goes on the blink during a telecast on the next Seven-Year Plan. Repair services are few, under-staffed, inadequately supplied and ill-organized. Corruption has not spared this nook of Soviet economic life either."[2]

* The author gratefully acknowledges the research assistance of John E. Machulak, a third-year law student at the University of Wisconsin-Madison. To the extent that part of the work on this article was done in Finland, the author's heartfelt thanks go to Mervi Tiensuu of the University of Helsinki.

More specifically, I found the relevant legal mechanisms were often skewed to favor producers and largely ineffectual as stimuli to quality for either this or other reasons. Contracts between trade organizations and producers for delivery of consumer goods were supposed to contain detailed terms governing product quality and thereby help raise its level through a semblance of bargaining. In addition, the State Committee on Standards, Measures, and Measuring Instruments Attached to the Council of Ministers of the USSR set minimum requirements for a number of products in its standards (*GOST*). In the event that the delivered goods did not meet the quality standards (whether consensual or regulatory), a trade organization was legally obligated to reject the shipment and refuse to pay for it, and to demand a contract penalty fixed by statute. Since the compromising of breaches of delivery contracts was illegal, the idea was that the purveyors of shoddy merchandise would suffer great monetary losses and, moreover, their default be noted by superior authorities. This would, in turn, awaken the rational maximizer in their breast. But enforcement of an organization's rights with respect to product quality was tempered by the familiar reluctance to treat fellow organizations with the full severity permitted (and even demanded) by law. Besides, many contracts were drafted purely as a formality and did not, consequently, create enforceable obligations. And there was still another hitch. To raise a distributor's quality consciousness, a manufacturer should have been answerable to a trade organization for breaches of express guarantees accompanying the product to the ultimate buyers. However, under the somewhat confusing set of rules in effect in the early 1960's the trade organization had no real opportunity (even if it wanted) to recover from its supplier for defects that appeared only in use. After the sale, the merchandise left the purview of the store and, henceforth, non-dealer repair shops were watching over the quality of the goods in consumers' hands and, to some extent, insulating the retailers from liability to their buyers. The "warranty" provisions of the 1922 RSFSR Civil Code and the 1961 USSR Principles of Civil Law, on their face, gave the buyer of a defective product four kinds of remedies (exchange, reduction in price, rescission with damages, and repair at seller's expense) but limited the buyer's recourse to the immediate seller. This requirement of "privity" typically insulated the manufacturer from direct liability and, presumably, blunted its possible deterrent effect. Even worse, under 1956 departmental regulations promulgated under dubious statutory authority, a buyer—as a general rule—enjoyed neither the right to proceed directly against the retailer nor the choice of the type of relief. The buyer initially had to deal with repair shops affiliated with manufacturing plants. And when a plant could eventually be deemed to have breached its obligation, several complicating factors (statutes of limitations, rules governing proper parties defendant, jurisdictional problems) made its actual exposure to liability quite unlikely. The deterrent effect of criminal liability was also questionable. Although the law provided for criminal sanctions for serious transgressions against product quality at the distribution stage, they were invoked exceedingly sparingly, sometimes because it was hard to pinpoint the origin of the faulty product. The device of "production mark" was a trademark with a peculiarly Soviet twist. In a market-type economy a trademark is normally regarded as a valuable asset; it is displayed prominently on the holder's goods and jealously guarded against infringement. In such an economy, trademark contributes to deliberate individualization of products. By contrast, the Soviet producer characteristically preferred anonymity, since its output was nothing much to brag about. As a result, in the Soviet Union the affixing of a production mark was compulsory and served as a means of locating those who made products of bad quality.

The consumer sector has been receiving increasing attention since the early 1960's. This is borne out by target and performance figures of the economic plans as well as officially sanctioned rationalizations. Investments and the level of modernization are up; both staples and durable goods are more plentiful.[3]

The extensive pro-consumer references in the reports and resolutions of the recent Party Congresses, especially the 24th and the 25th, have encouraged theorizers and ideologues to change their tune. While Khrushchev still thought he had the final word on which way the world was going, private property mentality was the evil to beat. The future looked bright insofar as the projected capacity of the system to satisfy people's needs went. But restraint and modesty were expected to rule the expression of these needs, and institutions or mechanisms other than private ownership were to be the principal means of meeting them. A strand in the Soviet legal thought busied itself with social relations that suggested the atrophy of civil law forms and thereby put a mantle of actuality around the idea of the withering away of law. By the late 1970's, however, as Fiat *Zhiguli* were rolling off the assembly line in Togliatti and cases of Pepsi in Odessa, it dawned upon the philosophers that, when one came right down to it, rising consumer expectations and the formation of the new Soviet person were entirely compatible. The image of the Soviet proletariat's clenched fist could be conveniently replaced by outstretched arm and hand grasping a Big Mac.

A recent article in the *Kommunist* takes issue with the view it attributes to "leftist" critics of capitalism (including the followers of Marcuse) and "left-liberal Western intellectuals" on the dangers of a "consumer society." The view under attack allegedly regards the rising living standards of the working people in some of the more advanced capitalist countries as the main reason for the working people's "bourgeoisification" and integration into the private ownership system. In other words, the satisfaction of people's material needs is intrinsically "counter-revolutionary." A milder version of the same view is said to hold that saturation of the market with inexpensive consumer goods is a socially and morally pernicious process resulting in "materialism," spiritual impoverishment, and "devaluation" of the human personality. According to the author of the article, however, the question whether increased consumption is an evil cannot be answered with simple "yes" or "no." It is all a question of what needs are being met and how they are being met. Human needs do not remain static throughout history. Scientific and technological progress inevitably elevates expectations. Confronted with this, capitalism not only fails to end material poverty but also spreads social and spiritual poverty through the dehumanization of social relations. By contrast, socialism (presumably, as it is believed to prevail in the Soviet Union) opens up broad horizons for the operation of the law of rising wants, the objective base for ennobling all relations and molding the new person. The author admonishes that critics should not try to make any mileage out of the fact the manifest Soviet position has shifted over time. The social demands and political slogans of a class at the early phases of its development change dialectically in the higher stages of social progress. The plebeian-proletarian asceticism loses its revolutionary character as modern productive forces increase the means of consumption and the proletariat becomes more revolutionary. Therefore, "leftist" theoreticians who knock the improvement of material incentives and the growth of the public welfare in socialist countries and extol crude egalitarian ideas as a means of combating a consumerist way of life are reactionary regurgigators of hopelessly outdated views. Working people who gripe about poor consumer goods have not, by that token, lost past revolutionary traditions and succumbed to petty bourgeois mentality. And be that as it may, the author hastens to add, the Party has no intention of retreating from the policy of substantially improving the people's standard of living which is a principal means of achieving the highest aim–the formation of the new person, a rounded (but not fat), well-educated, harmonious, and creative individual. Of course, there will be difficulties, the author concedes. Narrow consumerist habits persist. reflecting the petty bourgeois attitudes of some citizens. Ideological upbringing must be shored up to neutralize and overcome harmful influences from the outside. As long as the more developed capitalist countries still enjoy a certain superiority in producing various consumer goods and new kinds of technology, young people in the socialist countries are subjected to their subversive force. The author concludes that stepping up the production and distribution of consumer goods to match and surpass the capitalists is one of the most important strategies in the struggle against such subversion.[4]

Consonant with the new respectability of consumerism there has been a great deal of conceptualization regarding the consumer product quality issue. A search has been on for both an operational definition of product quality and a satisfactory identification and analysis of the means of achieving it.

A Soviet treatise on law and product quality starts with the proposition that any product of labor, as distinguished from a natural substance, possesses two most fundamental traits. It is characterized, first, by a multiplicity of objective technical and economic traits and, second, by definite social relations, including relations between the producers and those for whom the product is made. In the Soviet society, either administrative action or contract establishes particular legal relations between the two parties with respect to product quality. This leads to a definition of product quality in its legal aspect which looks to the level of correspondence between the technical and economic traits of a product, on the one hand, and its social requirements, insofar as they have been incorporated into law, on the other. The proponents acknowledge that their definition can be impugned for its orientation on the *status quo*. That is, in many instances quality requirements legally confirmed in state standards, norms, or other technical conditions, may insulate obsolescent products from criticism. This derives from the fact that the legal requirements *per se* do not ensure a higher product quality but guarantee a mere sameness at a permissible minimum level. Quality so perceived is no stimulus to enterprise to elevate their output to the level of the most advanced scientific and technological attainments worldwide. Of course, Soviet law makes it possible for a producer to make things of a quality above what the administrative regulations require but demands that the higher quality be provided for by contract. But, apparently, the critics of the proposed legal definition of product quality have been unable to offer a viable superior formulation. Thus, unless the state requirements and the matching desires of the contracting parties independently rise above the existing baselines, the quality of output stagnating at the administratively established levels cannot be challenged on legal grounds.[5]

Soviet literature also addresses the means of both raising the legal requirements of quality and realizing the legal requirements of quality having legal effect.

It stands to reason that an upward revision of the state standards, norms, and other technical conditions presupposes, above all, an adequate information flow to those empowered to revise and the allocation of sufficient human and material resources to accomplish the necessary revisions over a given period of time. Contractually fixed quality levels are apt to rise when the demand for a particular product is elastic enough to enable the buyers to reject products which, though complying with the present state requirements, nonetheless do not come up to their expectations and when the producers incur sanctions of one sort or another for unsold output. Investigation of demand would then be a seller's means of averting loss and, simultaneously, enhance voluntary commitments regarding product quality. Once the objectives of quality have been set, a number of devices are available to facilitate their attainment. One can think of both positive inducements for working toward the specified goals and negative sanctions for those who fall short. An attempt to divide the various means into non-legal (or extra-legal) and legal partakes of an exercise in metaphysics. While the mechanisms for imposing sanctions or conferring benefits with reference to more or less precise rules are dubbed "legal" by convention, it is less satisfactory to call the other means non-legal. As a rule, there are laws behind the mechanisms of this latter kind as well, authorizing or ordering their employment, providing for appropriations, etc. I do not believe the distinction, though typically maintained in Soviet literature, is useful and will not invoke it here for purposes of analysis.

2. Power to Set Requirements of Product Quality

The legal definition of product quality widely accepted in Soviet literature distinguishes between two kinds of powers to set requirements of product quality. First, there is the power of the parties to the legal transactions in the making and distribution of a product. It expresses itself in consensual and bargained terms regarding quality, arrived at between the personified links of the distributive chain. Second, contrasted with this, is the power of authorities external to the process of making and distributing products. *Ad hoc* determinations of quality requirements in the course of adjudication and generic requirements authoritatively established by administrative rule in advance are examples.

The distinction seems to apply not only to the Soviet situation but also to the Anglo-American experience. Obligors' promises as to performance, as well as assurances about conditions their performance could not affect, set the requirements of product quality in the earlier common law. Courts were called upon to decide what had been promised and/or assured and the extent of the obligor's compliance. The contract action, together with the adjunct action for breach of an express warranty, was the principal legal doctrinal device of this period. The concepts of implied warranty of merchantability and negligence (fault) in making or distributing a product arose with the passage of time. A product's merchantable quality was not a dickered term of sale but a requirement that law imposed irrespective of the will of the parties. A merchantable product had to be fit for the ordinary purposes for which such products were used. Negligence was the failure to use such care as a reasonable and prudent person would have under the circumstances (the failure to take cost-justified precautions) to avert the making or distribution of a product of insufficient quality. In both types of cases, the courts applied an external test and thereby became the promulgators of *ad hoc* standards of quality. Yet only vague generalizations about these standards could be extracted from the decided cases and employed as guides to future conduct. The recent development of strict seller and supplier tort liability at common law for losses arising out of the acquisition or use of defective products have left the role of the courts unchanged in these respects.

In deciding what was unmerchantable, defective, or conduct unbecoming a reasonable and prudent person, the courts took into account what those who were most intimately associated with the particular category of products either generally practiced or expected from others. Subconformity with trade custom (including voluntary private standards) and violation of the ordinary expectations of consumers and users regarding product quality, as a rule, led to a finding of insufficient quality. Conformity, while not always conclusively establishing sufficient quality, was deemed relevant to the issue. Thus, although the courts did not purport to be autonomous in this area, they did, in fact, retain a vast judging power over the existence and nature of trade custom, consumer expectations, and the essence of ordinary care. Eventually, however, a pressure in support of *ex ante* generic requirements caused the center of authority to shift from the judiciary to the other two coordinate branches of government. Increasingly, the legislatures asserted their power to set quality standards for whole categories of products, however, typically leaving the actual elaboration of the technical details to regulatory agencies. Nonetheless, the courts remain a significant force in the area of product quality determination in the United States. To be sure, their sphere of action is limited to some extent by the express provisions of the legislative-administrative standards and to some extent by judicial choice rooted in tradition. As to the latter, the courts will, for instance, generally consider a product unmerchantable or defective, or the conduct leading to its genesis and marketing incompatible with ordinary care, if it violates an applicable governmental safety standard. At the same time, they insist on second-guessing the bureaucrats when compliance with a standard is raised defensively in certain kinds of civil litigation. That is, such compliance will not necessarily assure a finding of merchantability, non-defectiveness, or the requisite care. Finally, legislative-administrative standard setting draws on sources that courts had once directly relied on. The most recent legislation—such as the Consumer Product Safety Act of 1972—envisions conscious reception and incorporation of extra-governmental experience. Voluntary private standards as well as non-business expertise must be solicited and considered in the standard-setting process.

The Soviet history of struggle for product quality through law is short by comparison. Discernment of secular trends might be a figment of an outside observer's wishful thinking. All in all, it seems, the power of authorities external to the process of the making and distribution of products has been dominant. The power of parties to transactions in the distributive chain has been relatively limited, although broader now than ever since the end of the New Economic Policy. As between the two kinds of external authorities, adjudication (whether in the courts or *arbitrazh*) has played a far less significant role than its Anglo-American counterpart. The principal authority has invariably been the legislative-administrative. In the early decades, this authority may have been exercised crudely and sporadically at the whim of individuals occupying influential political (even non-governmental) positions within the system. Today, its exercise is immeasurably more institutionalized on the basis of purported legal rationality.

3. Legislative-Administrative Standards as a Means of Raising Product Quality

The USSR Constitution of 1936 confirmed the broad competence of the federal government in economic affairs.[6] It did not specifically refer to product standardization, however. Until 1970, a Committee on Standards, Measures, and Measuring Instruments Attached to the Council of Ministers of the USSR and created by the Council pursuant to Article 68(f) of the Constitution exercised the overall guidance in matters relating to governmental standards. An amendment to the Constitution adopted that year[7] transformed the agency into a constitutional organ—the State Committee on Standards of the Council of Ministers of the USSR (*Gosstandart*)—specifically named in Article 70. The new Constitution of the USSR of 1977 retains this framework essentially undisturbed.[8]

In the meantime, *Gosstandart* has been operating under an executive decree of December 9, 1968.[9] Leaving aside standards for especially important products (which are issued by the Council of Ministers of the USSR) and those governing building supplies and equipment (issued by *Gosstroi*), *Gosstandart* approves and promulgates all other standards of federal scope. It also plans and coordinates standardization of products, sets levels of quality, and checks on and enforces compliance. *Gosstandart* exercises its functions through a network of field offices, including testing laboratories, inspectorates, and republic administrations of the Committee. Other governmental bodies (*e.g.*, federal ministries and republic councils of ministers) issue standards of limited applicability.[10]

The term "product quality" can cover quite a lot. However, it seems that product quality in its ordinary meaning could be conceptualized in three aspects: the esthetic, the functional, and the safety. A product is a thing of quality in its *esthetic* aspect when it satisfies the subjective tastes of all or a large number of the potential consuming or using public. As one of a class, a product might be entirely acceptable to a segment of the public yet be rejected by the rest. The latter might perceive it as faulty on account of shape, color, flavor, or some such characteristic. Quality, in this sense, is very strongly culturally determined; people's preferences and expectations are crucial to its definition. Where the preferences are diverse and the expectations high, introduction of a variety at the margin, so to speak, without affecting the generic product's "essence" is likely to improve its esthetic quality. The *functional* quality of a product is its ability to serve its basic purpose over some reasonable period of time. Quality in this aspect is, thus, more objective then a matter of a personal whim. Automobiles that do not run and leak oil, shoes that shed their heels on the third day of normal wear, and liverwurst that is mostly starch functionally are not products of quality. Improvement in this aspect presupposes a higher degree of technological mastery and deliberate measures of quality control. Finally, the concern of the *safety* aspect of product quality is attainment of an optimal level of safety. The goal is to hold down product-related accidents and the associated accident losses. However, this goal is not pursued at any cost. Instead, the search is on for a level of loss reduction at an acceptable cost. This aspect of quality incorporates both strong objective and subjective elements. It might not be too heroic to assume that people in general do not desire incapacitating accidents in product use. Consequently, they could be expected collectively to try to master the relevant technology and take measures of quality control for this specific purpose. On the other hand, societies and their members widely differ in their perceptions of causality and over the method of analyzing the accident problem, including the proper weighting of the items to be included in calculating the cost of particular categories of accidents and the cost of their prevention.

In the Soviet Union, legislative-administrative standards are a means of raising product quality mainly in its functional aspect. A good deal of this involves the grading of various products and translating the grades into levels of expected performance. The safety aspect–except perhaps in connection with ingestible products–has been relatively neglected, although in many instances there might be a direct positive relationship between improvements in function and increased product safety. In the absence of standardized popular tastes, standards cannot advance the esthetic aspect of product quality. In fact, enforced product uniformity against a backdrop of differential preferences would probably backfire. The Soviets have thought of another device instead. On April 28, 1962, the Council of Ministers of the USSR decreed the formation of artistic design sections within production ministries. The decree entrusted the sections with the responsibility for evaluating the esthetic quality of manufactured goods still on the drawing boards. A ministry which disagreed with the conclusions of the design section was required to submit the matter to an interdepartmental council of experts attached to the All-Union Scientific Research Institute on Technological Esthetics whose decision was final. In addition, each enterprise was required, upon designation of the chief designer for a new product, to name his or her deputy for the artistic aspects. The scheme has proven to be pretty much a paper mansion, however. Many enterprises have no artistically-trained designers. And, in any event, the procedure has been disregarded in practice even where the necessary personnel are available.[11]

Soviet legislative-administrative standards are issued not only to raise product quality in one or more of the aspects decribed but also to achieve uniform description and interchangeability of materials and components used in production. Maintenance of accuracy in measurements is inextricably linked with product standardization in this sense. *Gosstandart*, therefore, partakes of the nature and functions of agencies such as the United States Department of Agriculture, Department of Health, Education, and Welfare, and Consumer Product Safety Commission, on the one hand, and the United States Bureau of Standards, on the other. *GOST* 1-68 titled "The State System of Standardization" and in effect since January 1, 1970, provides a detailed description of the meanings and objectives of standardization.[12] A governmental standard is an example of subsidiary legislation–a form of administrative regulation. It is enforceable as any other legal rule. That much is clear. What is not clear is whether a standard sets out the requisites of minimum quality or demands precise adherence to its specifications. According to the apparently accepted Soviet definition of product quality, strict compliance with a standard would exclude liability, unless the parties to the transaction had agreed to performance criteria exceeding those contained in the standard. Indeed, in the absence of such agreement, strict compliance with the standard would seem to be an implied term of the transaction. The question vexing Soviet lawyers, then, concerns the freedom of the parties to agree on "upward" deviations. While the quest for quality in its three aspects would seem to be entirely compatible with such agreements, the objective of product uniformity might make them undesirable in some instances. The theorization reduces itself to this: Uniformity *per se* might lead to higher quality products. Its value should be recognized for this reason. However, the pursuit of uniformity should never be carried on with such a single-minded zeal as to become a brake on improvement of product quality in other respects.[13]

There are both positive and negative incentives to stimulate compliance with legislative-administrative standards and, where appropriate, performance above the established norms. The certification (*attestatsiia*) of product quality is the principal positive incentive. Put into effect in 1970, certification is a testimonial of the Soviet state. Special commissions are empowered to certify the quality of whole lines of consumer goods at three grade levels: superior, first, and second grade. Products whose quality meets the highest achievements of science and technology at home and abroad are classified "superior grade," and may be affixed the "Seal of Quality" (*Znak kachestva*). In 1976, 8.5% of all goods manufactured that year were expected to earn the seal as compared with 7% in 1975.[14] Products which meet the existing up-to-date standards of quality yet fail to qualify as "superior" are considered "first grade". The "second grade" comprises products which, while formally complying, are in some ways obsolescent. Second grade products must be either upgraded by modernization or removed from production. New product lines must be either certified as "superior" or withheld from production. The certification of superior and first grade products is good for up to three years. Thereafter, the product lines are subject to review. Enterprises which earn the "Seal of Quality" for their products are monetarily rewarded. The State Committee on Prices of the Council of Ministers of the USSR raises the wholesale prices of the "superior" products which enables the producing enterprises to receive additional profits on the sale of such products. Conversely, producers of "second grade" goods have their wholesale prices reduced, presumably down to a point to make continuation of the same output not cost-justified.[15] The certification process is subject to the usual human limitations. The bureaucratic "experts'" judgment is not necessarily the same as that of the product users or consumers and cannot predict the actual experience with the product in the future. It can be a source of inefficiencies

> ". . . In State Quality Certification, the experts of the certification commission sit around the table and decide that the shoes of a certain kind should be evaluated on three criteria: durability, styling, and softness of leather. They then rank the new model of a shoe on a five-point scale for each of these qualitites on the basis of their judgment, and the price surcharge is set on the basis of the sum of points. Evaluations of this kind are a form of economic government for the consumer but not of and by the consumer. Like market research, they very likely increase the social value of what gets produced. But, at best, they are efforts to second-guess the ultimate customer. The consequences of bad guesses are less serious in the case of consumer goods than in the case of producer goods, however. They are not "distributed" as producer goods are but are placed on sale in a market-like arrangement. If the experts have guessed badly, the new shoes will simply remain unsold at the established price and will eventually be withdrawn from production. But in the case of producer goods, once a new product has been certified by a state certification commission, it will most certainly continue in production and eventually replace the older model that the experts have decreed to be of lower quality."[16]

Negative incentives have been provided to discourage production of goods in violation of state standards, a situation worse than "second grade" output. According to article 47 of the USSR Principles of Civil Law, a buyer has the duty to reject goods violating state standards and refuse payment. Payments already made are recoverable. The twin statutes on the delivery of producer goods[17] (sec. 61) and consumer goods[18] (sec. 62) incorporate like sanctions and add a provision for a penalty. The effectiveness of these remedies, however, largely depends on the willingness of the parties to a transaction to pursue them. A potentially important economic sanction is incorporated in the Decree of November 10, 1970, and enforceable by *Gosstandart*. Its thrust is that profit derived by enterprises and organizations from sales of substandard products is transferred to the state budget and the profit figure excluded from the calculation of the fulfillment of the sales plan of the offending entity.[19] Moreover, *Gosstandart* has the right to prohibit manufacturing enterprises from delivering substandard goods, and trading and supplier organizations from selling the same. However, this does not always work out. Time and time again, manufacturers allegedly ignore the orders of the State Committee, and consuming enterprises accept, pay for, and use products known to be substandard. *Gosstandart* is compelled to resort to drawn-out and often pointless correspondence with the superior organizations of the violators, since it has no independent enforcing power against either the enterprises themselves or the guilty officials. Such an enforcing power might help and has been proposed. Other proposals include *Gosstandart* power to order transportation enterprises to cease carrying substandard goods, and the offices of *Gosbank* to stop honoring demands for payments on transactions involving such goods.[20] The present Civil Code provisions, like their predecessors, state that the quality of goods delivered by one state organization to another must, in the absence of contract provisions to the contrary, correspond to state standards, technical specifications, or samples, and that, in the event of noncompliance, the recipient is obligated to refuse to accept or to pay for the goods, and to demand refund of payment already made. If the defects in the goods delivered can be removed without returning them to the supplier, the recipient has a right to demand of the supplier correction of the defects in the place where the goods are located or to correct the defects by its own means at the supplier's expense.[21] Corresponding provisions apply to sales by state retail trade organizations to individual consumers.[22] Finally, criminal prosecution for the issuance of substandard products under article 152 of the RSFSR Criminal Code is the most extreme and, perhaps for that reasons, a little used negative sanction.[23]

4. Adjudicatory Determinations as a Means of Raising Product Quality

Ad hoc governmental determinations of acceptable levels of product quality occur, in principle, in the course of adjudication in both civil and criminal cases. Indeed, there is some Soviet "decisional law" and supplemental commentary out of which one can extract something resembling the accumulated legal doctrine of the much longer Anglo-American experience.

Article 245 of the RSFSR Civil Code sets out the rule that "the quality of a product sold must correspond . . . to ordinary requirements." This is a residual rule which operates only when not preempted by legislative-administrative standards or contract specifications. It replaces the language of article 195 of the 1922 RSFSR Civil Code which spoke of "fitness for the ordinary purposes"—a formulation akin to the concept of warranty of merchantability in American law. The present wording has been viewed as more precise and correct, "since we must inevitably resort to an objective comparison of the ordinary requirements, say, of automobiles sold at the contract price with the objectively ascertainable wear and tear of the automobile actually being sold."[24] This emphasizes the interplay of two factors: the seller's assurances regarding the level of quality inferable from the price charged, on the one hand, and the ordinary buyers' quality-related expectations when they part with a certain sum of money. The used-goods' example also suggests that the Soviet legal system is cognizant of either actual or potential "implied warranty of merchantability" disputes between private citizens. The adjudicatory determination of the requisite level of quality would, however, equally operate in sales (deliveries) involving at least one socialist enterprise as a party to the transaction. Another Soviet commentary states:

> "The phrase 'ordinary requirements' should be understood to mean requirements associated with the normal use of a thing for its designated purpose. Thus, for example, an electric iron should heat up within the limits needed for ironing and be, in other respects as well, fit for the designated use; a length of fabric should not have cuts, stains, or other defects hindering or making more difficult the designated use."[25]

In theory, one of the fundamental principles of liability for breach of obligation in Soviet civil law is the fault principle (article 222 of the RSFSR Civil Code). Consequently, liability for breach arises only when there is some fault, *i.e.*, unlawful intent or negligence, in the conduct of the obligor. But unlike guilt in the context of a criminal case, on which the prosecution has the burden of proof, fault is initially presumed. But, the same civil code article allows the party in breach to rebut the presumption. In a litigation over product quality the recipient of goods having made out a product defect is, as a result, in the position of a plaintiff assisted by something resembling a more limited variant of the doctrine of *res ipsa loquitur*. As might be expected, the obligees do not necessarily place their full trust in this evidentiary rule. They frequently take the burden upon themselves and, to the maximum extent possible, offer specific proofs of conduct leading to the defect.[26] A plaintiff is further helped on the fault issue by the rules that make the defendant vicariously liable for the fault of its obligors. The practice of *Gosarbitrazh* has fixed this type of liability for the so-called "principal supplier" (at least, in the cases of contracts of delivery) when breach has occurred not because of the supplier's own conduct but because of that of its cooperating entities, such as suppliers of materials or component part manufacturers. To exonerate itself from liability in these cases, the principal supplier must show the absence of not only its own fault but also the fault of these accessories.[27] As anyone familiar with the American law of liability for defective products probably knows, the proofs of fault, defectiveness, and causation, while doctrinally distinguishable, appear intertwined both in trial practice and in the attempts by courts to explain their decisions. The Soviets try to maintain the distinction, however, since the rebuttable presumption favors the plaintiff on one of the issues but is not supposed to have any effect on the others. Before the person allegedly in breach of an obligation can be required to prove the absence of fault on its part, the very fact of breach must be established; until improper performance of the obligation has been proved, it is deemed premature (so the argument goes) to presume anyone's fault. But it may be difficult to prove that a manufacturer-supplier breached its obligation with respect to product quality; the nature and origin of the defect must be shown (assembly, storage, transportation, etc.). This inquiry is deemed to require the identification of the person responsible for the breach, which becomes particularly complicated when several activities have converged to render the goods defective. *Gosarbitrazh* has come to the rescue, however. Apparently, proceeding from the general proposition that the fault of the obligor in breach is presumed, *Gosarbitrazh* explained in 1967 that the impossibility of establishing the cause of product failure (as, for instance, in the event of its destruction in an accident) did not exonerate the product manufacturer. Since the manufacturer was now unable to show it had not been at fault, the liability for the loss, in the opinion of *Gosarbitrazh*, was its. Doctrinal purists point out a lapse in logic here. The fact of accident in itself does not mean that either the manufacturer or some third person has improperly performed an obligation. That is, the manufacturer may have released goods of unimpeachable quality; latent defects may have arisen as a result of improper storage by the recipient. Or, by way of another example, the recipient may have either unskillfully assembled a complex product or misused a finished product. To inject Anglo-American terminology, the party invoking *res ipsa* should prove the defendant's "exclusive control." These critics conclude that, if the cause of the loss of goods has not been established, it is inappropriate to speak of the fact of breach by a particular person. In their view, the rules applicable to the accidental loss of things should govern: the party who had operational control over the thing should bear the loss.[28] In sum, it is not clear if the *Gosarbitrazh* decision is a jurisprudential mistake or represents a considered choice to shift the loss.

Article 152 of the RSFSR Criminal Code likewise contains residual proscriptive language next to the specific prohibitions relating to the issuance of nonstandard or incomplete goods by industrial enterprises. More specifically, the article punishes key officials of industrial enterprises that issue "poor quality goods" repeatedly or in large amounts. In a fairly recent guiding decree, the Supreme Court of the USSR interpreted the quoted phrase as describing goods that cannot–without substantial modification–be used for their designated purpose at all, as well as goods that—under conditions of proper use—do not stand up to the periods or other terms of any accompanying guarantee.[29] Court decisions have not, however, paid much attention to the question of how a particular product's lack of quality might be proved under this definition. Both the decided cases and scholarly commentary have focussed more on the other elements of the criminal statute.[30]

As we observed earlier, prosecutions under article 152 are rare. The reluctance of the prosecuting authorities to direct the wrath of criminal law against their confreres on the "economic front" is evident. The spirit of forgiveness is, thus, not only common among the members of the managerial class but also cuts across bureaucratic divisions. One might hypothesize that the perceptions of the two groups concerning the operation of the economy, and the position and the sphere of legitimate action of those who manage it, are about the same. Suggestions found in Soviet legal literature regarding specific improvements in the technical aspects of reporting this crime may be natural to make but perhaps off the mark.[31]

An article parallel to article 152 prohibits and punishes "the issuance for sale in trade enterprises, repeatedly or in large amounts of goods known to be of poor quality, nonstandard, or incomplete, by the manager of a store, depot, warehouse, or section, or by a marketing specialist or specialist in sorting spoiled goods" (article 157 of the RSFSR Criminal Code). This article raises issues that are for the most part identical with those arising under its counterpart.[32] The only apparent differences are between the lists of persons potentially liable under the two articles. But, again, perhaps more important is the phenomenon of nonenforcement.

> ". . . The State Trade Inspectorate, state laboratories supervising compliance with standards, and ministerial inspectorates of product quality have the right selectively to verify compliance with standards and product quality, prohibit the marketing of poor quality goods, and transmit materials on the issuance for sale of poor quality, substandard, and incomplete goods to investigative agencies. However, these organizations of supervision do not report every noticed instance of poor quality goods to the procuracy. Moreover, even when such reports are received, they comparatively rarely give rise to judicial proceedings. The procuracy frequently declines to commence a case for reasons of insignificance of the matter or inexpediency of criminal prosecution, reasons not founded on law at all."[33]

5. Contractual Arrangements as a Means of Raising Product Quality

Contractual arrangements impinge upon the process of raising product quality at two stages. At the *first* stage, there are contracts that serve to move products from the initial steps in their development and manufacture to the point of their distribution to the consuming public. The contracts by which the products are actually distributed to the consumers constitute the *second* stage.

State enterprises which participate in the design, manufacture, and distribution of consumer goods may conclude contracts specifying their quality insofar as establishment of consensual relations is not precluded by the economic plans or other preemptive legislation. We are not interested here in contract clauses that merely "concretize" or restate quality requirements embodied in, say, governmental standards. Such clauses do not independently seek higher levels of product quality but only make possible the application of civil law sanctions (in addition to administrative and criminal sanctions) to the offenders against quality defined by other means.[34] The contract clauses we are interested in are of two types. One type sets specific requirements for design, manufacture, and the manner of distribution with the esthetic, functional, or safety aspects of product quality in mind. Another type more generally requires that the product satisfactorily perform its function or retain certain characteristics over at least a reasonable period of time. In neither instance does the mere existence of a relevant governmental standard exclude the possibility of contract clauses providing for a higher level of quality.[35] There is, boldly speaking, very little law peculiar to the governance of the operation of the clauses of the first type. Technical specifications form their contents. The "deep background" law of contracts of delivery makes up the rest. The legal situation of clauses of the second type is distinguishable to some extent, it seems. For one, the contracting parties have a considerable leeway of agreement regarding the length of the periods over which the products to be delivered are "guaranteed" to perform or retain certain characteristics. As a further difference, the consequences of the parties' agreement on this point are quite extensively spelled out in legislation generally applicable to guarantee periods in contracts of delivery.

Periods of guarantee on consumer goods delivered from one socialist entity to another begin to run from the moment of their sale through the retail trade network–the last socialist link in the chain of distribution. This kind of guarantee is, in effect, an assurance that the article will perform or retain certain characteristics *in use*. If, on the other hand, the contract of delivery makes representations concerning a product's fitness (*godnost'*), the period of fitness is calculated from the day of manufacture and has the effect somewhat akin to product *dating*.[36] These are periods within which the recipient of a product must establish the fact of breach of the supplier's obligations as to quality. They are to be distinguished from the six-month statutory period of limitations of actions running from the date the recipient establishes in a proper manner the existence of breach.[37] As is the case with obligations in Soviet law generally, the supplier's breach must be attributed to its fault or no liability will follow. That is to say, one should not be fooled by the similarities between the Soviet guarantee and the express warranty in American law, the breach of which is treated as resulting in liability without fault. Of course, one should remember what we said about proof of fault earlier in the section on "Adjudicatory Determinations as a Means of Raising Product Quality." A rebuttable presumption of fault favoring the plaintiff entity operates here as well. The supplier is required to correct the defects in goods for which a guarantee period has been established at its expense or to replace the goods, unless it shows that the defects have arisen as a result of a violation by the recipient of the rules governing the use or storage of the goods.[38] For guaranteed goods, the period of guarantee is extended to compensate for the time during which they could not be used because of defect. And as a further bonus, the guarantee period on replacement goods begins to run from the day of replacement.[39]

Neither the correction of defects nor the replacement of defective goods within the guarantee period exonerates the supplier from paying a statutory penalty and the damages caused by the faulty delivery, calculated without deducting the penalty.[40] The parties are not permitted to agree to limit liability, if its extent has been specified in the existing legislation.[41] But the seemingly stringent provisions are not always put to work. It is an extremely rare occurrence that the recipients of goods make an attempt to collect damages. The upshot of this reticence is that the recovered penalties actually serve as a substitute for compensatory damages. The non-pursuit of the damages remedy, therefore, is said to lead to a blurring of the distinction between the categories of monetary sanctions and be ineffective in attaining the higher level of liability (in the form of an additional penalty) provided for by law for the violation of contract terms on product quality. A prominent Soviet commentator ascribes the atrophy of compensatory damages to the complexity of defining the correct amount of compensation. As a rule, *Gosarbitrazh* will not entertain suits for damages expressed in approximate figures, notwithstanding the fact that it might be impossible to establish a more exact amount.[42]

A recipient entity might, of course, be able to discover defects in the goods upon their delivery and prior to sale to the public. Such an entity can go after its supplier when it appears that the goods they passed on do not stand up to the requisite level of quality in use. But the recipient must act expeditiously lest its discovery of defects be of no legal consequence. Section 9 of the Instruction on the Acceptance of Producer and Consumer Goods as to Quality[43] requires a report on hidden defects in goods prepared within five days of the discovery but, in any event, no later than four months from the day of acceptance, unless special rules applicable to the particular transaction fix other periods. In the case of guaranteed goods, the four-month period is replaced by the period of the guarantee, and even though the period begins to run from the moment of retail sale, the recipient may prepare its report at any time during the pre-sale storage irrespective of the date of acceptance. "Hidden defects" for purposes of section 9 are defects that cannot be discovered by the usual inspection of goods of that kind and are revealed only in processing, assembling, use, or storage. Defects which do not qualify as "hidden" must be reported within much shorter periods calculated from the moment of acceptance.[44] These firm periods have not escaped criticism. Since the periods of guarantee vary in length depending on the nature of the product, the flat four-month period should likewise yield to appropriately differentiated terms. Besides, four months is not a very long time. By contrast, article 247 of the RSFSR Civil Code sets a six-month period for the discovery and reporting of hidden defects in goods transferred under a contract of sale. Criticism has also been directed at the concomitant situation wherein a supplier (manufacturer) of defective goods is completely freed of liability after the expiration of any of these periods, including the periods of guarantee. This is deemed particularly troubling because the preponderant volume of goods allegedly perform and retain other essential characteristics far beyond what the guarantee assures. Consequently, it has been proposed that suppliers be obligated to pay purely compensatory damages to the recipients of their goods which survive the guarantee period but fail within the life ordinarily assumed for purposes of accounting. Such proposals are, however, coupled with a notice taken of the continued phenomenon of mutual "amnesty" among economic managers who place "good relations" with their counterparts above the dictates of the struggle for product quality. The answer to this phenomenon is, in turn, more laws on compulsory vindication of rights under economic contracts and disciplinary sanctions for managers who practice calculated forgiveness.[45]

Consumer goods are ultimately distributed to the Soviet public through socialist retail trade enterprises under the rules governing contracts of sale, as some of our earlier remarks have indicated. The two bodies of contract law—delivery and sale—are alike in many respects. In a manner of speaking, sale is very much delivery stripped of features that are appropriate only to transactions executed under an imperative economic plan.

If a buyer is sold a product of quality below the level established by either a legislative-administrative, or adjudicatory authority or contract, and the seller has not beforehand disclosed its defects the buyer may, according to the code, elect to demand any one of four remedies: substitution of a product of proper quality (exchange); a proportionate reduction in the purchase price; correction of the defects by the seller without cost to the buyer or compensation for the expenses incurred by the buyer in correcting them; or rescission of the contract with compensatory damages to the buyer. These remedies attach to all sales regardless of the identity of the parties but may be modified by supplemental decrees for sales by retail trade enterprises to natural persons.[46] The seller's prior disclosure of defects would normally imply that the lower quality was part of the bargain. But if, as was assumed above, the seller has not made a timely disclosure, the buyer may present a claim against the seller immediately after discovery of a defect, but not later than six months from the date of delivery of the product. Here, too, associated decrees may establish different periods for presenting claims regarding defective products sold by retail trade organizations.[47]

The RSFSR Civil Code does not mention retailers' guarantees. The code only cites guarantee periods, established in accordance with article 263 and accompanying a delivery contract. The buyer may, during the period of the guarantee (calculated from the date of the retail sale), present a claim to the seller on the basis of defects which prevent the product's normal use. The list of buyer's remedies here is a bit shorter than under article 247. The seller is required to do one of three things: to repair without charge, to replace, or to accept a return and refund the purchase money, unless it is proved that the defects arose because the buyer violated the rules for the use or care of the product.[48] Notwithstanding the inconsistent wording of articles 246 and 248, the buyer's right to select the remedy seems to be preserved under both.[49]

Contrary to articles 246 and 247, article 248 does not expressly provide for implementing executive-administrative decrees or regulations. However, the 1974 Model Rules on the Exchange of Industrial Goods Purchased from the State and Cooperative Retail Trade Network[50] appear to have asserted dominance over matters dealt with by all three of them. The Rules of the USSR Ministry of Trade and *Gosstandart*, if issued under proper enabling authority, would override inconsistent republic law by virtue of federal legislative supremacy. But the existence of such authority seems to be in doubt. Articles 41 and 42 of the USSR Principles of Civil Law, which contain the matters covered by articles 245 through 248 of the RSFSR Civil Code, authorize subsidiary implementing legislation but only by union republics. In the instant case, a federal ministerial regulation purports to implement and even modify provisions of republic civil codes which are virtually carbon copies of an organic law enacted by the USSR Supreme Soviet. The Model Rules superimpose a set of provisions that purport to eclipse the buyer-consumer rights, spelled out in the Principles and codes, without any apparent awareness of or uneasiness about the contradiction. To add insult to injury, one of the co-issuers of the rules, the USSR Ministry of Trade, is the patron of the trade organizations which are bound to be among the beneficiaries of this apparent arrogation of power.

One might note that the paragraph of article 42 of the USSR Principles of Civil Law qualifying consumer remedies where guarantees have been given does not identify the implementing authority and that, therefore, the federal agencies may exercise some sort of inherent implementing power. However, when the Principles desire federal implementation, they specifically mention it time and time again throughout the entire text. And, in any event, only a portion of the Model Rules concerns sales with guarantees; part two covers exchanges of goods with no guarantees, which fall within the purview of article 41 and, consequently, republic implementing legislation.

Leaving aside the question of the validity of the subsidiary legislation, a problem which has occasionally perturbed the Soviet legal mind but not practice,[51] the fact remains that the Model Rules rather than civil codes supply many of the important answers. The rules are quite specific. Thus, the buyer of a black-and-white television set is not permitted to opt for an exchange at once. Instead, the manufacturer or a repair shop for guaranteed articles must be given first crack at fixing the set within ten days from the initial demand. Automobiles can be exchanged after an attempt at repairs, for up to two weeks, and only pursuant to a decision by a commission of automobile experts.[52] Part two of the rules implies that a buyer only has a choice between two remedies: exchange or refund of the purchase price upon return of the item.[53] Repairs, apparently, cannot be demanded, since repair facilities are meant to serve only guaranteed items. Common items such as wearing apparel, fabrics, furs, and rugs are not guaranteed but, then, their repair might be economically inefficient at any rate. However, the rules also seem to deny the buyer the remedy of proportionate price reduction provided for by both article 4 of the USSR Principles of Civil Law and article 246 of the RSFSR Civil Code.

6. Conclusions

The Soviet Union is moving into the age of high consumption. However the consumer products distributed very frequently suffer from deficiencies of quality in esthetic, functional, and safety aspects. Insofar as quality is not achieved through economic measures at the stages of product development, manufacture, and preparation for ultimate distribution, protection of the higher social and individual consumer interests in quality has been referred—by and large—to old civil law forms and a cumbersome machinery of direct government regulation.

One is left with the impression that the apparent gradual rise in Soviet consumer goods' quality is to be attributed to an improved technological base, a higher level of technical skill, and economic incentives which the state system maintains, in part, because of its inner logic and, in part, because of the country's more assertive presence on the world's markets. The devices ordinarily thought of as "legal" and which have been the main subject of this essay are not particularly innovative or effective to promote the policies behind them. They have served mainly as statements of high purpose and sources of ultimate sanction applied selectively and haphazardly.

NOTES

1. Z. L. Zile, "Law and the Distribution of Consumer Goods in the Soviet Union" in W. LaFave (ed.), *Law in the Soviet Society* (Urbana, 1965), p. 212.

2. *Id.*, p. 268.

3. "Povyshat' effektivnost' proizvodstva i kachestvo produktsii" (To Raise the Productive Efficiency and the Quality of Goods), *Planovoe khoziaistvo*, 1976, No. 4, 3-7.

4. V. Pechenev, "Rising Consumer Expectations and the Formation of the New Man," *Kommunist*, 1976, No. 18, 58-69, transl. and abstr. in *CDSP*, 29 (1977), No. 8, 5.

5. B. V. Ivanov *et al.* (eds.), *Pravo i kachestvo produktsii* (Law and the Quality of Goods), (Moscow, 1972), pp. 6-10.

6. USSR Constitution of 1936, Art. 14.

7. Edict of November 2, 1970, *Ved. V. S. SSSR*, 1970 No. 46, item 489.

8. See Arts. 73, 129, and 131.

9. *Sobr. Post. SSSR*, 1968, No. 23, item 168.

10. V. M. Ogryzkov, *Pravovoe regulirovanie kachestva produktsii* (Legal Regulation of the Quality of Goods), (Moscow, 1973), ch. IX; B. V. Ivanov *et al., op. cit.*, ch. 11, Sec. 2.

11. U. K. Ikhsanov, "Pravo i povyshenie esteticheskogo kachestva promyshlennykh izdelii" (Law and the Raising of the Esthetic Quality of Manufactured Articles), *SGiP*, 1973, No. 8, 54-59.

12. V. M. Ogryzkov, *op. cit.*, pp. 70-71.

13. *Id.*, pp. 76-79.

14. M. B. Emel'ianova, "Pravovoe regulirovanie attestatsii kachestva produktsii" (Legal Regulation of the Certification of the Quality of Goods), *SGiP*, 1976, No. 8, 45, 46.

15. V. M. Ogryzkov, *op. cit.*, pp. 104-109; B. V. Ivanov *et al., op. cit.*, pp. 49-53.

16. J. S. Berliner, *The Innovation Decision in Soviet Industry* (Cambridge, Mass., 1976), pp. 385-386.

17. *Sobr. Post. SSSR*, 1969, No. 11, item 64, in A. Iu. Kabalkin, *Grazhdanskoe zakonodatel'stvo: Sbornik normativnykh aktov* (Civil Legislation: Collection of Normative Acts), (Moscow, 1974), p. 388 (hereinafter cited as *Sbornik*).

18. *Sobr. Post. SSSR* 1969, No. 11, item 64, in *Sbornik*, p. 417.

19. V. M. Ogryzkov, *op cit.*, pp. 241, 244.

20. *Id.*, p. 242; B. V. Ivanov *et al., op. cit.*, pp. 70-76.

21. RSFSR Civil Code, art. 261.

22. RSFSR Civil Code, arts. 245, 246.

23. V. M. Ogryzkov, *op. cit.*, pp. 76, 179.

24. E. A. Fleishits (ed.), *Nauchno-prakticheskii kommentarii k GK RSFSR* (Scientific-Practical Commentary on the Civil Code of the RSFSR), (Moscow, 1966), p. 285 (hereinafter cited as *Kommentarii k GK*).

25. M. A. Vaksberg *et al.* (eds.), *Kommentarii k Grazhdanskomu kodeksu Kazakhskoi SSR* (Commentary on the Civil Code of the Kazakh SSR), (Alma-Ata, 1965), pp. 296-97.

26. V. M. Ogryzkov, *op. cit.*, p. 148.

27. *Kommentarii k GK*, p. 262.

28. V. M. Ogryzkov, *op. cit.*, pp. 149-150.

29. Guiding Decree No. 7 of the Plenum of the USSR Supreme Court of October 19, 1971, *Sov. Iust.*, 1971, No. 24, 21-22.

30. V. M. Ogryzkov, *op. cit.*, pp. 176-177.

31. Cf. *id.* at 179, 187-192.

32. See, *e.g.*, G. P. Tikhonova *et al.* (eds.), *Kommentarii k Ugolovnomu kodeksu RSFSR 1960 g.* (Commentary on the Criminal Code of the RSFSR of 1960), (Leningrad, 1962), pp. 288-89.

33. A. Belakhov, "Otvetstvennost' za vypusk v prodazhu nedobrokachestvennykh, nestandartnykh i nekomplektnykh tovarov" (Liability for the Issuance for Sale of Poor Quality, Substandard and Incomplete Goods), *Sov. Iust.*, 1973, No. 10, 10-11.

34. V. M. Ogryzkov, *op. cit.*, pp. 110-11; Statute on the Delivery of Consumer Goods, secs. 15, 36, *Sbornik*, pp. 423, 431-432.

35. RSFSR Civil Code, arts. 261, 263; Statute on the Delivery of Consumer Goods, secs. 36, 37, *Sbornik*, p. 432.

36. Statute on the Delivery of Consumer Goods, sec. 37, *Sbornik*, p. 432.

37. RSFSR Civil Code, art. 262.

38. RSFSR Civil Code, art. 263; Statute on the Delivery of Consumer Goods, sec. 38, *Sbornik*, pp. 432-33.

39. *Id.*

40. *Id.*, RSFSR Civil Code, art. 266.

41. Statute on the Delivery of Consumer Goods, sec. 87, *Sbornik*, p. 445.

42. V. M. Ogryzkov, *op. cit.*, pp. 145-46.

43. *Sbornik*, pp. 455, 458.

44. Instruction on the Acceptance of Producer and Consumer Goods as to Quality, sec. 6, *id.*, pp. 457-58.

45. L. Rutman, "Imushchestvennaia otvetstvennost' za postavku nekachestvennoi produktsii" (Property Liability for the Delivery of Goods of Poor Quality), *Sov. Iust.*, 1973, No. 24, 29-30.

46. RSFSR Civil Code, art. 246.

47. RSFSR Civil Code, art. 247.

48. RSFSR Civil Code, art. 248.

49. *Kommentarii k GK*, p. 288.

50. *Sbornik*, p. 379 (hereinafter cited as Model Rules).

51. See, *e.g.*, A. Vlasova, "Otvetstvennost' roznichnogo torgovogo predpriiatiia za kachestvo prodannogo tovara" (Liability of a Retail Trade Enterprise Regarding the Quality of a Product Sold), *Sov. Iust.*, 1970, No. 4, 11.

52. Model Rules, sec. 1, *Sbornik*, pp. 379-80.

53. Model Rules, sec. 11, *Sbornik*, p. 382.

LAW AND THE DELINQUENT FAMILY: REPRODUCTION AND UPBRINGING*

Peter H. Juviler

1. Introduction

Issues of how to influence families to have more children and to raise them better have confronted Soviet policy-makers since the mid-1930's.[1] The resolution of these issues of social replenishment and the implications of the resolution for Soviet law and practice are the central topics of this inquiry into Societ social engineering through law. Special attention is paid to the changing balance of compulsion and non-compulsive alternatives making up Soviet intervention to regulate the reproductive and educational functions of the family.

This is a vital matter for the Party. The success of its economic plans depends heavily on replenishment of the labor force. Replenishment has three dimensions:

1) the technical dimension of the "scientific organization of labor" and how planners and managers make use of the available working force;

2) the demographic dimension of birthrate, and how many persons are available, by age, sex, region to replenish that working force; and

3) the educational dimension of upbringing and how effectively the family, schools, and other sources of influence on the young, join to shape values and skills of the "new shift."

This chapter I devote to the demographic and educational dimensions of replenishment. There is considerable consensus abroad[2] and in the USSR that Soviet population problems have become, as the CPSU General Secretary put it, "more urgent recently" and call for "an effective population policy."[3] The issue has been, what policy? As for the educational dimension of family policy, it has posed the issue of how in law and practice to make parents liable for their own delinquency as upbringers and for the delinquency[4] of their children. Dealing with delinquent families is a component part of the

* I thank for their contributions to this article my commentator, Professor Wesley A. Fisher, and other discussants of my draft.

Soviet search for the law and order which the Party sees as important for the success of its economic development programs.[5] The experts are far from laying all blame for juvenile drunkenness, indiscipline, and lawbreaking at the door of the family.[6] Still, the family has figured prominently in Soviet assumptions about causes of and remedies for crime since Stalin's turnabout to familism in 1935. "Failures on the part of the family" are cited as a "leading cause" of juvenile delinquency and crime.[7] This chapter explores, then, the content and the application of the law in governmental responses to reproductive and educational delinquencies of the family. What changes have appeared since Stalin in the balance of direct legal compulsion and indirect broad programs, punishment and alternatives, and the scope of intervention, by the Soviet agencies responsible for social mobilization and control?

2. The Demographic Dimension

Declining Fertility

There are optimists in law and demography who talk about stabilizing birthrates or see recent birthrate drops as temporary echoes of the disastrous population depletions during World War II.[8] The Party seems to accept, rather, the more pessimistic analysis of leading demographers. They do not deny the delayed results of past disasters. But they espy also a tendency among more and more families to plan births and to have only one or two children, meaning an aging population and the possibility of zero growth rate if this keeps up.[9] The natural increase of the population dropped 21% between 1965 and 1975 (From 11.1 per 1000 to 8.8 per 1000; 8.9 per 1000 in 1976). There has been a fall in the birthrate among the older childbearing ages, when one expects the third and fourth child to be born. The number of children per 1000 women up to age 50 has been decreasing toward levels "barely sufficient to reproduce the population" and then mainly owing to the rural population. But the rural population is shrinking and becoming less fertile, even in parts of the Caucasus and Central Asia.[10]

Compulsion and "Demographic Legislation"

Experts and higher Party officials debated during the early 1970's whether or not to return to direct compulsion, to forcing the family to put a higher goal ahead of its private goals.[11] At a "round table" discussion on demographic policy called by "Soviet State and Law" (*Sovetskoe Gosudarstvo i Pravo*)–the leading Soviet law journal–the opening speaker, the journal's editor-in-chief, presented both alternatives for consideration. Law, he said, could exercise "a certain influence" on demographic processes both by "giving form to economic decisions (for example by establishing in law the size of family allowances, etc.)" and by expressing "judicial decisions in the form of prohibiting or encouraging certain actions of members of society."[12]

None of the other round table speakers appears to have supported the second, compulsive alternative. In fact, they never mentioned criminal law among the many branches of law they said can influence the birthrate. One speaker, a sociologist in the influential legal research and legislative drafting center, the Research Institute of Soviet Legislation of the USSR Ministry of Justice, stated that: "Above all, we are convinced of the complete ineffectiveness of attempts to influence the birthrate via direct proscriptions which reflect the freedom of demographic (reproductive) behavior of the family (via abortion bans, limiting the sale of contraceptives, etc.). . ." [13] Prior to the "round table," a few jurists had proposed to separate out into a single, unified collection of "demographic legislation" all legal norms directly regulating demographic processes like reproduction and migration. [14] Their suggestion some policy-seekers greeted either as futile duplication or as a wrenching of specific measures out of their broader legislative context and a step toward compulsion. "One cannot agree with such a proposal," said the above-mentioned sociologist at the Institute of Soviet Legislation. "In that sphere, 'direct regulation' is ineffectual as is well known. The artificial separation of 'demographic legislation' could only distract attention away from the demographic aspect of economic, labor, and family legislation." Neither this speaker nor his other colleagues invited to the discussion there or later accepted that any one pro-natalist measure had actually succeeded in raising birthrates, at least without an unbearable social cost. Leading demographers and most interested jurists have come to believe that (1) people cannot be forced to have more children than they want, and (2) the best approach to birthrate boosting is to lower the now unacceptable "costs" of having a second or third child. [15]

Neo-Statism

If compulsion is ruled out for the prevailing groups of experts, so do they rule out abandoning the birthrate to spontaneous choice. The trend in expert thinking reflects the political climate of neo-statism prevailing under the present régime. By statism, I mean an attitude toward social engineering which is based on the assumption that the state is virtually omnipotent in the right hands, that it can and should solve any problem from crime to labor shortages. I use "neo-statism" to describe the emerging post-Stalin approach to social engineering: less compulsive than Stalin's, more ready to consult experts and analyze carefully before issuing orders and laws, placing more reliance on positive incentives to influence behavior (though these were by no means lacking under Stalin). Neo-statism in demographic policy takes into account social and legal novelties in the situation since World War II. Socially, the novelty in the demographic situation since World War II has been the spread to many world regions of conscious family planning of the birth of each child (be it by mutual agreement or women's choice). [16] Legally, the novelty in the demographic situation is that "the social function of law is changing under conditions of socialist social relations and the scientific and technical revolution. Normative regulation moves over from primarily protective influence on social relations toward a more active influence on their formation,"[17] from rules of behavior toward social management and a greater variety of measures to encourage desired behavior.

"If we are justified in turning to the use of juridical acts in various branches of law which influence population movement but have as their direct goal the regulation of other social occurrences," a Soviet demographer states, "it is precisely because of the organic nature of the interconnection between demographic behavior and social system; living standards; family, property and social relations among people; the state of health services, of social insurance and provisions for everyday services; with migration processes and social changes."[18] And as organic interconnections are accepted between law and among various spheres of Soviet social life, so jurists join in a group, indisciplinary advisory effort headed by demographers but drawing in specialists from the fields of political economics, sociology, economics, law, social and general psychology, ethnography, medical science, physiology, anatomy, genetics, etc.[19] Clearly, the Soviet consultants on demographic policy are taken with systems analysis.[20] The hierarchy of systems, along with their interrelated parts, which bear on birthrates include, in this analysis:

1) *The family* as the primary subsystem.

2) The subsystem of variables involved with *demographic policy*. Demographic policy seeks the quantitative management of population. To maximize its availability for the economy (the chief Soviet concern) means to deal with birthrates, death rates (rising among working age persons, especially men), rates of occupational illness and accident, migration directions and intensities, infant mortality (which has been rising recently), the utilization of pensioners and housewives, population distribution and urban agglomerations. All these variables directly affect the quantity of available labor power and must be considered together and along with laws, social conditions and behavior, and the demographic "echoes" of past losses and birthrate fluctuations.

3) The more inclusive, or "higher" social subsystem involved with *population policy* as a whole and made up of *quantitative*, demographic policy, and policy aimed at improving the "quality" of the population, that is the mental capacity of people for work–as influenced by their upbringing, education, training, and social environment, and manifested in their skills and knowledge, attitudes to marriage and to family and work obligations, morality and social discipline.

4) Population policy is a constituent part of the *social and economic program* approved by the Party and legislated by the state. Socio-economic policy includes many social welfare measures, such as maternity leaves and family

allowances which serve also demographic purposes and must be adapted increasingly to demographic needs.[21]

Systems analysis serves the Party neo-statists as a means, less compulsive than the old statism, to combat the growing tendencies to autonomy in individual and organizational choices as Soviet society urbanizes and gets more complex. On this function rests its durability as more than simply a fad. Systems analysis is accepted as compatible with Marxism-Leninism.[22] Both deny the autonomy of society from politics and economics. Both deal with policy, law, social behavior, and economic development as parts of sets of interrelated variables which add up to more than the sum of each part.

Legitimated by Party ideologists, systems analysis in turn legitimizes the demographers' de-Stalinization of population analysis. Compulsion becomes only a small part of managing reproduction, migration, etc. And population management becomes possible in the Soviet system, according to the analysts, because "all social and economic levers influencing the intensity of demographic processes are concentrated in the hands of socialist society."[23] Neo-statism means "overcoming the autonomy of society," to quote one demographer. It is possible only with the economic power and resources at the disposal of the socialist state. They "create the possibility of purposefully managing all processes of social development on a society-wide scale." This neo-statism differs from Stalin's statism. (1) It is less compulsive. (2) It relies more on incentives. (3) It is more comprehensive and penetrating in its measures. (4) It is more cautious about the difficulties and slowness of changing individual choices by conscious state management.[24] (5) It is more tolerant of, aware of, and subject to the pluralistic clash of priorities and interests involving current issues; *e.g.*, how may women be liberated and best utilized from an economic, demographic, and ethical viewpoint; and how may authority and resources pass from central industrial ministries to local government so as more generously and better to provide everyday amenities for the workers in new factories and institutions.[25] (6) It involves more consultation of experts and has resulted in their urging that they be regularly consulted over matters like demographic policy,[26] on their research findings in the Center for Population Studies of Moscow University, the Institute of State and Law of the USSR Academy of Sciences, the Research Institute of Soviet Legislation of the USSR Ministry of Justice, the Central Statistical Board, and other centers.

The demographers' research leads them to a pivotal policy issue. It is, how to induce families actually having one or two children, the norm in many regions, to have the family ideal of two or three children. Their advice so far tends to be: (1) "legislative regulation of family behavior" must, above all, "reconcile work functions and the functions of reproduction." It must create conditions materially "favoring the raising of two or three children in the family." (2) Law can bring this about only when it creates for the family conditions where children "come to occupy a place serving the interests of both the family and society."[27]

In a frank, searching article, a much-published commentator urges that the "cost" of having the second or third child be reduced for today's psychologically emancipated but overworked Soviet women, among whom parenthood's prestige has been slipping and career opportunities become ever more valued. Women's unequal share of housework and child raising hits them with lower pay and positions and sickness rates about twice those for men–50% higher again for mothers. The financial and housing difficulties of young couples and their high breakup rates only unbearably add to the cost of any children beyond the first. Women's overwork and inequality, rather than material difficulties *per se*, remain the "key components" of that cost.

The drop in birthrates is women's spontaneous

> "response to their excessive work load and lack of equality with men–a response that consists of eliminating the single factor over which they have greatest control. The falling birthrate is an important–in fact, indispensable–lever that women can use in their efforts to achieve full equality with men . . . [by] reducing the time they must devote to the rearing of children. The lower birthrate alleviates the conflict between women's roles as housewife and worker, lightens their total work load, and saves many urban women from neurosis and ill health; at the same time, it permits them to take a more active part in production and in the management of society . . . the lower birthrate is an essential factor in an enormous social revolution–the transition from a patriarchate to a 'biarchate,' in which the two sexes are equally sovereign."[28]

First (and Last?) Steps

A modest legal consequence of consultations with experts appeared as the first Soviet child-support allowance for low income families of September 25, 1974.[29] Reporting on the Tenth Five-Year Plan, 1976-1980, to the Central Committee of the CPSU, Secretary General Brezhnev alluded to measures to improve the situation of women and children: the expanding pre-school facilities, and the new optional maternity leave grants.[30] It is planned to increase places in nurseries and kindergartens by almost three million places, or 30%, and extend to all working mothers a partially paid leave beyond the present 112 fully paid days of maternity leave, until a child reaches the age of one year, without loss of seniority. Housing is planned to experience the largest absolute addition of new space to date, 550 million square meters. Real incomes, including social fund measures like family allowances, are to increase by 21%.[31] These measures remain much less grandiose, so far, than are the demographers' projects of systems analysis and long term predictions.

This modest Soviet pro-natalist legislation follows in some ways the lead of the East European socialist countries. Drops in birthrates—as steep as or steeper than those occurring in the USSR—prompted in the 1960's a variety of birth-stimulating measures ranging from student mother scholarships and leaves (Bulgaria) to cut-rate train fares for families (East Germany). In Bulgaria, East Germany, and Rumania, women with young children may work a short day, and working mothers get earlier pensions in many cases. East European socialist countries give even longer maternity leaves than does the USSR. In Bulgaria, paid maternity leave increases from 120 days for the first child, to 150 for the second, and 180 for the third (120 for the fourth and later children). Czechoslovakia and Hungary offer mothers partially paid leave to raise a child up to 2 or $2\frac{1}{2}$ years old, respectively, without loss of seniority. Bulgaria offers similar, though shorter leaves. Some East European countries have stayed also with compulsion. Rumania reimposed a ban on non-medical abortions in 1966, after a nine-year moratorium. That country also restricts contraceptive sales and makes divorces expensive and lengthy. Bulgaria, Hungary, and Czechoslovakia limit non-medical abortions.[32] But a Soviet return to compulsion in divorce and abortions seems unlikely for the near future at least. In fact, non-medical abortions have been legalized for a large portion of Soviet rule—from 1920 to 1936 and, again, since 1955.

If not compulsion, then other matters remain to be resolved. Firstly, the equality of women with men, guaranteed by Article 35 of the 1977 USSR Constitution, is negated by the very additions made to that article during the discussion of the draft constitution. To the list of guarantors of women's equality was added: "creating conditions permitting women to combine work and motherhood," and "the gradual shortening of the work week for women with small children." Along with the guarantor of "paid leaves for mothers," all this means that the government has committed itself for now at least to bypassing the Cuban route (seen in mass education efforts and the family code of 1975) of achieving women's equality by having men shoulder a fair share of mother's work in the home. Under the Soviet approach, women still face career disadvantages exacerbated—not eliminated—by long post-natal leaves. My Cuban visit in November served as a reminder, also, that the USSR and Eastern Europe socialist countries lack the system of mass boarding schools for the last six pre-college grades that pass to the state much of the responsibility for the care of hundreds of thousands of Cuban teen-agers.

Secondly, there is the problem of low fertility among college students. Five and a half million day college students began the 1976/1977 school year. Though they belong in relatively fertile age cohorts, the college students produce relatively few children. How is their lot to be improved so as to encourage them to have more children, and is this the best thing to do from a wider viewpoint?[33]

Construction sites and new settlements have many more young men than young women. How best are the planners to turn "bachelor cities" into "newlyweds' cities?"[34] One out of four persons 25 through 29 years old is unmarried, according to the 1970 census. How are single men and women to be gotten together so that a dent can be made in the figure of 50 million single people 16 and older?[35] Unmarried mothers, especially the large share of them who live alone because the fathers have left, carry even heavier financial and psychological burdens than married mothers do.[36] How may men be induced or compelled to assume a greater share of that burden and where should the state now step in to help?

Finally here, though this may not exhaust the list of policy issues still unresolved, what is to be done about the fact that birthrates and family sizes are roughly twice as great in Central Asia and other relatively rural areas of non-European, mainly Moslem cultures? There, "costs" figure hardly at all. Women expect to have many children. My impression from careful reading of detailed recent Soviet population studies is that Soviet demographers are less "alarmed" about high non-European birthrates than is depicted in some quarters. True, the Soviet response is ambivalent. On the one hand the high non-European birthrates point to a growing weight of non-Europeans in the population and the potential for growing pressures from non-European peoples of Central Asia and the Caucasus, especially the Uzbeks, Kirgiz, Karakalpaks, Tadzhiks, Turkmens, Kazakhs, Chechen-Ingushi, Kalmyks, and Azerbaidzhani. The average number of children expected among these peoples ranges from 6.26 (Uzbeks) to 4.89 (Azerbaidzhani) as compared with 2.00 for Russians, 1.99 for the Latvians, and 1.71 for the Jews, the lowest of all. By the end of the 20th century, Russians could well have slipped from majority to plurality in the total Soviet population.[37] The slowness of non-European peoples to assimilate, the persistence of their adherence to their native tongues as first language, the explosive potentials of nationalism even—and especially—among partially assimilated and modernized non-European intelligentsia, the political sensitivity of Soviet spokespersons asserting the friendliness among Soviet peoples, singling out "bourgeois nationalism" as a baneful vanishing "survival," all point indirectly to the possibilities of Soviet political unease with the childbearing feats of their non-European compatriots.

On the other hand, one may with equal reason speculate that Soviet leaders welcome the burgeoning, along the Chinese frontiers, of people not noted for their friendliness with the Chinese. Moreover, Soviet demographers point to the important contribution of many non-European peoples to the Soviet national birthrate and seem to warn rather than exult that the birthrate is beginning to fall even in the most fertile non-European areas.[38]

Suggestions appear from time to time to make laws specially for republics with lowest birthrates, like the RSFSR, the Ukraine, Belorussia, and the Baltic republics, to provide separate apartments for newlyweds and for other measures to help them in the early years of their married life.[39] It is possible that opponents of high non-European birthrates exist among makers of such suggestions. In any event, differentiation in birth-stimulation expenditures can be taken as discrimination by those republics not receiving the extra largesse. Secondly, some demographers are likely to oppose such differentiation because it ignores the importance of keeping up non-European birthrates.

Soviet population policy is only one example of Soviet neo-statism in the form of broad, centrally formulated and orchestrated programs after careful consultation of expert opinion and reconciliation of often conflicting economic and political motivations, down to this latter question of the Central Asians' high fertility. This neo-statism of the "scientific and technical revolution" meant a more derivative, economic, non-compulsive population policy than had existed under Stalin.

3. The Educational Dimension

So far, I have passed over the qualitative implications for the family of the Soviet concern replenishment. "The quality of the population is closely connected with the formation in the younger generation of the most diverse creative capacities, a lofty spiritual side when it comes to ethical, esthetic, and other values . . . with improving the upbringing and education of the younger generation and training it in every way for active participation in every sphere of our economic and social life."[40] What are the implications for law under conditions of post-Stalin neo-statism of the Soviet effort to hold the family to a high quality educational role? How is law used to deal with delinquent children, parents of delinquents, and delinquent parents–and how does the trend in this use of law to influence how the family performs its reproductive function compare with the trend in the use of law to influence how the family performs its educational function?

Lawbreaking and the Family

The millions of crime-prone homeless waifs, *besprizornye*, have long since left the streets, markets, and railroad stations they frequented in the wake of two world wars and collectivization. But juvenile lawbreaking–delinquency and crime–continues to be the subject of concern and experimentation in the law. "It is clear," a veteran specialist writes, "that since the number of juveniles [persons under 18] in the Soviet population has about doubled," in the 1960's, "the country will experience an increase in juvenile lawbreaking." Another demographic reason for rising totals of juvenile crime is "the considerable increase in the urban population in the last 15 years." Countermeasures to date do not go far enough; "we must still try to do a lot more if we are to achieve palpable results in crime eradication."[41] This view is widely shared. Juvenile lawbreaking is singled out by the USSR Minister of Justice as one of three keys to crime prevention (the others being alcoholism and theft of state property).[42] According to criminologists, juvenile crime is indeed a key to crime in general because of the large share contributed by juveniles in crimes against persons and property and because the careers of habitual criminals begin often when they are teen-agers:[43] from a fifth to nearly a half of the careers of samples of repeaters interviewed for Table 1 (see below).

Table 1. *The Family Background of Especially Dangerous Repeaters and the Ages at Which They Committed Their First Crimes*

Family Background	Age at Which First Crimes Were Committed			Total
	Under 15	16-17	18 and Older	Total
Convict grew up with both parents in normal family	4.8	14.5	80.7	100
Convict grew up with both parents in abnormal family (drunkenness, beatings, running away, etc.)	18.2	27.3	54.5	100
Convict left with one parent before reaching the age of 18	9.7	18.1	72.2	100
Convict lost both parents before reaching the age of 18	13.2	31.5	55.3	100

Source: A.A. Gertsenzon, *et al., Kriminologiia*, 3rd ed. (Moscow, 1976), p. 275. Sample size and date are unspecified.

This table also implicates nominally "complete" but "unhealthy" families among the causes of juvenile and adult crime. Less than a fifth of the hardened criminals' careers began before 18 in "normal" families, but nearly half did in "abnormal" families. "Abnormal" families loomed larger in criminal careers than broken families did, larger even than completely shattered families did. Not so much divorces themselves (now running at 800,000 a year, or one for every three marriages and much higher in big cities)[44] as the various family conflicts leading to them owing to drunkenness, women's overwork, and numerous other sources of strain, tend to demoralize the children. "Whether or not such discords bring divorce in their wake is not so important. But it is awfully important that they leave broken people, especially children. . . The solution to this problem is just as much a *political* one as is eradicating drunkenness."[45]

Solutions for these crime-breeding family tensions belong in the category of so-called "general prevention" of juvenile crime. They require expenditures, hence are eminently "political." They speak to the strains, the non-antagonistic contradictions" of development, such as cultural and social inequality, and the contradictions between people's aspirations and "difficulties in job placement, unfavorable housing conditions, unsatisfactory daily living conditions . . . substantial differences between one's own living standards and the living standards of one's neighbors,"[46] the tendency for children of relatively under-educated parents to be least likely to go to regular secondary schools and most likely to be convicted of a crime.[47] Vocational school students are found to be six times more likely to be convicted of a crime than are secondary school students, working youths nine times more likely and youths neither working nor studying, 24 times more likely.[48]

Punishing Juveniles

The full profile of prevention spans both "general measures of prevention" and the "special measures of prevention" which respond directly to crime and which seek to both remove crime-breeding influences on juveniles before they break the law and to deal with the juveniles who have broken the law.[49] Punishment became "the main driving force against juvenile crime"[50] under Stalin, beginning with the crackdown of 1935.[51] Punishment, also, became virtually the same for juveniles as it was for adults in the *Gulag* labor camp empire where professional criminals recruited juveniles into the underworld.[52] Ambitious programs of grass roots prevention and measures to call adult instigators to account went by the board.[53] Stalin's legacy was punitiveness which tended to spare juvenile criminals' parents, moribund community controls, serious juvenile drunkenness, and crime.[54]

Twenty-five years later, crime prevention had changed more to emphasize measures other than punishment of the juveniles: more attention to "general measures of prevention;"[55] compulsory measures of community influence other than deprivation of freedom; and intervening against delinquent parents, on whom some of the onus of punishment therefore shifted. In sum, juvenile crime prevention after Stalin shifted to less punishment for juveniles[56] and more intervention and punishment for the family.

Families in the Network

With the uneven practices from one region or city to another, parents may possibly experience local intervention by the authorities or volunteer activists under their control:

1) before the children break the law because the parents need help or their behavior causes alarm as a threat to social order or their children's upbringing; or

2) after the fact of their children's delinquency or crime.[57]

The first contacts with parents about their behavior or the behavior of their children will come from somewhere in the community network: an array of state and public, paid and volunteer agencies operating under prodding and guidance of the local (rural settlement, district, or town without districts) Party Committee.[58] Maybe a teacher from school will drop by, or, more seriously, someone from the guardianship and trusteeship agency of the local education department in the Soviet. A parent may be approached by a volunteer activist group at work known as something like "the commission to help the family and the school." From the direction of the *MVD* there may turn up a children's inspector, a message from the reception and distribution center that the runaway child has been taken in there,[59] or a pointed reminder from the children's room at the militia precinct house that the child stole Ivan K.'s skates or was picked up playing hookey and has been registered with them as a lawbreaker. Perhaps there is a block committee or one of the 1,400 new "strongpoints of public order" nearby and a strongpoint or committee volunteer, a neighbor from the same housing project visits to carry out his function of "individual work with morally unstable people."[60] The visitor may be a People's Guard with junior in tow or a member of a Council of People's Assessors under the local People's Court. The parents may receive a notice to appear in that court for one of the actions I shall later describe.

The notice may come, rather, from the residential or workplace comrades' court. There are about 300,000 comrades' courts–140,000 in the RSFSR. These non-professional. volunteer agencies were reactivated in 1977, just as they seemed to be faiding out of action.[61] The 1977 reform gives them more explicit authority than they had under the 1967 statutes to hear complaints against family-related offenses like "public drunkenness, making homebrew . . . insults, slander, beatings and light injuries not harmful to health if inflicted for the first time, foul language . . . nonfulfillment or improper fulfillment by parents or guardians of their obligations to bring up children; unworthy behavior toward parents; unworthy behavior in the family. . ."[62] Beyond apologies, reprimands, and censure, the family offenders before the comrades' court face fines up to 50 rubles, and the possible recommendation to management that they lose year-end bonuses, privileged trip tickets, and their place on the apartment waiting list.[63]

Last, but not least important, the family may be visited by a "social inspector" or "social counselor," volunteers working under the local Soviet's Commission on Juvenile Affairs (CJA), or a notice may arrive to appear before the CJA. It is an unpaid board which intervenes in many ways to help place, decide on the parole of and the firing of minors, and which hears of lawbreaking by those apprehended juveniles not tried in comrades' court or the People's Court. "Coordinating centers for all community organizations concerned with upbringing and the prevention of juvenile lawbreaking,"[64] CJA's are state agencies under local Soviets, revived by union republic statutes of 1961-1962 as revised in 1967.[65]

CJA's have extensive powers for action against parents or substitute parents of juvenile lawbreakers, found to have abused or neglected them: "public censure; obligate them to make good damages inflicted by the juvenile up to 20 rubles; fine them up to 30 rubles; refer the case of the parents or their substitutes to a comrade's court; petition the People's Court to deprive them of parental rights," a measure I shall discuss separately. Without parental consent, CJA's may send juveniles to special medical-educational institutions and to special schools for problem juveniles in need of tight supervision and smaller classes (special general schools to finish elementary education through eight grade, and special vocational schools for grades 9 and 10), though a prosecutor must be present during the commitment hearing. When parents are long absent, sick, sentenced to confinement or otherwise prevented from supervising their children, the CJA may send the children to ordinary boarding schools or children's homes without parents' consent. The parents must contribute toward their children's upkeep to the extent they are able.[66] The most frequent CJA measures against parents appear to be fines, informing parents' place of employment, warning, censure, and referral to comrades' court.[67] Appeal of CJA decisions is to the local Soviet. Since the CJA chair is the secretary of deputy chair of the Soviet executive committee, the procedure is structured against the appellant.[68]

Law is one thing, practice another, as we have already indicated and shall have to again. All policy choices involve practical difficulties. It is all very well to divert juveniles increasingly away from corrections and the often faulty parole procedures associated with them. But then this places additional burdens on community alternatives to corrections–an amateur affair of families, volunteers, and "collectives." It obliges courts to see that the juveniles they set free undergo community rehabilitation. The system can be leaky. Of 18 minors tried by Khabarovsk courts and sentenced to punishment without deprivation of freedom and who showed up in this study of repeaters, only 4 had been put under the charge of a collective or a social counselor. The Kanavin District People's Court in Gorkii knew that Sitdikov's parents had lost control of him, that he did not go home at night, and that he got drunk. For habitual pilfering, it sentenced him to one year's correctional labor, meaning a 10% pay cut, but did not entrust him to a collective or order appointment of a social counselor. The construction organization where he went to work the day after his sentence was not informed about his conviction. He went on drinking and breaking the law and ended up with a two year sentence for stealing state property.[69]

Making Parents Liable

Unlike criminal law, civil law may put the burden of proof on the defendant. The new civil codes of the 1960's relieve parents of liability for damage caused by their minor children if they can show that they, the parents, were not at fault. With children 15-18 years old at the time they caused the damage, an additional condition for liability is that the children themselves have insufficient earnings to make restitution.[70]

Now that more families own cars, the perennial problems arising from junior's using the family car engage judicial attention, as in the case of *Mrs. N. v. P. and Parents*. The widow of N., killed in a January 3, 1977, car accident along with his father, sued the culprit, P., and his parents to recover damages for loss of breadwinner, funeral expenses, and costs of repair to the family car. The Irkutsk Regional Court found in favor of Mrs. N. P. and his parents appealed. P. denied fault from his place of confinement where he was serving criminal sentence for vehicular homicide. P.'s parents claimed they were not responsible for their sons's actions. The Civil Bench of the RSFSR Supreme Court apparently did not find that P.'s parents had disproved their own share of fault (the published decision is silent on this). It stated that, under the Civil Code just cited, parents must make up that share of restitution which their children are unable to pay. Plaintiff asked for restitution of N.'s salary of 421.50 rubles a month since their daughter received only a 60 ruble monthly loss of breadwinner pension. The court assessed P. for 300 rubles lump sum and 20 rubles a month until she reached age 16, or age 18 if studying. Plaintiff asked 443.50 for funeral expenses and 307.08 rubles for car repairs. The Court assessed P.'s father the full 443.50 for funeral expenses and P.'s mother 290.18 rubles for car repairs.[71]

Drunkenness–the bane of traffic safety seekers–figures largely in problems of social order and family upbringing. From the Party viewpoint, "Drunkenness causes large losses of working time, lowering of labor productivity. Drunkenness destroys the family, has a deleterious effect on the upbringing of the younger generation. It is one of the chief causes of crime."[72] Drunkenness has been associated with two-thirds of murders, three-fourths of aggravated assaults, snatching (*grabezh*), and robbery (*razboi*), one-half of the thefts of personal property, and two-thirds of auto accidents. Drunkenness, the criminologists say also, makes crime victims more vulnerable.[73]

Alcohol abuse prompts much of the social network's intervention into family life. B. and his wife both liked to drink. B. was called into school after his son, 14, began boasting there about how his father, B., included him in the heavy family drinking. The school interview had no effect. Then the school parents and teachers committee initiated a case against B. in the comrades' court where B. lived and got the son to go away to pioneer camp for the whole summer. B. meanwhile was finally prevailed upon to leave his son out of the family drinking. The son "began to study well and drinks no more."[74] Had B.'s son appeared in public places "in a state of intoxication offensive to human dignity and public morality," Mr. and Mrs. B. would have been liable under 1966 legislation to a fine of 3-10 rubles because their son was under 16. A 1972 addition extended the fining to cases simply where the under-16 child drinks in public. It shifted the fining from the police to the CJA. Parents (always add here–"or persons substituting for them") may be fined 10-30 rubles for the petty hooliganism (administrative offense) or hooliganism (criminal misdemeanor) of their children under 16. If the hooligan children are 16 to 18 years old, and have no earning, then their parents, again, must pay the fine and the cost of room and board for administrative arrest in cases of petty hooliganism. [75] "Thus, parents in these cases are liable not for their guilt but for the guilt of their children." [76]

Some of the armory of measures against alcohol and drug abuse initiated in the 1960's and 1970's both protects and deprives families. Administrative law of uncertain application directs workplace administrations to deprive of privileged trip tickets, year-end bonuses, and places on apartment waiting lists, employees failing for a year to respond to various means of community persuasion to stop abusing alcohol. [77] The present union republic criminal codes contain new provisions for court-appointed trustees over criminal offenders not sentenced to deprivation of freedom, when their drinking habit "puts the family in a serious material position." Revisions of 1968 further extended outside intervention under the law by adding drug abuse as a cause for appointing a trustee and expanding the list of agencies that may petition to have the trustee appointed. [78] The criminal codes specifically provide also for the courts to sentence abusers of alcohol and drugs (excepting pregnant and overage persons) to compulsory cures along with the regular criminal punishment. [79] Another extension of the state's legal reach came in 1967. It prescribes commitment to compulsory cure in medical labor prophylactoria, even without a crime having been committed, of alcohol abusers who either refuse voluntary cure in ambulatory clinics or who remain uncured after such treatment. [80] That is the law. Its wide non-application and its misapplication are another matter. [81]

Following the new criminal codes, the new civil codes added a measure of family protection–the procedure under which a court may order the limitation of the legal competence of persons so abusing alcohol or drugs as "to place their families in a difficult material position." This served among other things to divert wages from the drunkard to a trusteeship (who could be, for instance, the other spouse–usually the wife). To rub the lesson in, cases like this may be heard in visiting session where the drunkard works. [82] Sometimes, the trial court properly conducts a meaningful case and sends a special finding to the drunkard's workplace so that he may be watched or penalized there. At other times, visiting sessions flop as morality plays. The People's Court of the Soviet District, Voronezh, scheduled in visiting session the case of two alcohol abusers, S. and B., without verifying ahead of time that the competence-limiting action still was needed. The wives of S. and B. showed up at the sessions and asked that the sessions be terminated since their husbands had reformed.[83] Sometimes, far too many visiting session cases are heard to bring out circumstances surrounding alcohol abuse:

> "The People's Court of Krolevetskii District, Sumskaia Province heard 18 suits to limit the legal competence of persons working on the collective farm in one session December 9, 1974, at the Dubovichi Village Club. The People's Court of Burynskii District of the same province heard similar actions in the cases of 16 persons, many of them working in one collective farm, at a single visiting session. In none of these cases did the courts issue a special finding about improving educational work in the kolkhoz and confined themselves to establish the fact of citizens' alcohol abuse."[84]

To the list of attempted protections for the child-rearing parent, I should add the criminal liability of alimony defaulters[85] and the family law provision for the court's allotting less than half of the community property (normally divided evenly in cases of dispute) to a spouse "refusing to do socially useful work or squandering community property at the expense of family interests."[86] A People's Court gave Mr. P. less than half the community property after establishing that Mr. P. "abused alcoholic beverages, spent all his wages on liquor, sold for the same purpose things belonging to his wife and children for next to nothing, thus putting the family in serious financial straits."[87]

Where parents are found guilty of contributing to a child's delinquency, penalties may be more serious than civil limitations or fines. The criminal codes prescribe up to five years deprivation of freedom for adults drawing minors into criminal activity, into beggary, prostitution, gambling, or using a minor for the purpose of leading a parasitic existence. This is an adaptation of penalties first introduced by the decree of April 7, 1935. In an extension of intervention, drunkenness was added to the list before beggary in 1965,[88] and in 1972 the anti-drunkenness measures added an administrative penalty of fine up to 30 rubles levied against adults by the CJA or administrative commission of the local Soviet for single instances of their getting juveniles drunk (the criminal penalties being reserved for cases where the enticement to drunkenness is systematic).[89]

Again, that is the law. Practice seems to lag far behind. As in Stalin's day, courts seem disposed toward mechanically trying juveniles, and establishing their guilt and sentence, and stopping short of exposing and bringing to justice adults involved in their drunkenness and crime. The first deputy chairman of the RSFSR Supreme Court says that "extremely rarely is a criminal case initiated against adults guilty of drawing juveniles into drunkenness."[90] A stream of articles and supreme court directives testify both to the régime's determination to get at adult instigators of juvenile drunkenness, crime, and other deviance, and to the difficulties of getting law enforcement agencies and the courts to expose and prosecute the guilty adults.[91] Sometimes, the social network around families enfolds them in a close knit and restraining mesh supportive of their educational function.[92] I was given examples of this in the summer of 1977 in the USSR by a leading activist volunteer in the Kiev "Arsenal" factory, the chair of the Leningrad City CJA, and the chair of the Vasileostrov District CJA in Leningrad. A visit elsewhere brought out difficulties encountered in curbing drunkenness and thefts. The talks confirmed my impression from reading: the practice of community intervention is uneven. One veteran juvenile crime expert went so far a few years ago as to say that measures on the books "are rarely applied" by the CJA's, courts, etc., to call delinquent parents on the carpet before social organizations and collectives or to enact the civil and criminal penalties required by law.[93] But never has the régime fostered such a determined effort to promote social prevention and non-punitive, or non-incarcerating rehabilitation without isolation from the community, as it has since the late 1950's.[94]

Taking away Parental Rights

Communist visionaries have planned the demise of the family as an educational and economic unit. Lawmakers, however, have had to deal with social realities, consistently giving space–since the first 1918 Russian Family Code–to mutual support obligations in the family and to parents' obligations to raise their children to be useful members of the society. Rights have been always delegated to parents to be exercised only in the interests of the children and the society awaiting them.[95] "In handing over to you a certain authority," a famous educator told parents, "the Soviet state demands from you the correct upbringing of future citizens."[96] The mounting state concern for the replenishing function of the family eventuated in two articles devoted to the family in the USSR Constitution of 1977. The draft of Article 66 provided: "Citizens of the USSR are obligated to care for their children's upbringing, to prepare them for socially useful work, to raise worthy members of socialist society."[97] (The final version of this article goes on to proclaim the converse family law obligation, that of children "to care for and help their parents.") For the first time, in 1968, family law carried a statement of its educational purpose "to insure a family upbringing of children, linked organically with public education, in the spirit of devotion to the motherland, communist attitude to labor and the preparation of children for active participation in building a communist society."[98]

Deviations from such ideal upbringing that catch the attention of the community network may bring on either correctional measures without removing the children involved in ways already mentioned, or removal of the children, or deprivation of parental rights with or without removal of the children.[99] In the latter event, the CJA, prosecutor, or organs of guardianship and trusteeship of the local Soviet education department (or absent an education department, then the village or settlement Soviet executive committee),[100] may petition the People's Court to take away parental rights of one or both parents after careful investigation and perusal of a full report from the guardianship and trustee section. Deciding on this, the court must order the child removed, or approve removal already made in cases of danger to the child, and must award child support to the parent not deprived of rights and retaining custody, or to the substitute parent, where neither parent is left with parental rights or custody. Deprivation of parental rights may be only on specific grounds:[101] "if the court has established that the parents refuse to fulfill their obligations to educate their children or abuse their parental rights; are cruel to their children; have a harmful influence on their children through their immoral, antisocial behavior; and also if the parents are chronic alcoholics or drug addicts."[102]

The last two grounds appear in Soviet family law explicitly for the first time (though this does not exclude their citation in practice before 1968).[103] They formally extend the state's authority to intervene. Loose women seem to fall within the broad reach of "harmful influence on their children through their immoral, antisocial behavior," as in the case of *Kvalyn City CJA v. P.*

> "The Kvalyn City People's Court of Saratov Province examined the suit of the CJA against Citizeness P. to deprive her of parental rights over 2 children. It established that the children's mother works nowhere, is constantly drunk, leads an immoral life, neglects her children's upbringing. The father is characterized positively, cares for his children. The children love him, and the court deprived only the defendant of parental rights. The children remained in their father's custody."[104]

Prostitution is not a crime in the USSR. So, deprivation of this woman's parental rights served in effect as a penalty for prostitution as well as a protection for the children.

The parent(s) deprived of rights lose them only in regard to the child or children involved in the neglect, abuse, or corruption.[105] Presumably, if rights are taken away for a parent's drunkenness or drug addiction, this will be with regard to all children living with that parent. With far-reaching addition in 1968 of alcoholism and drug addiction as grounds for depriving a parent of his/her rights, for the first time in family law (as opposed to practice) alcoholism and drug addiction, though recognized as illnesses, are distinguished from other incapacitating illnesses, which may result in removal of children but are not considered to be the parents' fault and do not legally entail deprivation of parental rights.[106] Deprivation of parental rights is meant to protect children, punish the parents, and provide an object lesson to other parents.[107] It is consistently labeled an "extreme" and "exceptional" measure. In many interviews with Soviet judges and scholars, I received the same impression. Deprivation of parental rights is not supposed to be resorted to until available "measures of social influences" through school, the CJA, a comrades' court, or social organizations, have been tried and have failed to bring desirable results.[108]

On deprivation of parental rights, as on many other aspects of controls over the family, the RSFSR Family Code is not always a sure guide to rules in other union republics. Deprivation of rights is *only a civil action* against parents in the RSFSR, Belorussia, Uzbekistan, and Lithuania. For no apparent reason in the 11 other republics, deprivation of parental rights can be a supplementary punishment in a criminal trial, as under the old criminal codes,[109] without all the safeguards of a special separate civil action. To make matters worse, the grounds for such supplementary punishment vary confusingly from republic to republic. They include "non-payment of support," "abuse of rights," "malicious abuse of rights," "malicious evasion of parental obligations," "committing a crime against children," and in Moldavia, any abuse or omission resulting in children's drunkenness, debauchery, vagrancy, or other socially dangerous behavior.[110] Parents found delinquent under the family code may be deprived of just one or a few rights, such as custody or visitation rights.[111] A parent fully deprived of all parental rights loses both the non-material rights (*e.g.*, participation in child's upbringing or to adopt a child) and material rights (*e.g.*, to inheritance and support, and in some cases to continue living with the child).[112]

That is the law. What about the practice in both non-political and political cases? More often than not, CJA's and guardian and trusteeship sections act against delinquent parents only after damage is done and, for example, the child is already following in his father's (or mother's) footsteps, drinks heavily, and has committed his first known crime.[113] A Latvian Supreme Court Justice found, in the results of a survey of half a year of the juvenile criminal cases in his republic, that parents' indifference and failure to supervise their children figured as a frequent apparent cause of their lawbreaking. The findings implicated also agencies like CJA's in the community network for their accompanying indifference. The case of *The Latvian SSR v. Boris D.* told a story "unfortunately typical in many ways." Boris came to justice for robbing a youth his age of 48 rubles under threat of violence in a railroad station waiting room at 1 AM. In his drunken state, he collided with another man on his way out, hit him, robbed him too of some change, and went for 3 years' deprivation of freedom in an educational labor colony of ordinary régime by sentence of the Lundza City People's Court. Boris had a long record of bad schoolwork, truancy, and thefts, for which he was registered with the militia children's room. Boris seemed reformed briefly before the crimes for which he was convicted. His father left before Boris was born. His mother, the case materials reported, regarded her son as an annoying hindrance, paid no heed to his wellbeing and upbringing, and led a dissipated life. As a result, the court reported, Boris spent much of his time on the street in a circle of friends of shady reputation. Meanwhile at home, his mother presented him with the spectacle of her endless drinking bouts and a procession of visiting men. Not until just before Boris committed the railroad station crimes was action taken against his mother to deprive her of parental rights.[114]

I attended the case of Andrei, sentenced to 2 years in an educational labor colony for attacking two men in a cafe restroom while drunk and taking the watch of one of them. The Moscow court, noted in print for its experienced handling of juvenile cases,[115] brought out that neither busy parent deigned to come to support Andrei at his trial. Andrei, estranged from his mother, lived alone though only 16. The trial did not cause his mother, head of the methodological section of the State Committee on Radio and Television, where Andrei worked as a technician, to postpone her business trip abroad. His father, an army officer divorced and remarried, did not come west to be at the trial. Andrei's childhood, the trial judge noted, "was such a joyless one. Both this parents were working. Instead of giving him love, they bought him luxurious presents. He was a very unhappy boy," and a very unsupervised one. Yet at no time, apparently, had anyone approached the parents about Andrei to pressure them to pay more heed to him. The judge sent no special finding to the State Committee as far as I know. I am not saying that this was a case clearly presenting grounds for deprivation of rights. Rather, it seems the sort of borderline case where intervention ordinarily would not occur and deprivation of parental rights at this point neither served Andrei's cause nor was legally a foregone conclusion (aside from any consideration of the parent's privileged positions).[116]

Practice strays from law and directives also in the court hearings of suits to deprive parents of their rights. These lapses range from casual decisions, based on incomplete information and without required guardianship and trusteeship section reports, to unfounded deprivation of rights of persons failing to supervise children because of circumstances beyond their control.[117]

When it comes to deprivation of parental rights for ideological reasons, we may recall that far and wide parents have been deprived of rights and the custody of their children or otherwise penalized for reasons of life style, beliefs, or race.[118] So have dissident parents faced possible and actual deprivation of rights and loss of children recently in the USSR. First, though, a word about religion and the law in order to show once again that the use of legal compulsion has been part of an extension of intervention farther into family life after Stalin in the educational dimension of social replenishment. Always a cutting edge in social engineering, Soviet family, criminal, and administrative law is enlisted to help foster what the Party leadership deems to be desirable new customs and traditions and to combat undesirable ones. "Soviet law serves as an important means of struggle in overcoming old traditions and customs–harmful survivals of the past."[119] One of these "harmful survivals" is religion. The Communist Party aims eventually to wipe it out by intensive propaganda [120] and by legal compulsion. Stalin completed the legal foundation for today's intervention against religion by a 1929 decree on religious cults. Among other things, it restricted religious organizations to conducting worship, forbade religious propaganda, and thus originated the present truncated constitutional guarantee of "freedom of religion and anti-religious propaganda." [121] Stalin's last years brought toleration and lackadaisical anti-religious propaganda. But, the meaning of law depends on the political interpretation given it at any one time by the Party and local authorities. [122] Khrushchev applied and amended Soviet laws in a campaign of unprecedented reach, severity, and even brutality between 1960 and 1964. [123]

Criminal codes are the single most important area of Party interpretation. [124] Khrushchev and, in moderated form, his successors not only applied criminal code enforcements of religious proscriptions more vigorously, they gave them broader sweep under the new criminal codes in effect between 1960 and 1962 and edicts of 1966. The codes hit widely against parents organizing religious instruction for their children, taking them to religious worship, counseling them to avoid social participation and civic obligations, and performing rites such as baptism which the authorities interpreted as having been injurious to the children's health. [125] To help enforce legal restrictions and uncover violators, the governments of most union republics organized some form of commissions of volunteer activists under local soviets. [126]

An official rationale for the campaign is that many members of dissident religious sects are disloyal to the Soviet régime [127] and are "religious fanatics . . . who, under the guise of religion, attempt to perpetrate anti-social illegal acts, incite co-believers to refuse to fulfill civic obligations, to perform rituals injurious to health . . . declare the Soviet system 'an arm of the devil,' 'satan's world' ... summon them to annihilation in a holy war (Armageddon) ... to refuse to participate in elections, census taking ... prevent children from going to school, the movies, from watching TV, reading literature, newspapers, and magazines . . . urge co-religionists not to work in enterprises, collective farms, institutions, and instill contempt for socially useful work." [128]

The family is crucial in the anti-religious campaign because: "The family is the most important channel through which the churches seek to disseminate their influence upon the young." [129] Intervention into family life under the religious and criminal law goes far beyond the desultory efforts of Stalin's day. The pattern was set under Khrushchev's intense campaign of 1960-1964. 1) Believer's homes were invaded by agitators and by educational authorities and the courts teaming up to remove children and to visit other compulsion on resisting parents;

2) Children under 18 were barred by decrees passed in 1961-1963 from membership in religious organizations or participating in religious services or ceremonies of any kind. In the 1930's drive, at worst parents were forbidden to compel children to attend services against their own will;
3) Also unprecedented is the complete ban on organized religious instruction to children. Under Stalin, priests might instruct groups of no more than three and teach catechism upon parents' invitation;
4) It seems a quibble, in the light of what Stalin's collectivization and purges did to shatter millions of families, but on the religious front, it was not until after Stalin in the 1960's and 1970's that the practice began of removing children from believing parents to boarding schools and depriving the latter of their parental rights[130] under the flexible provisions of family law.[131] Here is an example of a deprivation of rights of an activist religious dissident:

> "Iakov Nikolaevich Pavlov, born in 1935, worked until 1973 as a technical planner for a local government body in Taldy-Kurgan in Kazakhstan. He is the father of eight children and a member of the dissenting wing of the Evangelical and Christian Baptists. The dissenting Baptists refuse to accept some of the restrictions officially placed on religious activity in the early 1960s, particularly the restriction on their right to instruct their children in religion."

Mr. Pavlov was arrested in the fall of 1973 and charged with violating laws on the separation of church and state, school and church, and with disseminating lies defaming the Soviet state and system. The prosecutor charged at the trial of Mr. Pavlov and five co-defendants in February 1974, among other things, that Mr. Pavlov and two co-defendants had admitted that they had jointly "organized religious lessons for their under-age children," allegedly a violation of the laws on separation of church from state, and school from church. Mr. Pavlov denied some charges but admitted to several including the charge of having taught religious principles to his children, "but said that a faithful Christian was obliged to do so, just as a dedicated Marxist-Leninist was obligated by conscience to instruct his children in the principles of communism. He reminded the court that Lenin had defended the right of each person to profess and to preach his faith." Mr. Pavlov was found guilty and sentenced to five years' confinement in a corrective labor colony. Also, the court deprived Mr. Pavlov of his parental rights over four of his eight children. Three co-defendants likewise were deprived of parental rights over some of their children.[132] Reports of parents being stripped of their rights because of their Baptist, Adventist, Pentecostalist, and other religions stopped after the Helsinki Conference of August 1975.[133] But the armory of laws limiting religious practices remains in effect, and a massive campaign of atheistic propaganda and introducing new secular rituals for important family and public occasions continues.[134]

Similarly, no instances of depriving would-be Jewish emigrants of parental rights have been recently reported. Two years prior to Helsinki, twenty-eight Soviet Jews appealed abroad for protests against the Soviet authorities' practice of taking parental rights away from some Jews who apply to emigrate to Israel. The courts used against the Jews article 18 of the FPLMF and article 52 of the CMF of the RSFSR which obligate parents "to raise their children in the spirit of the moral code of builders of communism." [135] That was the article cited by the District Department of Education, Leningrad, when supporting the suit against Solomon Dreizer brought by his first wife to deprive him of his parental rights after he applied to emigrate. Another ground for the suit: Dreizer had been sentenced to three years' confinement. The decision to strip him of his parental rights was upheld on appeal. [136] Post-Stalin changes in criminal, civil administrative, and family law amount to a dramatic increase in parental liability for their own delinquency and their children's.

The union republics of Central Asia, Kazakhstan (not now part of Central Asia in Soviet parlance), the Caucasus, and the RSFSR list in their criminal codes various "crimes constituting survivals of local custom"–crimes reflecting enduring religious and ethnic traditions. But their new codes of the 1960's feature a reduction of some 20 items previously listed. These omissions follow the virtual disappearance of some crimes like *baranta* (theft of cattle to enforce claims), dispensing traditional court justice, and religious taxing. [137] The RSFSR Criminal Code, uniquely, has a special chapter on crimes which are survivals of local customs. Formally, the articles of this chapter are applicable only in regions where they are considered such survivals. The chapter lists ten crimes. (CC's of the other republics have similar articles. Relatively few are listed in the Georgian CC.) Several of the crimes listed directly concern the family and parents. These are: refusal of relatives of the victim to be reconciled in a blood feud, acceptance and payment of a bride price (*kalym*), compelling a woman to marry or stay married or abducting a bride, concluding marital agreements according to local custom with a person under marriage age. [138]

These crimes and polygamy persist, owing to support in local economic conditions and local customs. Turkmenia seems to nurture the liveliest survivals of traditonal crimes–some 8 to 10% of all crimes in Turkmenia in the years 1960-1966. [139] Republic CC's contain also some articles of general as well as specifically anti-traditionalist purpose, such as articles making it a crime forcibly to prevent women from achieving equality by blocking their participation in state, public, or cultural life. [140] But the recent furor in Turkmenia has been against the "feudal bey survivals" of crimes growing out of custom. A Party-prodded campaign in Turkmenia has attacked "the hateful *kalym*" and has led to the reintroduction into the Turkmenian CC of an article against the once supposedly vanished practice of *kaitarma* (taking back a bride until *kalym* is paid).[141]

4. Conclusions

Soviet efforts to shape through law the family's replenishing functions add support to the impression gathered from other post-Stalin reforms in social engineering. It appears that the passing of Stalin's lethal totalitarianism has brought not a slackening but an intensification of state and community intervention into certain crucial areas of family life, even while the blunt weapon of mass terror has been discarded in favor of more selective police methods. I have reviewed here many changes in the framework of Soviet law governing court practice, parent's duties and rights, and the statutes of numerous state and social institutions ranging from CJA's and comrades' courts to the *MVD*'s correctional and enforcement arms and unpaid social volunteers. As colleagues have surmised, the intensification of state and community intervention into family life may be offset by its privatization in separate apartments and the family automobile.

My previous chapter for this project on Soviet law since Stalin dealt with the legal regulation of conjugal relations. It presented evidence of:
1) less arbitrariness in law-creation (though new possibilities of it in law-application);
2) a shift of compulsive intervention away from divorce and abortion toward more legal and administrative regulation of marriage, paternity, civil registration, support assessments, and the protection of pregnant and divorced spouses.

Similar trends emerge from the materials of the present chapter:
1) less arbitrariness in law-creation (though new possibilities in law application, again inherent in the nature of interventions involved in new approaches); and
2) a shift of intervention away from direct legal pressure to stimulate the birthrate (already touched upon in the previous chapter but elaborated on here) and toward pressuring delinquent parents–and the parents of delinquents.

Demographic policy has followed the social welfare leads of the East European socialist countries; *e.g.*, in adding a long partly-paid maternity leave of absence, but not the leads of those countries that retain elements of legal compulsion in the regulation of abortions, contraceptives, and divorce. The Soviet policy debates so far have brought defeat for proponents of direct legal action to stimulate the birthrate and a victory for proponents of studying and influencing the aspirations of millions of Soviet parents to reproduce up to the level of their ideals of two or three per family, instead of the actuality of one or two in many parts of the USSR. The outcome of the demographic debates meant also a rejection of the suggested assemblage of "demographic legislation."

Soviet approaches to both population policy and crime prevention evidence once again what I call a neo-statism, to distinguish it from Stalinist statism. Both outlooks center on beliefs in the capacity of the socialist state eventually to solve pressing social problems like falling birthrates and crime. Neo-statism is less compulsive than statism, though this does not rule out selective reliance on compulsion. We saw that the compulsive reach of the law has lengthened in many ways when it comes to parents' liability for their own or their children's deviance from norms of communist morality. Neo-statism as compared with statism is more comprehensive and penetrating in social management, more cautious about the costs complexities and difficulties of social engineering, more pluralistic and open and research-oriented in policy formation, and more reliant on the advice of experts.

Demographic neo-statism exists more in research theory and method than in still modest government policy. But, most importantly, specialists have pursuaded the Party leadership of the rightness of their analytical and complex systems approach, at least for now. Prime evidence of this lies directly in the speeches of the Secretary General of the Communist Party. Neo-statism in the regulation of the family's educational functions exists more in research, law, directives, and commentary than it does in the very uneven judicial and community practices of compulsion and influence. But it would be a mistake to liken the present gap between law and practice, regarding delinquent families, with the situation under Stalin. Then, law emphasized punishment and obliterated the substantive and procedural safeguards that now differentiate juvenile justice from justice for adults. Then, practice saw not simply malfunctioning of an elaborate network of agencies of community intervention and rehabilitation, but the absence of such a network. A stranger's knock on the door then was more likely than not to announce the arrival of the secret police at 2 AM. A stranger's knock on the door now is more likely, for the average family, to be announcing the visit of a teacher, social counselor, or volunteer guardian of public order, come to talk about a child's misconduct in school or in their neighborhood.

Several related questions, here unanswered, would extend the limited scope of this present inquiry. Firstly, there is the question of regulating the economic functions of the family in the still lively spheres of production and private enterprise.[142] A second question concerns other uses of family, administrative, and other branches of law against dissidents and their families. A third question, raised by colleagues, concerns the possibility that enforcing the greater responsibility of parents may have the unintended effect of discouraging parenthood and undercutting birthrates. This may be an unanswerable question. In any event, the mass nature of family choices in parenthood and the limited and imperfect nature of educational intervention indicate that the unintended effects on the birthrate of penalizing delinquent parents may be presumed to be small, especially when compared with the widespread de-fertilizing effects of urbanization and assimilation out of the progenitally profilic traditional ways of life in both Russian and non-Russian areas of the Soviet Union.

NOTES

1. For background over the entire Soviet period to the late 1960's, see H. Kent Geiger, *The Family in Soviet Russia* (Cambridge, Mass., 1968).

2. "CIA, in a report to a Congressional Committee, Predicts an Economic Slowdown in Soviet Union," *The New York Times*, Aug. 9, p. 3.

3. A. Ia. Kvasha (ed.), *Upravlenie razvitiem narodonaseleniia v SSSR (Problemy i perspektivy)* (Managing Population Growth in the USSR: Problems and Prospects), (Moscow, 1977), p. 3. "Rech' tovarischa L. I. Brezhneva na plenume TsK KPSS 25 Oktiabria 1976 goda" (Speech of Comrade L. I. Brezhchnev at the Plenum of the Communist Party of the Soviet Union of October 25, 1976), *Pravda* Oct. 26, 1976, p. 1.

4. By delinquency I mean any action, including lawbreaking and its legally most serious form, crime, to which the authorities react unfavorably.

5. L. Ponomarev, "I metody ubezhdeniia, i sila zakona" (Both Methods of Persuasion and the Force of Law), *Sov. Iust.*, 1977, No. 12, 1.

6. A. A. Gertsenzon *et al.*, *Kriminologiia* (Criminology), (hereafter, *Kriminologiia*), 3rd. ed. (Moscow, 1976), pp. 292-298; V. S. Tadevosian, "Otvetstvennost' roditelei za vospitanie detei" (Parents' Responsibility for the Upbringing of Their Children), in V. S. Tadevosian (ed.), *Pravovye voprosy sem'i i vospitaniia detei* (Legal Questions of the Family and the Upbringing of Children), (Moscow, 1968), pp. 69-70.

7. Ponomarev, *op. cit.*, p. 1.

8. V. Perevedentsev responds to this viewpoint in "Edinstvennyi v sem'e" (The Only One in the Family), *LG*, Mar. 16, 1977, p. 12. See also V. S. Tadevosian in "Kruglyi stol' 'Sovetskogo gosudarstva i pravo': Pravovye aspekty demograficheskoi politiki" (Round Table of 'Soviet State and Law': Legal Aspects of Demographic Policy), *SGiP*, 1975, No. 1, 28, at 31-32. (Hereafter cited as "Kruglyi stol.")

9. D. I. Valentei (Director of the Center for Population Study), *ibid.*, p. 29; Kvasha, *op. cit.*, pp. 90-110; D. Valentei and A. Kvasha, "Sotsial'no-ekonomicheskie problemy narodonaseleniia SSSR v dolgosrochnom perspective" (Social and Economic Problems of the USSR Population in Long-term Perspective), in D. Valentei (ed.), *Demograficheskaia situatsiia v SSSR* (The Demographic Situation in the USSR), (Moscow, 1976), pp. 1-6.

10. Perevedentsev, *op. cit.*, p. 12; *Narodnoe khoziaistvo SSSR v 1975 godu* (The USSR Economy in 1975), (Moscow, 1976), p. 43; *Narodnoe khoziaistvo SSSR za 60 let* (The USSR Economy for 60 years), (Moscow, 1977), p. 73.

11. Helen Desfosses, "Women and Pro-Natalism in the USSR," Conference Paper No. 25, Stanford University Conference on Women in Russia, May 29-June 1, 1975, p. 3.

12. "Legal Aspects of Demographic Policy," June 1974, arranged in collaboration with the Center for Population Study of the Economics Faculty, Moscow State University, a center authorized by decree of USSR *Gosplan*, State Committee of the USSR Council of Ministers on Science and Technology, and Presidium of the USSR Academy of Sciences to be "the leading organization for working out the social and economic principles and for regulating population growth. "Kruglyi stol," note 8 above.

13. G. A. Zlobin, *ibid.*, p. 32; D. I. Valentei, *ibid.*, p. 29; G. I. Litvinova, *ibid.*, p. 33.

14. R. Iu. Kandisberg and Ia. I. Rubin, "Demograficheskoe zakonodatel'stvo: poniatie i effektivnost' " (Demographic Legislation: Meaning and Effectiveness), *SGiP*,

1973, No. 12, 118-121; E. A. Pavlodskii, "Sistemnyi podkhod k poniatiiu demograficheskogo zakonodatel'stva" (The Systems Approach to Understanding Demographic Legislation), *SGiP*, 1976, No. 6, 131.

15. Zlobin, in "Kruglyi stol," note 8 above, p. 33.

16. Desfosses in "Kruglyi stol," note 8 above, pp. 13-15; Pavlodskii, *op. cit.*, p. 131; Zlobin, in "Kruglyi stol," note 8 above, p. 32.

17. *Ibid.*, p. 33.

18. Pavlodskii, *op. cit.*, p. 133.

19. Kvasha, *op. cit.*, pp. 17-18.

20. On the application of systems analysis in law see Peter H. Juviler, *Revolutionary Law and Order: Politics and Social Change in the USSR* (New York, 1976), pp. 158-160.

21. Kvasha, *op. cit.*, pp. 5-89.

22. *Ibid.*, pp. 13-18.

23. *Ibid.*, p. 8.

24. Bodrova, in "Kruglyi stol," note 8 above, p. 31; Zlobin, *ibid.*, p. 33; Valentei, *ibid.*, p. 29; Pavlodskii, *op. cit.*, p. 131.

25. V. P. Korchagin, in "Kruglyi stol," note 8 above, p. 33.

26. Pavlodskii, *op. cit.*, p. 133; Bodnov, in "Kruglyi stol," note 8 above, p. 31.

27. Kvasha, in "Kruglyi stol," note 8 above, p. 30.

28. Iu. V. Riurikov, "Children and Society–On Certain Aspects of Demographic Policy," *Voprosy filosofii*, (Problems of Philosophy), 1977, No. 4, 111-121, abstracted in *CDSP*, 1977, No. 29, 8.

29. *Ved. V. S. SSSR*, 1974, No. 40, item 63. It set 12 rubles a month for each child 7 years old or younger when per capita family income is below 50 rubles. See proscript comment of *SGiP* that this confirms thinking at the round table, *SGiP*, 1975, No. 1, 35.

30. "Rech' tovarishcha L. I. Brezhneva," note 4 above, p. 1.

31. Law of October 29, 1976, *Pravda, Izvestiia*, Oct. 30, 1976.

32. V. V. Bodrova, *Narodonaselenie evropeiskikh sotsialisticheskikh stran* (The Population of European Socialist Countries), (Moscow, 1976), pp. 7, 11-12, 59-64, 129-166; V. V. Bodrova, in "Kruglyi stol," note 8 above, p. 31.

33. A. Vyshnevskii, "I uchit'sia i zhenit'sia" (Both Study and Marry), *LG*, Jan. 12, 1977, p. 3.

34. V. Perevedentsev, "Goroda zhenikhov" (Bachelor Cities), *LG*, Feb. 16, 1977, p. 13.

35. Egborg Radzinskii, "Raznye liki odinochestva" (Various Aspects of Being Single), *LG*, Jan. 12, 1977, p. 13.

36. "Dochki-materi" (Young Daughter-Mothers), *LG*, Jun. 15, 1977, p. 12, writing against the suggestion of Leonid Zhukovitskii that encouraging unmarried mothers to have children is a way to raise the birthrate, in "Liubov' i demografiia" (Love and Demography), *LG*, May 4, 1977, p. 12.

37. Roman Szporliuk, "Why Some Soviet Sociologists Are Alarmed," *The New York Times*, Aug. 27, 1977; Edward L. Keenan, "Soviet Time Bomb: A Majority of Suppressed Minorities," *The New Republic*, Aug. 21 and 28, 1976, pp. 17-21.

38. Kvasha was cited in "Kruglyi stol," note 8 above, p. 30, as saying that a drop in Central Asian birthrates "may considerably complicate the demographic situation."

39. V. S. Tadevosian, "Demograficheskaia politika i pravo" (Demographic Policy and Law), *SGiP*, 1975, No. 8, 24.

40. Kvasha, *op. cit.*, p. 21-22.

41. Tadevosian, *op. cit* , p. 25.

42. "Nash zakon i ego garantii: Na voprosy chitatelei 'Truda' otvechaet Ministr iustitsii SSSR Vladimir Ivanovich Terebilov" (Our Law and Its Guarantees: USSR Minister of Justice Vladimir Ivanovich Terebilov Answers Questions of *Trud's* Readers), Mar. 2, 1970, p. 2.

43. G. Min'kovskii, "Problemy deistvitel'nye i mnimye (prestupnost' nesovershennoletnikh)" (Actual and Illusory Problems: Juvenile Crime), *Nauka i zhizn'*, 1968, No. 9, 76; *Kriminologiia*, note 6 above, pp. 37, 275 and *ibid.*, 2nd ed. 1968, p. 320; L. N. Moskvichev *et al.* (eds.), *Preemstvennost' pokolenii kak sotsiologicheskaia problema* (The Continuity of Generations As a Sociological Problem), (Moscow, 1973), pp.3-4, 78.

44. *Narodnoe khoziaistvo SSSR v 1975 g.*, note 10 above, pp. 7, 44; George St. George, *Our Soviet Sister* (Washington-New York, 1973), p. 142.

45. Quote is from A. Valentinov, "Spor s nastoiashchim muzhchinoi" (Argument with a Real Man), *Izvestiia*, Mar. 6, 1966. On divorce and on women's burden, see N. V. Gavrilova, "Problemnaia sem'ia kak ob"ekt sotsiologicheskogo issledovaniia" (The Problem Family As an Object of Sociological Research), *Sotsial'nye issledovaniia* (Social Research), 1971, No. 7, 157-169; A. G. Kharchev and S. I. Golod, *Professional'naia rabota zhenshchin i sem'ia* (Women's Careers and the Family), (Leningrad, 1971), pp. 29-30, 173-177; Hiram J. Grogan, "The Criminogenic Family: Does Chronic Tension Trigger Delinquency?" *Crime and Delinquency*, 1968, No. 14, 225.

46. *Kriminologiia*, note 6 above, pp. 68, 76, 156, 179.

47. M. N. Rutkevich, *The Career Plans of Youth,* transl. and ed. by Murray Yanowich (White Plains, NY, 1969), p. 160.

48. *Kriminologiia*, note 6 above, p. 289.

49. *Ibid.*, pp. 302-307.

50. *Pravda* editorial, Apr. 19, 1935.

51. Decree of April 7, 1935 lowering minimum age of criminal liability of juveniles from 16 to 12 and penalizing adults instigating juvenile crime with no less than 5 years' confinement, *Sov. Iust.*, 1935, No. 13, 11-12; decree of May 31, 1935 aimed at eliminating vagabondage and non-supervision of children, liquidating Commissions on Juvenile Affairs and calling for community prevention efforts, *Sobr. Zak. SSSR,* 1935, No. 32; item 252; John N. Hazard, *Law and Social Change in the USSR* (Toronto, 1953), pp. 252-253.

52. Z. A. Astemirov, "Iz istorii razvitiia uchrezhdenii dlia nesovershennoletnikh pravonarushitelei v SSSR" (From the History of the Development of Soviet Institutions for Juvenile Lawbreakers), in V. N. Kudriavtsev *et al.* (eds.), *Preduprezhdenie prestupnosti nesovershennoletnikh* (Preventing Juvenile Crime), (Moscow, 1965), p. 267; David J. Dallin and Boris I. Nicolaevskii, *Forced Labor in Soviet Russia* (New Haven, 1947), pp. 4, 237-238; Aleksandr Solzhenitsyn, *Arkhipelag gulag, 1918-1956: Opyt khudozhestvennogo issledovaniia*, (Gulag Archipelago, 1918-1956: Results of Literary Research), Parts I-II, (Paris, 1973), p. 543.

53. V. S. Tadevosian, "Zakon 7 aprelia 1935 g. i bor'ba s prestupnost'iu sredi nesovershennoletnikh" (The Law of April 7, 1935, and the Struggle Against Crime Among Juveniles), *Sov. Iust.*, 1937, No. 10-11, 48-50; his "Piat' Let Zakona 'O merakh bor'by s prestupnost'iu sredi nesovershennoletnikh' " (Five Years of the Law "On Means of Struggling Against Crimes among Juveniles"), *Sots. Zak.*, 1940, No. 5, 14-20; F. Nakhimson, "Bor'ba s detskoi prestupnost'iu v SSSR" (Struggle Against Juvenile Crime in the USSR), *Sov. Iust.*, 1937, No. 22, 29; his "K voprosu o bor'be s prestupnost'iu nesovershennoletnikh" (On the Question of the Struggle Against Juvenile Crime), *Problemy ugolovnoi politiki,* (Problems of Criminal Policy), 1937, no. 3, p. 91; S. B., "Vsesoiuznoe

soveshchanie prokurorov po delam nesovershennoletnikh" (All-Union Conference of Prosecutors for Juvenile Cases), *Sots. Zak.*, 1945, No. 11-12, 53-57.

54. Mark G. Field, "Alcoholism, Crime and Delinquency in Soviet Society," *Social Problems,* 3 (1955), 100-109.

55. A. P. Borodonkov, S. I. Kat'kalo, *Sovetskii zakon na strazhe chesti i dostoinstva zhenshchiny* (Soviet Law in the Defense of the Honor and Dignity of Women), (Leningrad, 1977), pp. 4-11; Iu. N. Korshunov, R. Z. Livshits, M. S. Rumiantseva, *Sovetskoe zakonodatel'stvo o trude: Spravochnaia kniga dlia profaktiva* (Soviet Labor Legislation: Handbook for Trade Union Activists), (Moscow, 1976), pp. 477-502; *Kriminologiia*, note 6 above, pp. 301-302.

56. Piecemeal post-Stalin reforms, incorporated into the Fundamental Principles of Criminal Law of the USSR and Union Republics (hereafter FPCL) in 1958 and the union republic criminal codes in effect 1960-1962, ended punishments of exile and banishment and the possibility of the death penalty for juveniles, set their maximum sentence at ten years (it was 25 years under Stalin) and raised the minimum age of criminal liability from 12 to 14, reintroduced partially mandatory parole as it worked out after a tightening in 1969. FPCL arts. 10, 22, 23-2, 24 paragraphs 3&4, 45; CC RSFSR (1975), *Ugolovnyi kodeks RSFSR s izmeneniami i dopolneniami na 1 ianvaria 1975 goda* (RSFSR Criminal Code as Amended up to January 1, 1975), (Moscow, 1975), arts. 10, 23-26; *Kriminologiia*, note 6 above, pp. 305-307. For useful source on criminal and non-criminal liability of juveniles, see M. P. Evteev and V. A. Kirin, *Zakonodatel'stvo ob otvetstvennosti nesovershennoletnikh* (Legislation on the Liability of Juveniles), (Moscow, 1970); "O zadachakh sudov po vypolneniiu ukazov i postanovlenii prezidiuma Verkhovnogo Soveta SSSR ot 8 i 15 fevralia 1977 g." (On the Task of the Courts in Applying Edicts and Decrees of the USSR Supreme Soviet Presidium of February 8 and 15, 1977), Directive No. 1 of the USSR Supreme Court Plenum, *BVS SSSR*, 1977, No. 2, 7-9.

57. *Kriminologiia*, note 6 above, pp. 302-307; Tadevosian, "Otvetstvennost' . . . ," note 6 above, pp. 74-75.

58. S. E. Zhilinskii, *Rol' KPSS v ukreplenii zakonnosti na sovremennom etape* (Role of the CPSU in Strengthening Legality at the Present Period), (Moscow, 1977); D. S. Karev, *Izuchenie i preduprezhdenie pravonarushenii sredi nesovershennoletnikh* (The Study and Prevention of Juvenile Lawbreaking), (Moscow, 1970), pp. 62-79.

59. *Ibid., passim*; Edict of February 15, 1977, *Ved. V.S. SSSR*, 1977, No. 8, item 138; Juviler, note 20 above, pp. 74-82.

60. I. Karpets, "Sovetskii obraz zhizni i pravoporiadok" (The Soviet Way of Life and Law and Order), *Partiinaia zhizn'* (Party Life), 1976, No. 19, 58.

61. "Polozhenie o tovarishcheskikh sudakh" (Statute on Comrades' Courts), Edict of the RSFSR Supreme Soviet of March 11, 1977, *Sov. Iust.*, 1977, No. 10, 23-26; "Sovershenstvovat' deiatel'nost' tovarishcheskikh sudov" (Improve the Functioning of Comrades' Courts), *Sov. Iust.*, 1977, No. 10, 4-5. The RSFSR comrades' court statute was preceded by a USSR act in the form of a USSR Supreme Soviet decree of February 8, 1977 *(Ved. V.S. SSSR*, 1977, No. 7, item 121) which ordered the formation of Community Councils on the Work of Comrades' Courts, to help them and coordinate their work. Among other changes, the decree provided for "broadening the competence of comrades' courts by giving them the right, in particular, to hear cases of unworthy conduct in the family . . ."

62. "Polozhenie . . .," note 61 above, article 11. Compare with 1961 statute article 5, para. 3, CMF RSFSR (1975), p. 98.

63. "Polozhenie . . .," note 61 above, article 16.

64. V. S. Pronina, *Kommentarii k polozheniiu o komissiiakh po delam nesovershennoletnikh* (Commentary on CJA Statute), (Moscow, 1968), p. 10.

65. E. V. Boldyrev, *Mery preduprezhdeniia prestupnosti nesovershennoletnikh v SSSR* (Means of Preventing Juvenile Crime in the USSR), (Moscow, 1964), pp. 41-44.

66. Statute of CJA of June 3, 1967, *Ved. V.S. RSFSR*, 1967, No. 23, item 536, reprinted as revised through 1969 in Evteev and Kirin, *op. cit.*, pp. 111-130, arts. 17, 19; Pronina, *op. cit.*, pp. 8-14.

67. Boldyrev, *op. cit.*, p. 155.

68. Statute of CJA, note 66 above, article 5.

69. "Bor'ba s retsidivnoi prestupnost'iu nesovershennoletnikh (obzor sudebnoi praktiki)" (The Struggle against Juvenile Recidivism (Survey of Court Practice)), *BVS SSSR*, 1975, No. 1, 32-41.

70. *Grazhdanskii kodeks RSFSR s izmeneniami i dopolneniami na 1 dekabria 1975 goda* (RSFSR Civil Code Amended as of December 1, 1975), (Moscow, 1976), articles 450, 451. Under the earlier statute of May 31, 1935, parents were liable, at fault or not. Tadevosian, *op. cit.*, pp. 76-77.

71. *BVS RSFSR*, 1977, No. 5, 1.

72. N. Ponomarev (Head, Department of Administrative Agencies, Moscow City Party Committee), "Za obraztsovyi obshchestvennyi poriadok" (For Exemplary Public Order), *Sov. Iust.*, 1977, No. 1, 4.

73. *Kriminologiia*, note 6 above, pp. 314-315.

74. M. M Babaev and A. E. Zhalinskii, *Kogda starshie v otvete* (When Elders Are Responsible), (Moscow, 1972), pp. 49-50.

75. Anti-hooliganism edict of July 26, 1966, *Ved. V.S. SSSR*, 1966, No. 30, item 595 articles 12, 14; "O merakh po usileniiu bor'by protiv p'ianstva i alkogolizma" (On Means of Intensifying the Struggle against Drunkenness and Alcoholism), edict of June 21, 1972, reprinted in L. L. Dedkov and N. A Stoliar, *Zakonodatel'nye akty ob administrativnoi otvetstvennosti* (Legislation on Administrative Liability), (Minsk, 1977), pp. 178-183.

76. Tadevosian, *op. cit.,* p. 74.

77. "O merakh . . .," note 75 above, article 3.

78. CCP RSFSR (1964), articles 62-65, and CCP RSFSR (1975), articles 62-65.

79. CC RSFSR (1975), article 62.

80. Edict of April 8, 1967, *Ved. V.S. RSFSR*, 1967, No. 15, item 33; *ibid.*, 1974, No. 10, item 287; M. Maslennikov, "Postanovlenie suda po delam o primenenii k alkogolikam prinuditel'nykh mer meditsinskogo kharaktera" (Court Decision in Cases of Applying Compulsory Cures to Alcoholics), *Sov. Iust.*, 1977, No. 3, 18-19.

81. Juviler, note 20 above, p. 91.

82. CC RSFSR (1975), article 16; CCP RSFSR (1975), *Grazhdanskii protsessual'nyi kodeks RSFSR s izmeneniami i dopolneniami na 20 dekabria 1974 g.* (RSFSR Code of Civil Procedure with Amendments to December 20, 1974), (Moscow, 1975), articles 258-263; Directive No. 34 of the Plenum of the RSFSR Supreme Court, *BVS RSFSR*, 1967, No. 1, 4-6; Directive No. 6 of the Plenum of the USSR Supreme Court, *BVS SSSR*, 1975, No. 6, article 12.

83. *Ibid.,* article 13-14; "Priznanie ogranichenno deesposobnymi grazhdan zloupotrebliaiushchikh spirtnymi napitkami (obzor sudebnoi praktiki)" (Limiting Legal Competence of Citizens Who Abuse Alcoholic Beverages (Survey of Court Practise)), *BVS SSSR*, 1976, No. 3, 40-41.

84. *Ibid.*, pp. 39-40.

85. CC RSFSR (1975), article 122.

86. FPLMF (1968), article 17, para. 3; CMF RSFSR (1975), article 21, para. 1.

87. L. Drozdova, "*Usloviia otvetstvennosti po sovetskomu semeinomu pravu*" (Conditions Creating Liability under Soviet Family Law), *Sov. Iust.*, 1977, No. 5, 25-26.

88. CC RSFSR (1975), article 73, para. 2, added April 7, 1935, prescribes "no less than 5 years" for inciting juveniles or drawing them to participate in crimes and for compelling juveniles to engage in speculation, prostitution, beggary, etc. The new codes prescribe *up to* 5 years deprivation of freedom. CC RSFSR (1964), (1970), and (1975), article 210.

89. "O merakh . . . ," note 75 above, p. 179.

90. N. Mal'shkov (First Deputy Chairman, RSFSR Supreme Court), "Rassmotreniiu del o prestupleniiakh nesovershennoletnikh–osoboe vnimanie" (Pay Special Attention to Juvenile Criminal Cases), *Sov. Iust.*, 1976, No. 24, p. 2; Ponomarev, *op. cit.*, p. 2.

91. "O praktike primeneniia sudami zakonodatel'stva po delam o prestupleniiakh nesovershennoletnikh i o vovlechenii ikh v prestupnuiu deiatel'nost' " (On Court Practice in Applying Legislation on Juvenile Criminal Cases and on Cases of Drawing Them into Criminal and Other Antisocial Activity), Directive No. 16 of the Plenum of the USSR Supreme Court of December 3, 1976, *BVS SSSR*, 1977, No. 1, article 22 (its article 24 lists previous such directives from 1963-1974); Directive of the RSFSR Supreme Court, February 28, 1968, *BVS RSFSR*, 1968, No. 6, 4-5; Directive No. 6 of the Plenum of the USSR Supreme Court, note 82 above, p. 12; A. M. Filatov (member USSR Supreme Court), "Praktika rassmotreniia del o prestupleniiakh nesovershennoletnikh" (Court Practise in Hearing Juvenile Criminal Cases), *Sots. Zak.*, 1977, No. 4, 21, 23; G. Min'kovskii and L. Korevskii, "Bor'ba s vovlecheniem nesovershennoletnikh v prestupnuiu deiatel'nost–vazhnoe napravlenie profilakticheskoi raboty" (The Struggle against Drawing Juveniles into Criminal Activity Is an Important Part of Prevention), *Sov. Iust.* 1976, No. 18, 20-21.

92. Ponomarev, *op. cit.*; D. Riabov, "Sud i vospitanie nesovershennoletnikh pravonarushitelei" (The Court and the Education of Juvenile Lawbreakers), *Sov. Iust.*, 1968, No. 10, 18.

93. Tadevosian, *op. cit.*, p. 72.

94. Pronina, *op. cit.*; Ponomarev, *op. cit.*, p. 3. On the importance of, but uneven use of, court special findings see, *e.g.*, K. Prikhodko, "Vyiavlenie i ustranenie prichin retsidivnoi prestupnosti nesovershennoletnikh" (Ascertaining and Eliminating Causes of Juvenile Recidivism), *Sov. Iust.*, 1974, No. 4, 21-22; G. I. Solomakha, "Profilakticheskoe znachenie chastnykh opredelenii po delam nesovershennoletnikh" (Preventive Significance of Special Findings in Juvenile Cases), in Karev (ed.), *Izuchenie*, note 58 above, p. 140; "Nauchno-prakticheskaia konferentsiia v Sverdlovske" (Conference on Theory and Practice in Sverdlovsk), *Sov. Iust.*, 1977, No. 12, inside front cover.

95. CMF RSFSR (1918), articles 149, 153, and 154; CMF RSFSR (1926), articles 33, 41, 46, and 51 obligate parents to see to children's upbringing, say that parental rights may be exercised only in the interests of the children, and specify loss of those rights if they are abused. CMF RSFSR (1918) appeared in *Sobr. Uzak. RSFSR*, 1918, Nos. 76-77, item 88. CMF RSFSR (1926) appeared in many revisions, keeping these articles. *Sobr. Uzak. RSFSR* 1926, No. 82, item 612, and see, *e.g.* its 1961 edition (Moscow, 1961).

96. A. S. Makarenko, *The Collective Family: A Handbook for Russian Parents* (Garden City, N.Y, 1967), p. 27. Source supplied by student Marc Berman.

97. *Pravda, Izvestiia*, Jun. 4, 1977.

98. FPLMF, articles 1-3.

99. CMF RSFSR (1975), articles 59, 64.

100. V. A. Riasentsev, *Semeinoe pravo* (Family Law), (Moscow, 1971), p. 195; FPLMF, article 19, para. 2.

101. "O praktike . . .,' note 91 above, article 22; FPLMF articles 19, para. 3 and 19, para. 4; CMF RSFSR (1975), articles 60, 61, 64; "Nekotorye voprosy sudebnoi praktiki

po delam o lishenii roditel'skikh prav i otobranii detei u lits, zloupotrebliaiushchikh spirtnymi napitkami" (Some Questions of Court Practice in Cases of Deprivation of Parental Rights of and Removing Children from Persons Abusing Alcoholic Beverages), *BVS RSFSR*, 1973, No. 10, 3-6.

102. FPLMF, article 19, para. 1; CMF RSFSR (1975), article 59, para. 1. A parent may not be deprived of rights simply for living apart or non-payment of support. K. K. Cherviakov, "Vliianie lisheniia roditel'skikh prav na roditel'skikh pravootnosheniiakh" (Consequences of Deprivation of Parental Rights for the Legal Relationships of Parents), *SGiP*, 1975, No. 7, 130-133.

103. CMF RSFSR (1961), articles 33, 46.

104. A. M. Beliakova and E. M. Vorozheikin, *Sovetskoe semeinoe pravo* (Soviet Family Law), (Moscow, 1974), pp. 217-218.

105 "O praktike . . .," note 91 above, article 23; Riasentsev, *op. cit.*, pp. 199-200.

106. Parental rights may be restored on occasion. CMF RSFSR (1975), article 63.

107. N. Ershova, "Nauncho-prakticheskie kommentarii: Lishenie roditel'skikh prav" (Commentary on Theory and Practice: Deprivation of Parental Rights), *Sots. Zak.*, 1971, No. 4, p. 46.

108. Riasentsev, *op. cit.*, p. 195; Beliakova and Vorozheikin, *op. cit.* p. 221.

109. CC RSFSR (1957), article 31(e).

110. V. N. Ivanov, *Ugolovnoe zakonodatel'stvo Soiuza SSSR i soiuznykh respublik: Edinstvo i osobennosti* (Criminal Legislation of the USSR and Union Republics: Uniformity and Peculiarities), (Moscow, 1973), pp. 34-37.

111. FPLMF, articles 19, para. 4, 24, para. 4; "Nekotorye voprosy . . .," note 101 above, articles 15, 16; Riasentsev, *op. cit.*, p. 198.

112. Cherviakov, note 102 above; CMF RSFSR (1975), articles 53, 56, 58, 60, 78, 99, 100, 126; *Grazhdanskii kodeks RSFSR*, note 82 above, article 333; "O nekotorykh voprosakh, voznikshikh v praktike primeneniia sudami kodeksa o brake i sem'e" (On Some Questions Arising in the Application by the Courts of the Code on Marriage and the Family), Directive of the RSFSR Supreme Court, February 21, 1973, *BVS RSFSR*, 1973, No. 5, 5-8, articles 15, 16.

113. R. Bashkirova, "Sudebnaia zashchita prav detei" (Judicial Protection of Children's Rights), *Sov. Iust.*, 1975, No. 4, 12-13.

114. V. Kauke, "Kogda podrostok bez nadzora" (When an Adolescent Is Without Supervision), *Chelovek i zakon*, 1976, No. 12, 53-55.

115. Riabov, *op. cit.*, p. 18.

116. "Nekotorye voprosy . . .," note 101 above, pp. 3-6; see also the sources cited in note 94.

117. See note 116.

118. Without intentions to compare anything more than the fact of ideological motivation, one recalls a loving but unconventional father's loss of his son to his dead wife's Iowan parents, described in Hal Painter, *Mark, I Love You* (New York, 1967); the Nazi's abduction of "racially good types" of East European children for Himmler's *Lebensborn* SS program of racial replenishment described in Hans Peter Bleuel, *Sex and Society in Nazi Germany* (Philadelphia, 1973), p. 166.

119. M. N. Kulazhnikov, *Pravo, traditsii i obychai v sovetskom obshchestve* (Law, Traditions, and Customs in Soviet Society), (Rostov, 1972), p. 154.

120. An unusual insight on governmental attitudes is in the report of a speech by Vice Chairman Furin of the Council on Religious Affairs of the USSR Council of Ministers, delivered in May 1976. *Chronicle of Human Rights in the USSR*, 1976, No. 22, 21; excerpts of increasingly harsh Party Central Committee Resolutions between 1954 and 1963 in the invaluable collection *Zakonodatel'stvo o religioznykh kul'takh:*

sbornik materialov i dokumentov (Legislation on Religious Cults: Collection of Materials and Documents), labeled ' Dlia sluzhebnogo ispol'zovaniia" (For Official Use), 2nd. enl. ed. (Moscow, 1971), pp. 36-38.

121. *Ibid.*, pp. 96-99; Joshua Rothenberg, "The Legal Status of Religion in the Soviet Union," in Richard H. Marshall, Jr., Thomas Bird, and Andrew Q. Blaine (eds.), *Aspects of Religion in the Soviet Union 1917-1967* (Chicago, 1971), pp. 61-102; *O religioznykh ob"edineniiakh. Postanovlenie VTsIK i SNK RSFSR ot 8 aprelia 1929 goda s izmeneniiami, vnesennymi Ukazom Prezidiuma Verkhovnogo Soveta RSFSR 23 iiunia 1975g.* (On Religious Associations: Decree of the VTsIK and SNK RSFSR of April 8, 1929, with Amendments Introduced by the Edict of the RSFSR Supreme Soviet Presidium June 23, 1975), (New York, 1975).

122. Rothenberg, *op. cit.*, pp. 96-99.

123. Donald A. Lowrie and William C. Fletcher, "Khrushchev's Religious Policy," in Marshall, *op. cit.*, pp. 131-135; Barbara Wolfe Jancar, "Religious Dissent in the USSR," in Rudolf L. Tökes (ed.), *Dissent in the USSR: Politics, Ideology, and People* (Baltimore, 1975), pp. 191-194, 209-211.

124. Rothenberg, *op. cit.*, p. 102.

125. CC RSFSR (1975), article 142, penalizes violation of laws on separation of church and state and so do analogous codes in the other republics. Edict of March 18, 1966, adds higher penalties, up to 3 years, in *Ved. V.S. RSFSR*, 1966, No. 12, item 220. The decree of March 18, 1966 (*ibid.*, item 221, reprinted in CMF RSFSR (1975), p. 198) has a list of violations, including "organizing and systematically conducting religious instruction of minors in violation of rules established by law." There are analogous explicit decrees in the other union republics (*Zakonodatel'stvo* ..., note 123 above, p. 271. It gives, in all cases, article numbers of analogous rules in criminal codes of the other republics). As for the rule not to be violated when teaching children, it is in the Statute of the Secondary School of September 8, 1970, article 3: ". . . Believing parents may give religious instruction by mutual agreement to their own children, but under the one essential precondition that this instruction should not take the form of group studies, but should involve only one's own children on a strictly individual basis without the invitation of teachers." A. Sediulin, *Zakonodatel'stvo o religioznykh kul'takh* (Legislation on Religious Cults), (Moscow, 1974), p. 31.

Article 143, CC RSFSR (1975), and analogous articles of CC's of the other republics, specify correctional labor up to 6 months or public censure for interfering with the conduct of lawful religious worship.

Article 227, CC RSFSR (1975), and analogous articles of CC's of the other republics, as the legislation around article 142, show an extension of state intervention under Khrushchev and Brezhnev. Article 227 originally penalized organizing or leading the conduct of rituals injurious to health or involving sexual licentiousness. An RSFSR Law of July 25, 1962, amended the article by (1) changing its wording to extend the list of offensive actions to read "injurious to health, or violating rights or inciting to refuse social activity or performance of civic obligations and drawing minors into the group." This greatly extended the reach against parents. (2) The 1962 law added a new section, article 227-2, which extended criminal penalties to persons actively participating in a group where these offensive actions allegedly occurred. *Ved. V.S. RSFSR*, 1962, No. 29, item 449, and similar articles of the republics. *Zakonodatel'stvo. . .*, note 120 above, p. 272. Apparently to make it feasible to penalize lesser offenders without throwing the criminal book at them (the first time anyway), the regime added administrative penalties for the actions covered in article 227 of fine up to 50 rubles payable to local Soviets' administrative commissions. Edict of March 18, 1966, *Ved. V.S. RSFSR*, 1966, No. 12, item 219, and similar legislation in the other republics. *Zakonodatel'stvo* . . ., note 120 above, pp. 259-260. On meaning of "injurious to health" and mention of baptism in icy water, see G. Z. Anashkin *et al.* (eds.), *Kommentarii k ugolovnomu kodeksu RSFSR* (Commentary on the RSFSR Criminal Code), (Moscow, 1971), p. 476 and Lowerie, note 123 above, pp. 138-139, mentioning also various forms of pressure on parents not to let their children be baptized.

For an idea of greater scope over previous legislation under Stalin, see comparison with CC RSFSR (1957), articles 122-127.

126. Model statute of Commissions to Help Executive Committees of Soviets of Toilers' Deputies on the Observance of Legislation on Religious Cults, November 26, 1966, No. 3020, recommended by the Council on Affairs of Religion of the USSR Council of Ministers, and some similar republic statutes, *Zakonodatel'stvo* . . ., note 120 above, pp. 161-169, 234-238.

127. *Chronicle of Human Rights* . . ., note 120 above, p. 21.

128. Sediulin, *op. cit.*, pp. 26-28.

129. E. F. Muravev and Y. V. Dmitrev "Atheism and Religion in the USSR," *Voprosy filosofii* (Problems of Philosophy), March 1961, transl. in *Soviet Review*, 1961, No. 2, p. 491, quoted in Lowerie, *op. cit.*, p. 142.

130. *Ibid.*, pp 143 145, Jancar, note 123 above, pp. 210-211.

131. CMF RSFSR (1975), article 52:

> "Parents must raise their children in the spirit of the moral code of a builder of communism, care for their physical development, training, and preparation for socially useful activity.
>
> Parental rights may not be exercised against the interests of the children."

This, plus article 59, on grounds makes a broad legal basis for deprivation of rights.

132. Amnesty International, *Prisoners of Conscience in the USSR: Their Treatment and Conditions* (London, 1975), p. 12.

133. *Chronicle of Human Rights in the USSR*, 1976, No. 22, p. 39.

134. Sediulin, *op. cit.*, pp. 89-91, and Kulazhnikov, *op. cit.*, *passim.*

135. *Chronicle of Human Rights in the USSR*, 1973, No. 4, pp. 44-45.

136. *Ibid.*, pp. 13-14; detailed account with documents of case of *Raiskaia v. Temkin*, No. 2-1822, January 17, 1973 in *Chronicle of Human Rights in the USSR*, 1973, No. 2, pp. 34-35.

137. F. J. M. Feldbrugge, "Criminal Law and Traditional Society: The Role of Law in the Integration of Non-Slavic Peoples," *Review of Socialist Law*, 3 (1977), No. 1, 11-32, 38, 42.

138. CC RSFSR (1975), articles 231-234.

139. Feldbrugge, *op. cit.*, pp. 38-40.

140. CC RSFSR, article 134.

141. Toushan Esenova, "Nenavistnyi kalym" (Hateful *kalym*), *LG*, May 22, 1974; "Rezonans: 'Nenavistnyi kalym': Redaktsiia 'Literaturnoi gazety' poluchila pis'mo pervogo sekretaria TsK KP Turkmenistana M. G. Gapurova" (Followup: 'Hateful *kalym*': Editors of LG have received a letter from the First Secretary of the CC CP of Turkmenistan M. G. Gapurov), *LG*, Jul. 24, 1974; Toushan Esenova, "Protiv perezhitkov proshlogo: Vsem mirom" (Against Survivals of the Past: To the Whole World), *LG*, May 28, 1975; M. G. Gapurov's report in *Turkmenskaia iskra*, May 30, 1976, transl. in *CDSP*, 1976, No. 23, 2, where he states that "the measures taken" since the furor began "still have not yielded any appreciable results."

142. My previous chapter for this project, in the parts on motives for marriage and divorce and on support, and the quite non-socialist nature of the Soviet laws on inheritance under the civil law reforms of 1961-1964 (see Alice Erh-Soon Tay, "The Law of

Inheritance in the New Russian Civil Code of 1964," *International and Comparative Law Quarterly*, 1968, 472-500) show the family yet a long way from the FPLMF ideal of "family relations free from material calculations." True, the economic function of the family has so shrunk since 1917 that it has lost much of its productive character and become mainly consumerist. (N. V. Orlova, "Nekotorye voprosy semeinogo prava v period stroitel'stva kommunizma," in Tadevosian, *Pravovye voprosy* . . ., note 6 above, p. 3.) But private commercial activities are much more extensive than civil and criminal law would indicate. (For a useful introduction to facts and sources, see Gregory Grossman, "The 'Second Economy' of the USSR," *Problems of Communism*, 1977, No. 5, pp. 25-40). And here we have to deal not only with the vital family garden plots, including the collective farm household operations (in civil law, see *e.g.*, articles 113, 126-132 of the RSFSR Civil Code). Garden plots, collective farm and otherwise, accounted for 59% of all potatoes grown in 1975, 34% of vegetables, 31% of meat, 31% of milk and 39% of eggs (*Narodnoe* . . ., note 44 above, p. 321)–according to Grossman (p. 26), the staggering total of over one-quarter of gross agricultural output all told. The dividing line between tolerated private production and prosecutable acts of money-grubbing "scum" (G. Iakovlev, "Nakip" (Scum), *Pravda*, Jun. 18, 1976, p. 3) seems a fuzzy one. Considerations of Soviet socialist ethics and of control dictate stringent application of laws against speculative acquisition and use of personal property, to say nothing of the loss of authority of the law and the massive stealing of public property involved in private operations (S. Marakov, "A Letter from the village of Izosimovo," *Komsomolskaia pravda*, Jan. 10 and 14, 1975, abstracted in *CDSP*, 1975, No. 27, 4-5). Khrushchev moved to intervene to stop many forms of family speculation and enterprise. (Hiroshi Kimura, "Personal Property in the Soviet Union, With Particular Emphasis on the Khrushchev Era, II," in English, *Surabu kenkyu* (Slavic Studies-Sapporo), 1970, No. 14, 81-88.

ADMINISTRATIVE JUSTICE AND JUDICIAL REVIEW IN SOVIET ADMINISTRATIVE LAW

Donald D. Barry*

1. Introduction

Definitions of administrative law by Soviet jurists are not very helpful in explaining the nature and content of the subject. They typically describe it as "a branch of Soviet law representing the totality of legal norms which regulate social relations established in the process of state administration"[1] or words to that effect. These words *do* suggest a conception of administrative law different from that normally employed in the United States, however, and closer to the continental European usage of the term. As Wolfgang Friedmann has pointed out, administrative law in the United States (and, to a lesser extent, in England as well) has "tended to remain narrowly confined to procedural methods and safeguards."[2] It does not include, in the words of Kenneth Culp Davis, "the enormous mass of substantive law produced by the agencies such as tax law, labor law, antitrust law, public utility law . . . and the like"[3] The continental European conception, by contrast, is much broader, embracing substantive law of this kind as well as "such matters of substance as public law contracts, domains and principles of public ownership, principles of legal responsibility on the part of government and other public authorities."[4] This broader conception of the field has been referred to as "the law relating to public administration."[5]

A cursory review of any Soviet administrative law textbook will demonstrate the extremely broad scope of the subject as understood there. Coverage typically includes a detailed exposition of the following: the principles of governmental administration and the law regulating it; state and social organs that make up the administrative apparatus and their officials, the civil service;

* The author wishes to acknowledge the valuable comments made by Professors Peter Solomon and Peter Maggs, and to thank Professor Gordon Smith for making available to the author his unpublished work on judicial review in Soviet administrative law.

the general forms of administrative activity and the means for keeping this activity within legal bounds; and the particular kinds of substantive administrative activity carried on by the various organs of the Soviet state, including economic administration, social-cultural administration, political-administrative functions, administration of external affairs, and inter-branch coordination such as planning, finance, record-keeping, and the like.[6] What will be examined in this paper, then, represents only a small part of Soviet administrative law.

"Administrative justice" is a term that has recently re-emerged in discussions of Soviet administrative law. It was in wide use during the 1920's but was condemned as a bourgeois adaptation at the end of the decade and ceased to be discussed in reference to Soviet law for several decades. Its mixed reception by scholars during the present decade epitomizes to some extent the status of Soviet administrative law as a whole, one of the less-developed areas of Soviet law. Unlike criminal law and procedure, civil law and procedure, family law, labor law, and a host of other fields, no overall codification of administrative law has taken place. Scholars are far from being in agreement on a number of basic questions about the subject. And there is even controversy as to whether a body of administrative procedural legislation, separate from the civil procedural law, ought to be adopted. Brezhnev indicated at the 25th Party Congress that codification of administrative law was under way,[7] but apparently this will only cover one aspect of the subject, that of administrative liability.[8]

Since administrative justice in Soviet parlance refers to *court* control over administrative activities rather than procuratorial control or other arrangements for checking the propriety of bureaucratic acts, major attention will also be devoted to judicial review. But these two matters–administrative justice and judicial review–will be treated in separate sections of the paper, since many Soviet jurists have discussed and still discuss the expansion of judicial review of administrative acts without mentioning administrative justice. In the section on judicial review, I will take several of the important questions that arise in American administrative law and look at the extent to which these matters are important in Soviet administrative law and how they have been handled. The emphasis will be largely on procedural questions rather than substantive law, and I will concentrate on the rights of Soviet citizens in their relations with Soviet officialdom rather than on economic administration or some other part of the subject.

There is a final point to make with regard to judicial review. As will be shown, the wide availability of judicial review has come to be one of the cornerstones of American administrative law. This is definitely not the case in Soviet administrative law. Other mechanisms of control over administrative action have been devised and emphasized, with the result that the availability of judicial review constitutes very much the exception rather than the rule.

Much of the attention in this paper centers on the efforts of Soviet jurists to make judicial review the preferred mechanism, or at least a more widely-used mechanism, for control over administrative activity.

The original intention in this paper was to use a framework of concepts familiar to students of American administrative law to discuss a number of problems of Soviet administrative law, among them those referred to above. That plan has had to be abandoned because of space limitations on the present paper. This study should be looked upon, therefore, as the beginning of a more comprehensive analysis that will go on to examine matters such as delegation of power, rulemaking, adjudication and the right to a hearing, bias and separation of functions, and administrative discretion and its control. In this paper, I have been able only to refer briefly to several of these matters. In using this terminology, it is not implied that Soviet law is developing legal principles similar to those that have evolved in American law. In some cases, these terms or their equivalents have not acquired currency among Soviet jurists. What does seem clear to me is that Soviet lawyers are becoming cognizant of problems in their administrative process that these terms represent and that their American counterparts have been confronted with over the past several decades.

2. Administrative Justice

As suggested above, the concept of administrative justice has had a spotty career in Soviet law. In the early 1920's, many jurists wrote of the desirability of developing a system of administrative justice in Soviet Russia.[9] Later, however, the concept came under considerable criticism and, by the end of the decade, "it went without saying that under the conditions of socialism there was no place for administrative justice."[10]

The problem was that the concept came to be seen as having a "bourgeois character" more appropriate for an "individualistic state" than a socialist one. Moreover, as one writer put it, the idea of needing to resolve conflicts between workers and the administration so soon after the achievement of socialism "would seem to constitute a dissonance, testifying to the fact that . . . not everything is going well." Another jurist argued that under socialism "there is no motivation of any kind for the creation of checks and balances" to the exercise of administrative powers, since the individual in a socialist society "is not something of value in itself. It is only a cog in a huge machine. Therefore, guaranteeing its rights is of secondary importance."[11]

So discredited was administrative justice that it took more than four decades for the concept again to be viewed as having possible application in Soviet law. The 1956 *Legal Dictionary* simply stated that "in the USSR administrative justice does not exist,"[12] while a similar publication of nine years later only allowed as how "some elements" of administrative justice might be acceptable in Soviet law[13] (the writer of these words wrote five years later, however, in 1970, that administrative justice "is in no way alien to socialist society."[14] It was not until the 1970's that administrative justice began to gain wider acceptance among legal scholars. Undoubtedly the major contribution to this development was D. M. Chechot's *Administrativnaia iustitsiia*, a spirited and well-argued piece of advocacy for the concept.[15] Chechot was not alone as a proponent, however,[16] and one defender of the term even went so far as to say that one should not reject a concept only because an analogous principle exists in a bourgeois state.[17] But the acceptance was not unanimous. V. A. Loriia published an article in 1970 entitled "Does Administrative Justice Exist in Soviet Law?" He answered the question strongly in the negative, asserting that administrative justice does not conform with democratic centralism and "contradicts the principles of socialist state administration."[18]

What is the precise meaning of this term, which has generated so much controversy over the years among Soviet jurists? In England and the United States, when the term is used at all, it appears to have no very definite meaning but embraces the general idea that administrative activity ought to be executed justly with regard to the private parties it affects.[19] In the Soviet Union, the term has been used somewhat more narrowly and seems always to refer to the judicial assessment of the propriety of administrative acts. Chechot defines administrative justice as "the arrangement for review and resolution in judicial procedural form of disputes arising in the sphere of administration between citizens or juristic persons on the one hand and administrative organs on the other, which is carried out by organs having jurisdiction which are specially created for solving legal disputes."[20] Chechot's definition is deliberately vague with regard to "organs having jurisdiction" to hear administrative law disputes because the context of his discussion includes foreign legal systems such as France and the Federal Republic of Germany, where administrative courts decide such disputes. Chechot and most other contemporary Soviet writers reject special administrative courts for the Soviet Union, advocating instead increased judicial review of administrative action by the regular courts.

As it happens, however, the connection in many Soviet writers' minds between administrative justice and the use of administrative courts may explain part of the antipathy toward the concept. The idea of administrative justice and the term itself seem to have come into Russian law from the countries having administrative courts, most notably France and Germany.[21] The Provisional Government in 1917 tried to establish a system of administrative courts. A number of Soviet writers of the 1920's, who wrote about administrative justice, favored administrative courts for the Soviet Union.[22] In fact, a system of such courts apparently came close to being established. In 1918, the People's Commissariat of State Control drafted a proposal for the creation of a "high administrative court," a 22-member Committee for the Review of Complaints that would have been essentially a judicial body. In the government's announcement rejecting the proposal, it was stated that "the establishment of an administrative court is untimely and too complex." Instead, the Soviet state created a Bureau of Complaints, which used the informal, non-judicial approach that remains the principal mechanism for reviewing possible abuses of official authority in the Soviet Union to this day.[23]

When the reaction against administrative justice set in in the late 1920's, then, it was in part a rejection of the idea of a separate set of administrative tribunals. Armed with quotes from Engels and Lenin, opponents showed that these founding fathers of socialism supported the right of the citizen to go to the regular courts for redress of abuses suffered at the hands of the bureaucracy. But opposition to administrative courts constituted only part of the campaign against administrative justice, and appears to have been used by some writers to mask other motivations. As already suggested, the attacks on administrative justice came at a time when Soviet officialdom had begun to downgrade or understate the influence on Soviet law of borrowings from the West. In this context, both administrative courts and administrative justice became unpopular concepts. Moreover, as mentioned, it was suggested that: 1) since there was no contradiction between the worker and his government, there was no need for an independent check on the latter and, 2) since the socialist state emphasized collectivism rather than individualism, there was no particular need to protect the rights of the individual against the state.[24] Finally, there was definite opposition among some Soviet lawyers and officials to increasing the ambit of judicial review of administrative action. This opposition sometimes took the form of rather forthright statements that "in Soviet law there cannot be suits against the administration,"[25] but more often it involved the objection to the courts' second-guessing the administrative organs and substituting their judgment for that of administrators. This has to do with what is called scope of judicial review in American administrative law, and will be discussed in the next section.

What it comes down to, then, is that those who have recently been trying to re-introduce the concept of administrative justice into Soviet law are, in reality, merely attempting to increase the sphere of *judicial* review of administrative acts. As Chechot has put it,

> "we suggest that the review and resolution of administrative disputes within the framework of the administration itself cannot be viewed qualitatively as a form of administrative justice . . . nor can procuratorial supervision or administrative control be placed in the category of 'instruments' of administrative justice. One can speak of administrative justice only when the resolution of administrative disputes is carried

out by a special organ which is separated from the so-called active administration and acts within the framework of an appropriate *judicial* procedure."[26]

The advocates of administrative justice, and especially Chechot, might have been better advised to abandon the term because of its unfortunate past and concentrate simply on recommendations for increasing judicial review.[27] Several writers sympathetic with the ends of administrative justice have suggested that more neutral terms such as "judicial control in administration," "judicial review of complaints of citizens arising from administrative law relations," and "the procedure for review of complaints" might be preferable to administrative justice.[28] And this point seems well taken, since numerous jurists have advocated the broadening of judicial review of administrative acts without mentioning administrative justice. The term can be downright confusing to Soviet writers even today. V. A. Loriia was quoted above as opposing administrative justice and arguing that no such thing exists in the USSR, and yet he advocates the widest possible judicial review of administrative acts, supporting the view expressed by V. M. Chkhikvadze that "every citizen" should have "the right to go to court in case of the violation of any rights and freedoms by any organ or person."[29] A critic of Loriia's view has called it "completely inconsistent,"[30] and so it is, but the inconsistency is traceable to a misunderstanding (either unconscious or deliberate) of the meaning of administrative justice. Still, the term seems to have gained currency among a considerable number of contemporary Soviet jurists. If it is not, as Chechot avers, "in the process of formation,"[31] then at least it seems to be an issue that will be debated by Soviet jurists for some time to come.

What is more important than the semantic confusions surrounding administrative justice is the amount and kind of judicial review of administrative acts that those responsible for the development of Soviet law are prepared to accept, and this is the matter to which we now turn.

3. Judicial Review

Three basic issues need to be examined in this section: the degree to which judicial review of administrative acts is now possible under Soviet law; the recommendations recently offered for broadening review; and the kind of judicial review proponents of this mechanism have in mind. Before addressing these matters, however, another problem must be discussed. There are two differing conceptions of what the administrative process embraces in Soviet law. This matter is not central to our concern, but bears importantly on judicial review, so the basic nature of the disagreement must be reviewed briefly.

Some Soviet jurists view the administrative process as embracing the totality of procedural rules by which administrative organs carry out their tasks. Others hold that the administrative process only involves the procedure for applying measures of administrative compulsion (*mery administrativnogo prinuzhdeniia*). These "wide" and "narrow" conceptions of the administrative process have been debated for years, with the proponents of each side apparently sticking to their guns.[32] To me, the broader conception of the administrative process seems more consonant with the functions administrative agencies perform in any developed country, including the Soviet Union. P. E. Nedbailo and V. M. Gorsheneva, in a 1976 book, have captured the sense of this point particularly well. They write not only of the "law-preserving" (*pravookhranitel'nye*) activities of the administration, where regulatory measures or measures of compulsion are applied, but also of the state's "law-providing" or "right-providing" (*pravonadelitel'nye*) functions. The latter are "associated with the positive satisfaction of a variety of needs of members of a socialist society" which "should be organized so that results are achieved effectively, swiftly, and with maximum comfort for all concerned." This is possible, they assert, only "when there exist finished rules which define the whole procedure for this kind of activity."[33] It is this last point that may be most important in the differences between those advocating the wide and the narrow views of the administrative process. For the latter, there seems to be no need to adopt detailed administrative-procedural legislation. They are content to have administrative procedural norms contained in the civil procedural codes.[34] Like Nedbailo and Gorsheneva, the other advocates of the wide conception recommend codification of detailed administrative procedure legislation. This difference of opinion seems to have two practical implications. *First*, it makes a difference in the extent to which one favors extension of judicial review of administrative acts: those advocating the narrow conception favor piecemeal extension of judicial review but not a general presumption of reviewability, the position toward which the advocates of the wider conception of administrative procedure tend. *Second*, those who oppose the separate codification of administrative procedural law are quite concerned about extending judicial review, but express little interest in the development of a consistent and reasonable set of administrative procedures prior to the court review stage, *i.e.*, within the administrative organs themselves, while some of the advocates of separate codification have expressed concern about both of these matters. It might be mentioned in passing that the question of separate codification of administrative procedural law seems to some extent to be an issue of territoriality among Soviet jurists, with the civilists and a few specialists in administrative law opposing the development, and the administrativists favoring it.[35]

Soviet jurists disagree as to the degree of judicial review of administrative acts presently available under Soviet law for two reasons: first, because legal provisions governing such review are contained in a number of individual statutes, and commentators do not always come up with the same list of statutes; and, more importantly, because there is some difference of opinion among jurists as to the actual scope of administrative law. Some writers argue that any dispute in which an administrative organ is a party is, by definition, an administrative law matter. A number of Soviet jurists object to this viewpoint, however, including such well-known scholars as D. M. Chechot and S. N. Bratus'.[36] They argue that such a criterion is unacceptable, since acts of administrative organs may engender both administrative law and civil law results. Thus, for instance, it is said that the process of issuing an *order* for living quarters is an act by an administrative organ (a local soviet executive committee) but it is one which creates a subjective civil right for the citizen receiving the *order*, and any dispute that might arise out of this process would involve civil law rather than administrative law.[37] In a narrow technical sense this is true. Article 25 of the RSFSR Civil Procedural Code provides that as a general rule all cases involving civil, family, labor, and kolkhoz law, in which at least one of the parties is a citizen, are subject to court review. It also provides that the small number of administrative law cases enumerated in article 231 of the Code are also subject to court review. Since administrative law disputes, as a rule, are not subject to court review, so this argument goes, article 231 constitutes an exception to the general rule. Therefore, if all disputes such as the one involving the housing order mentioned above were considered to be administrative law rather than civil law, there would have to be special statutory provisions in each case allowing for such court review. The problem with this line of reasoning is that in virtually all such cases there *is* a special statutory provision allowing for judicial review. Proponents of this viewpoint are hard put to find examples where this is not the case.[38] Moreover, to me this amounts to excessive concern as to which branch of law a given problem falls into, perhaps based on the same kind of interest in protecting one's turf that was mentioned above. In any case, it only clouds the answer to a question that needs to be addressed, namely, the degree to which acts of administrative organs actually are reviewable by Soviet courts.

Fortunately, some jurists avoid this problem by simply discussing judicial control over governmental administration and leaving aside the question of whether or not the matters being examined fall within administrative law.[39] We will follow the same approach, basing our analysis on the categories of reviewable acts developed by other writers. As far as is known to the author, only one person writing in English has recently analyzed the judicial role in reviewing administrative acts. This was George Ginsburgs, in an article published in 1968. Ginsburgs takes the broad approach to judicial review discussed above, and his findings have served as the basis for part of our analysis.[40]

One writer has stated that there are "about 30 categories of cases" in which "a judicial assessment of the legality and validity of individual decisions of the state administration which involve the subjective rights of citizens" is possible.[41] He does not list the thirty categories, and it has not been possible for this author to compile that many, but a composite list based on the suggestions of a number of sources, including Ginsburgs' article in English, would include the following:[42]

1) The cases mentioned in article 231 of the RSFSR Civil Procedural Code. Article 231 is the first article of the part of the code dealing with "Procedure for Cases Arising from Administrative Law Relations." It mentions three categories of court review: a) complaints about errors in electoral rolls; b) cases involving the seizure of property to cover defaults on government and local taxes, mandatory wage insurance, and self-taxation; c) "complaints about the actions of administrative organs." This last part of article 231 does not specify particular administrative acts that are reviewable, but the recent *Commentary on the RSFSR Civil Procedural Code* and other sources are in accord that only two kinds of cases are relevant: fines imposed on citizens under an edict of the Presidium of the USSR Supreme Soviet of June 21, 1961, and the revocation of drivers' licenses for driving while intoxicated under an edict of the Presidium of the RSFSR Supreme Soviet of June 19, 1968 and similar legislation in the other republics.[43]

2) Suits to compel the correction of errors in civil status records (date of birth, sex, etc.) under article 268 of the RSFSR Civil Procedural Code.

3) Cases involving a contested *order* for housing issued by a local soviet executive committee under article 296 of the RSFSR Civil Code.

4) A group of related cases in the field of labor law involving improper application of disciplinary penalties or improper dismissal.[44]

5) Cases concerning the refusal to grant permission for exchange of living quarters under article 325 of the RSFSR Civil Code.

6) Cases involving complaints concerning actions of notaries under articles 271-273 of the RSFSR Civil Procedural Code.

7) Cases involving complaints about the acts of bailiffs in connection with the execution or refusal to execute a property judgment under article 428 of the RSFSR Civil Procedural Code.

8) Cases involving complaints about the improper issuance of copyrights and patents.[45]

9) Cases involving suits seeking the exclusion of property from an inventory of property subject to confiscation under article 368 of the RSFSR Civil Procedural Code and the decree of the USSR Supreme Court of June 24, 1968, No. 6.

10) Cases involving complaints concerning the refusal to reserve housing quarters for tenants temporarily transferred from the area under article 307 of the RSFSR Civil Code.

11) Cases involving confiscation without compensation of houses built in violation of the law under article 109 of the RSFSR Civil Code.

12) Cases involving confiscation without compensation of houses built or acquired with unearned income under the edict of the Presidium of the RSFSR Supreme Soviet of July 26, 1962.
13) Cases involving damage suits against governmental organs for improper administrative acts by officials under article 446 of the RSFSR Civil Code.
14) Cases contesting adoption orders by local soviet executive committees under article 111 of the RSFSR Code on Marriage and the Family.
15) Finally, there is a group of what are referred to as "administrative infractions" *(administrativnye prostupki)* "which, based on the degree of their social danger, border on being crimes."[46] These infractions, which include petty hooliganism, petty speculation, petty theft, disobedience of police or volunteer people's guards, illegal construction and use of radio transmission equipment, and others,[47] are heard by a people's judge sitting alone and processing the case under a more informal procedure, not regular criminal procedure.[48] These cases do not actually involve judicial review, since it is the judge who makes the initial decision in the case and has the power to fine the offender or sentence him to a short period of detention. The judge's decision is not subject to appeal. As some Soviet jurists have put it, these are cases in which the judge is acting as an administrator.

The procedures used in the fifteen categories just listed vary widely. In some cases, judicial review is mandatory while in others it is at the option of the plaintiff. For some categories, appeal to a higher judicial body is provided for, while in others it is prohibited. A common recommendation from scholars is that more uniformity be brought to the judicial review procedure. What has been of more concern to jurists in recent years is the lack of a coherent principle or principles relating to reviewability. What persuasive reasons are there for the above categories of cases being reviewable while others are not? Several authors have pointed out glaring inconsistencies,[49] while others have indicated that some of the categories of reviewable administrative acts, such as complaints about errors in electoral rolls and actions involving default on taxes, are practically of no significance, since such cases almost never come to court any more.[50] Thus, while there is a considerable number of cases where review is possible, there are also a great many where it is precluded. Numerous writings have raised the question of expanding judicial review of administrative acts in recent years. In fact, it appears to be a sentiment about which Soviet jurists are near to unanimous. In the research work on this paper, the author found no Soviet writer who expressed the view that the number of categories of administrative acts subject to judicial review was adequate.

We will examine below some of the recommendations for expanding judicial review, but the question might be raised at this point as to why there is such strong sentiment in this direction. A number of writers have addressed this question. V. M. Chkhikvadze calls judicial review "the most effective means of defending the personal rights of citizens."[51] Among the specific advantages of the court, various writers have mentioned the openness of the proceedings, the equality of the parties, the elective character of the judges, the collegiality of the review, the participation of the public (people's assessors), the fact that the courts are designated by law as independent and only subject to the law, the requirement of the issuance of a reasoned opinion, and the rigorousness and detailed nature of the judicial procedure.[52]

This preference for judicial review also reflects a sense of the shortcomings in the other procedures available for defending citizen rights against the administration. It is said that correction of abuses by the procuracy comes slowly, unless the media get into the act as well.[53] Newspapers have no rights to correct legal abuses, and for this reason they have been referred to by a leading jurist as "an extraordinary and non-normal method for eliminating violations of legality."[54] The alternatives of writing letters of complaint or complaining in person to various governmental organs is encouraged by many Soviet leaders, and much has been written about this mechanism. But limited survey data seem to show that the people have little faith in this procedure, many choosing alternatives (going to the Party or the media) or not pursuing their complaint at all. Moreover, for at least some categories of complaints, the percentage of times the complaint is adjudged to be justified is extremely low.[55] On the other hand, it is pointed out that the courts rule in favor of the plaintiff in a high percentage of the cases brought by citizens against administrative organs where judicial review is possible.[56] The general advantages of the courts over other control mechanisms are summed up by Bakhrakh and Bonner in the following way:

> "The judicial form of defense of rights possesses a series of important advantages: the high legal qualifications of the judges, their independence, and also the special procedure for deciding disputes with its openness, directness, adversary procedure. Judicial proceedings constitute a qualitatively more finished form of defense of personal rights. The organs of the procuracy, peoples' control, and state inspection are less suitable to this kind of activity [because] here the citizen appears only as a complainant. By contrast the court is oriented toward the legal action [*isk*]. In court the citizen appears as a plaintiff, as an equal party in the dispute."[57]

With regard to the administrative appeal process, analysts point out other shortcomings. One of these is the potentiality of rendering an unfair decision because the official responsible for checking the legality of an administrative act is part of the organization that made the original decision. This involves, as one writer put it, "the well known 'departmental bias' (*vedomstvennost'*) of administrative control. Administrative organs, which are given control authority, comprise a part of the system of administrative organs and are subordinate in this system to the established hierarchy."[58] Another problem is that the methods of administrative review (informal checking, inspection, etc.) are said to be inferior to judicial procedure, "which makes it possible more thoroughly and comprehensively to elucidate a case and render a correct decision."[59] Finally, administrative review is said often to take longer than the time provided by law, while court review in administrative law suits is typically quite expeditious.[60]

It would seem that one of the answers to these problems would be improved procedural rules for administrative review, and this solution has been recommended. Remnev points out that detailed rules concerning the content and form of judicial decisions are contained in the republican codes of civil procedure. By contrast, the 1968 legislation concerning citizen complaints, applications, and recommendations only requires an organ "to issue well-grounded (*obosnovannye*) decisions." As a result, "in practice decisions are often issued by administrative organs which lack the necessary logical and legal basis, which often leads to repeated petitions by citizens on the same question." The answer, he says, is more detailed legislation "to define procedural rules that are consistent and [that explain] the conditions for review of complaints by administrative organs."[61]

As a matter of fact, this kind of legislation does exist on a limited basis, as applied to the work of the administrative commissions of the local soviets. In their current form, administrative commissions were instituted as part of the 1961 Supreme Soviet Presidium edict "Concerning the Further Limitation on the Application of Fines Assessed in Administrative Proceedings." Their powers and duties were further spelled out in subsequent republican legislation.[62] The 1961 legislation limiting administrative fines is looked upon as a landmark and a kind of model for future administrative-procedural legislation because of the detailed provisions it contains concerning administrative fines subject to judicial review as a general rule. This law and the legislation on administrative commissions contain a series of procedural provisions that approach judicial procedure in their nature: open proceedings, the right of the person accused of the infraction to participate in the proceedings, to acquaint himself with materials relevant to the case, to explain his side of the story and to submit information on his own behalf, and to appeal the decision reached.[63] This procedure is not dissimilar to that used in adjudicatory hearings by many US administrative agencies. But it is not typical in Soviet administrative practice, and in a sense it is less necessary in cases involving administrative fines than it would be in other areas of administrative law, because all cases involving fines are subject to judicial review.

Proposals for Increasing Judicial Review

The lack of general provisions on administrative procedure make the broadening of judicial review even more important than it otherwise would be, and many writers continue to advocate reform in this area. I mentioned above that Soviet jurists invoked Engels and Lenin in support of the use of regular courts rather than administrative courts to review administrative acts. These same quotations serve to buttress pleas for increasing the number of kinds of administrative acts subject to judicial review. Engels considered the first condition of freedom "the liability of all officials for all of their official acts before the regular courts and according to general law." Lenin recommended "providing every citizen the right to pursue any official in court, without complaint to his superior."[64] Note that both of these quotations suggest the idea of general and complete access to courts: Engels speaks of "all officials" and "all official acts," while Lenin mentions "every citizen" and "any official." In spite of these words, not all Soviet jurists favor such a complete citizen access to the courts. In fact, it appears that the majority of recommendations for broadening review stop short of advocating general reviewability.[65] I have already quoted Chkhikvadze's statement in his 1967 book that "every citizen" should have "the right to go to court in case of the violation of any rights and freedoms by any organ or person."[66] More or less similar statements have been made more recently by a number of others: Bonner and Kvitkin, writing in 1973, support "the possibility of going to court in any administrative dispute involving the personal rights of a citizen."[67] Nedbailo and Gorsheneva, in a 1976 publication, advocate a statute allowing a court "to declare void any acts of administrative organs which violate the rights and legal interests of citizens" and which gives "to every Soviet citizen the right to go to court in case of the violation of any (but particularly constitutional) rights and legal interests by administrative organs and officials."[68] And there are others of this persuasion.[69]

These formulations are extremely broad and are not likely to be adopted in the near future. It seems very unlikely, for instance, that the Soviet system will soon allow court review of a citizen's claim that an administrative organ such as the police or *KGB* has denied his constitutional right of freedom of speech. The unlikelihood of achieving such general reviewability probably explains in part why recommendations for piecemeal broadening of review are more numerous.

Another reason for rejecting a general law of reviewability is the "flood of litigation" idea that is sometimes heard in American discussions of law reform, *i.e.*, that the number of administrative appeals would overwhelm the courts.[70] Moreover, the traditions and habits of a country with regard to judicial review in certain areas are said to be relevant to this question. Chechot, in advancing this argument, says that "for example, we have never used the court as an organ to defend the personal rights of citizens in the sphere of activity of the USSR Ministry of Defense and the Ministry of Higher and Intermediate Special Education." [71]

Perhaps the most persuasive justification for rejecting the principle of unlimited judicial review, however, is the view that there are certain matters which simply are not appropriate for court review. As one Soviet writer has put it, "not every administrative complaint by content may be reviewed by a court." [72] This is a position taken by some leading commentators on American administrative law as well, and a point to which we shall return.

If these are some of the considerations on which opposition to a general law on reviewability are based, what are the grounds for piecemeal broadening of review? Put differently, what are the criteria by which advocates would determine where expansion of judicial review would take place? Some have suggested that review should be available only on the "most important" or "most essential" personal rights. But this formulation is rightly criticized as too vague: "for every citizen, any violation of a right or even an interest is always essential." [73] Other suggested criteria have included the degree of likelihood that the right in question will be violated, the value in ruble terms of the loss to be incurred by the citizen as a result of the administrative act, and the effectiveness and degree of legality of present administrative review in the area in question. But no one or combination of these criteria has found consensus among Soviet lawyers. [74] Most seem to resist the idea, suggested by at least one jurist, [75] that it is impossible to find objective criteria for determining which administrative acts should be reviewable in court. They want to avoid the conclusion that "everything is determined by the discretion of the legislature and depends exclusively on political considerations." [76] But it is also acknowledged that "political motives indisputably play a significant role" and that any recommendations for broadening review should realistically consider what is possible for the authorities to accept. [77] This realization no doubt contributes to the modesty of some of the recommendations.

A great many suggestions for piecemeal increases in judicial review have been put forward in recent years. Since there are no agreed-upon criteria for judging the significance of these categories, we will merely list them before making some concluding remarks. For convenience, these recommendations will be divided into two categories. First, there are a number of serious sanctions and measures of administrative compulsion *(vzyskaniia* and *peresecheniia*) for which judicial review or expanded judicial review is recommended: administrative arrest (in Russian, *arest*), confiscation of property, corrective works, administrative eviction, administrative detention (*zaderzhanie*), compulsory treatment, the taking of property and documents, and the razing of structures built without permission. [78] As Studenikina puts it, both administrative sanctions and measures of administrative compulsion—because of their potentially severe negative consequences—constitute very grave penalties for those to whom they are applied, and therefore, their use should be accompanied by the maximum procedural guarantees.[79] It occurs to me that these are the kind of penalties for which considerations of due process in American law would very likely require an administrative hearing, with a high level of procedural safeguards, but since the formal administrative hearing is not well-developed in Soviet law, the Soviet jurists discussing these matters recommend judicial review as a mechanism to achieve the same end.

Somewhat set apart from the above list are categories which often involve the refusal of permission by administrators or administrative failure to act. The most often-mentioned of these are: acts of the organs of guardianship and trusteeship; acts of the police organs on questions of residence permits; acts of the organs of social security on the awarding and size of pensions; violations of the waiting list to receive housing; failure of housing organs to fulfill certain obligations, for instance in carrying out capital repair; acts of the educational organs in providing places for children in nurseries, kindergartens, and boarding schools; the decisions of local soviets in providing plots of land for building individual houses; the decisions of administrative organs in depriving citizens of the right to keep cattle, fowl, etc.[80]

It seems probable that if broadening of judicial review is to come in the near future, it will be with regard to some of the items on this second list. But not all of them are equally likely to be considered seriously. The Soviet authorities seem particularly sensitive about bringing the legal practices in several of these categories out into the open, and it is improbable that they would condone judicial review of such administrative acts. The one that stands out in this regard is the residence permit (*propiska*) system[81] (with the arrangements for distributing housing and providing plots of land for building individual houses running a close second). It is interesting to note, therefore, that in the most thorough recent discussion of judicial review of administrative acts, by Chechot, it is recommended that the *propiska* system be excluded from review because of the desirability of maintaining a high level of administrative discretion. His reasoning on this matter is worth examining in more detail.

Chechot notes that while some Soviet laws use the phrase "right to a residence permit" (*pravo na propisku*), the Law on Passports, the basic normative act on the question, does not use this term. He says that the organs responsible for issuing residence permits have been given wide authority in deciding questions concerning the *propiska*, "and in practice it is possible for them to grant a residence permit in the absence of grounds provided for in the departmental normative acts *and not to grant it even if such grounds exist*."[82] Because of this wide discretion, says Chechot, the "right to a residence permit" is not a genuine personal right. This, he says, creates a "substantial barrier" to establishing judicial review on the question. He states that "the problem of a *propiska* is a real one only in certain large cities, resorts, and border localities," not noting that the first two are precisely the places where large numbers of Soviet citizens want to live. He says that limiting the growth of large cities has become "particularly acute" and may be achieved only by the combination of flexible legal and economic policies, "so that the local organs of power can make decisions concerning residence permits at their own discretion, taking into consideration local conditions." He repeats what he has said elsewhere in the book, that "there is no basis for substituting judicial discretion for administrative discretion." Thus, for the present and the foreseeable future, "the discretion of the administrative organs will always play an essential role in this question." [83]

This is the first time administrative discretion has come up in our discussion, and it deserves some comment. The problem of striking a balance between the degree of discretion necessary for an administrator to do his job and an uncontrolled abuse of discretion is a problem that is faced in all developed legal systems. It is only beginning to be recognized as a problem in current Soviet law, although some writers of the 1920's wrote of it in a sophisticated way. [84] Since Soviet law has developed so little in the direction of thorough-going review of administrative acts, it has made little progress in developing mechanisms for checking simple abuses of discretion. What Chechot is talking about is something a bit different, however. He seems to be saying, in effect, that if an area of administration is important enough or sensitive enough or "political" enough, it ought to be handled exclusively by the administrative agencies involved and be beyond the reach of the courts* (or other control mechanisms such as the procuracy as well, for that matter). In other words, the issue in question would be "so far committed to agency discretion as to be unreviewable." The words quoted are those of a leading authority on American administrative law, Kenneth Culp Davis, in describing what I believe to be an analogous category of acts not subject to judicial review in American law. [85] They include such matters as foreign policy, military activity, intelligence activity, and a handful of domestic administrative acts such as a US attorney's decision to prosecute or not to prosecute. [86] These categories of unreviewable acts are not static. Some acts considered unreviewable in the past are now reviewable, and this trend is likely to continue. As Davis puts it, the "area of review is much larger than it was at the beginning of the twentieth century and it is probably still growing." [87]

But still a residue remains of unreviewable administrative acts, even acts that might represent an abuse of discretion, and "the problem of determining what action is so committed [to agency discretion] and what is not is often subtle, elusive, and unclear." [88] American lawyers and other specialists differ on these matters, and we learn whether certain previously unreviewable ad-

* He even appears to condone the abuse of discretion by administrators when he says, as quoted above, that it is possible for the authorities "not to grant it [a residence permit] even if such [legal] grounds exist."

ministrative acts are still unreviewable as they are tested out in court. Davis thinks that "some issues seem clearly inappropriate for judicial determination," and that "the best generalization may be that the courts limit themselves to issues appropriate for judicial determination."[89] This is essentially what the Soviet jurist quoted above was suggesting when he wrote that "not every administrative complaint by content may be reviewed by a court."[90] These subjects not appropriate to judicial determination will not be identical in the Soviet and American systems, although there are probably some common elements, for instance on issues involving foreign affairs and military activity. Moreover, not all Soviet specialists will agree on which administrative acts of this kind should be beyond judicial review. S. N. Bratus', who praises much of Chechot's analysis, believes that "it would be reasonable and just if the grounds for the refusal of a residence permit . . . could be checked by a court."[91] Finally, if the obvious needs noting, much of the development in American law discussed above has been by the case-by-case evolution of precedents characteristic of a common law system. Developments in Soviet law will not come this way, but will emerge largely through statutory changes, influenced in part, by some of the writing discussed in this paper. Soviet law is a long way from what is presently characterized as a "presumption of reviewability" in American law.[92] But even if and when Soviet law develops that far, there will no doubt still remain a kernel of administrative activity such as that described above that will be considered inappropriate for judicial review.

The proponents of increased judicial review received some encouragement with the adoption of the new USSR Constitution in October, 1977. Article 58 of the Constitution contains three relevant paragraphs, only the second of which deals with the judicial review of administrative acts. The first paragraph provides citizens with the right "to complain against actions of officials and of state and social organizations." This right has long existed in Soviet law although, as Professor M. S. Strogovich noted in his comment on the draft version of Article 58, it was not mentioned in the 1936 Constitution.[93] The right to complain appears to be in no way expanded by this provision, however, which goes on to state that "complaints must be reviewed in a manner and within time-limits established by law."

The second paragraph of Article 58 provides: "Action of officials performed in violation of the law, exceeding their authority, impinging on the rights of citizens may be appealed to a court in a manner prescribed by law." Soviet commentators see this provision as being significant, but the question of how significant is a tricky one. As Professor S. N. Bratus' commented in his discussion of the draft version of Article 58, it could be said that it "only provides a constitutional basis for rules already existing in the civil procedural codes" and "it does not involve a broadening of judicial review of administrative acts." This is the interpretation of the new provision toward which this author would incline. But Bratus' prefers to see it as more significant. He calls on the words of Brezhnev in discussing the Constitution draft: "The Constitution provides enormous creative potential. And it must be used creatively"; says Bratus', "the creative potential of Article 58 of the draft must also be used maximally."[94]

The problem, of course, is the passage in the paragraph providing for judicial review "in a manner prescribed by law." This indicates that further legislation will be required to expand judicial review beyond its present boundaries, and both Strogovich and Bratus', the foremost commentators on the draft version of Article 58, recommend that such legislation be adopted.

This brings the analysis to the third paragraph of Article 58. It provides: "Citizens of the USSR shall have the right to compensation for damages inflicted by unlawful actions of state and social organizations, and likewise by officials in the performance of their duties." In the draft version, this paragraph also contained a phrase similar to those in the other two paragraphs, to the effect that the right to compensation shall be exercised "in a manner and within limits defined by law." But this phrase was removed in the final version of Article 58, although the similar phrases were retained in the first two paragraphs of the Article. It is not certain why these words were dropped, but a guess may be made. Like the provision in paragraph one on the right to complain, the right to sue for damages in paragraph three is not new. Its substance is contained in article 89 of the Principles of Civil Legislation of the USSR and the Union Republics, which was adopted in 1961. This article, which provided for the general liability of state institutions for damages for the first time in Soviet history, was a significant advance in Soviet law.[95] And it is this general principle that the third paragraph of Article 58 of the new USSR Constitution repeats in substance. Thus, there is no real need in this new provision to mention subsidiary legislation. But article 89 of the 1961 law contains an escape clause for certain state institutions, the organs of inquiry, preliminary investigation, the procuracy, and the courts, whose liability was to be based on special legislation to be adopted subsequently. In spite of the passage of seventeen years and the appeal from numerous Soviet jurists for implementation of the provision, such special legislation has never been adopted. To include similar language about the need for special legislation in the new USSR Constitution, therefore, would not only have been redundant, but it would also have been a pointed reminder that the 1961 law had never been fully implemented. Thus, the removal of this phrase from the final version of the constitution.

Given the fact that the authorities have been so slow to adopt implementing legislation on the 1961 law, can one expect further legislation for expanding judicial review as envisaged in paragraph two of Article 58 in the near future? One could argue the matter either way, but space constraints do not permit further speculation within the context of this chapter. It can be said, however, that this constitutional promise of increased judicial review–and at this point it is only a promise–gives proponents of such a development a convenient and unchallengeable authority to invoke in their continued advocacy of greater judicial control over the administrative organs.

The Scope of Judicial Review

A final matter for discussion in this paper is what is called scope of review in American law. Given reviewability, how closely will the court scrutinize the act in question and what kind of action is it prepared to take if it finds shortcomings in the way the administrator handled the problem? As Davis puts it, scope of review "indicates the degree of intensity of judicial inquiry."[96] Scope of review remains an issue of some importance in American administrative law, and Soviet jurists have spelled out quite definite ideas on analogous subjects in recent years.

On this question we begin again with Chechot. Chechot starts from the position that "the task of the court in reviewing cases arising from administrative law relations consists of checking the legality and validity [*zakonnost'* and *obosnovannost'*]* of the acts of administrative organs."[97] Other authors generally agree on this.[98] What causes some disagreement is whether the court should go beyond these two criteria to pass judgment on the *tselesoobraznost'*, the advisability or expediency, of the act in question. Some more specific meaning for these terms is required. According to Chechot, "legality and advisability" are often used together in legal discussions. The advisability of an act indicates "its correspondence with defined objectives. An advisable act secures the achievement of the objectives by the best (the optimal) means." But, he says, in any discussion of legality and advisability, legality must come first: "No kind of advisability beyond the limits of the statute is allowed . . . advisable but illegal decisions cannot be. This means that, in checking the legality of a decision, we are at the same time checking its advisability (in the sense indicated above)."[99]

But Chechot allows that there is another kind of situation–in which the administrator has wide discretion–where simply raising the question of legality is insufficient:

> ". . . the statute cannot regulate in an exhaustive way all possible variants of behavior and foresee every step of a person applying the law. Within the framework of the statute, discretion is possible. . . Obviously, in such a case the judgment about the legality of a solution cannot predetermine the conclusion about its advisability, since the statute itself

* Validity is only an approximation of the meaning of *obosnovannost'* although it is the first meaning given in Smirnitskii's Russian-English dictionary. More accurate might be "well-groundedness," and I have translated the adjectival form, *obosnovannyi*, as "well-grounded" above (see text accompanying note 60).

permits the possibility of a choice of several solutions, each of which would be legal."[100]

This is where the concept of validity comes into play. Validity, says Chechot, "is associated with the full and faithful establishment of the factual circumstances of the case, with the correct conclusions based on the established circumstances." Legality "is defined as the correctness of the application of the norms of substantive and procedural law."[101]

Under these definitions, the job of Soviet courts in judicial review seems fairly close to that of the American court in performing the same function: the American court is required to check whether the agency has applied the law correctly[102] ("legality" in Soviet parlance) and whether, as to the facts of the case, it finds that the administrative determination is "supported by substantial evidence on the record considered as a whole"[103] (which approximates the Soviet idea of validity). In American law, both the commentators and the courts go on to point out that judicial review does not guarantee that the "right" result or the "most desirable" result will be achieved: as Gellhorn puts it, "the function of judicial review is not to ensure the correctness of the administrative decision. That is a matter of judgement which Congress has delegated to the administrator and not to the reviewing court . . . the court's role rather is confined to determining whether the administrator has acted within his delegated discretion."[104] Or, as the US Supreme Court states in the landmark case of *SEC v. Chenery Corporation*: "The wisdom of the principle adopted is none of our concern. . . Our duty is at an end when it becomes evident that the Commission's action is based upon substantial evidence and is consistent with the authority granted by Congress. The very breadth of the statutory language precludes a reversal of the Commission's judgment save where it has plainly abused its direction in these matters."[105]

To the extent that the Soviet "advisability" (*tselesoobraznost'*) parallels the American "correctness" or "wisdom," many Soviet lawyers are saying much the same thing: "Of course the court cannot decide the question of the advisability of an act adopted by an administrative organ, but it can and should check the legality of that act."[106] "It is impossible, however, to deny that a decision by the court on the advisability of an act would place the court above the administration, and this would be wrong."[107] But Chechot has written on this matter most fully:

> "In those cases where the execution of an administrative act depends exclusively on the discretion of the administrative organ, control by the judicial organs should be excluded. If judicial control in such cases were allowed, this would mean that the judicial organs would be able to . . . resolve a dispute not on the basis of the application of a legal norm but only on the basis of their discretion, *i.e.*, to execute acts

which are committed exclusively to the competence of the administrative organ."[108]

In other words, as so many American commentators and courts have said, the court should not substitute its judgement for that of the administrator. This point of view seems to be the prevailing one in both American and Soviet law. But, recently, in both countries some opinion has been expressed to the effect than an insistence on this level of judicial non-interference in all cases may be going too far. American courts have shown some tendency in recent years to attempt to force administrative agencies to structure and curb their discretion,[109] and have begun to question the fairness of some informal discretionary administrative acts.[110] This may not amount to substituting judgment, but it does suggest that not all US courts now automatically deny review once they determine that administrative discretion is involved. Moreover, some commentators are questioning the tendency of courts to underestimate their capacity to review the *legal* aspects of an administrator's decision because that decision may have been based on highly specialized knowledge. As Davis recently put it:

> "When administrators are specialists, when the subject matter is within their specialization, when the factors that may have influenced their discretionary determination are many and complex, and when the judges as generalists have little confidence in their capacity to provide a useful check, the natural tendency is to get rid of the challenge of administrators' discretion by reciting that the action is committed to agency discretion by law and that it is therefore unreviewable. Yet whenever a court so holds, a party who thinks that discretion has been abused is denied a meaningful judicial check. Does the natural tendency of courts to cut off review in these circumstances mean that injustice remains uncorrected?"[111]

In effect, Davis answers "yes" to this question, saying that while subject matter specialization may often be outside of a judge's competence, there may still be legal aspects of an official's conduct that judges are perfectly competent to review. This Davis labels "judicial underestimation of judicial capacity."[112]

The Soviet response to this problem has not been identical to the American, and since the possibility of judicial review is so much narrower in Soviet law, few commentators have bothered to examine the problem. But if the prevailing view is that the court should not substitute its judgement for that of the administrator, there has been at least one partial objection to this point of view. It has been expressed in the following way. Although most statutes allowing for judicial review of administrative acts provide only for the *voiding* or *vacating* of an illegal administrative act by a court, there are rare provisions which allow the court to *change* the administrative action (*i.e.*, to substitute its judgment for that of the administrative organ). The best example is the 1961 legislation on limiting administrative fines, under which a court may rescind or lower a fine assessed against an individual or substitute a warning in place of a fine.[113]

Most Soviet commentators think that this is wrong and would curtail the court's power to change administrative acts.[114] But Bonner and Kvitkin, who have written the other recent detailed analysis of judicial review of administrative acts besides that of Chechot's, disagree, in what amounts to a direct attack on the view of Chechot. They note the prevailing viewpoint concerning the "inadmissibility of wide judicial discretion in resolving administrative disputes" (Chechot's words), and they accept this position if the case in question involves matters in which the court does not have the specialized knowledge to make sound judgments. But, "the choice of a specific size of an administrative fine or other administrative sanction is defined by a framework limited by law, and the gravity of the violation committed, the personality of the violator and his property situation, this is common law-applying activity" for which the court is "excellently qualified." In fact, they argue, there are grounds for suggesting that the discretion that emerges from the process of judicial decision may be a significantly better mechanism than the "unreasoned and, at times, completely uncontrolled discretion of the administration." Contrary to other commentators, they recommend increasing judicial discretion in order to better control administrative discretion.[115] But, so far, the view of Bonner and Kvitkin is definitely in the minority.

4. Conclusions

The opportunity for judicial review has come to be a fundamental premise in American administrative law. A handful of exceptions to reviewability to the contrary notwithstanding, Louis L. Jaffe was able to write a dozen years ago: "in our system of remedies, an individual whose interest is acutely and immediately affected by an administrative action presumptively has a right to secure at some point a judicial determination of its validity. This is the teaching of our history and tradition. It is our common law, and in a lesser measure a corollary of our constitutions."[116]

Soviet law operates from no such tradition or presumption. Those who make legal policy deliberately chose a different direction, favoring the use of other mechanisms to check erroneous administrative acts and keeping judicial review to a minimum. But, the overwhelming consensus of Soviet jurists has recently been that the present system is inadequate (not all of them say so in so many words). Whether they call it administrative justice or simply judicial review, and whether they advocate a general presumption of reviewability or the extension of review to selected categories of cases, the direction of their recommendations is clear: they want a system in which the mechanism of judicial control plays a much more significant role. The unanimity of the demand suggests that it is one to which the political leadership will eventually yield to some extent.

NOTES

1. A. E. Lunev (ed.), *Administrativnoe pravo* (Administrative Law), (Moscow, 1967), p. 11. On the difficulty of defining Soviet administrative law with clarity, see F. J. M. Feldbrugge (ed.), *Encyclopedia of Soviet Law* (Leyden, 1973), Vol. I, p. 18.

2. W. Friedmann, *Law in a Changing Society*, abridged ed. (Baltimore, 1964), p. 278.

3. Kenneth Culp Davis, *Administrative Law: Cases, Text, Problems*, 6th ed. (St. Paul, Minn., 1977), p. 1 (hereinafter cited as Davis, 1977).

4. Friedmann, *op. cit.*

5. Bernard Schwartz, *French Administrative Law and the Common-Law World* (New York, 1954), p. 85.

6. See, *e.g.*, V. M. Manokhin (ed.), *Sovetskoe administrativnoe pravo* (Soviet Administrative Law), (Moscow, 1977); for a variation on this approach see Lunev (ed.), *op. cit.*

7. *Izvestiia*, Feb. 25, 1976, 9.

8. V. A. Ivanov, "Sovershenstvovanie garantii prav grazhdan v administrativnom protsesse" (The Perfection of the Guarantees of the Rights of Citizens in the Administrative Process), *SGiP*, 1977, No. 2, 28.

9. See *e.g.*, M. D. Zagriatskov, *Administrativnaia iustitsiia II: Pravo zhaloby v teorii i zakonodatel'stve* (Administrative Justice II: The Right to Complain in Theory and Legislation), 2nd ed., revised and significantly expanded (Moscow, 1925).

10. D. M. Chechot, *Administrativnaia iustitsiia* (Administrative Justice), (Leningrad, 1973), p. 26.

11. The quotations in this paragraph, and the jurists writing them in the 1920's who made them, are cited in V. I. Remnev, "Iz istorii razvitiia administrativnoi iustitsii v SSSR" (From the History of Administrative Justice in the USSR) in M. M. Boguslavskii *et al.* (eds.), *Problemy upravleniia i grazhdanskogo prava* (Problems of Administration and Civil Law), (Moscow, 1976), pp. 76-77 (hereinafter cited as Remnev, "Iz istorii . . .").

12. P. I. Kudriavtsev *et al.* (eds.), *Iuridicheskii slovar'* (Legal Dictionary), 2nd ed. (Moscow, 1956), Vol. I, p. 20.

13. S. N. Bratus' *et al.* (eds.), *Entsiklopedicheskii slovar' pravovykh znanii* (Encyclopedic Dictionary of Legal Knowledge), (Moscow, 1965), p. 12.

14. N. G. Salishcheva, *Grazhdanin i administrativnaia iurisdiktsiia v SSSR* (The Citizen and Administrative Jurisdiction in the USSR), (Moscow, 1970), p. 130.

15. See note 10 above.

16. Remnev, "Iz istorii . . .," and Salishcheva, *op. cit.*

17. M. S. Studenikina, "Sootnoshenie administrativnogo i sudebnogo kontrolia v sovetskom gosudarstvennom upravlenii" (The Interrelationship of Administrative and Judicial Control in Soviet State Administration), *UZ VNIISZ*, No. 22, 1970, pp. 81-82. Moreover, D. N. Bakhrakh and A. T. Bonner concluded in an essay on the subject that "it will also obviously not be unhelpful to make use of the positive and negative experience of countries with developed systems of administrative justice." "Administrativnaia iustitsiia: razvitie i problema sovershenstvovaniia" (Administrative Justice: Development and the Problem of Completion), *SGiP*, 1975, No. 8, 21.

18. V. A. Loriia, "Sushchestvuet li administrativnaia iustitsiia v sovetskom prave" (Does Administrative Justice Exist in Soviet Law), *Pravovedenie*, 1970, No. 1, 110-114.

19. See, *e.g.*, the use of the term by H. W. R. Wade in *Administrative Law*, 3rd ed. (Oxford, 1971), pp. 6 and 172-173. The author found no entry for "administrative justice" in the index of any of the leading American administrative law textbooks.

20. Chechot, *op. cit.*, p. 31.

21. Zagriatskov, *op. cit.*, esp. pp. 8 and 23. V. Kobalevskii, *Sovetskoe administrativnoe pravo* (Soviet Administrative Law), (Kharkhov, 1929), pp. 410-413.

22. Zagriatskov, *op. cit.*, p. 54; Kobalevskii, *op. cit.*, p. 410.

23. The information in this paragraph is based on Zagriatskov, *op. cit.*, pp. 50-53. On further efforts to establish administrative courts in Soviet Russia in the 1920's see Chechot, *op. cit.*, pp. 59-61.

24. See above, text accompanying note 11.

25. This is the title of an article by S. Abramov written in 1947: "V sovetskom prave ne mozhet byt' administrativnogo iska," *Sots. Zak.*, 1947, No. 3, 8.

26. Chechot, *op. cit.*, p. 31. Emphasis mine.

27. The views of Soviet opponents of administrative justice seem curiously reminiscent of that of the English jurist A. V. Dicey in his opposition to administrative law, based on his misunderstanding of the French *droit administratif.* Writing in 1885, Dicey stated that "there can be with us nothing really corresponding to the 'administrative law' or the 'administrative tribunals' of France. The notion which lies at the bottom of 'administrative law' . . . is that affairs or disputes in which the government or its servants are concerned are beyond the sphere of the civil courts and must be dealt with by special and more or less official bodies. This idea is utterly unknown to the law of England and, indeed, is fundamentally inconsistent with our traditions and customs." *Introduction to the Study of the Law of the Constitution*, 10th ed. (London, 1959), p. 203. For a recent comment on this view of Dicey see Wade, *op. cit.*, p. 7.

28. Remnev, "Iz istorii . . .," p. 76; A. T. Bonner and V. T. Kvitkin, *Sudebnyi Kontrol' v oblasti gosudarstvennogo upravleniia* (Judicial Control in the Field of State Administration), (Moscow, 1973), p. 109.

29. Loriia, *op. cit.*, p. 113.

30. Remnev, "Iz istorii . . .", p. 77.

31. Chechot, *op. cit.*, p. 133.

32. The discussion of the wide and narrow conceptions of the administrative process can be found in many sources. Within the context of a thorough recent discussion of administrative law, see, for instance, Manokhin (ed.), *op. cit.* p. 45.

33. P. E. Nedbailo and V. M. Gorsheneva (eds.), *Iuridicheskaia protsessual'naia forma* (Juridicial Procedural Form), (Moscow, 1976). The quotations are from p. 137, while discussions of the law-preserving and law-providing functions of administrative organs may be found in several parts of the book. See pp. 10-11, 22, 41, 43 and Chapter V, pp. 135-172.

34. Salishcheva, *op. cit.*, p. 123, and Chechot, *op. cit.*, p. 78.

35. This is the way that Salishcheva, among others, describes it. *Op. cit.*, p. 122.

36. See Chechot, *op. cit.*, p. 91, and S. N. Bratus', "Ob usilenii i rasshirenii sudebnoi zashchity prav grazhdan" (Concerning the Strengthening and Broadening of Judicial Defense of the Rights of Citizens), *Pravovedenie*, No. 5, 1975, 52.

37. Chechot, *op. cit.*, p. 91, and Bratus', *op. cit.*, p. 51.

38. See, for example, Chechot, *op. cit.*, pp. 90-93.

39. See, *e.g.*, Bonner and Kvitkin, *op. cit., passim.*

40. George Ginsburgs, "Judicial Controls over Administrative Acts in the Soviet Union–The Current Scene," *Osteuropa-Recht*, 14 (1968), 1-33.

41. Remnev, "Iz istorii . . .". p. 74.

42. Many sources provide a list of such reviewable acts. Our composite is based largely on the following: Chechot, *op. cit.*, pp. 89-90 and sources cited therein; Ginsburgs, *passim.*; Bonner and Kvitkin, *op. cit.*, p. 92; Manokhin (ed.), p. 263.

43. R. F. Kallistratova *et al.* (eds.), *Kommentarii k GPK RSFSR* (Commentary on the RSFSR Civil Procedural Code), (Moscow, 1976), p. 303. Reference to RSFSR legislation may be taken to include similar legislation in other republics, where it exists.

44. For details on statutory provisions see A. S. Pashkov (ed.), *Sovetskoe trudovoe pravo* (Soviet Labor Law), (Moscow, 1976), pp. 482-487.

45. For details see O. S. Ioffe and M. D. Shargorodskii, *Voprosy teorii prava* (Question on the Theory of Law), (Moscow, 1961), p. 304.

46. M. S. Studenikina, "Sudebnaia praktika i admininstrativnoe pravo" (Judicial Practice and Administrative Law) in S. N. Bratus' (ed.), *Sudebnaia praktika v sovetskoi pravovoi sisteme* (Judicial Practice in the Soviet Legal System), (Moscow, 1975), p. 226.

47. As Studenikina has indicated (*ibid.*, p. 227), a number of other administrative infractions such as petty theft, driving while intoxicated, keeping home brew, and others are on the books in one or several republics but not across the USSR as a whole.

48. On abuses resulting from the use of this simpler procedure see I. F. Bartykov *et al., Administrativnye pravonarusheniia rassmatrivaemye v sudebnom poriadke* (Administrative Offenses Reviewed in Judicial Procedure), (Moscow, 1964), pp. 116-118.

49. See, *e.g.*, Salishcheva, *op. cit.*, pp. 125-6.

50. See, *e.g.*, Chechot, *op. cit.*, pp. 99 and 113.

51. V. M. Chkhikvadze, "Lichnost' i gosudarstvo: vzaimnaia otvetstvennost' " (Personality and the State: Mutual Responsibility), *SGiP*, No. 1, 1971, 25.

52. *Ibid.*; Bonner and Kvitkin, *op. cit.*, p. 10; Bratus', *op. cit.*, pp. 47-48.

53. *Ibid.*, p. 43.

54. *Ibid.*, pp. 46-47.

55. Chechot, *op. cit.*, pp. 103-106; V. I. Remnev, "Povyshenie effektivnosti poriadka rassmotreniia obrashchenii grazhdan" (Raising the Effectiveness of the Procedure for Review of Petitions of Citizens), *SGiP*, No. 12, 1967, 31.

56. *Ibid.*, 31-32; Studenikina, "Sudebnaia . . .", p. 228; P. Bukhalov and L. Nikol'skii, "Zhaloby na administrativnye organy v sude," (Complaints About Administrative Organs in Court), *Sots. Zak.*, 1971, No. 4, 19.

57. Bakhrakh and Bonner, *op. cit.*, p. 18.

58. Studenikina, "Sootnoshenie . . .", p. 73.

59. *Ibid.*, p. 74; on these points see also Nedbailo and Gorsheneva (eds.), pp. 124-125.

60. Remnev, "Povyshenie . . .", p. 32.

61. *Ibid.*, pp. 30-31.

62. See A. P. Kliushnichenko and A. P. Shergin, *Administrativnye Komissii* (Administrative Commissions), (Moscow, 1975), pp. 4-5; also *Kommentarii k zakonodatel'stvu o shtrafakh, nalagaemykh v administrativnom poriadke* (Commentary on Legislation on Fines Assessed Administratively), (Moscow, 1968), pp. 91-108.

63. Bartykov and others, *op. cit.* p. 119.

64. One or both of these quotations may be found in: Bratus', *op. cit.*, p. 53; Bonner and Kvitkin, *op. cit.*, p. 14; Salishcheva, *op. cit.*, p. 118; Bakhrakh and Bonner, *op. cit.*, p. 18; V. M. Chkhikvadze, *Gosudarstvo, demokratiia, zakonnost'* (State, Democracy, Legality), (Moscow, 1967), p. 342; V. Z. Pul'ianov, "Administrativnaia iustitsiia v Anglii" (Administrative Justice in England), *UZ VNIISZ*, 1974, No. 30, 236.

65. This is the conclusion of Nedbailo and Gorsheneva (eds.), *op. cit.*, p. 125.

66. Chkhikvadze, *Gosudarstvo*, . . .,p. 341. Since writing these words, it appears

that Chkhikvadze may have backed off from this view to some extent. Writing in 1971, he advocated the formulation of a "uniform principle" concerning judicial review of administrative acts in which the law provides "a clear list of cases of that kind" which will be subject to review. "Lichnost' . . .", p. 26.

67. Bonner and Kvitkin, *op. cit.*, p. 105. I have translated "sub"ektivnye" in this context as "personal".

68. Nedbailo and Gorsheneva (eds.), *op. cit.*, p. 127.

69. See the citation of sources favoring like views in *ibid.*, note 1; Remnev, "Iz istorii . . .", p. 77; Bakhrakh and Bonner, *op. cit.*, p. 21 and sources cited in note 23; G. E. Petukhov, "Razvitie kompetentsii suda po obespecheniiu zakonnosti v gosudarstvennom upravlenii" (The Development of the Competence of the Court in Guaranteeing Legality in State Administration), *SGiP*, 1975, No. 3, 117; N. S. Malein, "Ob okhrane prav lichnosti" (On Preserving the Rights of the Person), in M. M. Boguslavskii *et al.*, *op. cit.*, p. 95. Both Bakhrakh and Bonner and Petukhov advocate a gradual increase in reviewability ending with a law providing general court access. Zagriatskov (*op. cit.*, p. 61), writing in the 1920's, favored unlimited access of citizens to court in such cases.

70. Remnev, "Povyshenie . . .", p. 32. Chechot, *op. cit.*, p. 107. Advocates of unlimited review reject this argument, however. See, *e.g.*, Chkhikvadze, "lichnost . . .", p. 26; Bakhrakh and Bonner, *op. cit.*, p. 19.

71. Chechot, *op. cit.*, p. 106. In a footnote, Chechot immediately takes back his point about the Ministry of Defense, mentioning cases involving release from the requirement of military service for religious reasons. Under a 1919 law, repealed in 1939, an inductee had the right to judicial review of his request to be excused from military service because of religious reasons. For more on this law and other laws not now on the books which provided for judicial review of administrative acts, see Remnev, "Iz istorii . . .", p. 70.

72. Remnev, "Povyshenie . . .", p. 32.

73. Studenikina, "Sootnoshenie . . .", p. 85.

74. Chechot, *op. cit.*, pp. 99-100; Bratus', *op. cit.*, pp. 52-53; Nedbailo and Gorsheneva (eds.), *op. cit.*, pp. 125-127.

75. V. T. Kvitkin as cited in Studenikina, "Sootnoshenie . . .", p. 85.

76. Chechot, *op. cit.*, p. 97.

77. *Ibid.*

78. This list is based on Nedbailo and Gorsheneva (eds.), *op. cit.*, pp. 125-126, and Studenikina, "Povyshenie . . .", pp. 85-86.

79. *Ibid.*, p. 86.

80. This list is based largely on the common elements in lists of Chechot, *op. cit.*, pp. 96-97, and Nedbailo and Gorsheneva (eds.), *op. cit.*, p. 126. There are citations in these sources to many other writers who favor judicial review of one or more of the items on the lists.

81. See, for instance, "Concerning Some Rules on Propiska of Citizens," published in Leon Lipson and Valery Chalidze (eds.), *Papers on Soviet Law*, 1977, No. 1, 183-187. The first four articles of this decree were published in *Sobr. Post. SSSR*, 1974, No. 19, item 110, while articles 5 through 10, as contained in *Papers on Soviet Law*, are designated "not for publication."

82. Emphasis mine.

83. Chechot, *op. cit.*, pp. 107-108.

84. See, *e.g.*, Zagriatskov, *op. cit.*, pp. 53-62.

85. Davis, *op. cit.*, p. 64. Davis is here interpreting the words in Section 701 of the Administrative Procedure Act, "except to the extent that . . . agency action is committed to agency discretion" to mean "so far committed as to be unreviewable."

86. For citations of relevant cases and discussion see *ibid.*, pp. 59, 60, 65, 74. See also Davis' *Administrative Law of the Seventies*, Supplementing *Administrative Law Treatise*, (Rochester, NY, 1976), pp. 630-635.

87. Davis, *Administrative Law: Cases, Text, Problems*, p. 56.

88. *Ibid.*, p. 64.

89. *Ibid.*, pp. 64, 65.

90. Remnev, see above, text accompanying note 72.

91. Bratus', *op. cit.*, p. 53. He adds that "discretion is also defined by the framework of the statute" and that, therefore, a check for an abuse of discretion can be made by a court.

92. Davis, *Administrative Law: Cases, Text, Problems*, p. 58. Ernest Gellhorn, *Administrative Law and Process in a Nutshell* (St. Paul, Minn., 1972), p. 245.

93. M. S. Strogovich, "Pravo grazhdanina" (The Right of the Citizen), *LG*, Jul. 20, 1977, p. 2.

94. S. Bratus', "Pravo na sudebnuiu zashchitu" (The Right to Judicial Defense), *LG*, Aug. 3, 1977, p. 2.

95. On the background and development of this law see Donald D. Barry (ed.), *Governmental Tort Liability* (Leyden, 1970), pp. 23-77.

96. Davis, *Administrative Law: Cases, Text, Problems*, p. 56.

97. Chechot, *op. cit.*, p. 83.

98. See, *e.g.*, Nedbailo and Gorsheneva (eds.), *op. cit.*, p. 126 and sources cited therein, note 4; Bratus', *op. cit.*, p. 51.

99. Chechot, *op. cit.*, pp. 83-84.

100. *Ibid.*, p. 84.

101. *Ibid.*, pp. 84-85.

102. This inquiry can have several elements in American administrative law. As Gellhorn puts it (*op. cit.*, p. 46), it involves "whether the agency (a) has exceeded its constitutional or statutory authority; (b) has properly interpreted the applicable law; (c) has conducted a fair hearing; and (d) has not acted capriciously or unreasonably."

103. *Ibid.*, p. 265; the case on which this quotation is based is *Universal Camera Corporation v. NLRB*, 340 US 474 (1951).

104. Gellhorn, *op. cit.*, pp. 45-6 and 49.

105. 332 US 194 at 207-208 (1947).

106. Nedbailo and Gorsheneva (eds.), p. 126.

107. Bratus'. *op. cit.*, p. 51. In accord on this point are Bakhrakh and Bonner, *op. cit.*, p. 20, and the Soviet writer of the 1920's Zagriatskov, *op. cit.*, pp. 59-60. I have not quoted Chechot on the matter of *tselesoobraznost'* because his analysis tends to confuse the issue. In his extended discussion of advisability and validity, he does not say, as Nedbailo and Gorsheneva, Bratus', and others do, that the court should not review the advisability of an administrative act. He says, in effect, that in checking a decision for validity, "the question of the advisability of a decision is fully covered . . ." (p. 85; see the context for this conclusion, pp. 84-86). In other words, court review of legality and validity would preclude the possibility of an inadvisable decision being upheld. This would be a very different view of the scope of judicial review from that prevailing in the United States.

108. Chechot, *op. cit.*, p. 75.

109. See, for instance, the cases cited in Davis, *Administrative Law: Cases, Text, Problems*, pp. 52-55 and 455-460.

110. See, *e.g.*, *Citizens to Preserve Overton Park v. Volpe*, 401 US 402, 28 L.Ed. 2d 136 (1971). See also Davis' comments on this case and the problems of judicial review of

informal administrative acts in *Administrative Law of the Seventies*, 677-683, 652-654, 316-322.

111. Davis, *Administrative Law: Cases, Text, Problems*, p. 65.

112. *Ibid.*, p. 72, and see the case used by Davis as an illustration of this point, *Kletschka v. Driver*, 411 F.2d 436 (2nd Cir., 1969).

113. *Kommentarii k zakonodatel'stvu . . .*, note 62 above, p. 204; Chechot, *op. cit.*, pp. 128-129; Bonner and Kvitkin, *op. cit.*, pp. 92-93.

114. Chechot, *op. cit.*, p. 129.

115. Bonner and Kvitkin, *op. cit.*, pp. 94-95.

116. Louis L. Jaffe, *Judicial Control of Administrative Action*, abridged student ed. (Boston, 1965), p. 336.

PROCURATORIAL SUPERVISION OF ECONOMIC VIOLATIONS IN THE USSR

Gordon B. Smith*

1. Introduction

Social engineering through law implies the specification and definition of behavior in ways that are consistent with the goals and norms of a society. Law, when viewed from this macro-analytic perspective, channels the behavior of the mainstream of society in accordance with certain norms.

However, just as law concerns itself with societal behavior in general, it concerns itself equally with the behavior of the individual. At this micro-level, we can speak of law as a mechanism of social control which is designed to affect the individual's decision-making calculus and, thus, his behavior. Law establishes a probability or risk of punishment for violations which is sufficiently costly for most individuals to deter anti-social acts. Unlike the function of law at the macro-level which is largely didactic, concerning itself with socialization of norms and striving towards universality, law at the micro-level is selectively enforced and concerned with relative compliance. The former aspires to "optimality" in social control, while the latter is satisfied with strategic control.

In this paper, we will examine the control function of the Procuracy in its supervision of economic violations. It is argued that procuratorial supervision of economic violations is an example of strategic control, despite claims to optimality by Soviet jurists.

2. Procuratorial Supervision and Economic Violations

The recent "Brezhnev Constitution," like the 1936 "Stalin Constitution" before it, assigns to the Procuracy the task of supervising the full and complete execution of laws by state and administrative organs, enterprises, social organizations, officials, and citizens.[1] This general supervisory function includes redressing grievances of citizens, as well as protecting state interests. In other words, the jurisdiction of the Procuracy includes the supervision of

* The author acknowledges the advice of Professor Harold Berman and the support of the Harvard University Russian Research Center and the Texas Christian University Research Foundation.

economic and administrative violations having detrimental effects for state interests.

The role of the Procuracy (*prokuratura*) in supervising economic violations arising from state administration encompasses several levels of activity. *First*, the *prokuratura* supervises the full execution of laws, decrees, instructions, and other normative acts of state organs, and the legality of actions of administrative and managerial officials. *Second*, the Procuracy is responsible for supervising the legality of actions of police, inspectors, and other investigatory officers as they attempt to uncover economic violations. *Third*, procurators in the Departments for the Review of Criminal and Civil Court Cases review the legality and well-foundedness of judicial decisions in cases of economic crimes and violations. *Fourth*, the Procuracy may institute criminal proceedings or recommend disciplinary or administrative punishments for persons accused of economic violations. *Finally*, the Procuracy is responsible for coordinating the activities of state inspection agencies, the police, *Gosarbitrazh, Gosstandart*, and other administrative organs investigating economic violations.

"Economic violations," as used here, refers to a classification of legal violations occuring in the economic sector which directly and adversely affect state economic interests. In Soviet legal parlance, most economic violations fall under the general heading "*pravonarusheniia zakonodatelstva ob okhrane sotsialisticheskoi sobstvennosti*–violations of legislation on the protection of social property." Examples of the specific economic violations with which we concern ourselves here include petty theft from factories, collective farms, and other enterprises, improper maintenance of state or collective property, and substandard production. Altering or padding accounts and records and graft by officials are designated as "economic crimes" in the criminal codes of each republic. However, lesser instances of these violations frequently are disposed of through the protests or representations of procurators and involve no criminal prosecution. We consider them here as falling within the precincts of "economic violations." Several types of labor violations also fall within the bounds of our definition of economic violations. In a socialist economy, labor is a raw material "owned" by the state. The illegal reduction of work hours, extension of allowable vacation time, poor work discipline, and inadequate supervision and control of workers involve the loss to the state of a valuable resource. The illegal firing of workers may or may not have a detrimental impact on the interests of state administration or may harm one agency while benefiting another. For example, after graduating from a medical institute, D. was assigned to work as a medical officer in a pioneer camp. One and one-half years later he was transferred to the Krasnodar *Krai* Health Department by order of the Ministry of Health of the RSFSR. D. brought suit to recover his former position. The Krasnodar *Krai* People's Court ruled that it could not uphold the directive of the Ministry. Citing the Statute on the Assignment of Young Specialists, the court declared that a person may not be released from his position without approval of the organization to which he is assigned.[2] In this case, approval was required from the Central Committee of the Komsomol. The court's actions benefited D. and the pioneer camp administration at the expense of the Ministry of Health.

In other cases, the arbitrary and illegal suspension of workers clearly does not serve state economic interests. For example, the director of food services for the Exhibition of Economic Achievements in Moscow twice fired a dispatcher K. for personal reasons. The Dzerzhinskii *Raion* People's Court in Moscow found the director guilty of violating Article 138 of the RSFSR Criminal Code and sentenced him to one year of corrective labor.[3] Rather than seeking to judge the facts of each case, the present discussion of economic violations excludes cases of illegal firings and suspensions.

Finally, the illegal enlargement of private land plots or improper use of collective or state land also involves a loss to the state of an economically valuable resource and, therefore, are considered economic violations.

As we will see, in recent years the Procuracy has devoted the largest portion of its resources to the detection and prosecution of these economic and administrative violations that detrimentally affect the state's economic interests.

3. Recent Trends in Procuratorial Supervision of Economic Violations

The present research draws on several data sources in addition to the secondary literature of Soviet legal scholars. We analyzed 496 cases of general supervision–published in the Procuracy's journal, *Sotsialisticheskaia Zakonnost'*, from 1955 through 1976[4] –to provide a detailed picture of the subjects of procuratorial action concerning economic violations and to point out changes over time. In addition, survey data collected from procurators by the scholars at the Laboratory for the Study of Procuratorial Supervision of the Law Faculty of Leningrad State University were analysed. Finally, consultations were conducted with several Soviet legal scholars and practicing procurators to obtain their responses to questions not covered in the literature.

The procurator applies four measures to control administrative violations: protests, representations (*predstavleniia*), proposals (*postanovleniia*), and warnings (*predosterezheniia*). Of these, protests and representations are by far the most frequent. The protest is issued against a specific act, frequently brought to the procurator's attention by an aggrieved citizen. In contrast, representations apply to a class of violations. Procurators issue a protest after a violation has come to light and attempt to establish prompt remedies for the grievance. When issuing representations, procurators frequently allow illegal administrative actions to continue unchecked until they gather materials and approach the actions collectively. The very nature of the two mechanisms is such that the procuratorial protest is better suited to redressing citizens' grievances arising from administrative activity, while the representation is better suited to controlling economic violations.

During the period 1955-1976, almost two-thirds of the cases published in *Sotsialisticheskaia Zakonnost'* involved protests, one-third involved representations. However, since 1968 the trend has been reversed; representations have averaged 71.2% of all procuratorial actions.

Soviet scholars advance several explanations for the decrease of protests relative to representations. *First*, the expansion of the economy has created a situation in which many violations occur within similar circumstances and can best be supervised by dealing with them as classes of violations. *Second*, representations go further than protests in preventing violations and altering those conditions which lead to legal violations. *Third*, the legal knowledge of administrative officials and enterprise managers has risen in recent years, lowering the number of isolated, unique violations that are better handled through protests.[5]

A *fourth* explanation for the relative decline of protests, but one not put forward by Soviet scholars, is that the representation is better suited for controlling economic violations. As we will see shortly, in recent years procurators have placed a heavy stress on supervision of economic violations.

The emergence of the representation as the major mechanism of procuratorial supervision is a relatively recent phenomenon. In 1941 representations constituted 41% of all procuratorial actions.[6] S. G. Berezovskaia of the Institute of the Procuracy of the USSR states that from 1955 to 1959 procurators submitted one-half as many representations as protests.[7] However, in our analysis of published cases from 1955-1976, we found only five representations prior to 1968. After 1968 representations outnumbered protests more than two to one. V. I. Chermenskii, Chief of the Department of General Supervision of the USSR Procuracy, confirms that this ratio is indicative of present procuratorial practice.[8] Berezovskaia links the dramatic shift in editorial policy of *Sotsialisticheskaia Zakonnost'* toward representations to the actions and decisions of a plenum of the Central Committee of the CPSU in 1968 which apparently criticized the journal's neglect of procuratorial representations especially pertaining to economic violations.[9] The increase of procuratorial attention to economic violations since 1968 is clearly indicated in Table I.

Economic violations constituted only a marginal subject of procuratorial activity until 1969. We have already suggested several reasons for the 1968 shift. During the period 1955-1969, procurators concerned themselves with issuing protests against cases of the illegal firings and other labor violations as well as the illegal imposition of administrative fines. The latter became the predominant concern of procurators during the campaign against improper fining following the issuance of a decree of the Presidium of the Supreme

Table 1. *Economic Violations, 1955-1976 (in percent)*

	1955	1958	1959	1960	1961	1962	1963	1964	1965	1966
Economic	0.0	8.3	20.0	0.0	6.3	13.0	8.0	6.5	5.9	15.2
Non-Economic	100.0	91.7	80.0	100.0	93.7	87.0	92.0	93.5	94.1	84.8

	1967	1968	1969	1970	1971	1972	1973	1974	1975	1976
Economic	7.7	10.3	48.4	43.3	30.8	24.2	27.3	50.0	73.9	58.8
Non-Economic	92.3	89.7	51.6	56.7	69.2	75.8	72.7	50.0	26.1	41.2

Soviet on June 21, 1961, "On the Further Limitation of Application of Fines, Imposed by Administrative Procedure."[10] But these factors alone are not sufficient to explain the dramatic shift from protests to representations and from non-economic to economic violations in 1969. The most plausible explanation lies in economic developments in late 1968 and early 1969.

The economic reforms which were announced by Premier Kosygin in late September 1965 were prompted by a deceleration in the rate of economic advance since 1958. During the period 1958-1966, the economic growth rate of the USSR slipped from 8.5% to 6.8%. From 1967 to 1968, growth in per capita income slipped from 6.7% to 6.1%. National income slowed from 8.6% to 7.5%. Industrial production dropped from 10% in 1967 to 8.1% in 1968. Finally, worker productivity fell from 6.6% to 5%.[11] The 1965 reforms recentralized economic management after Khrushchev, restoring the ministries and "branch" system of administration. In addition, the reforms incorporated sales and profits of enterprises as indicators of performance, reducing the number of centrally set indices. By the end of 1968, more than 26,000 industrial plants, producing three-quarters of the total industrial output of the Soviet Union, had been converted to the new system.[12] The greater autonomy for enterprise managers was expected to result in more efficient use of labor and equipment. It also necessitated better supervision and control of economic violations in industrial enterprises and state farms.

In response to the deteriorating economic performance in 1968 and 1969, Brezhnev presented a "confidential report" to the Supreme Soviet in December 1969 on the failures of the eighth Five-Year Plan. Brezhnev chided industrial managers and officials is several sectors of the economy. *Pravda* gave extensive coverage to Brezhnev's remarks and called for meetings of collectives to be organized in all productive enterprises to raise worker productivity and discipline.

In light of these developments, the change in focus of procuratorial supervision from issues primarily affecting individual aggrieved citizens to economic violations which damage the State's economic interests is more readily understandable.

With the completion of the eighth Five-Year Plan in 1970, procuratorial action on economic violations appears to have tapered off until 1973. However, the target figures of the ninth Five-Year Plan were uncommonly high. Thus, in 1974 and 1975, an intensive campaign was mounted leading up to the termination of the plan period on December 31, 1975. What we may be witnessing, then, is a regular pattern of ebb and flow of procuratorial activity governed by the economic plan. The intensity of procuratorial campaigns might also serve as a barometer of difficulties that are being experienced in the economy in general, and various sectors of the economy in particular.

As we see in Table 2 below, the subjects of procuratorial action in cases of economic violations are most frequently factory managers or directors of state enterprises at the regional and local levels. Ministerial officials constituted almost one-third of all procuratorial actions.

Table 2. *Subjects of Procuratorial Actions Against Economic Violations (in percent)*

Directors of factories and enterprises	37.2
Ministerial officials	30.6
Directors of collective and state farms	12.4
Officials of soviets and executive committees	12.4
Other officials	7.5
	100.1

There has been a tendency since 1974 to send representations to higher levels of state administration, especially republic ministries, as we see in Table 3 below.

Table 3. *Level of Subjects of Procuratorial Representations Issued Against Economic Violations, 1969-1976 (in percent)*

	1969	1970	1971	1972	1973	1974	1975	1976
Local	41.7	9.1	44.4	26.3	26.1	4.6	0.0	17.7
Oblast'	12.5	54.6	27.8	15.8	30.4	40.9	30.4	29.4
Republic	25.0	22.7	27.8	31.6	17.4	45.5	39.1	41.2
All-Union	20.8	13.6	0.0	26.3	26.1	9.1	30.4	11.8
	100.0	100.0	100.0	100.0	100.0	100.1	99.9	100.1

The specific economic violations prompting procuratorial action breakdown as follows:

Table 4. *Economic Violations, 1955-1976 (in percent)*

Theft of state property	21.5
Padding or altering records	16.5
Poor work discipline	12.4
Substandard production	11.6
Improper maintenance of state property	10.7
Violations of working hours	10.7
Violations of land allotments	9.1
Violations of vacations	4.1
Graft, accepting favors	2.5
Illegal expenditure of state or collective revenues	0.8
	100.1

Almost 90% of all economic violations fall within three general categories: theft and improper use and maintenance of state property; labor violations resulting in substandard production; and padding or altering accounting and plan fulfillment records. We now turn to a detailed examination of each of these three categories.

Theft of State Property

So common is the problem of petty theft from factories and enterprises that it is the subject of frequent cartoons in the satirical magazine *Krokodil* and other Soviet publications. However, it is difficult to get an accurate statistical estimate of the extent of theft in the USSR. Published Soviet data indicate that approximately 17% of all crime and 45% of all juvenile offenses involve theft.[13] However, Walter Connor feels these figures underrepresent the true level of theft from state enterprises.[14] Many thefts of a petty nature are handled through comrades' courts and do not appear in criminal statistics. In addition, the general tolerance of theft from state enterprises, in which workers may suspect that the managers are engaged in their own misappropriations, and the general scarcity of many goods in the Soviet economy, all lead to high incidence of theft. Much of the theft is never reported and, instead, is attributed to inventory "shrinkage."

During a campaign against theft from enterprises in the Lithuanian, Estonian, Uzbek, and Kazakh republics in 1969, 27.2% of all cases were referred to comrades' court.[15] However, comrades' courts did not appear to provide adequate consideration of the cases. Materials concerning the violations forwarded to comrades' courts by procurators were considered by the tribunals in only 40% of the cases.[16] This would indicate the need for more active procuratorial coordination and follow-up in the disposition of economic violations.

Repeated instances of theft from factories are common, and in recent years many Soviet scholars have advocated better accounting of thefts and other violations in labor books. Two scholars at the Saratov Law Institute, V. Gavrilov and V. Pimenov, cite the case of F. who was convicted of theft from a store in which she worked. She was subsequently hired as a clerk in another Saratov store and eventually was promoted to store manager. In a short period of time she embezzled more than 25,000 rubles.[17] Another investigation revealed that K. was fired three times, and V. four times, from Saratov commercial enterprises for systematically poor work discipline and each time, either by forging or altering their labor books, were hired again in supervisory positions. Gavrilov and Pimenov report that in order to avoid controversies, the managers of enterprises firing workers for theft or other violations frequently enter reasons for terminating employment in the labor books such as "for family reasons" or "at the worker's request."[18]

Of the total number of procuratorial representations issued against economic violations in Saratov *oblast'* from 1967 to 1971, approximately 73% concerned cases of theft of socialist property. Such cases constituted 87% of all representations of procurators in the RSFSR.[19]

In our sample of cases published in *Sotsialisticheskaia Zakonnost'*, 13.8% of all representations and 21.5% of all economic violations involved theft of socialist property. The supervisory activity of procurators in cases of theft of state property appears to be equally distributed among procurators at the *oblast'*, republic, and all-union levels. Local procurators issue significantly fewer representations against petty theft.

Substandard Production

An increasingly contentious problem for the Soviet economy is the production of goods which are defective or substandard. The Soviet theoretical journal *Kommunist* stated that, in the first six months of 1975, over six million pairs of defective shoes had been produced in Soviet factories. Of these, 5.4 million were returned to the factory for alteration. Over the same period, 423,000 items of defective hosiery were produced and 225,000 were returned.[20] The fact that such a large percentage of these defective goods were delivered indicates the existence of gross inadequacies in the detection of defective products within factories. Not only do such cases represent a significant economic loss to the state, they also can be harmful to consumers. For example, in 1974 the First Deputy Procurator-General of the USSR issued a representation to the Ministry of Machine Building for Light and Food Industry regarding the necessity of improving quality control in production. During the course of investigating signals of violations in enterprises subordinate to the Ministry, procurators found that as many as 15% of the sterilization machines produced by one factory were missing a crucial electrical element and were thus useless. The defective machines resulted in illnesses in several people. Criminal proceedings were instituted against the director and chief of the control department of the factory.[21]

Soviet scholars cite several causes of substandard production.[22] First, ministries and chiefs of departments are primarily concerned with plan fulfillment and insufficiently concerned with supervising the quality of production. Second, quality control departments are accorded low priority in most enterprises and factories, and suffer from personnel and equipment shortages. Third, economic sanctions for producing poor products are inadequate. When fines are levied, they frequently are passed on to the buyer. One investigation turned up the following letter from the deputy director of a Saratov factory to the first deputy chief of a technical supply department in the Georgian republic.

> "We will not object if you agree to pay us the fine [incurred for violations], in as much as we have many potential buyers and do not exclude the possibility that we could sell the goods to one of them. Agree and you will conclude the deal . . I hope that this arrangement will be mutually beneficial to our factory and your department."[23]

Fourth, within factories there is inadequate control of worker discipline which frequently results in waste and poor quality production. For example, enterprises subordinate to the Ministry of Industrial Construction Materials every year lose 70 million rubles through waste, of which only 60,000 rubles is ever recovered.[24] Fifth, control authority over substandard production is dispersed among more than ten agencies. Sixth, article 152 of the RSFSR Criminal Code limits criminal responsibility for substandard production and inadequate control to the director, chief engineer, and chief of technical control, and not to others such as deputy directors. Finally, procurators sometimes drop charges before an investigation in a factory has been completed.

Substandard quality workmanship has especially plagued the Soviet construction industry. V. Kim and L. Ivanov, procurators in the Kazakh republic, cite the primary cause as the desire of managers to fulfill the plan at any cost. In the Kazakh republic in 1973, only 48% of all new housing received good evaluations upon inspection. According to Kim and Ivanov, an extremely widespread cause of low quality construction is "storming." More than 35% of all housing starts were begun in the last quarter of the plan year. Of these, 70% were begun in the last week of December.[25] "Storming" often results in the exploitation of workers and even accidents.

Of the economic cases published in *Sotsialisticheskaia Zakonnost'* from 1955 to 1976, 11.6% concerned substandard production. However, it has only been in recent years that procurators have devoted much attention to cases of substandard production. From 1969 to 1973, few cases were published in procuratorial journals. Procuratorial investigations of substandard production began to increase in 1973, and by 1974 and 1975 constituted approximately one-fourth of all economic violations. This increase reflects the impact of a procuratorial campaign against substandard production coincident with the conclusion of the 1971-1975 Five-Year Plan.

What we see, then, are conditions in the Soviet economy which virtually insure the existence of legal violations—whether theft of state property or substandard production. Specifically, those conditions include "storming" to fulfill plan quotas, economic scarcity which insures outlets even for substandard goods, and planning which does not allow sufficient flexibility in establishing supply relations between producing units to account for inventory "shrinkages" caused by thefts. The combined effect of these factors causes managers to take shortcuts, risking detection and punishment. Optimal control of economic violations cannot be achieved as long as these systemic factors exist.

Padding and Altering Plan Records

Given the pressure to fulfill plan quotas and the built-in obstacles which impede the realization of that goal, it is likely that managers are tempted to alter or pad records concerning plan fulfillment.

Punishments for padding accounting records often are more severe than for other forms of economic violations because they usually involve the misappropriation of larger sums of money and the motive is always greed. For instance, *Bakinskii Rabochii*, the organ of the Azerbaidzhan Communist Party, reported in December 1975 that five Soviet citizens had been sentenced to death and 59 others to prison in an agricultural swindle that resulted in a loss to the state of about 15.6 million rubles.[26] The deal involved a vegetable canning factory in Lenkoran which illegally arranged to give land to several fish-processing enterprises for growing vegetables. No vegetables were ever grown and the director of the factory and local party officials pocketed more than 3.5 million rubles.

However, not all cases are so dramatic. V. Kuznetsov, procurator in Moscow, cites the case of a motorpool where drivers regulary tampered with odometers to register more miles than they actually drove.[27]

Padding or otherwise altering accounting records constituted 4.0% of all procuratorial actions from 1955 to 1976 and 16.5% of all economic violations. The most frequent subjects of procuratorial actions for altering accounting records are factory and enterprise managers at the *oblast'* level, followed by ministerial officials at the republic and all-union levels. The disclosure of misappropriations and falsification of records occurs most frequently at the *oblast'* level due to active auditing of industrial enterprises by *oblast'* auditing departments.

4. Uncovering Economic Violations

Procurators rely on two principal means of uncovering economic violations: citizens' complaints and investigations. Article 14 of the Statute on the Procuracy empowers procurators to receive and review citizens' complaints. Most protests are prompted by information from the press, citizens' complaints or "signals" received by procurators during the course of their contact with *oblast'* and regional organizations, soviets, auditing departments, tax offices and safety inspectorates, or attendance at meetings of worker collectives.

Citizens' complaints are most effective in cases of consumer fraud and substandard production. For example, in 1973, repeated complaints of citizens concerning consumer deception and substandard products prompted the First Deputy Procurator General of the USSR to issue a representation to the USSR Ministry of Trade. The subsequent investigation uncovered more than 260 cases of consumer deception in Oktiabrskii *raion* in Leningrad. In Kashkadar'inskaia *oblast'* in the Uzbek republic, 70% of all consumer complaints concerning poor quality food products were found to be legitimate.[28]

By far, the most common means of uncovering economic violations is periodic investigations. This is confirmed by an analysis of which organs are the most frequent objects of procuratorial investigations. Figures of the RSFSR Procuracy for 1972 indicate that the most frequent objects of procuratorial investigations are industrial enterprises and social organizations.

Procurators report that they frequently lack accurate information on the extent of economic violations in their regions. Procuratorial campaigns serve a dual purpose of uncovering cases of economic violations and providing procurators with some indication of how bad the situation is.

However, one major weakness of procuratorial supervision of economic violations is that procurators are trained to be generalists. Law curricula do not provide prospective procurators with sufficient training in auditing procedures or methodological techniques to exert meaningful supervision over complex economic activities. Whatever expertise procurators have is acquired solely by experience.

When conducting investigations of administrative departments and economic enterprises, procurators may enlist the aid of jurisconsults in those organs, technical experts associated with inspectorates or scientific-research institutes, and other specialists. Of 243 *raion* procurators surveyed, 44.4% use the legal services of enterprises and organizations.[29] Of those responding affirmatively, over half include the jurisconsults in investigations of legal violations and approximately one-fourth consult with jurisconsults concerning measures to prevent legal violations.[30]

When conducting investigations into economic-financial activities in enterprises and firms, 64.3% of the surveyed procurators claimed to use materials

Table 5. *Objects of Procuratorial Investigations in the RSFSR in 1972*

Enterprises and social organizations	130,964
Kolkhoz managers	42,078
Raion and city organs of administration	25,642
Agricultural and rural soviets	22,077
Raion and city executive committees	9,692
Krai, oblast', and autonomous republic administrative organs	2,641
All-union and republic ministries	870
Krai, oblast', and autonomous republic executive committees of soviets	211
Total	234,175

* In several cases, there were multiple objects of investigations. This accounts for the disparity between the figures in Table 5 and the aggregate figures presented previously.

Source: L.A. Nikolaeva, *Teoreticheskie i prakticheskie problemy obespecheniia zakonnosti v sovetskom gosudarstvennom upravlenii organami prokuratury i suda* (Unpublished doctoral dissertation, Leningrad State University, 1974), p. 181.

of control-auditing organs, while 35.7% demand documents and records directly from the enterprises and firms in question.[31] More than one-half of the procurators engage specialists in these investigations.

In other words, procurators are more likely to enlist the support of persons outside of the organs they are investigating than jurisconsults affiliated with those organs. Some procurators have criticized jurisconsults for allying themselves with the organs with which they are associated, thus obstructing procuratorial investigations.[32]

5. Punishment of Economic Violations

Article 15 of the Statute on the Procuracy establishes the power of the procurator to propose the imposition of criminal, disciplinary, or administrative sanctions on officials or citizens who have violated the law. Criminal charges are initiated when the procurator encounters a violation of the criminal codes. He transfers the case to the Department of Investigations and Prosecution of the Procuracy, and it eventually goes to the people's court. Disciplinary punishment may be imposed by administrative organs, economic enterprises, and social organizations, to sanction their own members. Finally, administrative punishments may be imposed only by special bodies invested with those powers (*e.g.*, the police, inspectorates, and game wardens).

Corrective relief frequently is sought in those cases in which someone has suffered material damages as a result of an illegal administrative action. For instance, procuratorial protests against the illegal firing of workers usually direct enterprises to reinstate workers and pay back wages. Corrective relief is frequently employed also when personal property has been illegally seized.

Soviet law also recognizes material responsibility of citizens, officials, and corporate bodies. In contrast to corrective relief, material responsibility is more symbolic than corrective in that it does not attempt to compensate for specific damages. Measures of material responsibility are imposed apart from administrative, disciplinary, or criminal punishments. The procurator poses the question of material responsibility, while the guilt of the person or institution—and the imposition of a fine or other punishment—is determined by the court or administrative commission. In practice, material responsibility has been used to strengthen penalties for official negligence concerning technical safety and anti-pollution regulations.

Aggregate figures are not available for the number of officials subjected to criminal, administrative, or disciplinary action each year. However, S. G. Berezovskaia and T. L. Markelov of the Institute of the Procuracy report that the number of people subjected to disciplinary or administrative sanctions increased by 12% from 1954 to 1973 and the number of officials held materially accountable for damages incurred as a result of illegal actions increased by more than 40%.[33] Figures for Voronezh *oblast'* suggest the extent of imposition of administrative and disciplinary punishments. In 1967, procurators recommended that administrative or disciplinary sanctions be directed against 218 officials.[34] This figure increased to 287 in 1968; 312 in 1969; 435 in 1970; and 637 in 1971. For the most part, persons subjected to disciplinary or administrative sanctions are young workers with few years on the job who are found guilty of theft of enterprise or communal property.[35]

During the period 1955 to 1976, *Sotsialisticheskaia Zakonnost'* reported administrative or disciplinary action taken in conjunction with 8.7% of all procuratorial protests and representations and criminal action in 4.8%.

Subsidiary action (criminal, administrative, or disciplinary) is initiated in almost one-third of all procuratorial representations. In contrast, subsidiary action is initiated in only 2.8% of all procuratorial protests.

Theft of state property is the most frequent cause of criminal prosecution, while theft and substandard production together account for the majority of disciplinary action by procurators. Table 6 below provides a complete breakdown for all categories of violations.

Procurators apply criminal, disciplinary, and administrative sanctions somewhat differently. Directors of enterprises, administrative offices, and departments, predominate as subjects of disciplinary or administrative action, while criminal action maintains a wider scope of application, more than one-half of all criminal proceedings being directed at other categories—ministerial officials, officials of soviets or executive committees, comrades' courts, etc.

The number of cases resulting in subsidiary action by procurators is substantially higher during campaigns against economic violations. In 1969

Table 6. *Objects of Criminal and Disciplinary Action, 1955-1976 (in percent)*

Violation	Criminal	Disciplinary
Theft of state property	41.2	26.7
Substandard production	23.5	26.7
Padding records	17.6	13.3
Improper maintenance of state property	5.9	10.0
Work discipline	5.9	20.0
Land violations	5.9	0.0
Graft	0.0	3.3
	100.0	100.0

procurators in the Lithuanian, Estonian, Uzbek, and Kazakh republics undertook an extensive investigation of theft from state enterprises. As a result of the investigations, administrative punishments were applied in 72.8% of all representations.[36] The specific punishments were: administrative arrest 46.2%, fine 36.9%, corrective labor 10.0%, and other administrative punishments 6.9%. The level of criminal prosecution of economic violations remained unchanged by the campaign–3.5% of all representations.

The figures on the imposition of sanctions on persons responsible for economic violations are inflated considerably by the practice of referring many minor cases to the comrades' courts. A study of 23 state enterprises indicated that 51% of the persons accused of committing thefts were judged before comrades' courts.[37]

In practice, procurators undertaking investigations and issuing representations concerning economic violations frequently send information notes (*informatsionnye zapiski*) to local Party organs. These notes may pertain to specific violations or general conditions of law enforcement in the region. Procurators usually initiate these notes; however, occasionally Party organs request procurators to compile information and statistics on law enforcement. In addition, procurators consult with members of the Party apparatus at all levels concerning problems affecting the Party itself and administrative, legislative, and legal problems of special interest to the political leadership.

In 1968 procurators in the RSFSR issued 4,260 notes. The number of information notes increased to 5,268 in 1971 and 5,731 in 1972.[38] In 1972 procurators issued information notes in conjunction with 10.7% of all procuratorial representations in the RSFSR. The increase in issuing information notes to Party organs in recent years can be seen from figures for Vornezh *oblast'*. In 1976 *raion* procurators in Voronezh sent 125 information notes to Party organs. This figure increased to 142 in 1968; 191 in 1969; 237 in 1970; and 295 in 1971 (a 136% increase in five years).[39]

We can obtain a more detailed picture of the objects and levels at which procurators issue information notes by examining the published cases from *Sotsialisticheskaia Zakonnost'*. Procurators informed Party organs in 9.2% of the representations published in *Sotsialisticheskaia Zakonnost'* from 1955 to 1976. More than 80% of the representations in which Party organs were informed involved economic violations, most commonly violations of labor discipline or padding of records. More than one-half of all violations resulting in information notes to Party officials were uncovered at the *oblast'* level, and about one-third of the cases at the republic level. These figures confirm the predominance of *oblast'* level Party-administrative interaction which Hough and Stewart found in regional studies of administration and Party organization.[40]

Finally, there is a tendency to notify Party organs in cases involving disciplinary action or criminal prosecution. Party organs were informed of one third of all cases resulting in criminal prosecution and more than one-half of all cases involving disciplinary or administrative action.

6. Assumptions of Procuratorial Supervision

Underlying the institution of procuratorial supervision of economic and administrative activity is a philosophical notion of "optimal control." Although not specifically referred to in those terms, Soviet jurists profess the hope that the Procuracy can indeed supervise the *full* and *exact* execution of *all* laws, decrees, instructions, and other normative acts by administrative officials.[41] This mechanistic and utopian appraisal of general supervision is typified by the statement of R. A. Rudenko, Procurator-General of the USSR:

> "The main goal now in the activity of the Procuracy in supervising the exact and unwavering observance of laws is to achieve results. Procuratorial supervision must be even more aggressive. The challenge is not merely one of promptly uncovering uneconomic activities, extravagances, provincialism, violations of state discipline, and other violations of the law, but also to stop them, eliminate their causes, and hold the guilty to account, even to criminal prosecution, and to foster in the society, in the collective of workers, a sense of responsibility for the prevention of legal violations. To fulfill this challenge completely, it is necessary for us assiduously to avoid limiting our actions to formal representations or becoming satisfied with bureaucratic replies."[42]

Given this basic orientation to view procuratorial supervision in optimal terms, it should be no surprise that some jurists have turned to cybernetic modelling of procuratorial processes. Inherent in cybernetic control models is the idea that an output may be evaluated in relation to a set of norms or standards and deviations can be systematically reduced until an optimal outcome is reached. K. F. Skvortsov of the Institute of the Procuracy of the USSR has developed a cybernetic procuratorial control model in which an administrative action is evaluated (supervised) by the Procuracy in relation to a set of standards (the law), and deviations (violations) are protested until an optimal (legal) result is achieved.[43] Several obvious difficulties arise in this formulation. *First*, Skvortsov is describing a closed cybernetic system which fails to account for exogenous variables such as citizens' complaints and actions of courts, comrades' courts, and Party and trade union organizations. *Second*, the cybernetic model assumes a well-developed and clearly defined set of norms by which outputs may be evaluated. However, Soviet jurists admit that in many areas of law, including economic relations and administrative accountability, codification is an extremely complex task because the law and regulations are so diverse and contradictory. Yet, procurators nevertheless tend to see their function as the mechanistic application of clearly defined laws to administrative acts. B. P. Kochetov, Chief of the Department of General Supervision of the Leningrad Procuracy, said, "We merely apply the law in searching for legal violations. Either there has been a violation of the law or not. When a point of law is unclear, we consult with legal experts to help clarify it."[44] *Third*, cybernetic systems apply automatic controls, free of personal motivations and biases. However, procuratorial action depends upon the judgment of the procurator to act and is exacerbated by efforts of managerial and administrative officials to cover up cases of maladministration. *Finally*, Soviet jurists fail to acknowledge the existence of a margin of error in their control processes. Unlike most sophisticated automatic control systems which define deviation in relation to a range of acceptable output, most Soviet jurists hold to a notion of absolute compliance with the law. Neither can it be safely concluded that legality constitutes the bottom line of acceptable activity in administration, since evidence exists that procurators frequently choose to ignore many minor violations.

What Soviet scholars and jurists steadfastly refuse to acknowledge publicly is that, for a rational factory manager interested in fulfilling his production quota, there may be an incentive to produce substandard or incomplete products. In such cases, the proper role of procuratorial supervision is to alter the decision-making calculus of the factory manager. This I choose to call "strategic" as opposed to "optimal control." Strategic control seeks to decrease deviating outputs to an acceptable level by increasing the probability of detection and punishment. The goal is not zero defects, or conversely, optimal output. Instead, it recognizes that some defects and errors will occur; it merely strives to limit the frequency and extent of such deviations.

As we have noted with regard to substandard production and theft, the Soviet economy contains structural inadequacies that virtually insure the occurrence of legal violations. In the rush to fulfil quarterly and yearly plans, quality of production typically tapers off. Soviet economic planning also is hindered by notions of optimality in assigning gross amounts of resources. No allowance is made for waste, inefficiency, error, or "shrinkage," thus causing dislocations for secondary producers. In such cases, there appears to be a relunctance to hold higher administrators (ministers and *Gosplan* officials) responsible. Rather, most administrative, disciplinary and criminal proceedings are initiated against directors of *oblast'*, regional, or city enterprises, departments, factories, or state farms.

As in so many other areas, Soviet theory regarding procuratorial supervision of economic violations differs from its practice. Although Soviet procurators advocate optimal control, in actuality they are achieving a selective and strategic level of control. Cases published in the popular press and legal journals often focus on particularly blatant violations. The high level of publicity and strict punishments given in cases of theft, substandard production, padding or altering accounting records, or other economic violations, indicate that procurators are trying to reduce the frequency of such violations by increasing the perceived risk of detection and punishment. The desire to alter the incentive structure for "cutting corners" by managers, officials, or factory employees, is especially evident in the campaigns against low labor productivity, theft of state property, and other economic violations which periodically dominate procuratorial and legal journals. Finally, the strategic nature of procuratorial control is indicated by the willingness of procurators to ignore minor violations. Selective enforcement frees procurators from the heavy burden of handling all cases, distracting them from major violations. However, it also creates some uncertainty concerning what the permissible parameters of behavior are. This uncertainty may serve to prompt administrative officials to be more cautious than they would otherwise be. However, it can also act as an open invitation to officials to violate regulations, but to do so moderately and discreetly.

From this perspective, the change in the emphasis of procuratorial supervision in 1969 can be seen as a rational attempt to narrow the broad-ranging focus of procuratorial supervision to those violations which result in the greatest loss to the state. But procuratorial supervision at best provides only prophylactic protection against economic violations. The succesful eradication of wide-spread economic violations in the Soviet Union will ultimately depend upon the creation of effective internal auditing and control mechanisms within factories and enterprises and the elimination of those systemic factors that create conditions conducive to the continued existence of economic violations.

NOTES

1. Article 164 of the 1977 USSR Constitution. An English translation of the new Soviet Constitution by F. J. M. Feldbrugge and William B. Simons has been published in *Review of Socialist Law*, 4 (1978), No. 1, 57-84.

2. Archive of the Krasnodar *Krai* Court, Case No. 3-16-67.

3. Cited in Iu. V. Feofanov, *Sto protsentov zakona* (One Hundred Percent of the Law), (Moscow, 1970), pp. 45-58.

4. A collection of translations into English of all the cases of general supervision published in *Sotsialisticheskaia zakonnost'*–beginning in 1937 up to and including those published in 1973–can be found in Leon Boim and Glenn G. Morgan, *The Soviet Procuracy Protests: 1937-1973* (Leyden, 1978).

5. These explanations were provided in consultations with several jurists including S. G. Berezovskaia, V. I. Chermenskii, A. D. Berenzon, L. A. Nikolaeva, Iu. M. Kozlov, and K. F. Skvortsov.

6. S. G. Berezovskaia, "Puti razvitiia obshchego nadzora," (The Road of Development of General Supervision), in R. A. Rudenko (ed.), *Na strazhe sovetskikh zakonov* (On Guard for Soviet Laws), (Moscow, 1972), pp. 213-214.

7. S. G. Berezovskaia, *Prokurorskii nadzor za zakonnost'iu pravovykh aktov organov upravleniia v SSSR* (Procuratorial Supervision of Legality of Legal Acts by Administrative Organs in the USSR), (Moscow, 1959), p. 107. The representations made in 1959 are not reflected in the cases reprinted in *Sotsialisticheskaia zakonnost'* for 1959 and analyzed here.

8. Consultation with V. I. Chermenskii, Chief of the Department of General Supervision, Procuracy of the USSR, Dec. 3, 1975.

9. Consultation with S. G. Berezovskaia, Institute of the Procuracy of the USSR, Moscow, November 26, 1975.

10. *Ved. V.S. SSSR* 1961, No. 35, item 368.

11. "Russia in Recession," *Economist*, Jan. 24, 1970, 10-12.

12. Karl W. Ryavec, "Soviet Industrial Managers, Their Superiors and the Attempt at Planned Behavioral Change," *Soviet Studies*, 21 (1969), 208-229.

13. S. S. Ostroumov, *Sovetskaia sudebnaia statistika* (Soviet Judicial Statistics), (Moscow, 1970), p. 248, and V. S. Karasev, "Nekotorye dannye, kharakterizuiushchie primenenie mer ugolovnogo nakazaniia k nesovershennoletnim prestupnikam" (Data, Characterizing the Application of Measures of Criminal Sanction to Juvenile Offenders), in *Preduprezhdenie prestupnosti nesovershennoletnikh* (Prevention of Juvenile Crime), (Moscow, 1965), p. 225.

14. Walter D. Connor, *Deviance in Soviet Society: Crime, Delinquency and Alcoholism* (New York, 1972), pp. 150-152.

15. B. M. Dubrovinskii, "Nekotorye voprosy prokurorskogo nadzora v bor'be s melkimi khishcheniiami" (Several Questions of Procuratorial Supervision in the Struggle Against Petty Theft), in *Voprosy prokurorskogo nadzora* (Questions of Procuratorial Supervision), (Moscow, 1972), p. 61.

16. *Ibid.*, p. 66.

17. V. V. Gavrilov and V. S. Pimenov, "Nekotorye voprosy prokurorskogo nadzora za ispolneniem zakonov pri prieme na material'no otvetstvennuiu rabotu v torgovle"

(Several Questions of Procuratorial Supervision of Execution of the Laws Upon Acceptance for Materially Responsible Work in Trade), in *Voprosy teorii i praktiki prokurorskogo nadzora* (Questions on the Theory and Practice of Procuratorial Supervision), (Saratov, 1974), p. 162.

18. *Ibid.*, p. 163.

19. *Ibid.*, p. 162.

20. "Bor'ba za kachestvo–vsenarodnoe delo" (Fight for Quality–A National Concern), *Kommunist*, 1975, No. 16, 8.

21. *Sots. Zak.*, 1974, No. 4, 89-90.

22. For example see G. Beloshapko, "Bor'bu s narusheniiami zakonodatel'stva o kachestve produktsii–na pervyi plan" (Struggle Against Violations of Legislation on Quality of Production–In the Foreground), *Sots. Zak.*, 1976, No. 3, 12-16.

23. *Ibid.*

24. *Ibid.*

25. V. Kim and L. Ivanov, "Nadzor za ispolneniem zakonov ob otvetstvennosti za nedobrokachestvennoe stroitel'stvo" (Supervision of Execution of Laws on Accountability for Poor Quality Construction), *Sots. Zak.* 1975, No. 5, 35-38.

26. Cited in *New York Times*, Dec. 28, 1975, p. 7.

27. V. Kuznetsov, "Prokurorskii nadzor v bor'be s propiskami" (Procuratorial Supervision in the Struggle Against Padding), *Sots. Zak.*, 1975, No. 7, 13.

28. *Sots. Zak.*, 1975, No. 2, 85-86.

29. Data provided by the Laboratory for the Study of Procuratorial Supervision, Law Faculty, Leningrad State University.

30. *Ibid.*

31. *Ibid.*

32. For example see V. G. Rozenfeld, *Prokurorskii nadzor za sobliudeniem zakonnosti dolzhnostnykh lits predpriiatii* (Procuratorial Supervision of Observance of Legality by Officials in Enterprises), (Voronezh, 1973), pp. 49-51.

33. S. G. Berezovskaia and T. L. Markelov, "Nadzor za zakonnost'iu aktov organov upravleniia" (Supervision of Legality of the Acts of Administrative Organs), *Sots. Zak.* 1974, No. 12, 18.

34. Rozenfeld, *op. cit.*, p. 161.

35. *Ibid.*, Chapter 3.

36. Dubrovinskii, *op. cit.*, p. 61.

37. *Ibid.*

38. L. A. Nikolaeva, *Teoreticheskie i prakticheskie problemy obespecheniia zakonnosti v sovetskom gosudarstvennom upravlenii organami prokuratury i suda* (Theoretical and Practical Problems of Guaranteeing Legality in the Organs of Soviet State Administration by the Procuracy and the Court), (Unpublished doctoral dissertation, Leningrad State University, 1974), pp. 219-220.

39. Rozenfeld, *op. cit.*, p. 150.

40. See Jerry Hough, *The Soviet Prefects* (Cambridge, Mass., 1969) Philip D. Stewart, *Political Power in the Soviet Union* (Indianapolis, Ind., 1968), and Joel C. Moses, *Regional Party Leadership and Policy-Making in the USSR* (New York, 1974).

41. See Statute on Procuratorial Supervision in the USSR, May 24, 1955, *Ved. V.S. SSSR*, 1955, No. 9, item 222.

42. R. A. Rudenko, "Leninskie idei sotsialisticheskoi zakonnosti i printsipi organizatsii deiatel'nosti sovetskoi prokuratury" (Lenin's Ideas on Socialist Legality and the Principles of Organization and Activity of the Soviet Procuracy), in *Na strazhe sovetskikh zakonov* (On Guard for Soviet Laws), (Moscow, 1972), pp. 35-36.

43. K. F. Skvortsov, "K postroeniiu modeli prestupnogo povedeniia" (Towards the

Construction of a Model of Criminal Behavior), in *Voprosy ugolovnogo prava, ugolovnogo protsessa i kriminologii* (Questions of Criminal Law, Criminal Procedure, and Criminology), (Dushanbe, 1966), pp. 158-166.

44. Consultation with B. P. Kochetov, Chief of the Department of General Supervision, Leningrad Procuracy, Apr. 26, 1976.

CRIMES AGAINST THE CENTRAL PLANNER: 'OCHKOVTIRATEL'STVO' [1]

Stanislaw Pomorski*

1. Introduction

The economy of socialist states,[2] its values, policies, and structure, have left a clear mark on criminal legislation. One of the best visible manifestations of that is, of course, the special superior protection afforded to socialist ownership.[3] Another is the law on 'economic crimes." Soviet criminal codes exemplify well the generalization once made by an American authority that,

> "the contrast between Marxian socialist definition of crime and that of non-Marxian lands suggests that novelty appears primarily in the category of 'economic crimes.' "[4]

The experience of socialist countries in general, and that of the Soviet Union in particular, seems to suggest that, by and large, massive intervention of criminal law into economic life is an inherent feature of socialism.[5] Socialist criminal codes have been more punitive towards what is perceived as economic deviance, and that for at least four reasons:

1) They protect *specifically socialist* values, institutions, and policies. Therefore, certain types of conduct deemed socially useful or even respectable in a non-socialist society are criminalized by socialist states. Let us take as an example so-called speculation, a type of conduct criminalized in all socialist countries.[6] It consists of "the buying up and reselling of goods or any other articles for the purpose of making a profit."[7] In non-socialist societies, during

* I am grateful to Professor George Ginsburgs, who read a manuscript of this article, for his inspiring comments. Professor Roman Jakobson's suggestions concerning the etymology of *ochkovtiratel'stvo* were invaluable. The article benefited from the discussion held at the Conference on Social Engineering Through Law in the USSR, held on October 28-30, 1977, in New York; in particular I would like gratefully to acknowledge the comments by Professors Walter D. Connor, George Ginsburgs, and Leon Lipson. Ms. Paula Lazarus, a third year student at Rutgers-Camden School of Law, was very helpful in my research, working under a grant from the School. My special appreciation goes to Ms. Sarah Campbell for her editorial contributions and excellent typing.

peacetime, such conduct is perceived as normal trading activity. Why should it be criminalized in socialist law? One can think of a few rationales: A speculator receives a profit without performing any socially useful labor. Thus, he violates the principle of distribution of income "to everybody according to his work."[8] At the same time, he upsets the planned distribution of goods. He is likely to exacerbate scarcity, as well as to cause an increase in prices, thereby injuring consumers.[9] Therefore, the mischief of speculation is twofold: it smacks of capitalism and is likely to injure the consumer. The values protected by the statutes criminalizing speculation are socialist principles of income distribution, as well as planned distribution of goods and the interests of the consumers.

2) Some kinds of socially undesirable conduct that are left to private law sanctioning in non-socialist societies, or are without any formal sanctions whatever, have been transformed by socialist countries into "public law" issues and made targets of criminal law. So, for example, mismanagement or the issuance of poor-quality production are usually of no concern to criminal law in capitalist societies. Adverse consequences come either from simple failure on the market or from a civil action. A socialist economy transforms such conduct into matters of public concern because it causes harm to state (cooperative) property and to central planning—the two pillars of the economic system. Moreover, the market mechanism is inoperative, and civil action under the circumstances is unlikely. Consequently, issuance of poor-quality production[10] or mismanagement are criminalized.[11] Indeed, the very concept of mismanagement is changed: because the basic indicator of successful performance is the fulfillment of the plan, the failure to fulfill the plan may be, at least *prima facie*, assessed as a case of mismanagement.[12]

3) The socialist economy, especially in systems based on central economic planning, has its own characteristic dysfunctionalities. Criminal law tries to remedy them and thereby creates new types of crimes unknown elsewhere. A good illustration of this is "making additions to and other distortions of accounts concerning fulfillment of plans" (CC RSFSR, article 152-1), a crime which makes sense only under the conditions of economic planning, Soviet-style. Another illustration of an economic crime which belongs in this category is "private entrepreneurial activity by utilization of state, cooperative, or other social forms."[13] The crime has typically been committed by sales personnel of state-owned bars and restaurants, who simply serve their own beverages to the customers. This way they collect the handsome difference between regular retail prices of vodka, wine, coffee, or tea, and the prices charged in the restaurants.[14] The practice has been notorious in various service establishments run by the state or cooperatives. Recently, much more colorful cases have been reported by the Soviet press, especially from the Georgian SSR, where whole state factories have been controlled and run by industrious racketeers as their private enterprises.[15]

4) Finally, the highly centralized methods of economic management—with heavy reliance on administrative orders (planning acts) sent by the planner to subordinate units—naturally generate punitive kinds of reaction to disobedience, that is, punitive types of sanctioning. On the other hand, systems which leave more of the decision-making power with the operational entities provide for their greater economic and legal autonomy, with greater orientation toward a compensatory kind of liability.[16] The Soviet system, by and large, has shown a definite preference for strong control by the central planner and consequently a preference for punitive sanctioning of failure, whether in the form of administrative/disciplinary or criminal penalties. Within the limits of this basic orientation, the Soviet system has undergone various changes and modifications which, most of the time, turned upon the issue of "decentralization" and use of "economic" rather than "administrative" methods of management. This evolutionary process has had some impact upon the degree of intervention by criminal law in the sphere of economic life. All in all, with all the zig-zags and regressions, the developmental trend seems to be toward more restrained use of criminal law.[17]

As I have tried to show, "economic crimes" represent one of the central themes of Soviet criminal legislation, law enforcement, and criminal law theory. It is impossible, therefore, in an article-length study even to survey, let alone cover, the entire subject matter. Under the circumstances, I propose to focus on one specific offense of fundamental importance; that is, on the crime of *ochkovtiratel'stvo* or eyewash, defined as "making additions and other distortions of accounts concerning fulfillments of plan." At least three coincident justifications of this choice come to mind: *First* of all, the relevant statutes are designed to protect values and institutions of the foremost importance for the system: central planning, development of the economy, cooperation between operational entities, and rational and efficient decision-making by the central executive. *Secondly*, the mischief the law tries to remedy, that is, misinforming the central planner by operative entities, seems to represent one of the most acute and persistent problems plaguing the system. It is difficult to overestimate its adverse impact upon the functioning of the economic system and upon the social mentality. *Thirdly*, the above mentioned phenomena put to the test some basic ideological assumptions of Marxism-Leninism about a socialist economy and society. Thus, our discussion will lead us from a description and analysis of legal materials to broader questions concerning the functioning of the Soviet economic and social system.

2. Lasik Roitschwantz and Chairman Pashaev: A Case Study

Ilya Ehrenburg, in his satirical novel written in the late 1920's, *The Stormy Life of Lasik Roitschwantz,*[18] treats us to the following delightful story of his anti-hero.

Lasik Roitschwantz was an outstanding cutter of men's trousers. Since making ends meet in his profession was impossible, Lasik found a position in the Department of Animal Breeding. His job was to supervise the increase of pure-bred rabbits in the entire Tula District. After a short and peaceful period on the job, Lasik received a questionnaire from the central office including seventeen questions, all of them on rabbit-breeding. The questionnaire was troublesome, inasmuch as there weren't any rabbits in the district, since a couple that had been dispatched to the district some time ago had died on their way. At first, Lasik decided to answer all the questions honestly and generated thereby the wrath of his supervisor, Comrade Petrov. Let Ehrenburg take over the narrative for a little while.

> "Comrade Petrov began to rage up and down the corridor cursing:
>
> 'Are you crazy? Do you know what that means? Firing of personnel!
>
> . . .
>
> 'You don't understand a thing! You want to ruin us all! How can anyone fill out an official questionnaire with such answers? One has to give this thing special importance, stress the achievements. Charts, surveys, diagrams. If you sent in this nonsense, we would all go to prison. Change it all at once. You have no understanding whatsoever of the needs of the state." [19]

After having received the reprimand, Lasik worked for five days on the questionnaire, and here is the result of his labor:

> " 'Since the late pair was dispatched to Tula on November 18, 1924, the population of rabbits for the entire district may be set at 11,726.5 heads. In regard to the normal occurring functions and the lack of lemonade, the number as of January 1, 1930, in this entire district, is 260,784. Parasites, such as groundsquirrels or phylloxera rastatrix, were not noticed. As to other diseases, aside from the tragic end of the first pair, and the possibility of an insignificant runny nose, thanks to the heroic attitude of the District Board of Health, we have no complaints. The rabbits are being kept in plantations and in other cupboards. The birth increase in the population swells enormously.'
>
> . . . After completion of his work, Lasik decided not to disturb Comrade Petrov . . . and he sent the document to Moscow. For two long weeks he enjoyed peace and tranquillity . . . But, one day, the corridor resounded with the noise of crashing boots. A commission from Moscow had arrived to study the model rabbit-breeding enterprise in Tula.

> 'First of all, we would like to congratulate you, Comrade. The number of rabbits in your district alone is greater than that of the entire Soviet Union . . . We want to convince ourselves, on the spot. Tomorrow we shall drive out to the agricultural, experimental stations. Tell us, please, in which region is the greatest number of rabbits to be found?'
>
> 'Where to find them? Not in the region, nor in the cupboard, but here.'
>
> And proudly Lasik pointed at his small head. The corridor resounded once more with the crashing of boots, but this time it was an ominous sound. Comrade Petrov . . . raged:
>
> 'You have made fun of everybody! To jail! To court!' "[20]

And there we are: in court, in the *real* court this time. But switching from the world of literary fiction and satire to the world of official court reports will not be difficult—the similarity of related events is striking. The author of *Lasik Roitschwantz*, otherwise an unattractive writer, was in the 1920's still a keen observer of Soviet reality. Too keen for the taste of contemporary Soviet critics, who consider this work "subversive and cynical in its ambiguous attitude toward the Soviet regime."[21] So, we are now in the very real court: it is the Supreme Court of the USSR, which, on January 20, 1962, heard and decided the Case of Pashaev,[22] convicted of forging accounts on plan fulfillment. But, rather, let the official reporter speak. He at least cannot be accused of being subversive and cynical in his ambiguous attitude toward the Soviet regime:

> "The Judicial Division for Criminal Cases of the Supreme Court of the Azerbaidzhan SSR, on September 30, 1961, condemned M. P. Pashaev under article 167, paragraph 1, and article 172 of the Criminal Code of the Azerbaidzhan SSR to a punishment which consisted in relieving him from the office that he occupied.[23]
>
> Having considered the case on the protest of the Procurator General of the USSR against the judgment on the grounds of the lightness of the measure of punishment assigned to Pashaev and the incompleteness of the preliminary investigation, the Judicial Division for Criminal Cases of the Supreme Court of the USSR has established the following:
>
> Pashaev was found guilty of systematically abusing his official position as chairman of a collective farm and engaging in eyewash [*ochkovtiratel'stvo*] and additions, submitting false data on fulfillment by the collective farm of the state supply plans. In particular, during 1959 and 1960, he bought butter in the stores of the district, and bought meat, eggs, wool, and cattle from various persons, and then supplied all these items in fulfillment of the state plan. In all, he bought and shipped for

state supply 4,921 kilograms of butter. Moreover, as a result of the fact that he bought the butter for 28-30 rubles a kilogram and sold it for 21 rubles a kilogram, the collective farm suffered a significant loss. During 1960, Pashaev bought 7,791 eggs from various persons and turned them over to the state. Likewise, he bought 394 kilograms of wool and 74 head of cattle, which he turned over to fulfill the state supply plan.

Thus as the result of Pashaev's illegal actions, besides the deception of the state, the collective farm suffered damages in the amount of 64,759 rubles.

Pashaev, illegally conspiring with the accountant of the collective farm, Maksimov, who was also convicted in the case, indicated 480 hectares of corn instead of 350 in his report to the statistical board.

The facts of [eyewash], additions to accounts, and presentation of intentionally distorted accounting data concerning the fulfillment of plans of supply of agricultural products, were actually present which Pashaev himself does not deny. However, the investigative agencies and the court, in finding Pashaev guilty of this crime, did not verify and did not clarify the circumstances and the reasons which caused him to commit these actions. Pashaev, both at the preliminary investigation and in court, while not denying the facts stated above, testified that the abuses and additions were made by him with the knowledge and on the direct instruction of individual leaders of the district, and that similar actions were taking place in other collective farms, also at the demand of the same leaders of the district. In support of this fact, Pashaev relied on a written statement, included in the file of the case, by an inspector of the Commission of Soviet Control of the Council of Ministers of the Azerbaidzhan SSR of March 9, 1961, in which it is indicated that a similar practice was going on in many collective farms of the district, and that the leaders of district organizations knew about it and were repeatedly warned of its impermissibility. In the same statement, it is noted that abuses were also permitted in the milk plant, where butter was accepted from the collective farms instead of milk, and the director of the milk plant, Kheirul, destroyed documents evidencing illegal actions. However, the investigative organizations, and later the court, left Pashaev's explanations without verification. Moreover, the investigative agencies and the court did not even interrogate those persons who, according to Pashaev's explanation, compelled him to commit the above-mentioned illegal actions.

The verification of the explanations of the convicted person concerning the circumstances and causes which led him to commit illegal actions is of substantial significance for the correct resolution of the case. Therefore, the Judicial Division considers that the preliminary and judicial investigations of the present case were carried out one-sidedly and incompletely.

At the same time, it should be noted that if on supplementary investigation of the case the circumstances are not established which, according to Pashaev's explanation, compelled him to commit the illegal actions, then the punishment to which he was sentenced by the court should be considered too light.

The Judicial Division, agreeing with the protest, has ruled:

The judgment with respect to M. P. Pashaev shall be vacated and the case concerning him referred for a new investigation."

The case includes two distinguishable, although closely related, layers: the *first* layer involves the personal liability of Pashaev and his co-defendant Maksimov; the *second* involves the actions of those under whose orders Pashaev allegedly acted, and whom the opinion of the court only vaguely identifies as "district leaders."

Pashaev was convicted on two counts. One of his offenses consisted of a plain falsehood: Pashaev, in conspiracy with accountant Maksimov, reported to the statistical board 130 more hectares of corn than the area actually cultivated by "his" collective farm. The false reporting apparently did not cause any immediate harm to the state property.[24] The mischief of the offense was simply in misleading the planning agencies as to the actual performance of the farm. Another offense of which Pashaev was convicted is a little more difficult to grasp. After all, the state received its due: the delivery of butter, eggs, wool, and cattle was actually made and made at the officially approved scale of prices. Nevertheless, the mischief is there: the state was again "deceived," as the opinion put it, because the delivery originated from the wrong source. The collective farm should deliver to the state only what it actually produces. Through the plans of delivery, the collective farm's performance is measured and responsibility fixed. Pashaev, who failed to produce enough to satisfy the quotas assigned, bought up the goods from retail stores and private individuals to deliver them to the state and, thereby, to cover up his failure. While doing so, he caused several economically undesirable consequences: he misled the planner as to the performance of the farm managed by him; he disturbed the planned distribution of goods, removing them from the retail stores and thereby depriving individual consumers of the desirable goods; thirdly, he caused a substantial monetary damage to the collective farm, which had to pay the difference between the higher retail or market prices and the lower delivery prices.

Only now we reach the second layer of the case. It follows from the report[25] that Pashaev did not deny any of these facts. He claimed, however, that all the distortions of the accounts on the plan fulfillment and other "abuses" were made by him "on the direct instructions of individual leaders of the district, and that similar actions were taking place in other collective farms also at the demand of the same leaders of the district." The defendant even indicated that these individuals "compelled him to commit the abovementioned illegal actions."[26] The investigators, as well as the trial court, remained unimpressed by the defendant's allegations, which to some extent were substantiated by the record of the case. Nothing was done to verify them. The persons who allegedly "compelled" Pashaev were not even interrogated. In other words, Pashaev claimed that in his district deceiving the central planner was not at all perceived as deviant behavior. To the contrary: it was an established pattern of doing business by all chairmen of the collective farms under the orders and guidance of "district leaders." In a sense, Pashaev was a conformist, not a deviant. Who these mysterious and powerful "district leaders" were the opinion does not say, but guessing is not difficult. They could not be anybody else but executive officers of the district Party committee or the executive committee of the district Soviet. Why they were interested in directing and coordinating the eyewash in the district is obvious: they were responsible for the agricultural production in their district. Their own performance was measured by the fulfillment of the plan of delivery by kolkhozes and sovkhozes in the district. Since chairmen of the collective farms are in fact–if not in law–totally dependent on the district Party committee executives, the latter have enough power to exert pressure on them. Pashaev probably exaggerated in saying that he was "compelled" to engage in report-padding. What happened between the district committee and him was certainly something short of duress: there was a pattern of behavior which the committee expected to be followed; given the substantial coincidence of interests between the committee and its agents–chairmen of the collective farms–and a total career dependence of the chairmen upon the committee, resistance could hardly be expected. Pashaev, as a member of the local elite group, simply played the role expected of him by those who led the group. Characteristically, the group perceived its interests as opposed to those of the system as a whole, represented by the central planner.

The opinion of the Supreme Court, without saying that Pasheav's story is true, suggests that it is highly plausible and, if true, should have "substantial significance for the correct resolution of the case." Consequently the judgment below was reversed, and the case remanded "for a new investigation."

The legal relevance of Pashaev's story does not follow clearly from the opinion. Suppose it checks out well at the new trial. Is the defendant entitled to exoneration? Such a result would be rather difficult to justify. Obviously, Pashaev did not act in a state of necessity. Neither can he excuse himself by relying on flagrantly unlawful orders. The opinion does not seem to suggest that. If anything, the opinion hints that Pashaev is guilty in any case.[27] The only open issue with respect to him is the sentence. If he really acted under orders from "the district leaders," the punishment imposed by the trial court may be sustained, but if this is not established, "then the punishment to which he was sentenced by the court should be considered too light." The implications of the opinion for Pashaev are unequivocal: either he will help in the prosecution of his former superiors or his sentence will be substantially increased. He cannot win, but he certainly can lose after the new trial. Pashaev, his liability, and his sentence are only a target of secondary importance for the USSR Supreme Court. The Court has a strong suspicion that Pashaev's case was only the tip of the iceberg, that it represents just a little fraction of a much broader conspiratorial scheme. The Court wants to expose the scheme, the whole local conspiracy against the planner, and to use Pashaev as a vehicle for that.

If this is the clearly marked leaning of the USSR Supreme Court, the republican trial court, as well as the agencies investigating the case, showed just the oppposite tendencies. They remained entirely insensitive to Pashaev's allegations. Literally nothing was done to check them. As the opinion of the Court put it, "the investigative agencies and the court did not even interrogate those persons who, according to Pashaev's explanation, compelled him to commit the above-mentioned illegal actions."[28] One cannot resist an impression that the republican agencies *did not want* to expose the conspiracy against the plan. They did not want to hurt the local establishment. Obviously they wanted to leave its members immune. What were their motives? We can only speculate: maybe it was a desire to avoid confrontation with *apparatchiki*; maybe the feeling of solidarity with the local establishment was stronger than loyalty to the central executive. Whatever their motives, they disposed of the case smoothly and swiftly. Two bottom-level culprits were convicted but not dealt with severely. Pashaev was given the most lenient of all possible sentences: relieving him from the office he occupied. Since the additional punishment of "prohibition from occupying offices of a given kind" was not imposed, Pashaev remained eligible for another appointment, which maybe was even quietly promised to him. Also, a monetary damage caused to the collective farm was not exacted from the defendant.

Leniency of sentence, very typical of this type of cases in general,[29] in this case might have been dictated by some additional tactical considerations: to give the scape-goated defendant little reason to protest his conviction vigorously and to avoid his bringing the case to the attention of higher authorities.

The strongly contrasting approaches by the USSR Supreme Court and Procurator General of the USSR, on the one hand, and by the republican law enforcement agencies on the other, seem to reflect some deeper differences. Is it not the case that we are witnessing here the clash of interests between the central and the local, between the system as a whole–represented by the central planner–and one of the sub-systems? And that, in this carefully disguised struggle, the federal law enforcement organs speak for the central planner, whereas the republican agencies are on the other side of the barricade?

We will return to these questions a little later.

3. The Eyewash: Magnitude and Phenomenology of the Problem

All available sources indicate that the case of Pashaev is very characteristic in its two aspects: it illustrates a typical pattern of managerial deviant behavior, as well as typical reaction to such deviance by the law enforcement agencies.

The primary questions, however, are the following. How common is such deviance among Soviet managers? How many factory managers, chairmen of collective farms, directors of supply offices, leaders of construction sites, as well as their superiors and collaborators, have tried to feed the central planner doctored information? How often have they engaged in such activities? And what has been the magnitude of the deception committed?

The issue is not a trivial one, since centrally planned economies function on the assumption that the planner has maximum valid information at his disposal. The claimed rationality of the centrally planned systems rests on such an assumption, since only a well-informed planner is able to make rational decisions. Need I say that there is no way of knowing exact answers to our fundamental questions, and all we can try for is some rough approximation.

Even the most routine source of information—criminal statistics—is not available; all we have is some fractional, entirely unsatisfactory data.[30] The gap in the case of eyewash is, however, not particularly damaging, since criminal statistics seem to be so far behind reality that we can say there is practically no correspondence between the two. Prosecution of report-padding has been extremely erratic. In some republics, the situation may be fairly identified as one of non-enforcement.[31]

The "real" picture emerges from political documents, legislative acts, official and semi-official statements, and newspaper articles. The picture is rather impressive and may be summarized as follows.

Soviet political leadership has, for decades, perceived eyewash as a plague on the national economy. From the high concern shown, as well as the intensity and caliber of the remedies applied, one is led to believe that the problem was perceived as one of the greatest magnitude.

In 1952 Khrushchev, addressing the XIX Congress of the CPSU, denounced managers who tried to "outsmart the Party and the state" by padding reports on plan fulfillment.[32] In January 1961, a plenary session of the CPSU Central Committee was held which, in large part, busied itself with the disease of the eyewash that plagued economic life, especially agriculture.

Khrushchev made many angry statements against those who tried to "deceive the Party."[33] Some practical remedies followed very soon. On May 19, 1961, the Central Committee and the USSR Council of Ministries passed a Decree on the Measures to Prevent Facts of Deception of the State and on the Increase of Control over the Reliability of Accounts on the Fulfillment of Plans and Obligations.[34] Hundreds of thousands of Party activists were mobilized to do the job.[35]

The campaign was backed up by a special criminal statute[36] which specifically denounced the mischief of eyewash as "anti-state actions."[37] The statute was later incorporated in all of the republican criminal codes.[38] Report padding had, of course, been punishable before the edict was passed, as a variation of official misconduct.[39] The purpose of the new enactment was two-fold: *first*, to single out and denounce with particular fanfare this specific kind of wrong doing in order to dramatize the issue, to focus the attention of law enforcement agencies and, perhaps, to achieve a better visibility of the crime; *secondly*, to increase the severity of the sanction.[40] The edict and its apparent deterrent/preventive impact was welcomed with due enthusiasm.[41] The enthusiasm, however, proved to be quite premature. Addressing the Plenary Session of the Party Central Committee in November 1962, Khrushchev again found eyewash a major threat to the economy;

> "An important task of the central agencies . . . is to block deception, account padding, local interest tendencies, bribery, the squandering and theft of state material values, etc.
>
> *Instances of this kind are unfortunately quite widespread.*
>
> One hundred and forty cases of account padding and misrepresentation in accounting to the state were found at collective and state farms of Kalinin Province in the first quarter of 1962 alone; 116 such cases were found at collective and state farms of Zaporozhe Province in the first six months of this year. At the collective farm of the village of Nadzhi, in Georgia's Dasheti District, alone, the annual report was padded by listing 46 nonexistent heads of cattle, 50 pigs, and 226 sheep and goats.
>
> In approximately one year, 38 cases of falsifying the amount of work performed were disclosed in construction organizations of the Chita Economic Council . . . if these phenomena are not disclosed and swept away, they could become *a serious hindrance to our development*" (emphasis added).[42]

The phnomena have not since been swept away. They have been troubling Khrushchev's successors up to the most recent time. There have been a number of official and semi-official statements to this effect.[43]

The leadership once again raised the issue at the XXV Congress of the CPSU,[44] being soon seconded by the USSR Procurator General Rudenko.[45]

Strikingly, Rudenko, while discussing the tasks of the procuracy in regard to the national economy, put the struggle against eyewash at the very top of the list of priorities, ahead of fighting poor quality of production, mismanagement, and stealing socialist property.[46] This order of priorities alone seems to say a lot about the official assessment of the problem. It is striking that the issue was once again raised by Brezhnev in his address to the Supreme Soviet on the new Soviet Constitution. Brezhnev emphatically pointed to *ochkovtiratel'stvo* as a major problem which should be treated with the "full severity of law."[47]

The phenomenology of eyewash has been rich and involves a great variety of tricks. The most common are probably crude quantitative additions to the reports having no correspondence to actual performance. Some of these cases are interesting because the falsehoods have been unusually bold: here is the head of the state grape-growing trust who reported establishing five new farms with over 5,000 hectares of land under cultivation. None of these farms ever actually existed.[48] Here is the head of a construction site who reported building a large loading platform, but actually never did.[49] In some cases the culprits show more ingenuity: for example, they report deliveries of large amounts of cotton or wool or grain which never occurred but at least they cover it up by obtaining fictitious receipts from the supply office, often for money.[50] A very common technique of making illegal additions is reporting production manufactured in the next planning period (month, quarter, year) as finished in the preceding planning period.[51] Managers of construction sites transfer incomplete buildings to the users and report them as completed constructions.[52]

Ochkovtiratel'stvo may also consist of other than quantitative misrepresentations about economic performance: for example, misrepresentations concerning quality of production[53] or even the very nature of economic activity.[54]

Ochkovtiratel'stvo often coincides with other crimes. Reporting feigned success in the fulfillment of plans often generates undeserved payments in bonuses. Therefore, report padding may become a method of stealing socialist property, even if the latter is not a primary purpose of the culprit but rather a by-product of the principal crime.[55] According to the USSR Supreme Court, even if report padding was not committed *with the purpose* of obtaining bonuses unlawfully, but in fact bonuses were paid with the culprit's knowledge, such facts would justify conviction under two counts: eyewash and stealing socialist property.[56]

Cases have also been reported where the primary purpose of the defendants was stealing socialist property and the method used was report padding.[57] Bribery is not an unusual concomitant of eyewash, such as a payment for forged documents and similar cover-up services.[58]

Report-padding is a classical white-collar crime, Soviet-style, a crime committed by economic managers. Technically, it has to involve managers of operative entities and their chief accountants, since only these officers have the right and duty to report formally on the fulfillment of plans.[59] It is also the managers who have a primary interest in the crime: since they are responsible for the fulfillment of the plans, they are interested in showing successful performance and in concealing failures. Their ability to keep managerial positions, their prestige and chances of promotion, as well as a substantial part of their earnings, depend upon the reporting of success. But the managers are by no means the only beneficiaries of *ochkovtiratel'stvo*. The people who surround them also benefit from the crime and hence have a strong personal stake in false reporting. The group of beneficiaries includes some of their subordinates whose professional careers and earnings also directly depend on plan fulfillment. Practically the whole administrative and technical staff of the enterprise is vitally interested in reporting successful performance. Then come formal and not so formal superiors who also have a stake in the victories and defeats of the enterprises, construction sites, or collective farms within their jurisdiction. The professional and political competence of the superiors is judged on the basis of the performance by the entities under their supervision. The group of superiors with vested interests is broad and diversified: here may be included not only officers of the apparatus of economic administration, but also executives of the local party committees and of local Soviets. There is a definite community of interests and goals among all these people, interests and goals which often do not coincide with those of the system as a whole, represented by the central planner. In view of the aforesaid, it is not surprising to find that the managers engaging in *ochkovtiratel'stvo* act in a very cooperative environment, that they enjoy a lot of support in their endeavors, ranging from friendly neutrality and acquiescence to explicit encouragement and even pressure. Under the circumstances, it becomes understandable why *ochkovtiratel'stvo* often becomes a routine practice, going on for years, pursued by broad conspiratorial groups having good working relations with the establishment. Indeed, local leaders of various ranks often surface as organizers and coordinators of *ochkovtiratel'stvo* in their districts,[60] cities, and provinces,[61] or even whole union republics.[62]

Local authorities, as a rule, show a great deal of tolerance towards *ochkovtiratel'stvo*, turning a deaf ear to various signals of criminal misreporting, trying to minimize and dismiss even proven cases of the crime.[63]

As Professor Hough correctly put it,

> "Although the local Party officials have a strong self-interest in preventing actions that will lead to plan non-fulfillment, they (like the managers they supervise) may also have a self-interest in illegal or quasi-illegal actions that improve the economic performance of their area or

create the appearance of better economic performance" (emphasis added).[64]

It seems that all this justifies a certain redefinition of *ochkovtiratel'stvo*: it is more than a white-collar crime by economic managers; it is a crime of local establishments aimed at the central planner.

The question arises why it is necessary for the managers, their associates, and superiors to resort to deception. Why are they unable to achieve genuine success in the fulfillment of plans? What are the causes? Do they lie in defective planning or in indolent execution of the plans?

4. Policies and Patterns of Law Enforcement

All of this has to have a definite impact upon law enforcement. Indeed, enforcement of article 152-1 CC RSFSR may serve as a classical example of law nullification. To be sure, the central judicial and prosecutorial authorities, following the Party line, have shown high concern about it. Prosecutors and courts of lower levels have been repeatedly and emphatically instructed[65] that:

1) *ochkovtiratel'stvo* is a crime representing substantial social danger and therefore should be fought vigorously;
2) it is a matter of foremost importance that cases of *ochkovtiratel'stvo* be *fully* investigated and prosecuted, that is, that in every case all incidents of criminal activity be brought to light, all guilty persons prosecuted, and underlying causes of crimes exposed;
3) it is particularly important that not only immediate executors of criminal schemes but, first of all, their *organizers* be punished;
4) sentences should be proportionate to the degree of harm done and to the contribution made by each culprit; by and large, sentencing practices have been much too lenient;
5) the additional punishment of "deprivation of the right to occupy specified offices or to engage in specified activity" should be applied as a matter of general rule;
6) compensation for material damages done to the state, first of all by unjustified payments in bonuses, should be exacted from the defendants.

The above-outlined guidelines have been coupled with strongly worded criticism of the lower courts for their excessive leniency. The courts and prosecutors remainded for years strikingly unresponsive to the criticism and directives from above. The number of court cases has remained extremely low.[66] Prosecutors would fail to institute investigations or would drop charges in serious cases with overwhelming evidence of guilt; they would do it without any justification or, sometimes, with justifications bordering on absurdity.[67]

Cases prosecuted in courts were most of the time of minor significance. Indictments never covered all of the guilty persons involved. Typically, only secondary figures were brought to responsibility, whereas the real architects of the criminal schemes were left immune.[68] The mood of permissiveness and compassion also prevailed in the courtrooms. One would notice the uncritical attitude of the courts toward conspicuously inadequate indictments,[69] judgments of acquittal contrary to the weight of evidence,[70] nullification of the statutory sanction through lenient sentencing practices,[71] negligent treatment of the monetary harm done to the state.[72] Perhaps the most striking and the best documented is judicial permissiveness in sentencing: one of the obvious purposes of the 1961 edict[73] was to increase the severity of sanction and to override judicial leniency by the introduction of mandatory deprivation of freedom as a penalty. Under the statutory scheme, non-custodial punishment may be applied only in view of "exceptional circumstances."[74] The courts managed to reverse the statutory scheme completely. According to the analysis of judicial practice done for the staff of the USSR Supreme Court, only 11.6% of the persons convicted of *ochkovtiratel'stvo* were sentenced to deprivation of freedom; with regard to the remaining 88.4%, the courts applied a variety of non-custodial sanctions – predominantly suspended sentences (40%) or correctional labor tasks to be served at the place of employment.[75] Many convicts continued to hold their managerial positions after conviction. From only 21% of the convicts did the courts exact compensation for the harm done, and only in the amounts collected by the defendants themselves.[76] The additional punishment of deprivation of the right to occupy specified offices or to engage in specified activity is very selectively applied. Therefore, the majority of convicted persons either keep their managerial jobs or are immediately eligible for another appointment. Given the highly punitive sentencing patterns of the Soviet courts in general,[77] the leniency shown toward persons guilty of *ochkovtiratel'stvo* is even more striking.

The explanation of the selectivity of enforcement, as well as judicial leniency, seems to be easy.

With respect to many architects and organizers of eyewash–notably local state and Party dignitaries, leaders of provincial elite groups–local procurators are utterly powerless. They simply do not have enough power to prosecute them. The same may be true with respect to many managers who enjoy the support and protection of the local leaders.[78] But even in cases where procurators are in a position to bring charges, they are likely to decide against it for a variety of reasons. Such charges tend to be unpopular with the local leaders. The prosecuted defendants may embarrass or compromise the local establishment while defending themselves against the charges. They may expose broader schemes. They may have close and friendly relations with the district/city or province Party committee. They may be useful to them. Prosecuting secondary culprits, while giving immunity to the real bosses, must give uncomfortable feelings to people who perceive themselves as officers of the law. Finally prosecutors, as members of the state bureaucracy, must feel socially close to the culprits and identify with them. It is unlikely that they perceive them as wrongdoers, since false reporting to the central planner seems to be widely practiced by members of this social group.

Selective prosecution executed against secondary, minor culprits, who occupy in the bureaucratic structure the bottom level, seems to be a compromise. This much and only this much are law enforcers able and willing to yield to the pressure from above. The tribute to the central executive is so modest, however, that it almost never puts in jeopardy the group interests of the local bureaucracy.

The above explanation of the prosecutorial attitudes is fairly well applicable to judicial behavior as well.

It may hardly be expected from the Soviet judge that he would eagerly send to a labor colony a respected comrade who engaged in what all comrades in his position are routinely engaging in every day. Moreover, such a comrade usually claims, not without good reason, that he is being scapegoated, since all of his crimes have been encouraged, ordered, or at least approved of by his superiors. Obedience to orders from the Party officers is a highly cherished virtue in the Soviet system; independence and personal integrity are not. Judges, as agents of the system, may not remain deaf to such claims.

5. Some General Reflections

The phenomenon of eyewash sketched in the preceding sections invites some general reflections on the functioning of the Soviet economic and social system. The official explanation of *ochkovtiratel'stvo* as actions of corrupt individuals who "sneaked into" the managerial elite can hardly be taken seriously in view of the facts. The persistence, pervasiveness, and highly organized, practically institutionalized, nature of eyewash suggests that it must have some deeper roots in the system. The phenomenon seems to be a manifestation of the conflicts arising between the system as a whole (represented by the central executive/central planner) and its subordinate component entities (enterprises, economic associations, etc.) as well as between the central and the local, between the super-elite and the local establishment groups and cliques.

One wonders why these conflicts and struggles have surfaced in the form of deception and misinformation. An explanatory hypothesis which I propose to consider rests upon fundamental ideological assumptions concerning the structure and functioning of the Soviet system.

The Soviet economy, indeed the Soviet society as a whole, is organized according to a machine model: one center of political and economic disposition, supplied with maximum relevant data and equipped with infallible tools for their interpretation, makes all the important decisions. The decisions, conveyed to various parts of the system, are faithfully carried out, and their implementation is quickly and exactly reported back to the center.

Underlying the machine model is a fundamental assumption, that is, the assumption of ideal cooperation. According to this assumption, each and every part of the system cooperates with other parts and carries out its function under the direction of the center of disposition. Ideal coordination and cooperation is assured by the community of substantive goals and rational division of labor. Harmonious cooperation, according to the assumption, makes the system highly efficient and superior to the chaotic and anarchic system of a capitalist economy.[79] In fact, however, the Soviet economic system does not function according to the assumption of ideal cooperation. Actually, various parts of the system (such as operational production entities, territorial entities, agencies of economic administration, agencies of Party bureaucracy, etc.), pursue their own goals and interests not necessarily consistent with each other or with the parts and interests of the system as a whole. The real relationships between various parts of the system quite often appear to be relationships of competition, bargaining, and struggle, rather than cooperation.[80] The malady of eyewash is a symptom of one particular category of conflicts, that is, primarily conflicts between the central executive (representing the system as a whole), on the one hand, and subordinate operational entities on the other. As can be seen from the preceding discussion, each of the "combatting" parties is involved in a system of alliances which help in carrying out the struggle. Sometimes allies identify so strongly with the cause that they take over and play a principal role. So it has happened in those districts where eyewash is organized and orchestrated by the local Party officers or members of the general state administration. Thus, it appears that the primary Party organization as well as local Party organs, by and large, have failed in fulfillment of a function expected of them, namely the function "to alleviate the persistent inability of administrators to obtain all the information they need in order to make intelligent decisions."[81] Indeed, in many cases local Party organs have presided over conspiracies aimed at misinforming the central planner.

It is easy to see why eyewash has become a dominant method of struggle. Since under the ideologically binding dogmas of ideal cooperation–"the leading role of the Party," "monolithic unity of the Party," and "democratic centralism" an open struggle against the decisions by the central executive is totally illegitimate, the struggle had to take on disguised forms. Their common core is misinformation, double talk, and playing with the labels.

The malady of eyewash undermines another assumption fundamental to the centrally planned economy, namely, the assumption that the central executive has at its disposal maximum relevant information and hence is able to make rational decisions. In fact the central planner is wrapped up in misinformation, surrounded by Potemkin's villages having little correspondence with reality. The planner is, of course, aware that subordinate entities try to cheat him, and he tries to make up for that by introducing various "corrections." Need we say that these "corrections," under the circumstances, cannot be precise and that oftentimes they must be entirely arbitrary. Consequently, the planner makes his decisions for the future on the ground of unreliable, incomplete, and distorted information. Plans drafted on the ground of such information cannot be realistic, and their honest fulfillment can hardly be expected. Therefore, it seems that eyewash carries strong self-perpetuating potential.

One can think of various responses to the malady of eyewash. More radical ones would lead to substantial modifications of the machine model by leaving more spontaneity and freedom to operational entities. This kind of response has not appeared feasible to the Soviet policymakers up till now. Soviet responses have always been conceptualized as further perfection of the machine model, rather than its dismantling. Every campaign against *ochkovtiratel'stvo* entailed increases in inspection activities, establishing new inspection agencies, mobilization of volunteer inspectors, etc. Inspection agencies in turn have been responsible for the production of more rules and regulations, more written standards, which in turn have generated even more violations and, in turn, more inspection activities. Hypertrophy of inspection activities, their low efficiency, high costs and their negative impact upon production processes have created a problem *per se*.[82] The recent campaigns against eyewash include direct involvement of the procuracy in the inspection processes. The procuracy is now expected to use its powers of "general supervision" for the enforcement of "planning and contractual discipline."[83] The development is not surprising. It represents the next stage in the history of "the machine model" in action: disappointment with inspection agencies set up by the economic administration and the Party apparatus has led to a direct involvement of the law enforcement agency in the economic processes.

Assumptions of ideal cooperation and total rationality of the system certainly reach beyond the purely organizational sphere. These assumptions have important implications for social psychology, for the types of human relationships under socialism. The experience of cooperation for the common cause is likely to generate feelings of trust and friendship and is likely to shape attitudes of loyalty and candor. And indeed, that is what Soviet moral doctrine preaches as ideals.[84]

The reality is, as we have shown, quite different. This reality, full of conflicting interests fought for under disguised forms of misinformation, has left a clear imprint upon the moral atmosphere and upon the surrounding economic, and broader, public life in the USSR.

The participants are constantly experiencing and confronting lies: either actively, in the case of those who make misrepresentations to their superiors, or passively, in the case of those to whom these misrepresentations are addressed and whose psychological profile is strongly colored by suspicion and distrust. This psychological experience–in which public life is first of all a game of appearances and suspicion–is by no means limited to the immediately participating parties. As we have seen in the preceding sections, the immediate participants are included in a complex network of collaborators and supporters who sometimes even run the game from behind the scene. Neither can we say that the experience of lies, distrust, and suspicion is shared by the elite members only. The masses are quite aware of what is going on since the game of appearances is being played out in the open. The inhabitants of Cheliabinsk were certainly aware that the success of the housing project was "slightly exaggerated," especially those who were offered apartments without roofs, walls, and doors.[85]

Needless to say, the phenomenon of *ochkovtiratel'stvo* is neither a Soviet discovery nor an exclusively Soviet problem. The bold undertakings of Prince Potemkin long preceded the birth of the Soviet state. Difficulty in receiving adequate information from lower levels has been troubling administrators of large bureaucratic organizations of the western world as well. American literature, for example, is full of discussions of eyewash in corporate and administrative life.[86] The point is that eyewash in the USSR, as well as in some other socialist countries, has become much more pervasive, almost omnipresent. The inevitable question is: why?

The most obvious explanation is the magnitude and pervasiveness of bureaucratic structures and procedures in the Soviet economy as well as its highly centralized nature. The whole economy of the country is managed by the state. The state plays the roles of a super-producer, super-distributor, and super-employer. Moreover, in this vast country the decision-making process is highly centralized: most decisions of any consequence are reserved for the central planner and his agents. Since eyewash is a by-product of bureaucratic organization and procedures, the all-embracing nature of such organization and procedures inevitably makes eyewash more pervasive in the Soviet Union than elsewhere.

Any economic system with such an enormous potential for bureaucratic eyewash should have inbuilt devices of self-correction, an effective signaling system able to discover misinformation. A great paradox of the Soviet system, however, is that its capacity for self-correction is much lower compared to the systems of the capitalist West and that at least for two reasons:

First of all, the market mechanism, which at some point could spontaneously, if ruthlessly, expose the failure of subordinate operative entities, has been switched off. All the attempts to use artificial substitutes such as "economic accountability" and "planned contracts," for whatever reason have proved to be ineffective. *Secondly*, severe restraints imposed upon freedom of expression reduce significantly the chances of *ochkovtiratel'stvo* by local establishment groups being exposed to public criticism. Therefore, two basic signalling mechanisms, one economic and the other political, have been discarded. The strong commitment of the Soviet system to "the machine ideal" appears therefore to be self-defeating.

Finally, we should look at *ochkovtiratel'stvo* from a broader perspective, as a part of a larger whole, as a fact of Soviet political culture. Misrepresentations as a fundamental experience of public life have been neither limited to the sphere of the national economy [87] nor have they been aimed exclusively against the superior authorities. Probably the most pervasive trait of public life in the Soviet Union and in Eastern European socialist countries is a dramatic discrepancy between various ideological principles on the one hand and social experience on the other. Here belongs, for example, the fundamental discrepancy between the ideology of popular participatory democracy [88] and the social experience of total control by the state-party apparatus. Here we can mention, to give another example, the discrepancy between the ideology of affluence and the social experience of scarcity. [89] The whole ideological work of the state-party, the whole enormous indoctrination effort is aimed at projecting an image of the real world consistent with current ideological assumptions. But, in order to do that, it is necessary to distort reality by banning important segments of information about public life as well as to engage in massive misrepresentations of it. Indeed, the public is fed every day all kinds of misinformation from numerous propaganda outlets. At the same time, censorship is busy trying to ban any information inconsistent with the officially projected image of the world. [90] This experience of living in a socialist society (of the Soviet type) was ably summarized by a distinguished Polish writer Andrzej Kijowski:

> "the essence of the system prevailing here lies not so much in its cruelty, as the liberal stereotype would have it, not in its exploitation, as the leftist stereotype would wish it, nor in the extermination of national and religious values, as the rightist stereotype proclaims. Its essence is a lie which permeates every sphere of our life." [91]

Since the experience of public life has basically been an experience of lies, the common man as well as members of the establishment share an assumption that the value of truth and moral norms related to it are simply irrelevant. There is no expectation of truth in public life. Candor, to be sure, remains a virtue cherished in the personal-life compartment, whereas in public life it is simply irrelevant, and if practiced would be perceived at least as naiveté or even as plain stupidity.

Considered in this broader context, *ochkovtiratel'stvo* as a form of managerial deviance fits well the over-all picture of public life in the Soviet Union. It is very much a part of the political culture of lies.

Last, but not least, there seem to exist certain currents in the Russian pre-revolutionary history showing clear kinship with *ochkovtiratel'stvo* Soviet-style. First, we have the lack of tradition of candor and loyalty toward the state. Judging from available historical and literary sources, it seems that deceiving the state or simply lying to the state was not only very common but also generally perceived as acceptable in imperial Russia. [92]

Second, there was a strong tendency to present things belonging to the realm of public life in a much better light than was true in reality: erecting façades to cover much gloomier substance. [93]

The two currents spectacularly coincided in the immortal enterprise of Prince Potemkin—a genius and founding father of *ochkovtiratel'stvo*—one of those imperial dignitaries who found swarms of able and willing disciples in the Soviet Union.

NOTES

1. The etymology of the word *ochkovtiratel'stvo* and of the underlying phrase *vteret' ochki* offers no particular difficulties. The phrase was already known in the nineteenth century. V. I. Dal' quotes it in his famous *Tolkovyi slovar' zhivago velikaruskago iazyka* and illustrates it with the expression *nadet' na kogo (komu na nos) ochki*—to put glasses on somebody (on somebody's nose), and interprets its meaning as *odurachit'*—to fool (somebody). Compare V. I. Dal', *Tolkovyi slovar' zhivago velika-ruskago iazyka* (Definitional Dictionary of the Living Great Russian Language), 2d ed. (Moscow, 1881), Vol. II, p. 664. This imagery of the idiom *vteret' ochki* seems, however, to be secondary. The first element of the compound *ochkovtiratel'stvo* must have referred rather not to *ochki*—glasses—but to the singular, *ochko*—pip (plural, *ochki*—pips), on cards or dice. Dal' himself in the same paragraph mentions a sharper's technique of rubbing in false pips to make a card higher. Apparently, the expression *vtirat' ochki* belonged originally to sharpers' argotism and later the derivative *ochkovtiratel'stvo*—eyewash—must have been formed and included in the journalistic, political, and forensic language. As to the current meaning of the word, compare quotations from the two standard dictionaries of the contemporary Russian:

> "Ochkovtiratel'stvo: Vtiranie ochkov, obman s tsel'iu predstavit' chto nb. v bolee vygodnom polozhenii, chem na samom dele.—*Ob"iavit' reshitel'nuiu bor'bu ochkovtiratel'stvu.*"

D. N. Ushakov (ed.), *Tolkovyi slovar' russkogo iazyka,* Vol. II (Moscow, 1938), 1035.

> "Ochkovtiratel'stvo: Namerenoe skryvanie nedostatkov, izobrazhenie chego-libo v bolee vygodnom svete, chem na samom dele, obman—*Rukovoditeli—to zdes'narod byvalyi, umeiut tovar litsom pokazat'. V odnoi MTS u nikh* [*v raione*] *kolkhozy bogatye, vsekh gostei tuda voziat . . . Staraia bolezn'—ochkovtiratel'stvo.* Ovechk. Raion. budni."

Slovar' sovremennogo russkogo literaturnogo iazyka, Vol. 8 (Moscow-Leningrad, 1959), p. 1815.

2. By "socialist states" I mean those states which adhere to a social order built upon the non-private ownership of the basic means of production. This operative definition is being employed rather than others which are committed for or against the concept, or are emotionally laden. See P. D. J. Wiles, *The Political Economy of Communism* (Cambridge, Mass., 1962), p. 31.

3. Compare S. Pomorski, "Criminal Law Protection of Socialist Property in the USSR" in D. Barry, G. Ginsburgs, P. Maggs (eds.), *Soviet Law After Stalin, Part I, The Citizen and the State in Contemporary Soviet Law* (Leyden, 1977), p. 353 ff.

4. J. N. Hazard, *Communists and their Law, A Search for the Common Core of the Legal Systems of the Marxian Socialist States* (Chicago and London, 1969), p. 478.

5. J. Andrejew, *Zarys prawa karnego państw socjalistycznych* (Outline of Criminal Law of Socialist States), (Warsaw, 1975), p. 110.

6. *Id.*, p. 112.

7. The 1960 Criminal Code of the RSFSR, hereafter CC RSFSR, art. 154, and corresponding provisions of criminal codes of other union republics.

8. A. A. Piontkovskii (ed.), *Kurs sovetskogo ugolovnogo prava, v shesti tomakh* (Handbook of Soviet Criminal Law in Six Volumes), (Moscow, 1970), Vol. V, p. 479; Hazard, *op. cit.*, p. 210. The same policy has surfaced in the prohibition of "activity as a commercial middleman carried on by private persons as a form of business for the purpose of enrichment" (CC RSFSR, art. 153, para. 2). The policy underlies another provision, which makes a crime of "private entrepreneurial activity by utilization of state, cooperative, or other social forms" (CC RSFSR, art. 153, para. 1). In the latter context, the policy certainly overlaps with other economic policies, such as protection of state resources against misuse for the purpose of making profit, and protection against illegal competition. The policy is also apparent from the prohibition against using hired labor (CC RSFSR, art. 162).

For a more recent general overview of "economic crimes," see V. Chalidze, *Ugolovnaia Rossiia* (Criminal Russia), (new York, 1977), p. 246 ff.

9. Piontkovskii, *op. cit.*, p. 479.

10. CC RSFSR, art. 152; for a general discussion, see A. L. Belakhov, *Ugolovnaia otvetstvennost' za vypusk nedobrokachestvennoi, nestandartnoi i nekomplektnoi produktsii* (Criminal Liability for the Issuance of Poor-Quality, Substandard and Incomplete Production), (Moscow, 1971).

11. Compare CC RSFSR, art. 172. For a further discussion see B. V. Zdravomyslov, *Dolzhnostnye prestupleniia. Poniatie i kvalifikatsiia* (Official Crimes. The Concept and Classification), (Moscow, 1975), particularly p. 120 ff.; Andrejew, *op. cit.*, p. 111.

12. Failure to fulfill the economic plan has been specifically criminalized by at least five of the Soviet republics. See Criminal Codes of Moldavia (art. 155); Georgia (art. 163); Uzbekistan (art. 171); Kazakhstan (art. 151), and Armenia (art. 152) in *Ugolovnoe zakonodatel'stvo Soiuza SSR i soiuznykh respublik* (Criminal Legislation of the USSR and the Union Republics), (Moscow, 1963).

13. Compare CC RSFSR, art. 153, para. 1; Polish CC, art. 223; Bulgarian CC, art. 226.

14. G. Feifer, *Justice in Moscow* (New York, 1964), p. 297 ff.

15. R. Kaiser, *Russia. The People and the Power* (New York, 1976), p. 111 ff. For an anecdotal account, see Y. Brokhin, *Hustling on Gorky Street* (New York, 1975), p. 35 ff.

16. G. Eörsi, "Law and Economic Reform in Hungary" in G. Eorsi and A. Harmathy (eds.), *Law and Economic Reform in Socialist Countries* (Budapest, 1971), p. 110 ff.

17. Andrejew, *op. cit.*, p. 113.

18. For the purpose of the present paper, I am using the 1960 New York edition of the book. No doubt in writing "The Stormy Life," Ehrenburg was strongly influenced by Jaroslav Hašek's *Adventures of the Brave Soldier Schweik*. Lasik, like Schweik, due to his apparently naive but in substance rationalistic attitude, exposes irrationalities, hypocrisy, and cruelties of the system.

19. Ehrenburg, *op. cit.*, p. 90.

20. *Id.*, p. 91 f.

21. M. Slonim, *Soviet Russian Literature. Writers and Problems, 1917-1967* (London, 1967), p. 212.

22. *BVS SSSR*, 1962, No. 2, p. 32-33; an English translation of the case by Professor Harold J. Berman appeared in *Soviet Statutes and Decisions*, 1 (1965), 125-127. The case is quoted in Professor Berman's translation.

23. Articles 167 and 172 of the Criminal Code of Azerbaidzhan SSR correspond to articles 170 and 175 of the CC RSFSR.

24. The eyewash was "plain" in the sense that the forged report did not generate any payments in bonuses. Analogous mischiefs committed by the managers of state

enterprises often result in illegitimate payments of bonuses to the culprits and/or to other employees.

25. Berman, *op. cit.*, p. 126.

26. *Id.*, p. 127.

27. Compare the syllabus of the decision, *id.*, p. 125.

28. *Id.*, p. 127.

29. See notes 63-64 and 73-74 and accompanying text.

30. We know, for example, that the whole group of "economic crimes," of which *ochkovtiratel'stvo* is just one, represented a few years ago 5% of the total caseload of the Soviet courts. S. Ostroumov, *Sovetskaia sudebnaia statistika* (Soviet Courts' Statistics), (Moscow, 1970), p. 248; W. D. Connor, *Deviance in Soviet Society. Crime, Delinquency and Alcoholism* (New York and London, 1972), pp. 150-152.

It has been reported that, in the two-month period of January-February 1962, courts of the seven union republics (including RSFSR) disposed of 37 cases of report-padding, while during the same period such cases were totally unknown to the courts of the remaining eight union republics. I. Iakimenko, "K itogam izucheniia sudebnoi praktiki po delam o pripiskakhi i drugikh iskazheniiakh otchetnosti" (Study of Judicial Practice in Cases on Additions and Other Distortions of Accounting), *BVS SSSR* 1962, No. 2, p. 41. Strikingly, the list of eight union republics without recorded cases of *ochkovtiratel'stvo* includes Tadzhik SSR, the land where all agriculture had been run on fraud for years. Compare V. Bulgarin, "Bor'ba s khishcheniiami sotsialisticheskoi sobstvennosti v sel'skom khoziaistve, sovershaemymi putem pripisok" (Fighting Stealing of Socialist Ownership in Agriculture Committed Through Additions), *Sots. Zak.*, 1963, No. 1, 33. Perhaps the most spicy detail reported by Bulargin, then the Procurator of the Tadzhik SSR, was that his predecessor in the office had been actively involved in *ochkovtiratel'stvo* on cotton deliveries.

31. V. Kulikov, "Iskazhenie otchetnykh dannykh–protivogosudarstvennoe deianie" (Distortion of Accounting Data–An Antistate Action), *Sots. Zak.*, 1973, No. 5, 9.

32. Quoted in V. Solovev, *Bor'ba s dolzhnostnymi zloupotrebleniiami, obmanom gosudarstva i pripiskami po sovetskomu ugolovnomu pravu* (Struggle Against Official Abuses, Deception of the State and Additions under Soviet Criminal Law), (Moscow, 1963), 16 f.

33. *Plenum Tsentral'nogo Komiteta Kommunisticheskoi partii Sovetskogo Soiuza. 10-18 ianvaria 1961 goda* (Plenary Session of the Central Committee of the Communist Party of the Soviet Union. January 10-18, 1961), (Moscow, 1961), p. 592 f. Khrushchev illustrated his criticism by giving several examples of eyewash by chairmen of collective farms and managers of state farms who had engaged in buying up meat or cattle from private individuals and then delivering them in the fulfillment of assigned quotas. Apparently, Pashaev was only following a well-established pattern.

34. B. Leontiev, *Otvetstvennost' za khoziaistvennye prestupleniia* (Liability for Economic Crimes), (Moscow, 1963), p. 10.

35. V. Zelenov, *Bor'ba s ochkovtiratel'stvom i pripiskami* (Struggle Against Eyewash and Additions), (Moscow, 1964), pp. 47-60.

36. Edict of the Presidium of the Supreme Soviet of the USSR, May 24, 1961 "On Liability for Additions and Other Distortions of Accounts Concerning Fulfillment of Plans," *Ved. V.S. SSSR*, 1961, No. 22, item 225.

37. *Id.*, preamble.

38. Leontiev, *op. cit.*, p. 11.

39. Solovev, *op. cit.*, p. 18.

40. *Id.*

41. Iakimenko, *op. cit.*, p. 40.

42. Pravda, Nov. 20, 1962, quoted in CDSP, 24 (1962), No. 48, p. 8.

43. Compare: Decree No. 6 of the Plenum of the Supreme Court of the RSFSR, December 2, 1961, "On Judicial Practice in the Cases of Additions and Other Distortions of State Accounting in Fulfillment of Plans" in *Postanovleniia Plenuma Verkhovnogo Suda RSFSR* (Decrees of the Plenum of the Supreme Court RSFSR), (Moscow, 1967), p. 28 ff.; Decree No. 1 of the Plenum of the Supreme Court of the USSR, January 12, 1973, "On Judicial Practice in the Cases of Additions and Other Distortions of Accounting on Fulfillment of Plans," *BVS SSSR*, 1973, No. 1, p. 7 ff; Decree No. 4 of the Plenum of the Supreme Court of the USSR, February 25, 1977, "On the Process of Implementation of the Decree of the Plenum of the Supreme Court of the USSR of January 12, 1973 'On Judicial Practice, etc.,' " *BVS SSSR*, 1977, No. 2, p. 13 ff; L. Brezhnev, Report of the Central Committee of the CPSU to the XXV Party Congress in *XXV s"ezd Kommunisticheskoi partii Sovetskogo Soiuza* (XXV Congress of the Communist Party of the Soviet Union), Vol. 1 (Moscow, 1976), p. 84; R. Rudenko, "XXV s"ezd KPSS i zadachi prokuratury" (The XXV Congress of the CPSU and Tasks of the Procuracy), *Sots. Zak.*, 1976, No. 5, p. 9 ff; Decree of the Plenum of the Supreme Court of the USSR, No. 1, March 26, 1976, "On the Elevation of the Level of Justice Administration in the Light of the Decisions of the XXV Congress of the CPSU," *BVS SSSR*, 1976, No. 3, p. 7 f; M. Maliarov, First Deputy Procurator General of the USSR, "Accountable in Rubles," *Izvestiia*, Jun. 11, 1974, *CDSP*, 26 (1974), No. 23, p. 27 f. See also recent remarks by L. Brezhnev included in his report to the USSR Supreme Soviet on the new Soviet Constitution. *Pravda*, Oct. 5, 1977, p. 2.

44. Brezhnev, *op. cit.*

45. R. Rudenko, *op. cit.*, p. 9.

46. *Id.*, p. 9 f.

47. *Pravda*, Oct. 5, 1977, p. 2.

48. Zelenov, *op. cit.*, p. 37.

49. Case of Krivorotov *et al.* in *Sbornik postanovlenii Verkhovnogo Suda RSFSR 1961-1963* (Collection of Decrees of the Supreme Court of the RSFSR 1961-1963), (Moscow, 1964), p. 201.

50. Zelenov, *op. cit.*, p. 60; Bulargin, *op. cit.*, p. 34 f; Case of Mylnikov and Popovchenko in *Sbornik*, note 49 above, p. 316.

51. Zelenov, *op. cit.*, p. 77.

52. "Deceivers Punished," *Pravda*, Mar. 30, 1961, cited in *CDSP*, 13 (1961), No. 13, p. 25 f; "Report Padding," *Izvestiia*, Jul. 16, 1974, cited in CDSP, 26 (1974), No. 28, p. 19.

53. Zelenov, *op. cit.*, p. 75.

54. Compare "Living Descendants of Lieut. Kizhe," *Izvestiia, May* 13, 1971; cited in *CDSP*, 23 (1971), No. 29, p. 28), reporting the following story:

> "The repair-and-construction administrations of the Rostov Everyday-Service Construction Trust have constantly received bonuses for overfulfilling the plan. But one day it was discovered that the trust does almost no repair-and-construction work; its administrations simply sell building materials and report the amounts obtained in this way as payments for services rendered to the population. In the past 18 months alone, the six administrations have reported the fulfillment of the plan for services to the public in the amount of 920,000 rubles! Steel, roofing, and lumber have been sold to collective and state farms, and then false documents have been drawn up stating that these materials were used in housing repairs."

55. Bulargin, *op. cit.*, p. 33.

56. Decree No. 4 of the Plenum of the Supreme Court of the USSR, February 25, 1977, note 43 above, p. 15.

57. Bulargin, *op. cit.*, p. 33 ff.

58. *Id.*

59. Decree No. 1 of the Plenum of the Supreme Court of the USSR, January 12, 1973, note 43 above, p. 9; Decree No. 4, note 43 above, p. 15.

60. G. Toporov, "Reshitel'no presekat' popytki obmana gosudarstva" (Decisive Prevention of Attempts at Deceiving the State), *Sots. Zak.*, 1961, No. 9, p. 11.

61. "Deceivers Punished," note 52 above, p. 25 f.

62. Bulargin, *op. cit.*, p. 33.

63. *Pravda*, Sept. 5, 1971, cited in *CDSP*, 23 (1971), No. 36, p. 26; *Pravda*, Nov. 20, 1971, cited in *CDSP*, 23 (1971), No. 47, p. 31.

64. J. F. Hough, *The Soviet Prefects: The Local Party Organs in Industrial Decision-making* (Cambridge, Mass., 1969), p. 200.

65. Compare: (1) Decree of the Plenum of the Supreme Court of the RSFSR, No. 6, December 2, 1961, note 43 above; (2) Decree No. 1, note 43 above; (3) Decree No. 4, note 43 above.

66. Kulikov, *op. cit.*, p. 9 f.

67. Kulikov, *op. cit.*, p. 10; N. Gorsheneva, "V bor'be s narusheniiami gosudarstvennoi distsipliny" (In the Struggle Against Violations of State Discipline), *Sots. Zak.*, 1975, No. 7, 10; Toporov, *op. cit.*, p. 12 f; Iakimenko, *op. cit.*, p. 42.

68. Toporov, *op. cit.*, p. 12; Decree No. 6, note 43 above, p. 29 f; Iakimenko, *op. cit.*, p. 42; Decree No. 1, note 43 above, p. 7; Decree No. 4, note 43 above, p. 13; "Rassmotrenie del o pripiskakh i drugikh iskazheniiakh otchetnosti o vypolnenii planov (obzor sudebnoi praktiki)" (Consideration of Cases of Additions and Other Distortions of Accounting on the Fulfillment of Plans) (Overview of Judicial Practice), *BVS SSR*, 1973, No. 2, p. 41.

69. Kulikov, *op. cit.*, p. 10; Gorsheneva, *op. cit.*, p. 10.

70. Case of Mylnikov and Popovchenko, note 50 above, p. 316; the case appeared in English translation by Professor H. J. Berman in *Soviet Statutes and Decisions*, 1 (1965), 80-83.

71. "Rassmotrenie," note 68 above, p. 41.

72. *Id.*, p. 42.

73. Note 36 above.

74. Compare CC RSFSR, arts. 43 and 152-1.

75. "Rassmotrenie," note 68 above, p. 41; Kulikov, *op. cit.*, p. 11.

76. "Rassmotrenie," note 68 above, p. 42.

77. S. Pomorski, "Communists and Their Criminal Law" (forthcoming).

78. Compare Kulikov, note 31 above, p. 10.

79. M. Hirszowicz, *Komunistyczny lewiatan* (Communist Leviathan), (Paris, 1973), p. 92 ff; S. Pomorski, "The Soviet Economic Associations: Some Problems of Legal Status and Organization after the 1973 Reform," *Review of Socialist Law*, 2 (1976), No. 3, 129, 157.

From Soviet writings see A. Volin, "Sotrudnichestvo i vzaimnaia pomoshch'–osnova sotsialisticheskikh otnoshenii mezhdu predpriiatiiami" (Cooperation and Mutual Help–A Foundation of Socialist Relations Between Enterprises), *Kommunist*, 1959, No. 3, p. 49 ff.

80. Hirszowicz, *op. cit.*, p. 94.

81. A. Hough, *op. cit.*, p. 99.

82. *Id.*

83. Gorsheneva, *op. cit.*, p. 10; N. Bezriadin, V. Rozenfeld, "Prokurorskii nadzor v

bor'be za ukreplenie trudovoi i gosudarstvennoi distsipliny" (Procuratorial Supervision in the Struggle to Strengthen Labor and State Discipline), *Sots. Zak.* 1977, No. 6, p. 8 ff. Compare the interesting statistics on procuratorial "general supervision" actions prompted by "economic violations" included in the paper in this volume by Gordon B. Smith, "Procuratorial Supervision of Economic Violations in the USSR," especially Tables 2 and 5.

84. Compare, The Moral Code of the Builder of Communism, Sections 5 and 6.

85. See notes 59-62 and accompanying text.

86. Hough, *op. cit.*, p. 99; H. A. Simon, *Administrative Behavior*, 3d ed. (New York, 1976), p. 163; A. Downs, *Inside Bureaucracy* (Boston, 1967), p. 118.

87. Compare, for instance, the rather impressive activity by the Moscow militia which suppressed information about a large proportion of reported juvenile offenses "by not putting them on the official record." Lt. Col. Mamykin, chief of the 130th Militia Precinct in Moscow, was quoted as saying:

> "If I were to send genuine figures about child crime in my precinct into the city militia headquarters, I would not last a day in my job. *This is what they all do*; I am not the only one" (emph. added).

Compare A. Shtromas, "Crime, Law, and Penal Practice in the USSR," *Review of Socialist Law*, 3 (1977), No. 3, p. 316.

88. Constitution (Fundamental Law) of the Union of Soviet Socialist Republics, *Izvestiia*, Oct. 8, 1977, Arts. 1-3, 48, Eng. transl. by F. J. M. Feldbrugge and William B. Simons in *Review of Socialist Law*, 4 (1978), No. 1, 57-84.

89. S. Pomorski, "Criminal Law Protection of Socialist Property in the USSR" in D. Barry, G. Ginsburgs, P. Maggs (eds.), *op. cit.*, p. 243.

90. Compare, for example, the following excerpts from Polish censorship documents:

> "The publication of information on the limitations of the freedom of action of communists in Egypt, Algeria, Sudan, Iraq, Libya, and Syria is forbidden."

> "There should be no disclosure about the increasing pollution of rivers flowing from Czechoslovakia."

Quoted in "How the Censors Build Up a False Picture of the World," *The Times* Sept. 26, 1977.

91. Quoted in S. Baranczak, "Poland's Unofficial Crusade: Publish and Be Free," *The Times*, Dec. 23, 1977, p. 10.

92. R. Hingley, *The Russian Mind* (New York, 1977), p. 93-94.

93. T. Szamuely, *The Russian Tradition* (New York, 1974), pp. 3-9; Hingley, *op. cit.*, p. 94.

LEGAL POLICY UNDER KHRUSHCHEV AND BREZHNEV: CONTINUITY AND CHANGE

Robert Sharlet

"Social engineering through law," the title of this volume, implies an instrumental conception of law used by the ruling elite to direct, control, regulate, and limit social change in the USSR. Within the scope of post-Stalinist legal instrumentalism, there has been room for considerable variation which has been perhaps best expressed in the contrast between Khrushchev's generally utopian predilection as projected in the 1961 Communist Party Program, and Brezhnev's fundamentally pragmatic outlook as reflected in the 1977 USSR Constitution.[1] Given our increasing awareness of the basic differences of style and policy between the Khrushchev (1953-1964) and Brezhnev (1964-) "administrations,"[2] it should not surprise us to find dissimilarities in "legal policy" or Party policy towards the "social regulation process"[3] of the Soviet system between the two leaders as well. Yet the record, in general, is not simply one of consistent change from the imputed subjectivism of Khrushchev to the implied pragmatism of Brezhnev. In the area of legal policy, in particular, a comparison of Khrushchev and Brezhnev reveals a complex picture of change and continuity.

Schematically, the broad similarities and differences between Khrushchev and Brezhnev can be initially seen in Soviet "meta-legal policy."[4] Under Khrushchev the general political policy of de-Stalinization was the principal meta-legal policy, impacting on the social regulation process at the outset through the tendency towards the elimination of terror. Cumulatively, Khrushchev's accelerating tempo of de-Stalinization had the effect of contracting the "prerogative" sphere of regulation, thereby creating the social "space" for a corresponding expansion of the "normative" sphere.[5] After 1964, Brezhnev maintained a fundamental commitment to de-Stalinization but sharply decelerated its tempo, both as a general policy and as a meta-legal policy. Basically, the realignment from prerogative to normative was sustained by Brezhnev but stabilized. The progressive reduction of the prerogative sphere was gradually arrested, culminating in the symbolic "rehabilitation" of the secret police in 1967, on the occasion of its 50th anniversary, and the emphasis shifted to consolidating and strengthening the normative sphere. Khrushchev's and Brezhnev's different attitudes towards de-Stalinization are perhaps most vividly expressed by the fact that Stalin's body was removed from the mausoleum and a monument to his victims even contemplated under Khrushchev, while Brezhnev installed a modest bust of the General Secretary before his niche in the Kremlin wall.

However, the cleavage in meta-legal policy is much more pronounced when one compares Khrushchev's cluster of political attitudes, orientations, and style, summarized in the term "populism" with Brezhnev's contrasting "realism". Khrushchev's populism as meta-legal policy manifested itself in the revival and expansion of popular justice by adding a regulatory substratum to the normative and prerogative spheres. Khrushchev's popular justice relied heavily on mass spontaneity in bringing horizontal, societal-level pressures to bear on socially deviant peers.[6] In sharp contrast, Khrushchev's peer stratum has been steadily subsumed by the normative and prerogative spheres under Brezhnev's realist influence. Popular justice has been progressively eroded and subordinated to professional legal controls with the emphasis now much more on "consciousness" from above rather than "spontaneity" from below.

Looking at the post-Stalin period historically, it can be said that a weak and somewhat polarized consensus exists between Khrushchev and Brezhnev on de-Stalinization as meta-legal policy in contrast to the conspicuous cleavage in Soviet meta-legal policy between Khrushchev's populism and Brezhnev's realism. In spite of this cleavage, both men have claimed Leninist legitimacy for their divergent attitudes, orientations, and style, and in fact both claims are valid since there were "several Lenins". Khrushchev's populism as meta-legal policy reflects the influence of the early, utopian Lenin in power, the Lenin of the *otmiranie* or the "withering away" of the state and law who presided over the post-revolutionary de-institutionalization of the tsarist legal system and the intended devolution of its "temporarily" necessary residual functions to minimal state institutions and simplified social organizations. A different Lenin is Brezhnev's model. His realism as meta-legal policy tends to draw its inspiration from the later (1919-1924), more pragmatic Lenin in power, the Lenin who spoke of the need for "temporary" restoration of the "machine called the state" and led the way to the re-legalization of Soviet society with the emphasis on social control from above.[7]

Khrushchev's and Brezhnev's consensus and cleavage in meta-legal policy have, in turn, led to continuity and change in the area of "structural legal policy."[8] From Khrushchev to Brezhnev, the two major themes of continuity (within their consensus, albeit weak, on de-Stalinization) have been what I have called "de-Vyshinskyization"[9] and a commitment to legal reform. In contrast, the elements of dissensus between Khrushchev and Brezhnev over the Stalin question have led to different usages and applications of the concept of "socialist legality." Finally, their populist-realist cleavage led predictably to dissimilar operational orientations towards the peer justice institutions.

First, I shall take up the continuities in structural legal policy under the two post-Stalin régimes. Under Brezhnev's régime, de-Vyshinskyization has continued, but with *two* qualifications:

1) Jurisprudential development of a theory of the all-people's state and law continues, but as only one of several lines of speculative legal thought and without the ideological impetus given it by Khrushchev's Party Program of 1961;[10]

2) The emphasis in legal education and legal scholarship has changed subtly during the Brezhnev years in the direction of more practice and less theory. Academic attention has been shifting from such Khrushchevian topics as "scientific communism" to more practical subjects exemplified by the great interest in economic law and the scientific and technical revolution.[11] In brief, there now seems to be less concern with legal theory as an explanatory device and predictive tool and more preoccupation with various conceptions of law as a mechanism for problem-solving and conflict resolution.

A second major area of continuity has been the post-Stalin leadership's uninterrupted commitment to an extensive and intensive program of legal reform which, it is assumed, has provided the content for the greatly expanded normative sphere, a hypothesis now generally confirmed by the first volume in this series.[12] The continuity of this commitment from the mid-1950's to the present seems to be qualified by only one noticeable difference. Under Khrushchev's leadership, the legal reform program involved at least nominal and symbolic participation by the mass public as well as the actual and substantive participation of the jurists in the legal policy-making process; whereas, during Brezhnev's régime there has been less "public" discussion and more specialist participation in legal policy-making.[13] Of course, it must be recognized that this trend has coincided with the fact that aside from the family and labor *osnovy* or fundamental principles of legislation of 1968 and 1970, respectively, (which largely completed the reform of the main areas of the inter-relationship of the individual and the state in Soviet law), it has fallen to Brezhnev to preside as Party leader over reform of the more technical branches of law involving primarily intra-state relations.[14] However, simultaneously, it should be added that this tendency conforms to a broader trend under Brezhnev towards granting greater access to, and relying more heavily on, specialist participation in policymaking in general.[15]

Now let me turn to the changes in structural legal policy from Khrushchev to Brezhnev. Flowing from the dissensual elements in their respective attitudes towards de-Stalinization, Khrushchev and Brezhnev have tended to assign different meanings to the term "socialist legality," a concept which in the post-Stalin years has transcended its descriptive function and metaphorized into a political symbol designed to express the régime's commitment to govern predominantly through the stabilized, formalized, and professionalized normative sector. In its primary meaning, "socialist legality" describes the relationship between the state and citizen; metaphorically, it connotes the emphasis and direction within this relationship as well. Predictably, Khrushchev, who made selective criticism of Stalinism the hallmark of his régime, basically construed "socialist legality" in a pro-individual, anti-arbitrariness direction, symbolizing his public commitment to the restoration and reinforcement of normative means at the expense of the Stalinist prerogative techniques. Conversely, Brezhnev, accepting the premise of a realigned social regulation process but muting further criticism of Stalin, has given precedence to the crime problem in Soviet society and tends to use the concept of "socialist legality" to signal his pro-state, anti-deviance orientation in the administration of criminal justice.[16]

Finally and inevitably, the populist-realist split in policy-making style and content between Khrushchev and Brezhnev leads directly to a major cleavage in structural legal policy between the former's derivative legal populism and the latter's conflicting legal realism. Operationally, this has meant dramatically different attitudes towards the social institutions of peer regulation. Revived or recreated under Khrushchev's aegis, these institutions reflected his legal populism through the institutionalization of public opinion (which substituted "social" for "official" arbitrariness) to induce social conformity and combat low-level deviance in the short run, while assisting in the "creation of the new man" during the then forthcoming "transition to communism." As a practical matter, this initially took the forms and shapes of anti-parasite's proceedings in the amorphous social assemblies, free-wheeling comrades' courts, and frequently overly zealous *druzhiny,* or people's guards, patrolling the streets and public places.[17]

Khrushchev's populist forums for justice drew criticism from the legal profession, which felt that the attitudes and behavior encouraged in these forums would erode respect for legality, which the jurists were charged with enhancing in the mind of the mass public. As a result of such criticism and no doubt other factors in the arena of leadership politics about which we know much less, the Khrushchev régime modified the peer justice institutions in the early 1960's by giving priority to quasi-legal form over populist content. Nevertheless, these institutions continued to be widely used as instruments of supervised spontaneity.[18]

After his succession, Brezhnev's diametrically opposed legal realism did not have an immediate impact on his predecessor's popular justice, but over time, *de facto* and *de jure* changes slowly accumulated which, while preserving the forms, limited the use of peer forums for social regulation. Their scope of operation and degree of activity restricted, the peer institutions have now been quietly coopted from above and integrated into the state's struggle against deviance.[19] Anti-parasite proceedings have been transferred to the reestablished *MVD*, comrades' courts are less widely and less frequently used and are subject to administrative supervision from above (*e.g.*, in the housing units), and the *druzhiny* are now less visible on the streets (frequently patrolling in the late-night, early-morning shift) and have come increasingly to resemble semi-professionalized militia auxiliaries.

In all three instances, gone is the Khrushchevian spontaneity and enthusiasm, the publicly proclaimed significance of peer pressure, and the ideological rhetoric on the gradual devolution of certain state functions to organizations of "social self government" which would serve as classrooms in the education of the "new Soviet man."[20] All of this now sounds strangely discordant in Brezhnev's "developed socialist society" where the order of the day is to increase productivity and modernize management by systematically carrying out "scientific-technological revolution" throughout Soviet society.[21]

Turning now to "substantive legal policy,"[22] of which the Party is the ultimate source within its overarching structural and meta-legal policies, there is evidence of both major continuity and major change from Khrushchev to Brezhnev. Within their joint commitment to the enlargement, increased stabilization, and greater formalization of the normative sector of social regulation, and their shared support for legal reform, Khrushchev and Brezhnev during their successive régimes have produced a steady stream of *Fundamental Principles* which have provided the frameworks for codification or recodification in nearly every branch of Soviet law as the first stage in the process of legal policy implementation. Essentially though, the enactment of *Fundamental Principles* affords the Party, at best, with infrequent opportunities to express its will in the form of substantive legal policy. Aside from these periodic occasions for the systemic revision of the basic principles for a particular branch of law, the bulk of the Party's substantive legal policy-making activity may well be expressed indirectly through the continuous, incremental process of scholarly commentary on, higher judicial interpretation of, and legislative amendments to, extant law.[23]

However, it remains to be seen whether these processes represent a more precise stage of policy implementation of the *Fundamental Principles* for a specific branch of law (beyond the enactment of the relevant union republic codes), or whether these micro changes in the law are having a feedback effect on the macro basic principles for legislation and thereby constitute an extension of the legal policy-making process. The eventual answer to the question may, in fact, be that this incrementalism represents both more refined implementation and extended policymaking, simultaneously, for the codes and the *Fundamental Principles* respectively. Meanwhile, an answer must await a series of longitudinal studies of the post-codification amending and interpreting processes in the various branches of Soviet law to determine how incremental changes in the law under Brezhnev may have affected the corresponding *Fundamental Principles* enacted under Khrushchev and beyond, to how post-Khrushchev incrementalism may have affected the *Fundamental Principles* enacted under Brezhnev. Whether, in the first instance, the legal marginalia will reveal continuity or change from Khrushchev to Brezhnev is difficult to forecast.

However, in another major area of substantive legal policy, "campaigning," the differences between Brezhnev and Khrushchev follow from their populist-realist dichotomy in general, and in particular in regard to the social regulation process, are unmistakable. Concentrating just on each one's major "campaign," there are conspicuous changes in style, technique, and general thrust from Khrushchev to Brezhnev. Khrushchev launched his major campaign for the *restoration* of socialist legality with the main emphasis on the elimination of official arbitrariness *vis-à-vis* the individual (a process sometimes described as liquidating the consequences of the "cult of personality"), and secondary stress on the control of deviance. Brezhnev, in contrast, has been presiding over his major campaign for the *maintenance* of socialist law and order, the essential focus of which is purely anti-deviance, without Khrushchev's ideological flourishes and historical referents.[24]

Khrushchev's campaign took a short term curative approach to arbitrariness and crime; Brezhnev's campaign has been fashioned around a middle-run curative approach and a longer term preventive perspective on crime and its causes. Khrushchev relied on the criminal justice system and the peer justice process, the two which overlapped in jurisdiction at points and frequently worked at cross purposes in terms of the spirit if not the letter of the campaign. Brezhnev, instead, has primarily used the criminal justice system (coordinated by the *MVD*) for his middle-run purposes and the evolving legal socialization process (directed by the reestablished Ministry of Justice) for his longer term goal in regard to the crime problem in Soviet society, with no apparent conflict between the two spearheads of his campaign.[25] In his campaign rhetoric, Khrushchev displayed a definite preoccupation with the shadow of the past while Brezhnev's references have been firmly rooted in the present with an opening to the not-too-distant future.

Both leaders evolved subcampaigns as spin-offs from their main efforts. Khrushchev's was an assault on "white collar" economic crime which, through the calculated use of publicity, quickly achieved such high visibility that it began to eclipse the socialist legality campaign and contravene its main restorationist theme. Among other things, the *KGB* was conscripted into the war against large-scale economic crime, no doubt because of the high political priority involved and possibly due to the inter-republic scope of the major cases.[26] Brezhnev, whose law and order campaign more routinely includes a drive against economic crime—both petty and large-scale—has generated his own specialized campaign against the various forms of dissent which have flowered in the Soviet Union in recent years. Similarly, Brezhnev's subcampaign has enlisted the now fully "rehabilitated" *KGB* who pursue a relatively small group of people (whose activities also frequently "cross" republic lines), in a relentlessly curative manner which has entailed an even greater volume of flagrant violations of Soviet due process than occurred during Khrushchev's specialized campaign.[27] In even greater contrast, though, Brezhnev's move against the dissidents has been of a relatively low profile (in terms of the internal public), utilizes administrative as well as judicial techniques of repression, and has been effectively compartmentalized within the dominant mass campaign for law and order.[28]

Finally, Khrushchev's and Brezhnev's campaigning styles are markedly dissimilar. Khrushchev's style was often personalistic, occasionally histrionic, and sometimes characterized by contradictory changes of strategy and tactics and abrupt redeployment of the "forces" in his clashing campaigns on the legal front. In a word – he was highly subjective as a legal campaigner. Brezhnev's style is far more bureaucratic and his campaign leadership far more pragmatic and decidedly less conspicuous, which has generally resulted in a comparatively better planned, more systematic, and more carefully orchestrated main and subcampaign against criminals and "politicals" respectively. Lest we leave this section on too discordant a note, it should be recorded that the two "campaigners," Brezhnev and Khrushchev, share a common experience: neither has succeeded in rooting out crime or even in eliminating the particular outgrowth which he found especially intolerable. Arbitrariness and crimes of all hues continue to flourish, and even dissent is becoming a hardy perennial in Soviet society.[29]

Lastly, I conclude on a particularly pernicious point of continuity from Khrushchev to Brezhnev—both have shown a penchant for carrying on the Stalinist tradition of resorting to the use of "*ad hoc* legal policy"[30] for the purpose of bypassing normative procedures in favor of taking expedient action against a political pariah or group heresy. In this respect, Khrushchev and Brezhnev are not only vestigial Stalinists but good Leninists as well in keeping faith with Lenin's dictum that dictatorship cannot be limited by law. In the context of the Soviet system, this means that the post-Stalin Communist Party continues to cast itself in the role of a metajuridical entity, above and spatially outside of the parameters of the Soviet "dual state". The Party in this role continues to function as the arbiter of jurisdiction within the Soviet system, allocating (and changing if necessary) to the normative and prerogative spheres their respective jurisdictions.

In effect, the Party remains the court of last resort for "official Russia" when it cannot achieve a particular objective through the legal system. The

Party's remedy is an *ad hoc* legal policy which circumvents the hierarchy of legal policies and the normative sphere in order to strike directly at a hapless individual or a group bereft of the thicket of rules and procedures normally intended to afford the citizen in post-Stalin Russia a degree of protection against the direct, arbitrary action of the state. In such cases (and they are no longer numerous since the death of Stalin), regardless of whether Brezhnev or Khrushchev presides, the Party is effectively declaring *deus ex machina* that *partiinost'* (Party-orientation) is higher than *zakonnost'* (legality), that political expedience may usurp formal legality in the relationship of state to citizen if it is deemed necessary. An *ad hoc* legal policy, then, tailored to "fit" a lone individual or a small group–be it a dissenter, a heinous murderer, a would-be emigrant, a spectacular swindler, a band of religious zealots, a group of ethnic extremists, or a putative political conspiracy–is the quintessence of a prerogative act. All of which should suggest, in spite of the steady development of the normative sphere in the USSR during the post-Stalin period, that prerogativism continues as a state of mind (and an inveterately rooted one) as well as a spatial concept in Soviet society.

Without a doubt, the Party since the late 1930's and especially under Khrushchev and Brezhnev has progressively "Romanized" the Soviet legal system, but simultaneously it has reserved to itself the inherent power of *ad hocism* enabling it to intervene at will in either "official Russia" or "popular Russia" in the spirit of Marxian flexibility. In the vocabulary of Western political philosophy, this is the essence of unlimited government.

Finally, we come to the new USSR Constitution of 1977 which exemplifies the combination of change and continuity in Soviet legal policy under Brezhnev and Khrushchev. As a meta-legal policy, the 1977 Constitution represents the post-Stalin compromise between Brezhnev and Khrushchev by codifying both the scope and limits of de-Stalinization in the accents of legal realism but with concessions to the populist spirit, especially in the preamble, the new political culture clause (Art. 9), the constitutional recognition of lay defenders and accusers (Art. 162), and the familiar section on the "new man" and the road to communism (Chap. 3) inspired by the 1961 Party Program. Functionally, the new document constitutes the culmination of over two decades of the Khrushchev-Brezhnev structural policy of legal reform through the subsumption and integration of the major principles of the substantive legal policies embodied in the post-Stalin Fundamental Principles, statutes, and codes. Last but not least, the new Soviet Constitution incorporates most of the caveats on the relation of citizen to state from the 1936 Constitution (and adds several more), which will continue to facilitate and now even more formally legitimate the régime's resort to *ad hoc* legal policy in political cases. In this tendency towards explicit political cooptation of formal legal process in Party-selected cases, the line of continuity extends from Lenin and Stalin through Khrushchev and Brezhnev.[31]

NOTES

1. See John N. Hazard, "A Constitution for 'Developed Socialism,' " in the present volume and Robert Sharlet, "The New Soviet Constitution," *Problems of Communism*, 26 (1977), No. 5, 1-24.

2. Compare Carl A. Linden, *Khrushchev and the Soviet Leadership, 1957-1964* (Baltimore, Md., 1966) and George W. Breslauer, "Khrushchev Reconsidered," *Problems of Communism*, 25 (1976), No. 5, 18-33, with Jerry F. Hough, "The Brezhnev Era: The Man and the System," *Problems of Communism*, 25 (1976), No. 2, 1-17, and Gail Warshofsky Lapidus, "The Brezhnev Regime and Directed Social Change: Depoliticization as Political Strategy," in Alexander Dallin (ed.), *The Twenty-Fifth Congress of the CPSU: Assessment and Context* (Stanford, Ca., 1977), ch. 3.

3. By social regulation process, I mean the process by which the norms of inter-personal relations and the relations between the citizen and the state are defined, sanctioned, and regulated through the legal system, the administrative control apparatus, and officially sponsored peer-group controls. See Robert Sharlet, "Law in the Political Development of a Communist System," in Roger E. Kanet (ed.), *The Behavioral Revolution and Communist Studies* (New York, 1971), ch. 10. For the most comprehensive and current study of the role of the Party in the Soviet legal policy-making process, see Peter Vanneman, *The Supreme Soviet: Politics and the Legislative Process in the Soviet Political System* (Durham, N.C., 1977), ch. 9.

4. Meta-legal policy has a significant impact on the social regulation process, although it is not intended to apply exclusively to that process. A meta-legal policy may be either a general political policy with system-wide application within which the social regulation process is subsumed, or a policy more limited in scope that is primarily directed toward another systemic process but has a "spillover" effect on the social regulation process or one of its component parts. See Robert Sharlet, "Soviet Legal Policy Making: A Preliminary Classification," in "Special Issue on Social System and Legal Process," *Sociological Inquiry*, 47 (1977), No. 3-4, 212.

5. On the normative and prerogative spheres of Soviet law, see "Introduction" and "Appendix I: The Framework for Analysis" in Donald D. Barry, George Ginsburgs, and Peter B. Maggs (eds.), *Soviet Law After Stalin, Part I: The Citizen and the State in Contemporary Soviet Law* (Leyden, 1977), pp. xiii-xv and 299-300.

6. On the peer-group controls under Khrushchev, see Harold J. Berman and James W. Spindler, "Soviet Comrades' Courts," *Washington Law Review*, 38 (1963), 842-910; Dennis M. O'Connor, "Soviet People's Guards: An Experiment with Civic Police," *New York University Law Review*, 39 (1964), 579-614; and Marianne Armstrong, "The Campaign Against Parasites," in Peter H. Juviler and Henry W. Morton (eds.), *Soviet Policy-making* (New York, 1967), ch. 7.

7. Both the utopian and the pragmatic Lenin are encompassed in John N. Hazard, *Settling Disputes in Soviet Society: The Formative Years of Legal Institutions* (New York, 1960). Lenin used the phrase the "machine called the state" in his lecture on "The State" at Sverdlov University in Moscow in 1919. See V. I. Lenin, "The State," in John N. Hazard (ed.), *Soviet Legal Philosophy* (Cambridge, Mass., 1951), p. 15. Soviet legal historical scholarship under Brezhnev has tended to emphasize Lenin's pragmatic role in shaping the normative sphere or legal system of the social regulation process. See, *e.g.*,

S.N. Bratus' and I. S. Samoshchenko (eds.), *Rol' V. I. Lenina v stanovlenii i razvitii sovetskogo zakonodatel'stva* (The Role of V. I. Lenin in the Making and Development of Soviet Legislation), (Moscow, 1969) and V. Davydov, *V. I. Lenin i razvitie grazhdanskogo zakonodatel'stva soiuznykh respublik* (V. I. Lenin and the Development of the Civil Legislation of the Union Republics), (Kishinev, 1970).

8. Structural legal policy is the policy type through which the Party, as the hegemonic policy-maker, addresses itself primarily and directly to problems of social regulation at a macroscopic level. Through this type of legal policy, the Party effects major structural changes in several different ways, including institutional or processual innovation; de-institutionalization or processual revision; reinforcement or refinement of existing institutions or procedures. The Party's legislative intent through structural legal change is to enhance its efficiency and effectiveness in attaining its posited purposes and goals. See Sharlet, "Soviet Legal Policy Making," *Sociological Inquiry, op. cit.*, p. 214. For two studies of problems of the structural legal policy type, see Donald D. Barry, "Soviet Housing Law: The Norms and Their Application," in Barry, Ginsburgs, and Maggs (eds.), *op. cit.*, pp. 1-32, and Barry, "Administrative Justice and Judicial Review in Soviet Administrative Law," in the present volume.

9. By this term, I mean first the reopening of theoretical discourse on the nature and functions of Soviet law, and then the reorientation of legal education and the revitalization of legal scholarship in the post-Stalin and post-Vyshinsky period of Soviet legal development. See Sharlet, *id.*, pp. 214-215.

10. See, *e.g.*, Roger E. Kanet, "The Rise and Fall of the 'All-People's State': Recent Changes in the Soviet Theory of the State." *Soviet Studies*, 20 (1968), No. 1, 81-93; B.N. Topornin, "Obshchenarodnoe gosudarstvo i sotsialisticheskaia demokratiia" (The All-People's State and Socialist Democracy), *Pravovedenie*, 1975, No. 2, pp. 7-17; and M.I. Baitin, "O klassovoi sushchnosti Sovetskogo obshchenarodnogo gosudarstva" (Concerning the Class Nature of the Soviet All-People's State), *SGiP*, 1976, No. 1, 5-13.

11. See, *e.g.*, Peter B. Maggs, "Improving the Legal Mechanisms for Economic Change" in the present volume; M. P. Rinz, "Pravo i nauchno-tekhnicheskii progress" (Law and Scientific and Technical Progress), in V.M. Chkhikvadze (ed.), *XXIV s"ezd KPSS i voprosy teorii gosudarstva i prava* (The Twenty-Fourth Congress of the CPSU and Questions of the Theory of State and Law), (Moscow, 1972); Erik P. Hoffmann, "Soviet Views of 'The Scientific-Technological Revolution,' " *World Politics*, 1978 forthcoming.

12. See Barry, Ginsburgs, and Maggs (eds.), *op. cit.*

13. Notwithstanding the public discussion of the draft constitution during 1977 which, in terms of the pre-ratification revisions, was clearly secondary in importance to the even more extensive specialized discussion which took place within the Soviet system and outside of the media. See Sharlet, "The New Soviet Constitution," *op. cit.*, 14-16.

14. For *e.g.*, the latest new fundamental principles were enacted for forest legislation in 1977. The on-going reform of Soviet product quality legislation is even more specialized and technical and therefore even less amenable to any kind of meaningful general public discussion. See, *e.g.*, Zigurds L. Zile, "Product Quality in Soviet Law: The Tested and the Changing," in the present volume.

15. See Jerry F. Hough, "Political Participation in the Soviet Union," in Hough, *The Soviet Union and Social Science Theory* (Cambridge, Mass., 1977), ch. 4.

16. See Peter H. Juviler, *Revolutionary Law and Order: Politics and Social Change in the USSR* (New York, 1976), pp. 85-109; and S.E. Zhilinskii, *Rol' KPSS v ukreplenii zakonnosti na sovremennom etape* (The Role of the CPSU in Strengthening Legality in the Contemporary Period), (Moscow, 1977).

17. See Glenn G. Morgan, "People's Justice: The Anti-Parasite Law, People's

Volunteer Militia and Comrade's Courts," in *Law in Eastern Europe* (Leyden, 1962), Vol. 7, pp. 49-81.

18. See Harold J. Berman and Donald D. Barry, "The Jurists," in H. Gordon Skilling and Franklyn Griffiths (eds.), *Interest Groups in Soviet Society* (Princeton, 1971), pp. 326-28; and John N. Hazard, "Soviet Law and Justice," in John W. Strong (ed.), *The Soviet Union Under Brezhnev and Kosygin* (New York, 1971), pp. 94-95 and 103-104.

19. See William E. Butler, "Comradely Justice Revised," and "Statute on Comrades' Courts," in *Review of Socialist Law*, 3 (1977), No. 3, 325-31 and 331-43 respectively. Also, see Peter H. Juviler, "Law and the Delinquent Family: Reproduction and Upbringing," in the present volume.

20. Some letters on behalf of including a specific reference to comrades' courts and people's guards in the draft constitution were published in the press during the public discussion of 1977, but the only response in the final document was the inclusion of the Khrushchevian phrase "social self-government" in the preamble.

21. See Robin F. Laird, " 'Developed' Socialist Society and the Dialectics of Development and Legitimation in the Soviet Union," *Soviet Union*, 4 (1977), No. 1, 130-49.

22. This type of legal policy is intended to affect Soviet society as a whole through a major component or subcomponent of the social regulation process. As such, it is relatively more specific, focussed, and content laden than structural legal policy, the context within which it is formulated. However, the degree of specificity of substantive legal policies can vary considerably, ranging from a sharply focused and narrowly applicable body of all-union fundamental principles of legislation to a more diffuse but widely applicable "campaign." See Sharlet, "Soviet Legal Policy Making," *op. cit.*, p. 216. For two substantive legal policy studies in the form of analyzing fundamental principles, see F. J. M. Feldbrugge, "Soviet Corrective Labor Law," and Peter H. Juviler, "Whom the State Has Joined: Family Ties in Soviet Law," both in Barry, Ginsburgs, and Maggs (eds.), *op. cit.*, pp. 33-69 and 119-157 respectively.

23. For a study of incremental substantive legal policy-making, see George Ginsburgs, "Soviet Court Reform, 1956-1958," in Barry, Ginsburgs and Maggs (eds.), *op. cit.*, pp. 77-104.

24. To compare "campaigning" under Khrushchev and Brezhnev, see respectively, Stanislaw Pomorski, "Communists and their Law," "Special Issue in Honor of Professor Helen Silving," in the *University of Puerto Rico Law Review*, 1978, forthcoming; and Gordon B. Smith, "Procuratorial Supervision of Economic Violations in the USSR," in the present volume.

25. On legal socialization of the mass public, see, *e.g.*, A. S. Pavlov, *Pravovoe vospitanie* (Legal Education), (Moscow, 1972); and N. Ia. Sokolov, *Organizatsiia pravovoi propagandy* (The Organization of Legal Propaganda), (Moscow, 1974).

26. See Stanislaw Pomorski, "Criminal Law Protection of Socialist Property in the USSR," in Barry, Ginsburgs, and Maggs (eds.), *op. cit.*, pp. 223-258, esp. pp. 234-238; and "Economic Crimes in the Soviet Union," *Journal of the International Commission of Jurists*, 5 (1964), 3-47.

27. See Christopher Osakwe, "Due Process of Law and Civil Rights Cases in the Soviet Union, in Barry, Ginsburgs, and Maggs, *op. cit.*, pp. 179-221, esp. pp. 205-214; Ivo Lapenna, "The Contempory Crisis of Legality in the Soviet Union: Substantive Criminal Law," *Review of Socialist Law*, 1 (1975), No. 2, 73-95.

28. See Robert Sharlet, "Dissent and Repression in the Soviet Union," *Current History*, 73 (1977), No. 430, 112-117 and 130; and Yuri Luryi, "The Role of Defence Counsel in Political Trials in the USSR," *Manitoba Law Journal*, 7 (1977), No. 4, 307-324.

29. On the roots of economic crime, see Stanislaw Pomorski, "Crimes Against the Central Planner: *Ochkovtiratel'stvo*," in the present volume; John M. Kramer, "Political Corruption in the USSR," *Western Political Quarterly*, 30 (1977), No. 2, 213-24; Aron Katsenelinboigen, "Coloured Markets in the Soviet Union," *Soviet Studies*, 29 (1977), No. 1, 62-85; and Gregory Grossman, "The 'Second Economy' of the USSR," *Problems of Communism*, 26 (1977), No. 5, 25-40. On the flourishing of political dissent, see Rudolf L. Tökes (ed.), *Dissent in the USSR: Politics, Ideology, & People* (Baltimore, Md., 1975); F. J. M. Feldbrugge, *Samizdat and Political Dissent in the Soviet Union* (Leyden, 1975); and Peter Reddaway, "Dissent in the Soviet Union," *Dissent*, 23 (1976), No. 2, 136-54.

30. *Ad hoc* legal policy is the means by which the Party reserves to itself the inherent power of dictatorship to bypass the normative sphere or legal system of the social regulation process by resorting to *ad hoc*, extra-legal action when it is deemed necessary. See Sharlet, "Soviet Legal Policy Making," *op. cit.*, pp. 218-219.

31. See Sharlet, "The New Soviet Constitution," *op. cit.*, pp. 1-6, and 24; V. Chalidze, "Human Rights in the New Soviet Constitution," in the present volume; and Sharlet, *The New Soviet Constitution of 1977: Analysis and Text* (Brunswick, Ohio, 1978).

INDEX